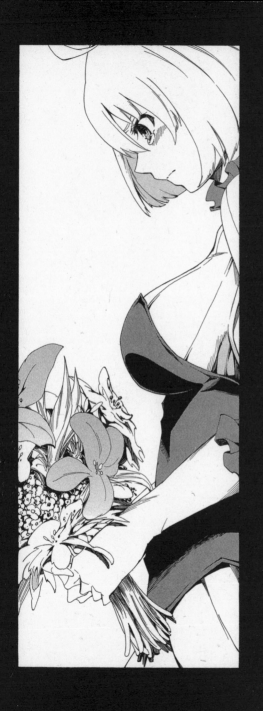

CHAPTER 14 RUINS

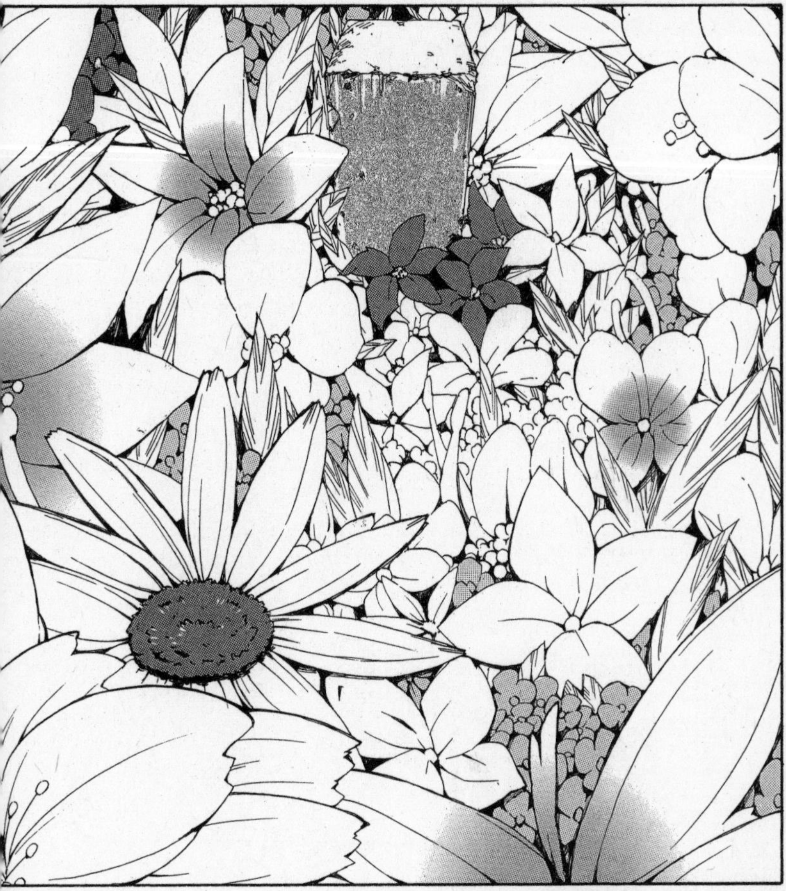

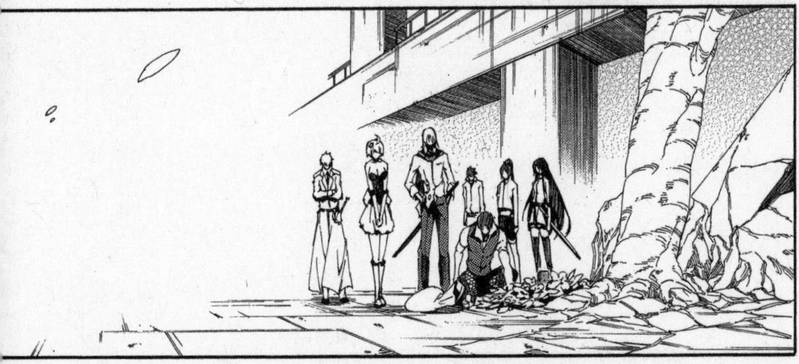

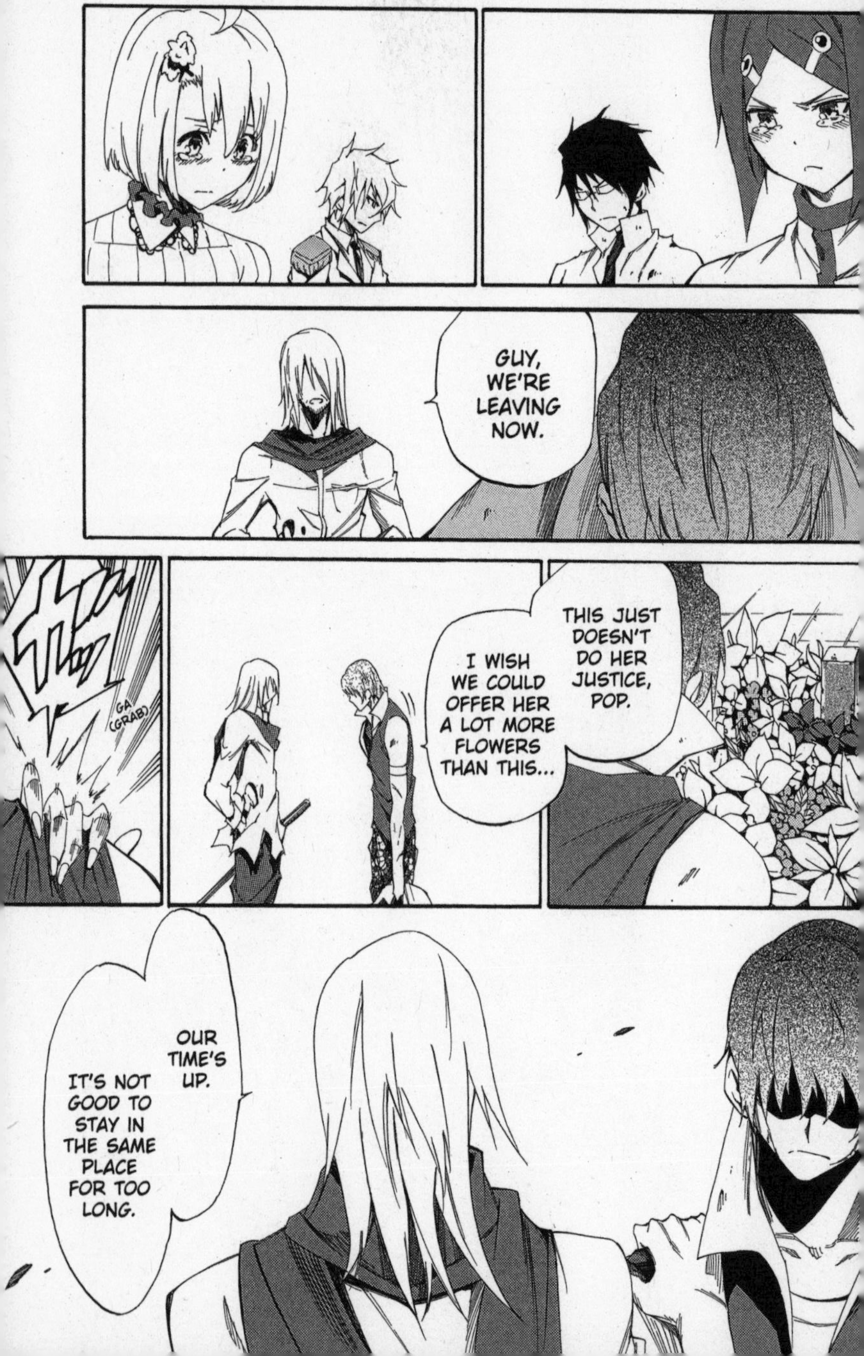
GUY, WE'RE LEAVING NOW.
THIS JUST DOESN'T DO HER JUSTICE, POP.
I WISH WE COULD OFFER HER A LOT MORE FLOWERS THAN THIS...
GA (GRAB)
OUR TIME'S UP.
IT'S NOT GOOD TO STAY IN THE SAME PLACE FOR TOO LONG.

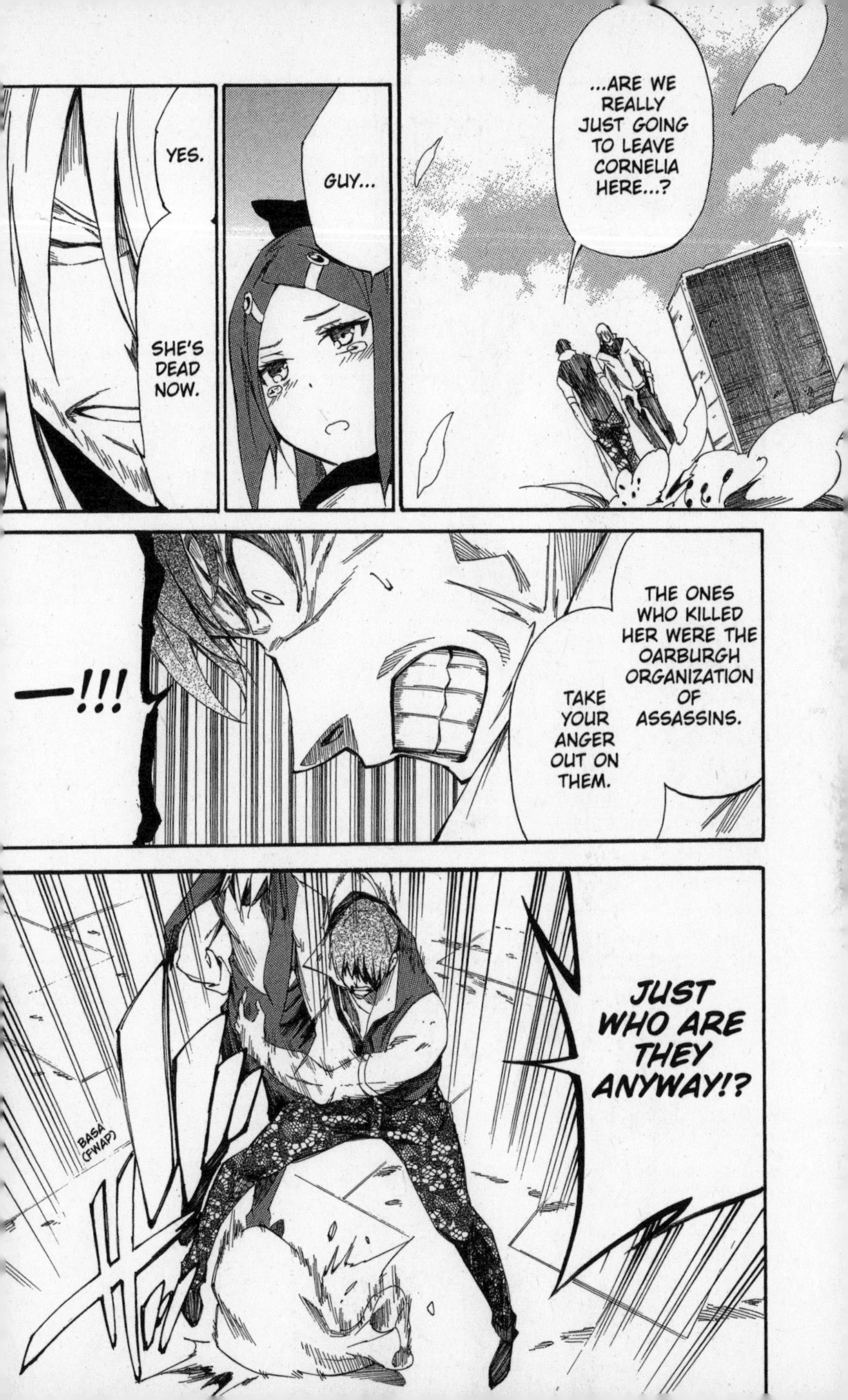
...ARE WE REALLY JUST GOING TO LEAVE CORNELIA HERE...?
GUY...
YES.
SHE'S DEAD NOW.
THE ONES WHO KILLED HER WERE THE OARBURGH ORGANIZATION OF ASSASSINS.
TAKE YOUR ANGER OUT ON THEM.
—!!!
JUST WHO ARE THEY ANYWAY!?
BASA (FWAP)

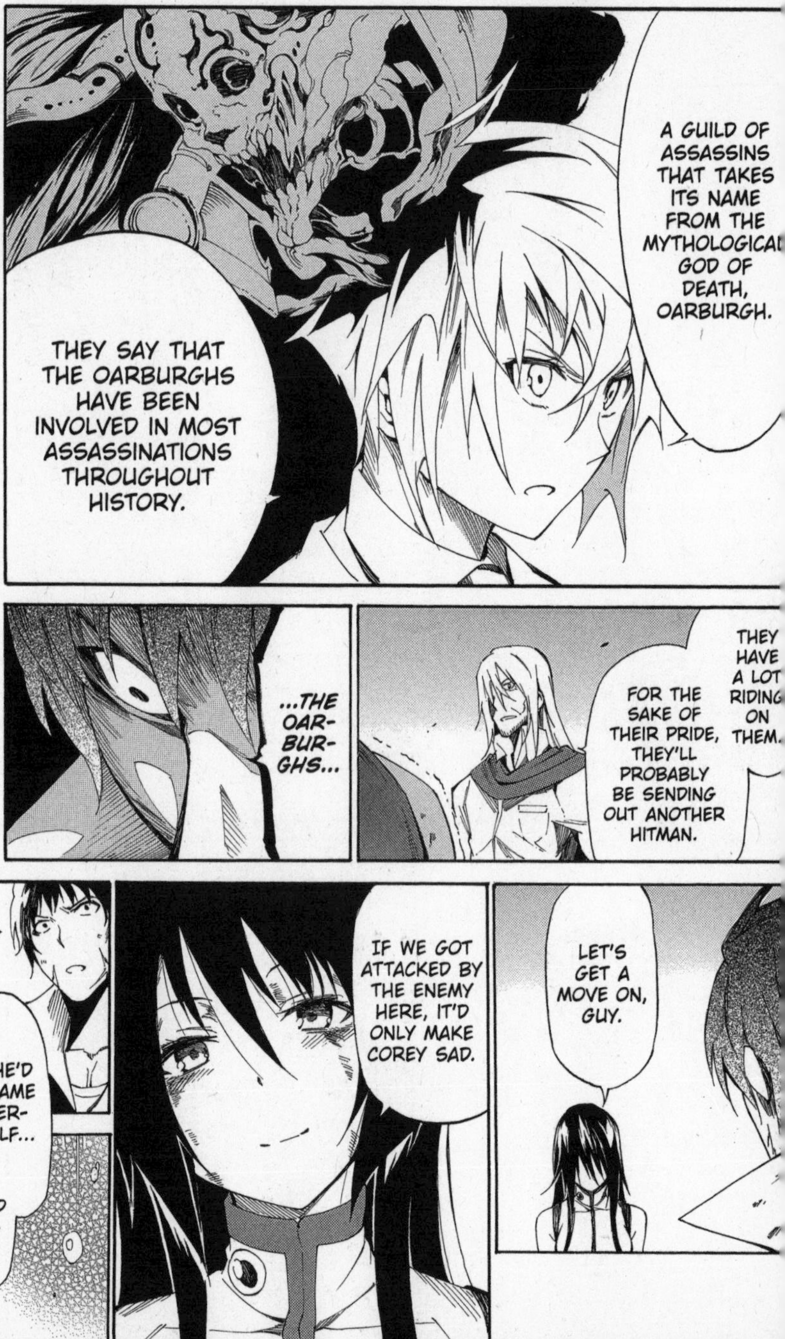
A GUILD OF ASSASSINS THAT TAKES ITS NAME FROM THE MYTHOLOGICAL GOD OF DEATH, OARBURGH.
THEY SAY THAT THE OARBURGHS HAVE BEEN INVOLVED IN MOST ASSASSINATIONS THROUGHOUT HISTORY.
THEY HAVE A LOT RIDING ON THEM.
FOR THE SAKE OF THEIR PRIDE, THEY'LL PROBABLY BE SENDING OUT ANOTHER HITMAN.
...THE OAR-BUR-GHS...
LET'S GET A MOVE ON, GUY.
IF WE GOT ATTACKED BY THE ENEMY HERE, IT'D ONLY MAKE COREY SAD.
SHE'D BLAME HER-SELF...
...AND FEEL AW-FUL.

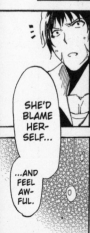

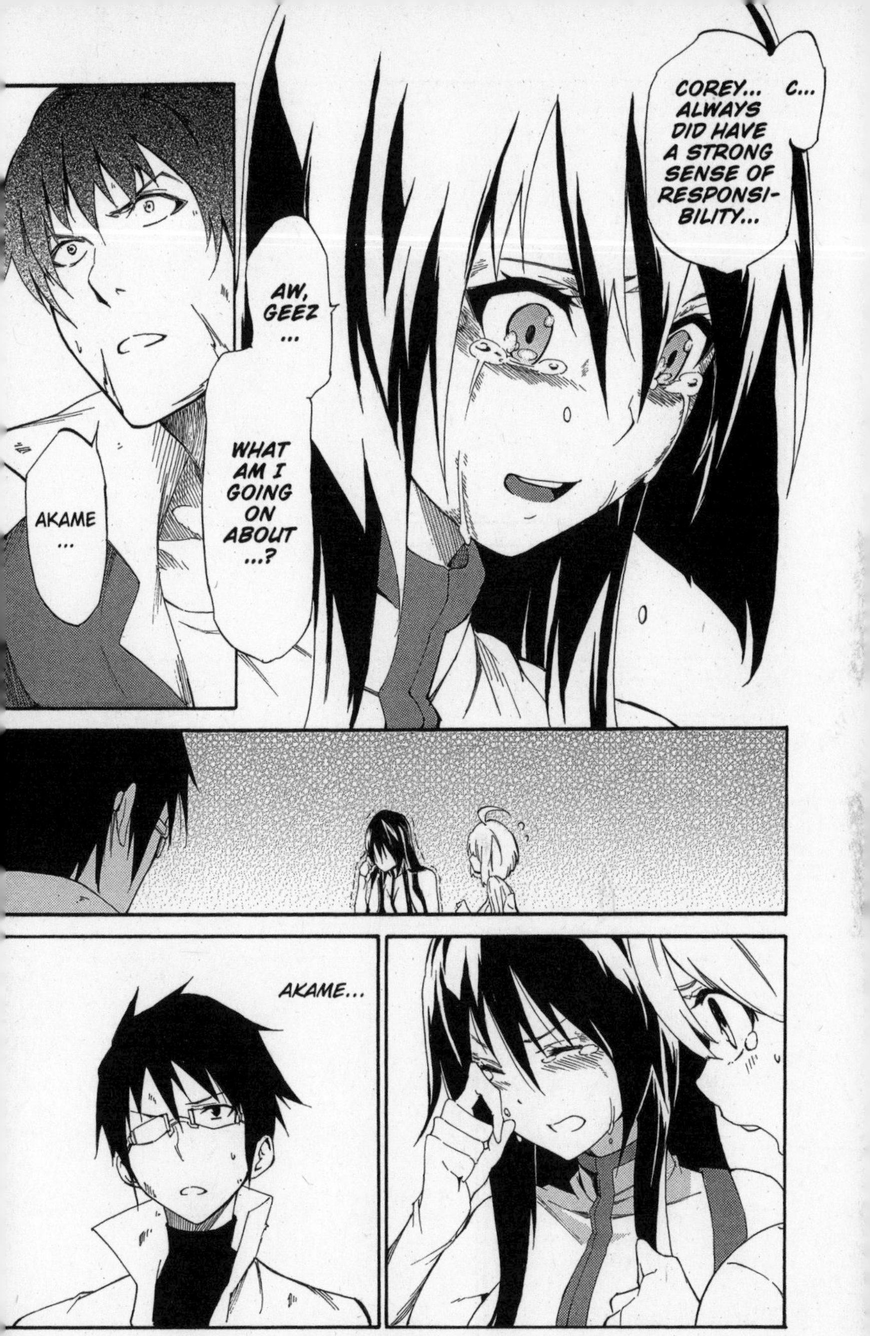
COREY... C... ALWAYS DID HAVE A STRONG SENSE OF RESPONSI-BILITY...
AW, GEEZ...
WHAT AM I GOING ON ABOUT...?
AKAME...
AKAME...

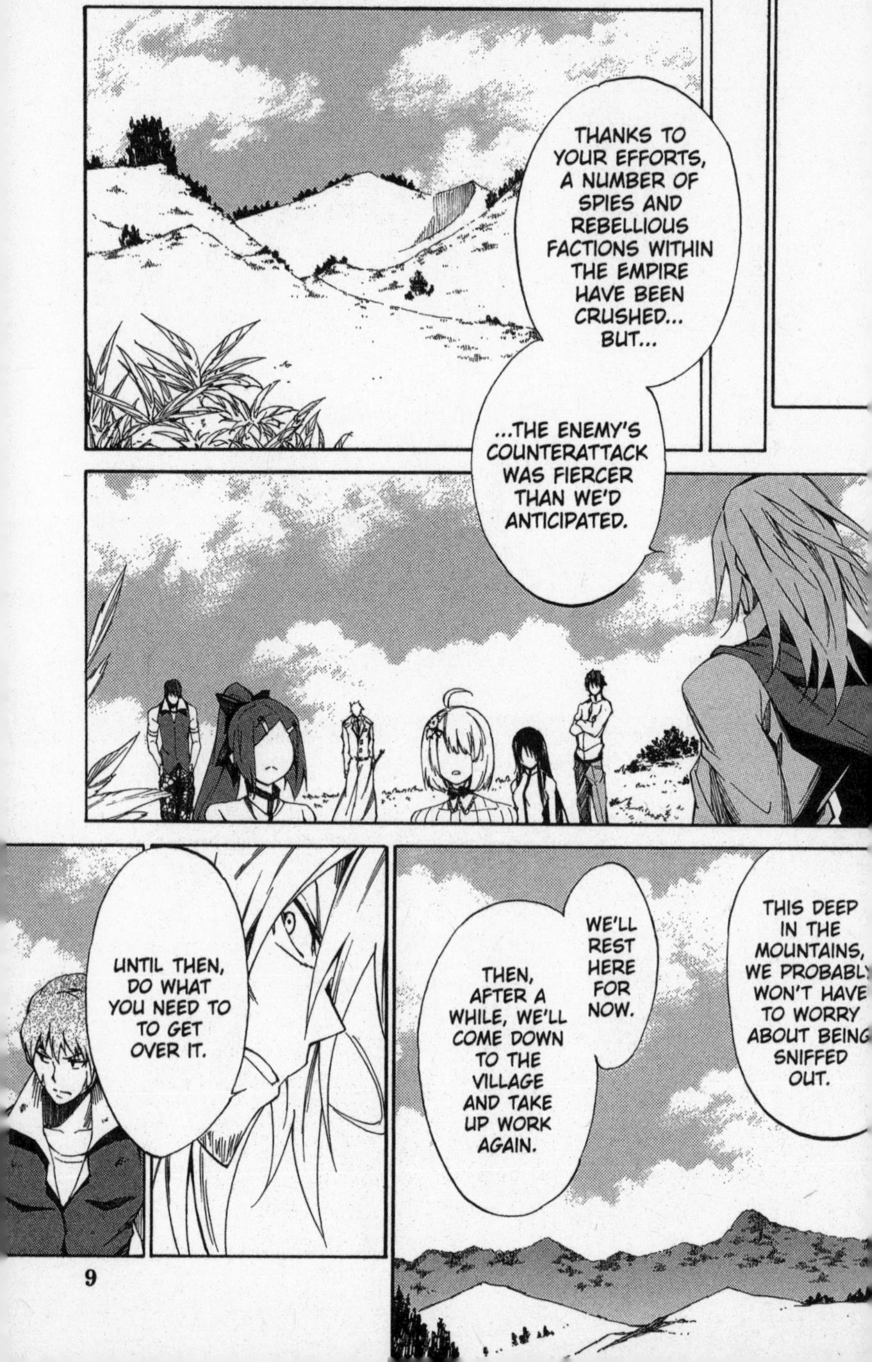
THANKS TO YOUR EFFORTS, A NUMBER OF SPIES AND REBELLIOUS FACTIONS WITHIN THE EMPIRE HAVE BEEN CRUSHED... BUT...
...THE ENEMY'S COUNTERATTACK WAS FIERCER THAN WE'D ANTICIPATED.
THIS DEEP IN THE MOUNTAINS, WE PROBABLY WON'T HAVE TO WORRY ABOUT BEING SNIFFED OUT.
WE'LL REST HERE FOR NOW.
THEN, AFTER A WHILE, WE'LL COME DOWN TO THE VILLAGE AND TAKE UP WORK AGAIN.
UNTIL THEN, DO WHAT YOU NEED TO TO GET OVER IT.

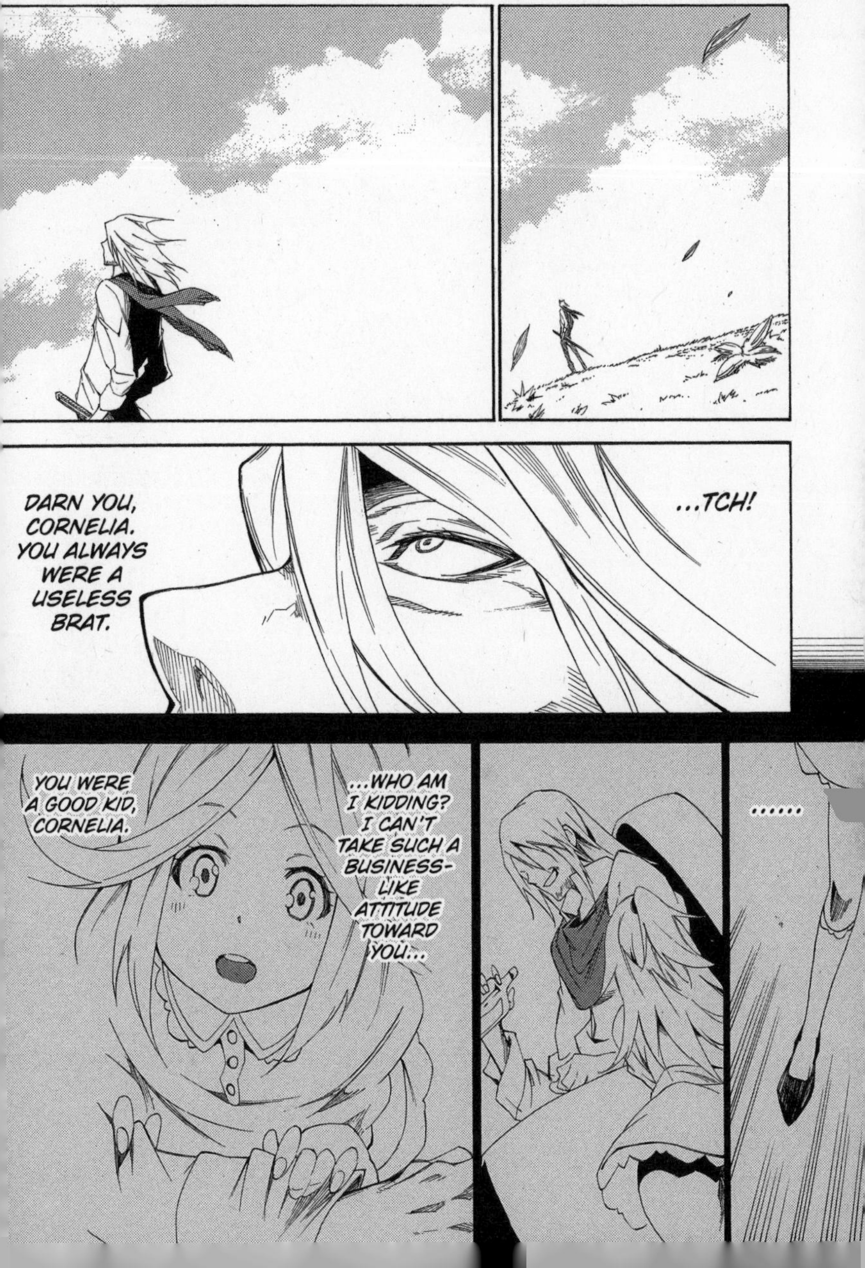
...TCH!
DARN YOU, CORNELIA. YOU ALWAYS WERE A USELESS BRAT.
......
...WHO AM I KIDDING? I CAN'T TAKE SUCH A BUSINESS-LIKE ATTITUDE TOWARD YOU...
YOU WERE A GOOD KID, CORNELIA.

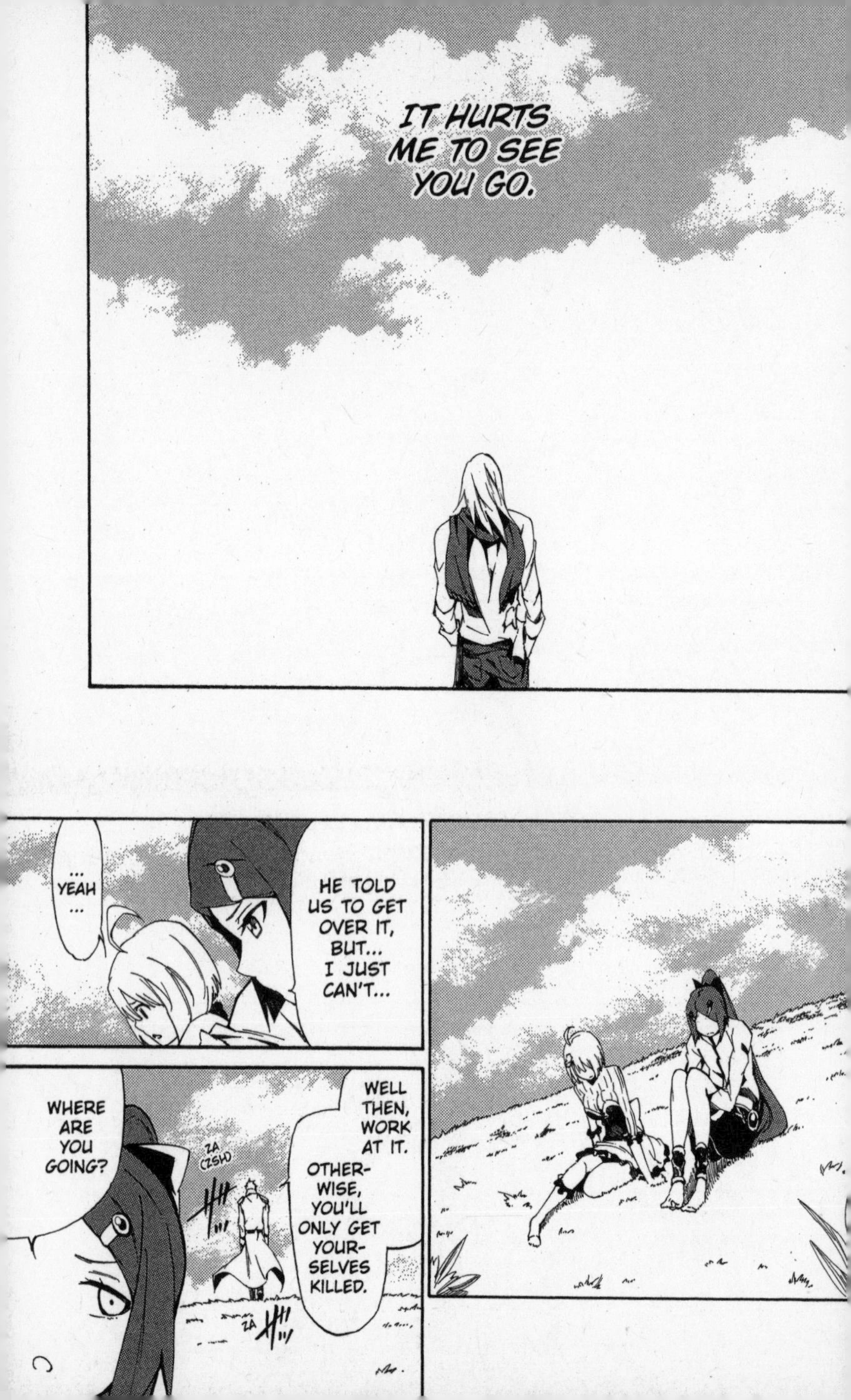
IT HURTS ME TO SEE YOU GO.
HE TOLD US TO GET OVER IT, BUT... I JUST CAN'T...
...YEAH...
WELL THEN, WORK AT IT.
OTHERWISE, YOU'LL ONLY GET YOURSELVES KILLED.
ZA (ZSH)
ZA
WHERE ARE YOU GOING?

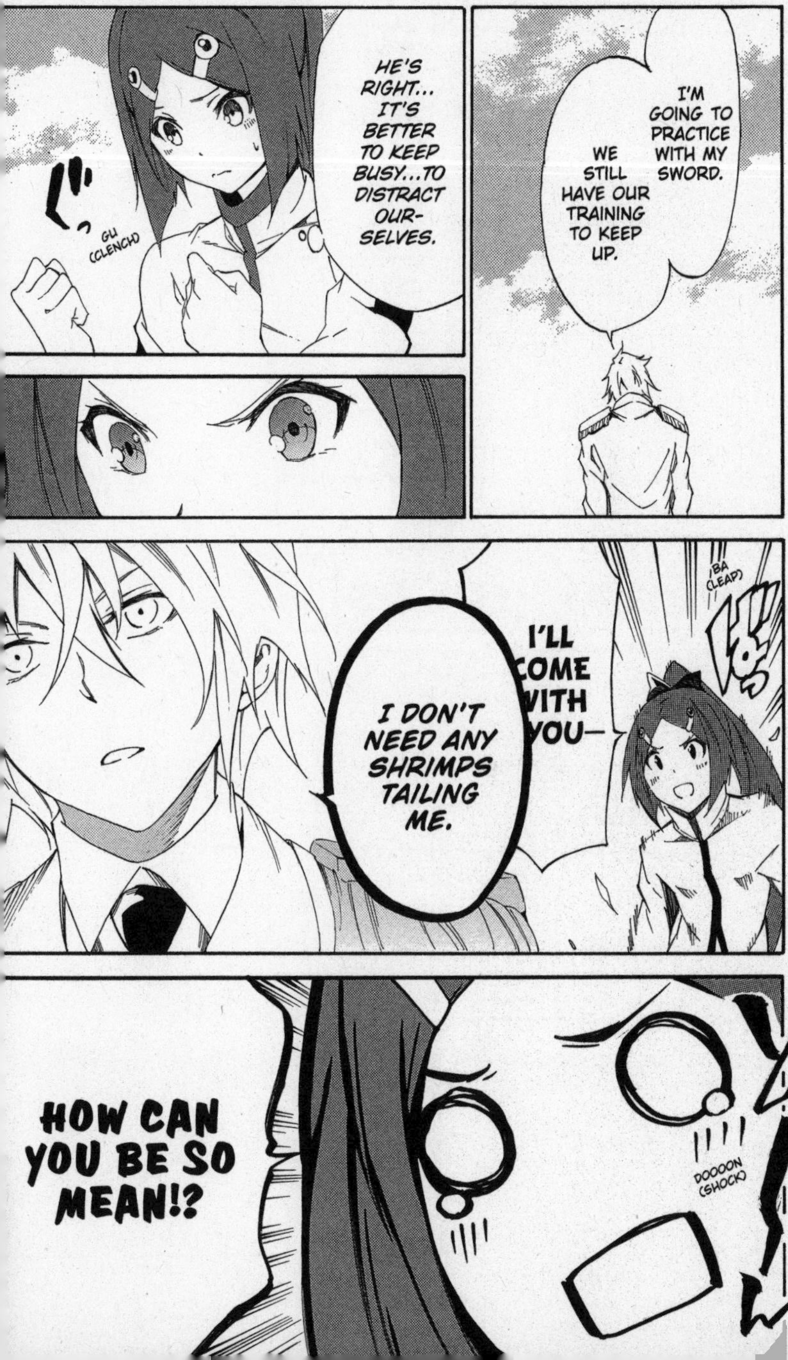
I'M GOING TO PRACTICE WITH MY SWORD.
WE STILL HAVE OUR TRAINING TO KEEP UP.
HE'S RIGHT... IT'S BETTER TO KEEP BUSY...TO DISTRACT OUR-SELVES.
GU (CLENCH)
BA (LEAP)
I'LL COME WITH YOU—
I DON'T NEED ANY SHRIMPS TAILING ME.
DOOOON (SHOCK)
HOW CAN YOU BE SO MEAN!?

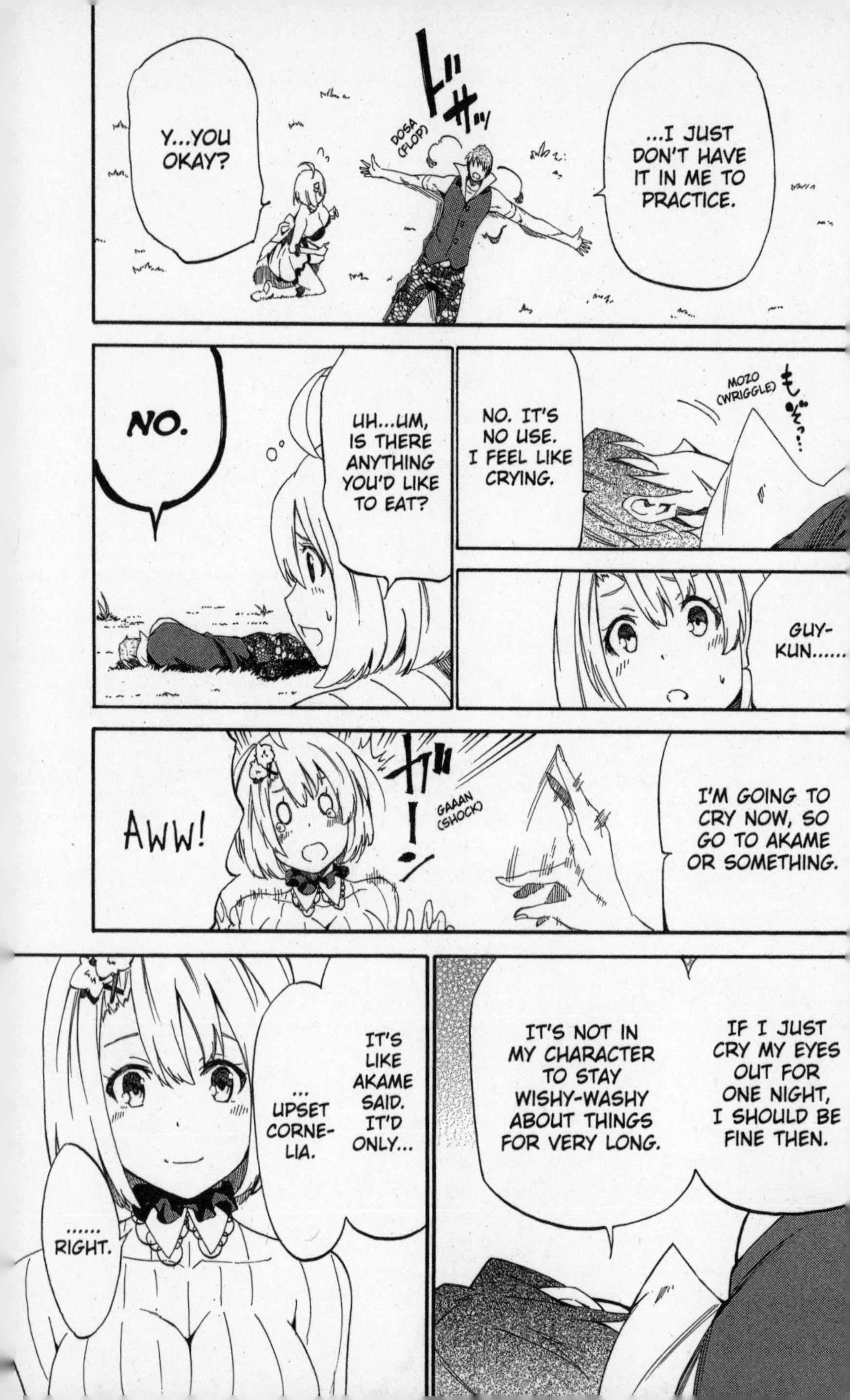
...I JUST DON'T HAVE IT IN ME TO PRACTICE.
DOSA (FLOP)
Y...YOU OKAY?
MOZO (WRIGGLE)
NO. IT'S NO USE. I FEEL LIKE CRYING.
GUY-KUN......
UH...UM, IS THERE ANYTHING YOU'D LIKE TO EAT?
NO.
I'M GOING TO CRY NOW, SO GO TO AKAME OR SOMETHING.
GAAAN (SHOCK)
AWW!
IF I JUST CRY MY EYES OUT FOR ONE NIGHT, I SHOULD BE FINE THEN.
IT'S NOT IN MY CHARACTER TO STAY WISHY-WASHY ABOUT THINGS FOR VERY LONG.
IT'S LIKE AKAME SAID. IT'D ONLY...
...UPSET CORNELIA.
......RIGHT.

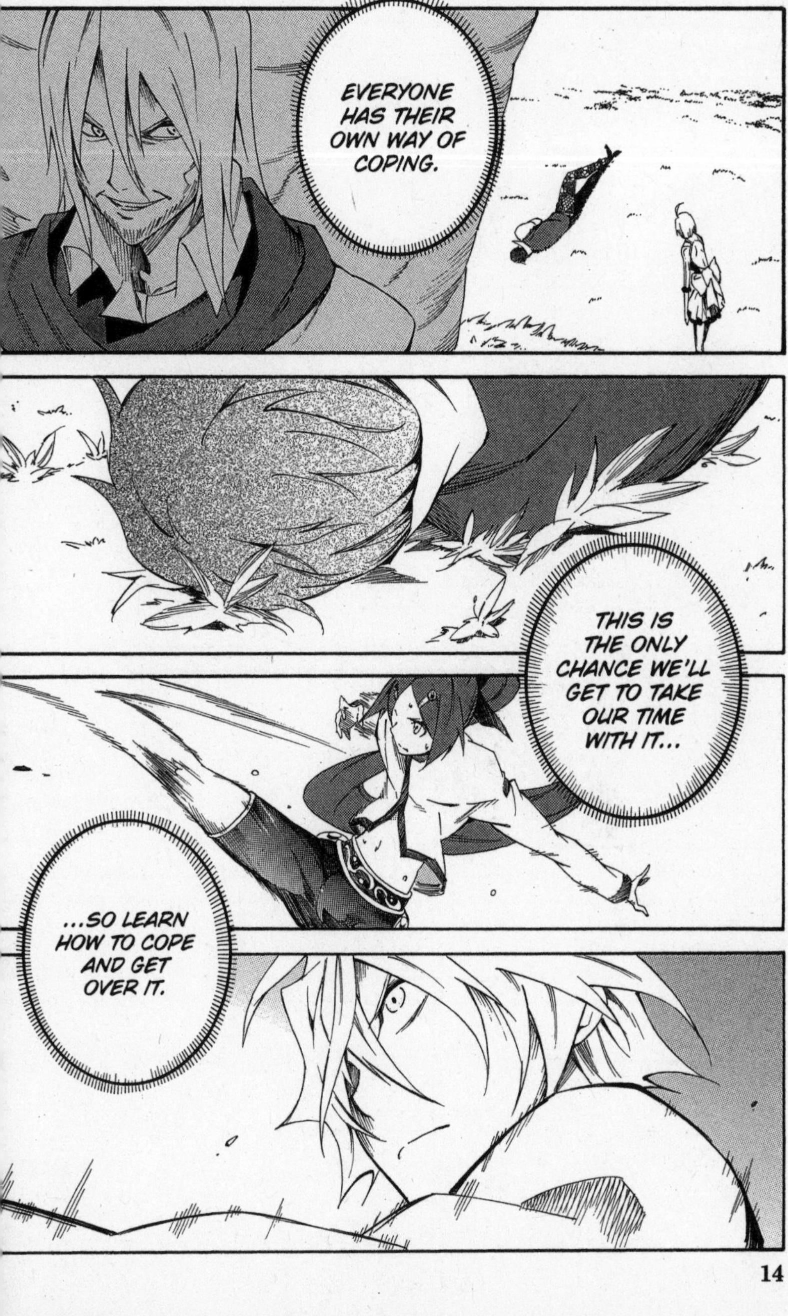
EVERYONE HAS THEIR OWN WAY OF COPING.
THIS IS THE ONLY CHANCE WE'LL GET TO TAKE OUR TIME WITH IT...
...SO LEARN HOW TO COPE AND GET OVER IT.

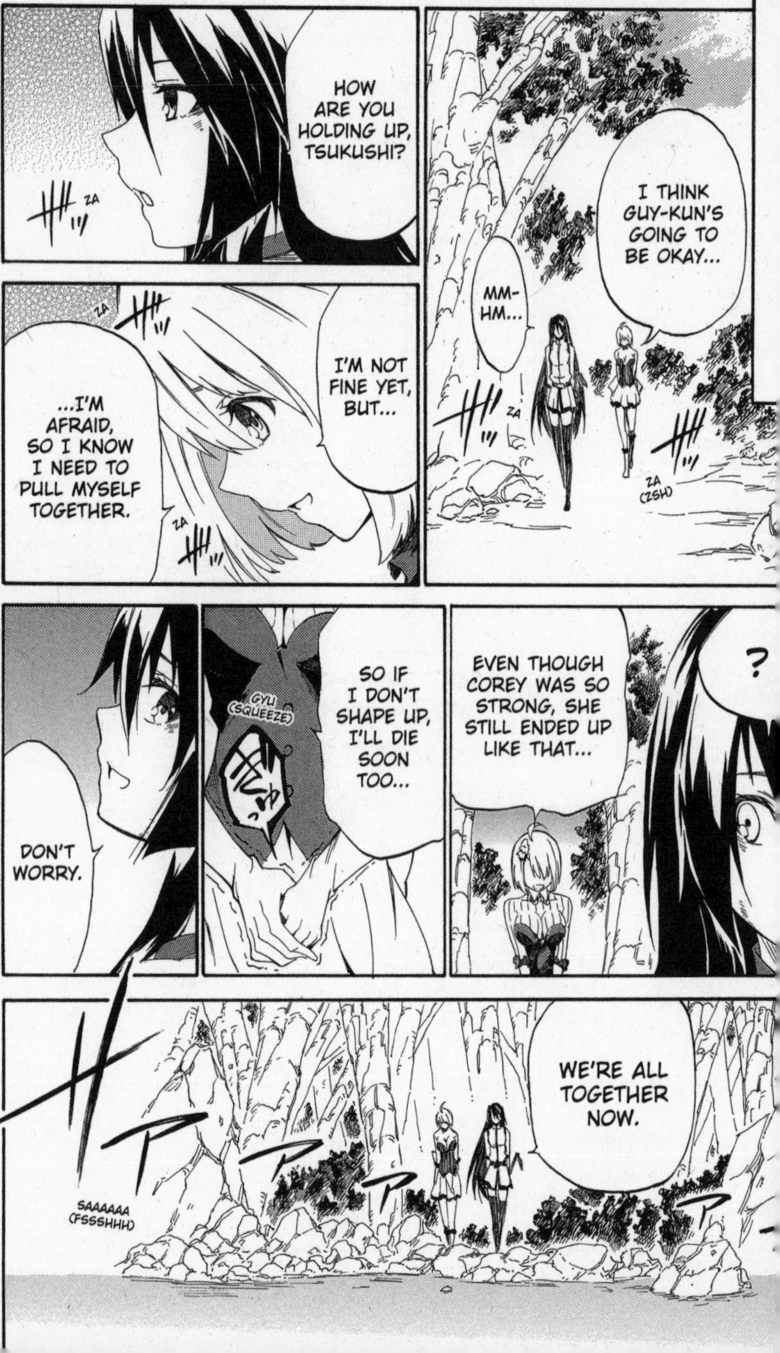
I THINK GUY-KUN'S GOING TO BE OKAY...
MM-HM...
ZA
ZA (ZSH)
HOW ARE YOU HOLDING UP, TSUKUSHI?
ZA
I'M NOT FINE YET, BUT...
ZA
...I'M AFRAID, SO I KNOW I NEED TO PULL MYSELF TOGETHER.
ZA
?
EVEN THOUGH COREY WAS SO STRONG, SHE STILL ENDED UP LIKE THAT...
SO IF I DON'T SHAPE UP, I'LL DIE SOON TOO...
GYU (SQUEEZE)
DON'T WORRY.
WE'RE ALL TOGETHER NOW.
SAAAAAA (FSSSHHH)

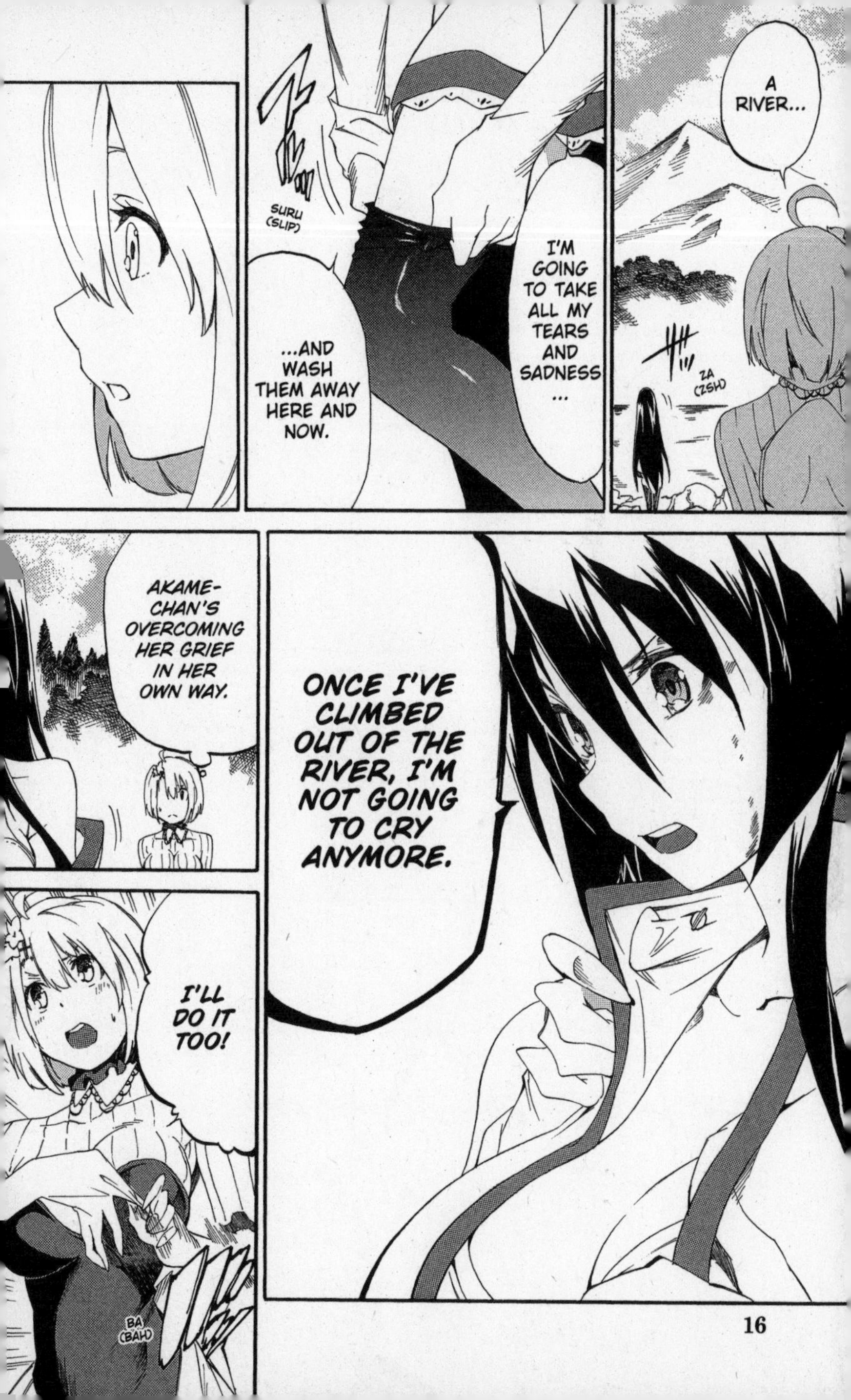
A RIVER...
ZA (ZSH)
I'M GOING TO TAKE ALL MY TEARS AND SADNESS...
...AND WASH THEM AWAY HERE AND NOW.
SURU (SLIP)
ONCE I'VE CLIMBED OUT OF THE RIVER, I'M NOT GOING TO CRY ANYMORE.
AKAME-CHAN'S OVERCOMING HER GRIEF IN HER OWN WAY.
I'LL DO IT TOO!
BA (BAH)

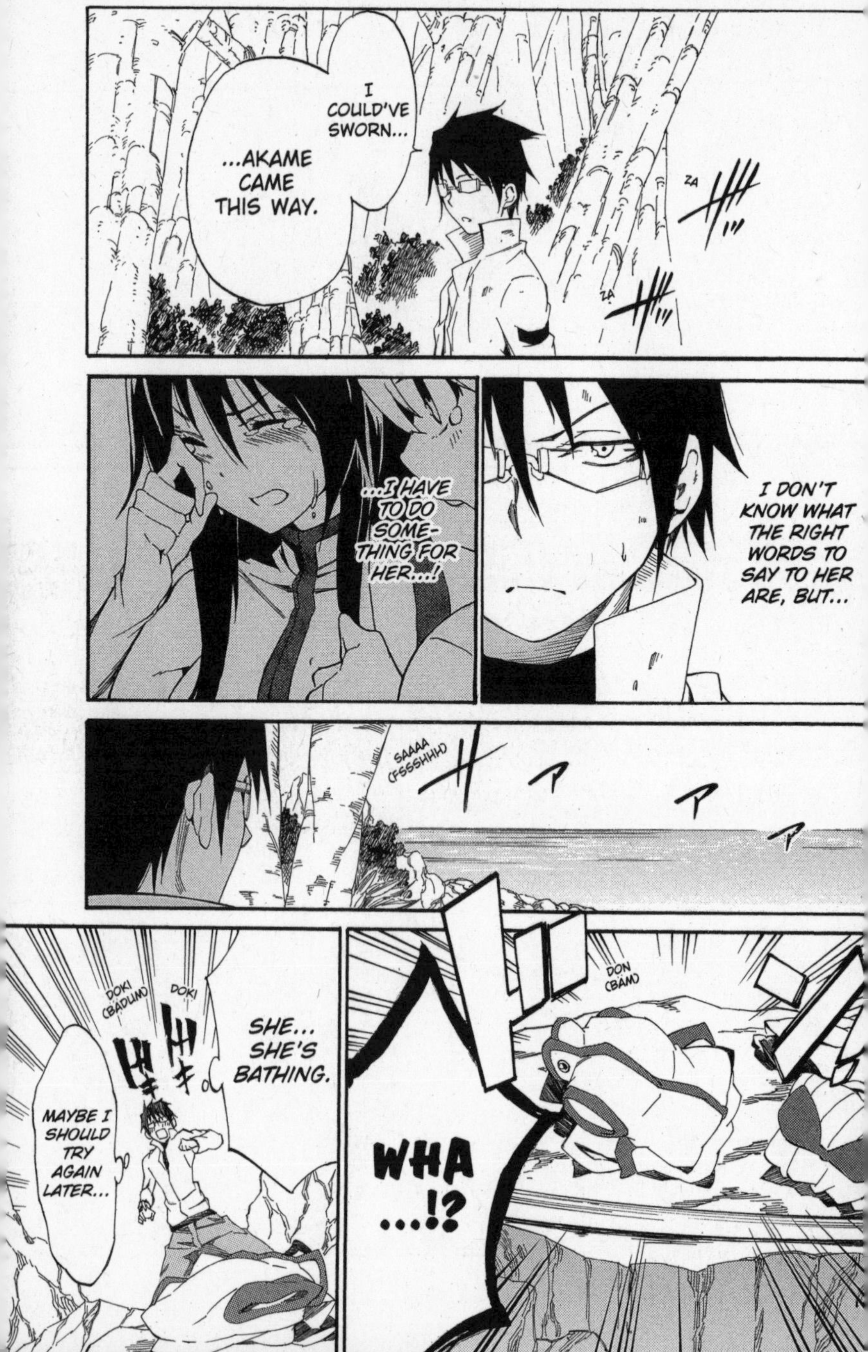
I COULD'VE SWORN...
...AKAME CAME THIS WAY.
ZA
ZA
I DON'T KNOW WHAT THE RIGHT WORDS TO SAY TO HER ARE, BUT...
...I HAVE TO DO SOME-THING FOR HER...!
SAAAA (FSSSHHH)
DON (BÄM)
WHA...!?
DOKI (BÄDUM) DOKI
SHE... SHE'S BATHING.
MAYBE I SHOULD TRY AGAIN LATER...

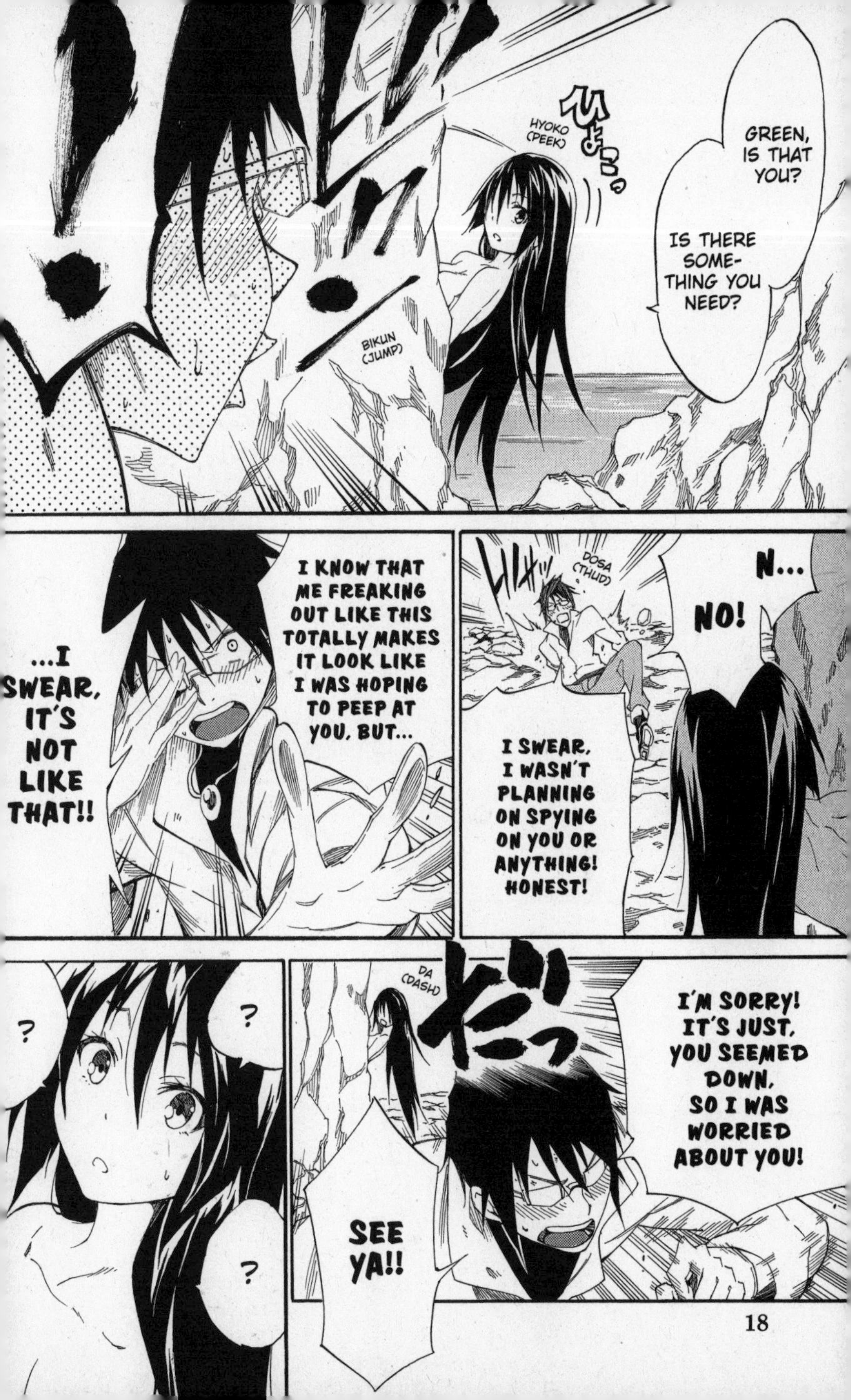
GREEN, IS THAT YOU?
IS THERE SOME-THING YOU NEED?
HYOKO (PEEK)
BIKUN (JUMP)
N...
NO!
DOSA (THUD)
I SWEAR, I WASN'T PLANNING ON SPYING ON YOU OR ANYTHING! HONEST!
I KNOW THAT ME FREAKING OUT LIKE THIS TOTALLY MAKES IT LOOK LIKE I WAS HOPING TO PEEP AT YOU, BUT...
...I SWEAR, IT'S NOT LIKE THAT!!
I'M SORRY! IT'S JUST, YOU SEEMED DOWN, SO I WAS WORRIED ABOUT YOU!
DA (DASH)
SEE YA!!
?
?
?

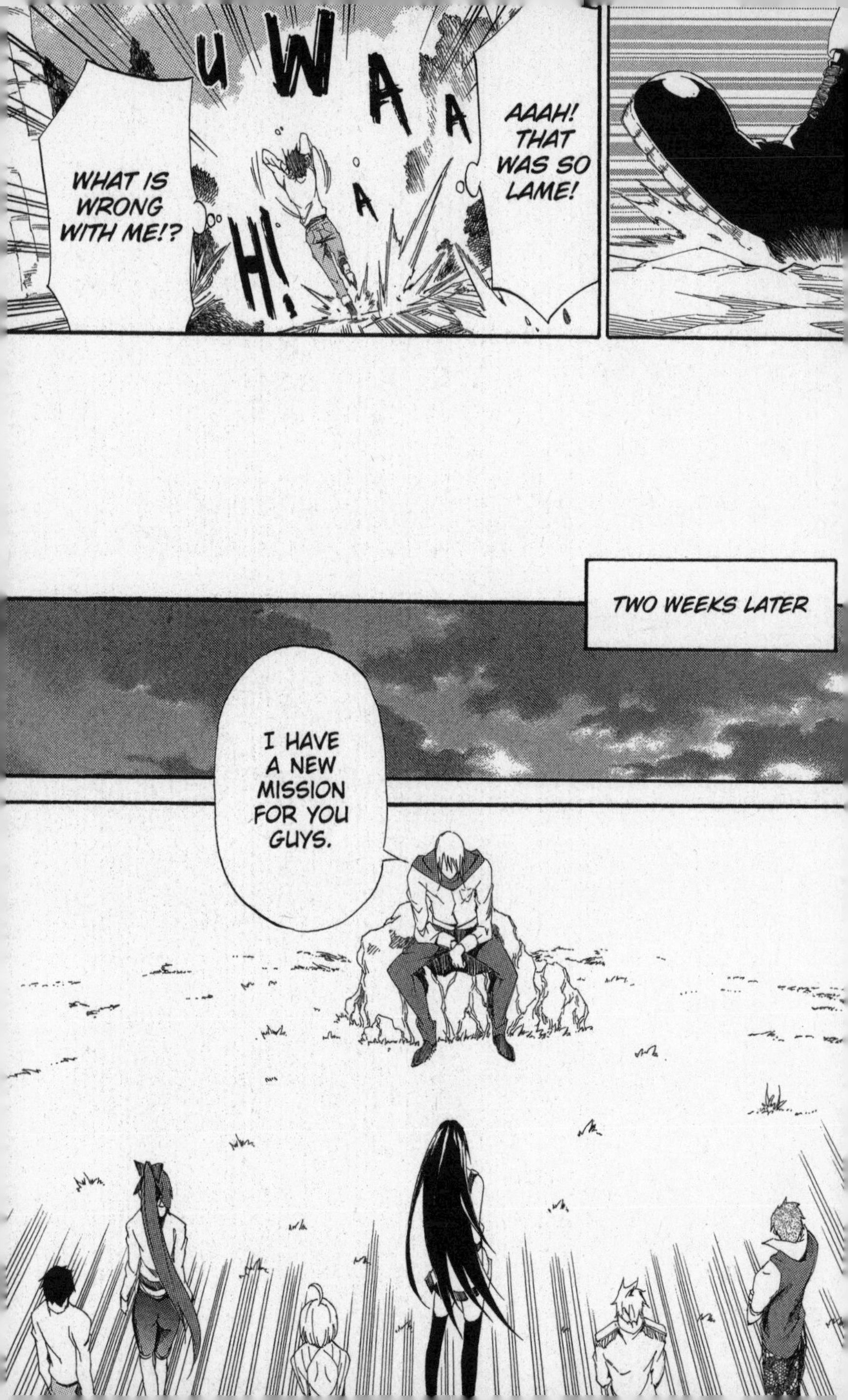
AAAH! THAT WAS SO LAME!
UWAAAH!
WHAT IS WRONG WITH ME!?
TWO WEEKS LATER
I HAVE A NEW MISSION FOR YOU GUYS.

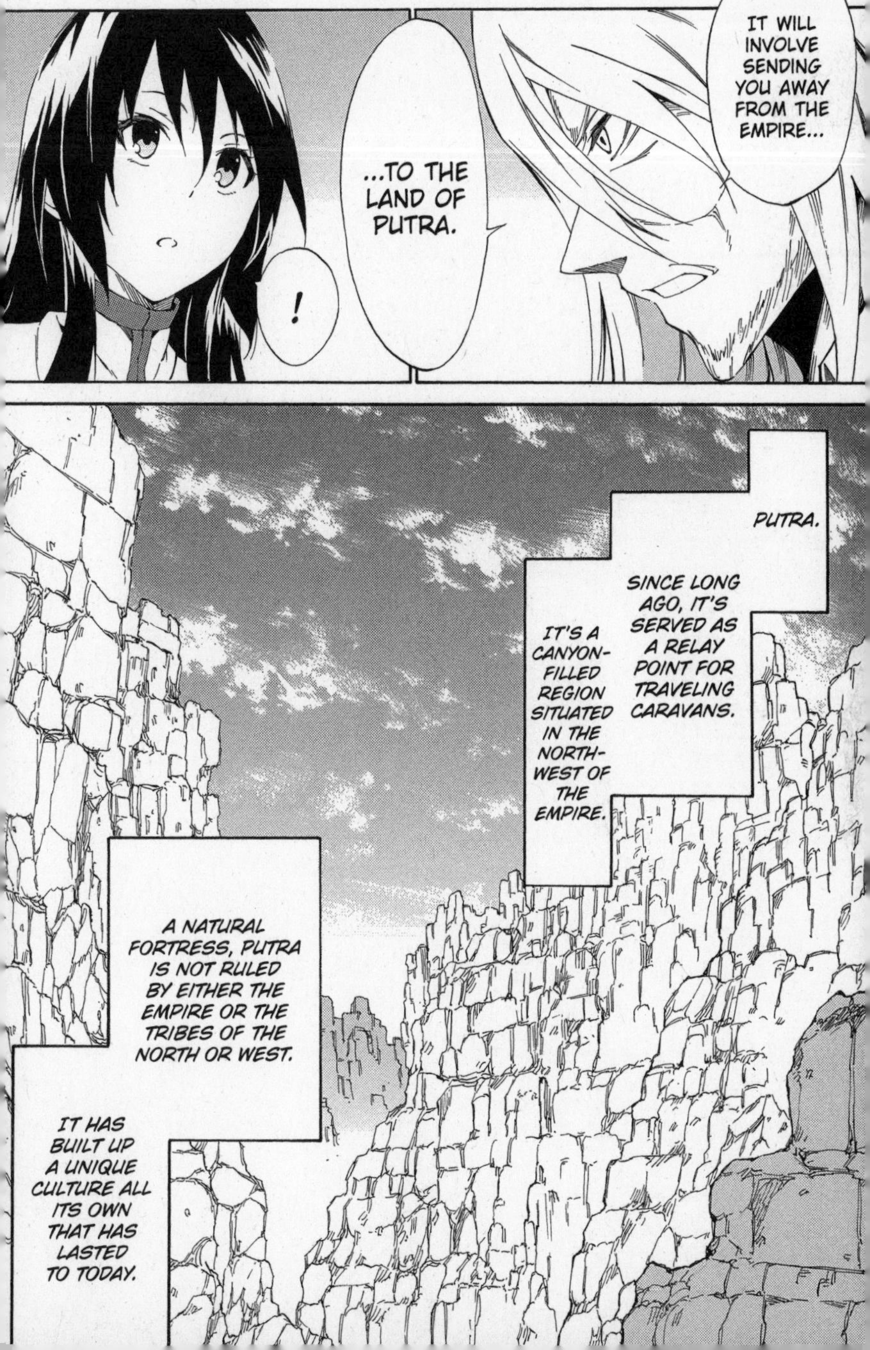
IT WILL INVOLVE SENDING YOU AWAY FROM THE EMPIRE...
...TO THE LAND OF PUTRA.
!
PUTRA.
SINCE LONG AGO, IT'S SERVED AS A RELAY POINT FOR TRAVELING CARAVANS.
IT'S A CANYON-FILLED REGION SITUATED IN THE NORTH-WEST OF THE EMPIRE.
A NATURAL FORTRESS, PUTRA IS NOT RULED BY EITHER THE EMPIRE OR THE TRIBES OF THE NORTH OR WEST.
IT HAS BUILT UP A UNIQUE CULTURE ALL ITS OWN THAT HAS LASTED TO TODAY.

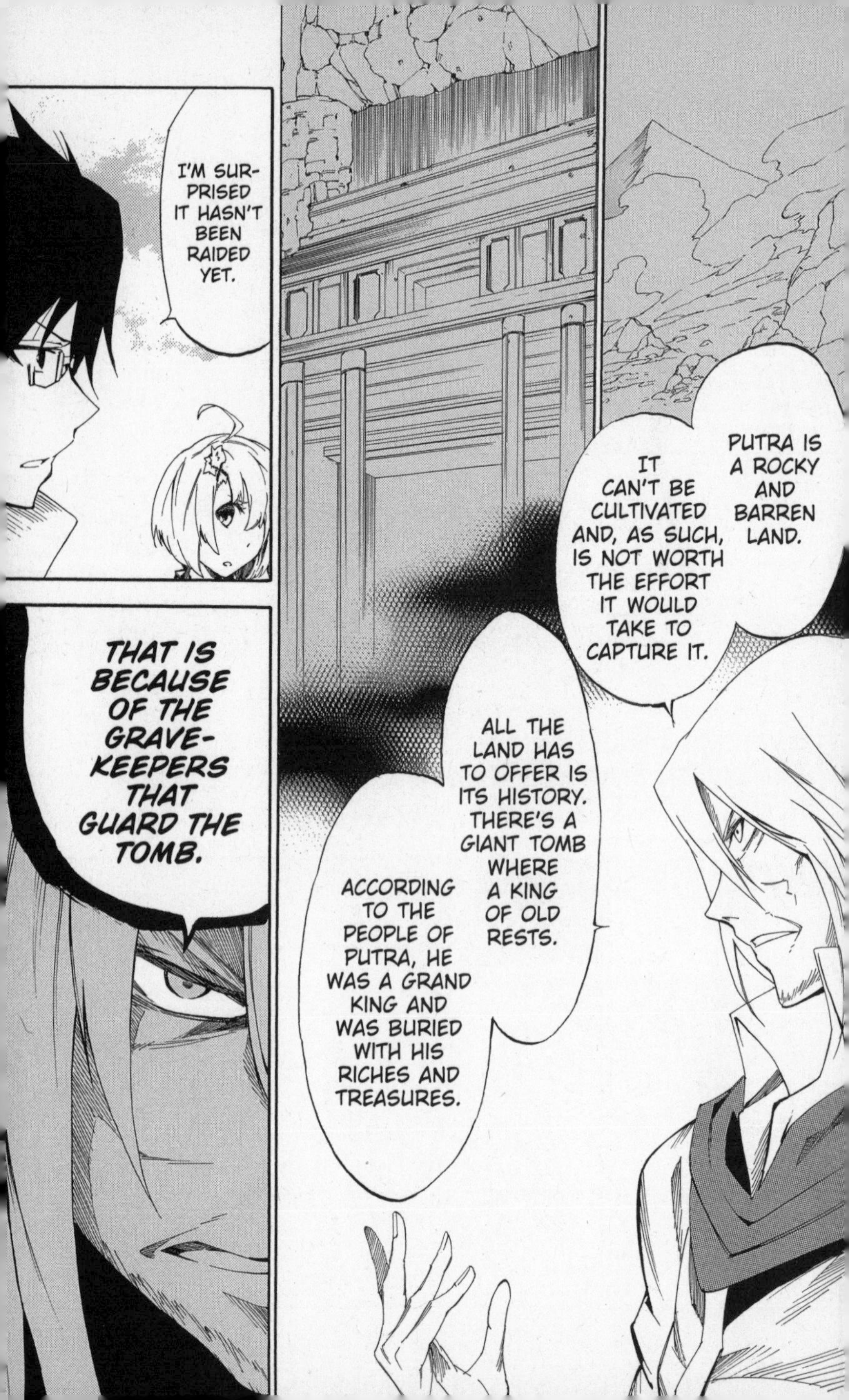
PUTRA IS A ROCKY AND BARREN LAND.
IT CAN'T BE CULTIVATED AND, AS SUCH, IS NOT WORTH THE EFFORT IT WOULD TAKE TO CAPTURE IT.
ALL THE LAND HAS TO OFFER IS ITS HISTORY. THERE'S A GIANT TOMB WHERE A KING OF OLD RESTS.
ACCORDING TO THE PEOPLE OF PUTRA, HE WAS A GRAND KING AND WAS BURIED WITH HIS RICHES AND TREASURES.
I'M SURPRISED IT HASN'T BEEN RAIDED YET.
THAT IS BECAUSE OF THE GRAVE-KEEPERS THAT GUARD THE TOMB.

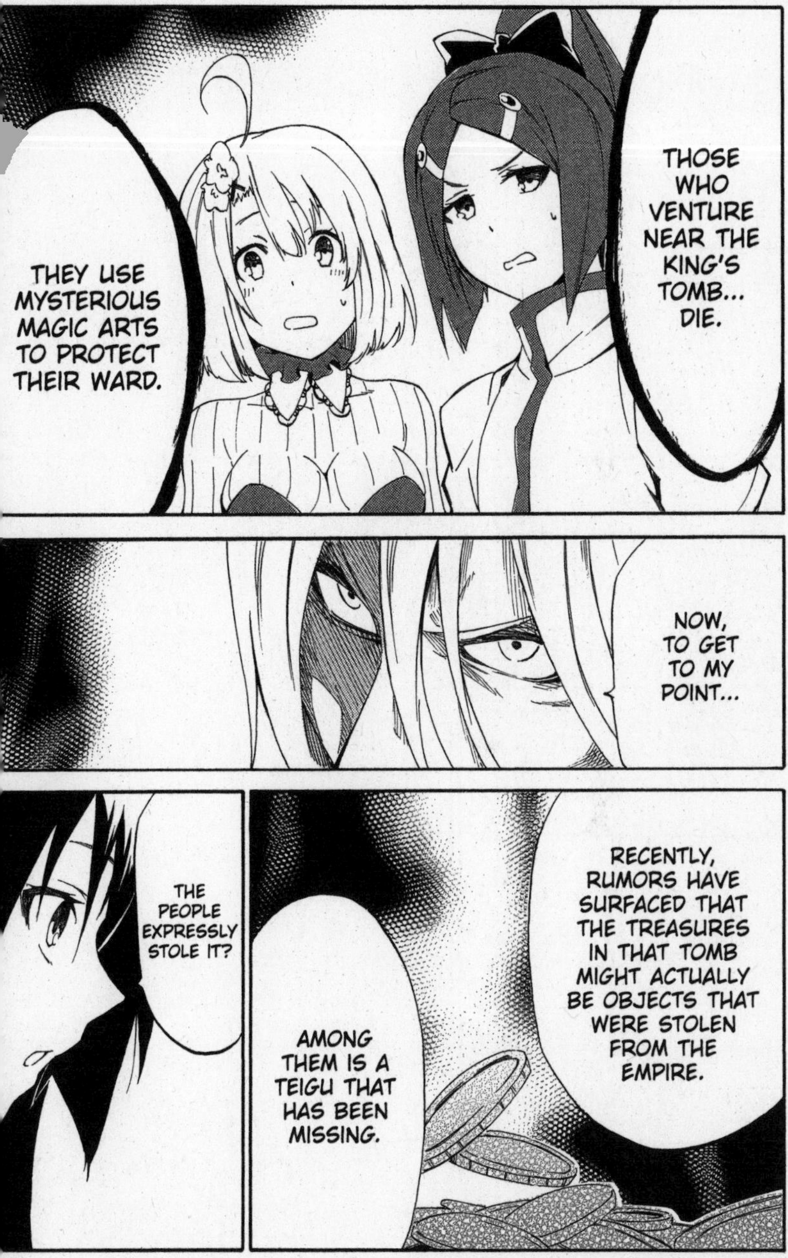
THOSE WHO VENTURE NEAR THE KING'S TOMB... DIE.
THEY USE MYSTERIOUS MAGIC ARTS TO PROTECT THEIR WARD.
NOW, TO GET TO MY POINT...
RECENTLY, RUMORS HAVE SURFACED THAT THE TREASURES IN THAT TOMB MIGHT ACTUALLY BE OBJECTS THAT WERE STOLEN FROM THE EMPIRE.
AMONG THEM IS A TEIGU THAT HAS BEEN MISSING.
THE PEOPLE EXPRESSLY STOLE IT?

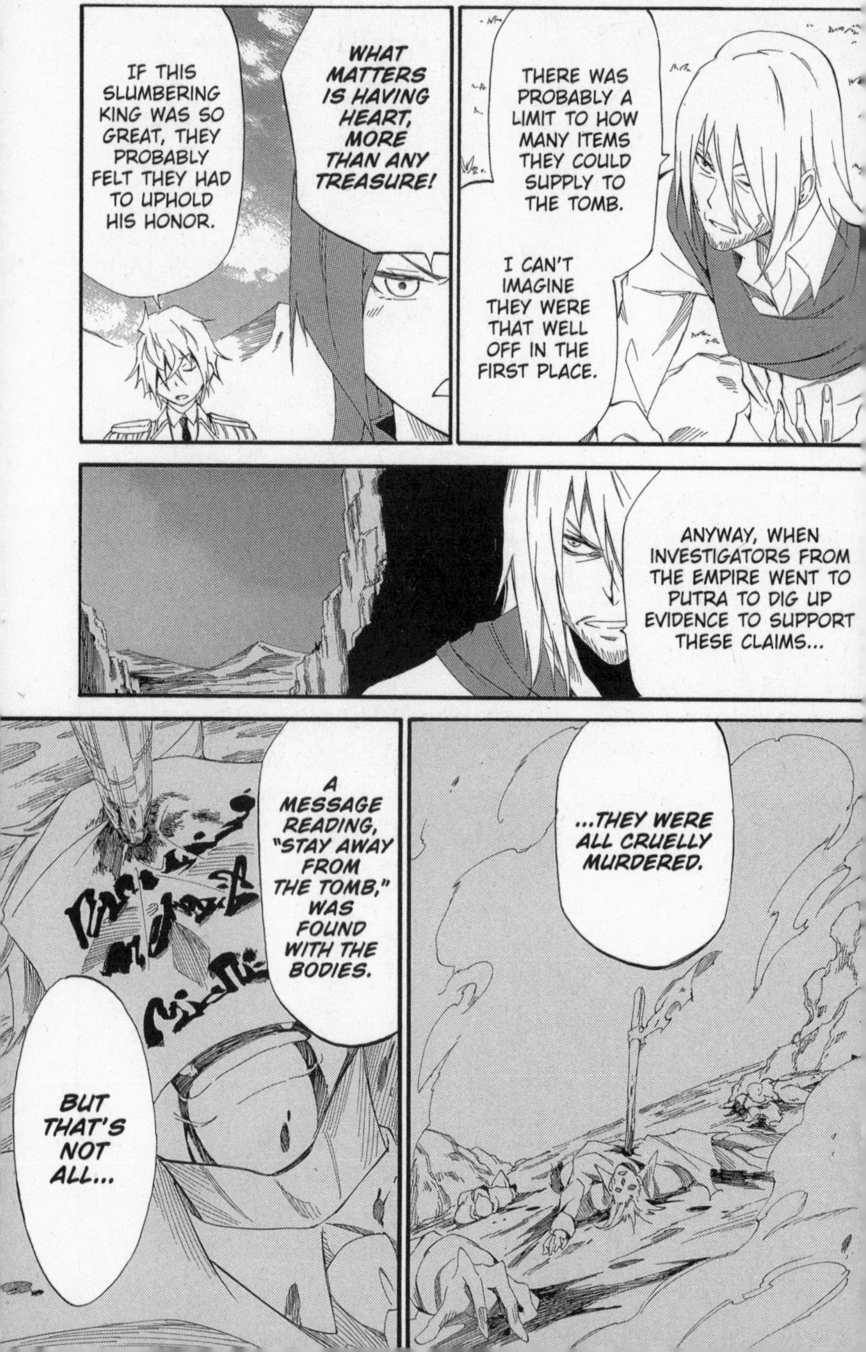
THERE WAS PROBABLY A LIMIT TO HOW MANY ITEMS THEY COULD SUPPLY TO THE TOMB.
I CAN'T IMAGINE THEY WERE THAT WELL OFF IN THE FIRST PLACE.
WHAT MATTERS IS HAVING HEART, MORE THAN ANY TREASURE!
IF THIS SLUMBERING KING WAS SO GREAT, THEY PROBABLY FELT THEY HAD TO UPHOLD HIS HONOR.
ANYWAY, WHEN INVESTIGATORS FROM THE EMPIRE WENT TO PUTRA TO DIG UP EVIDENCE TO SUPPORT THESE CLAIMS...
...THEY WERE ALL CRUELLY MURDERED.
A MESSAGE READING, "STAY AWAY FROM THE TOMB," WAS FOUND WITH THE BODIES.
BUT THAT'S NOT ALL...

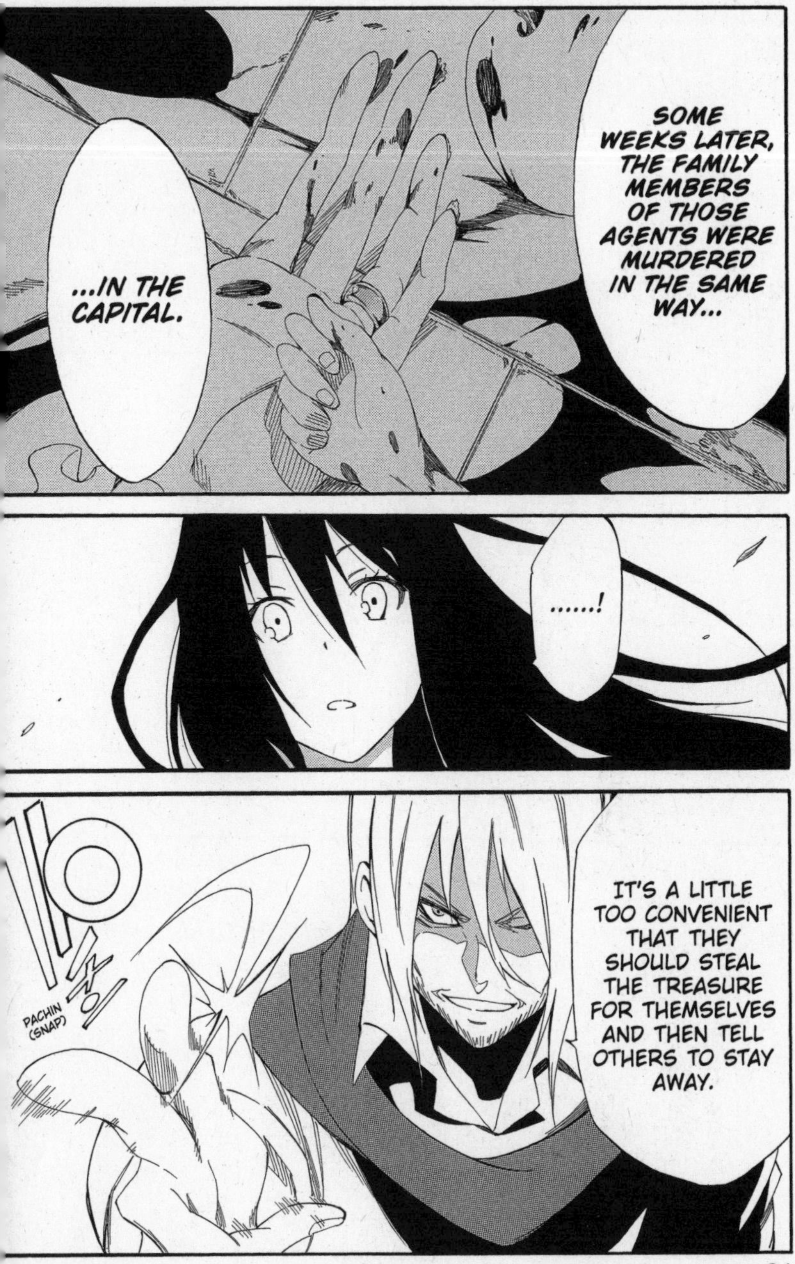
SOME WEEKS LATER, THE FAMILY MEMBERS OF THOSE AGENTS WERE MURDERED IN THE SAME WAY...
...IN THE CAPITAL.
......!
IT'S A LITTLE TOO CONVENIENT THAT THEY SHOULD STEAL THE TREASURE FOR THEMSELVES AND THEN TELL OTHERS TO STAY AWAY.
PACHIN (SNAP)

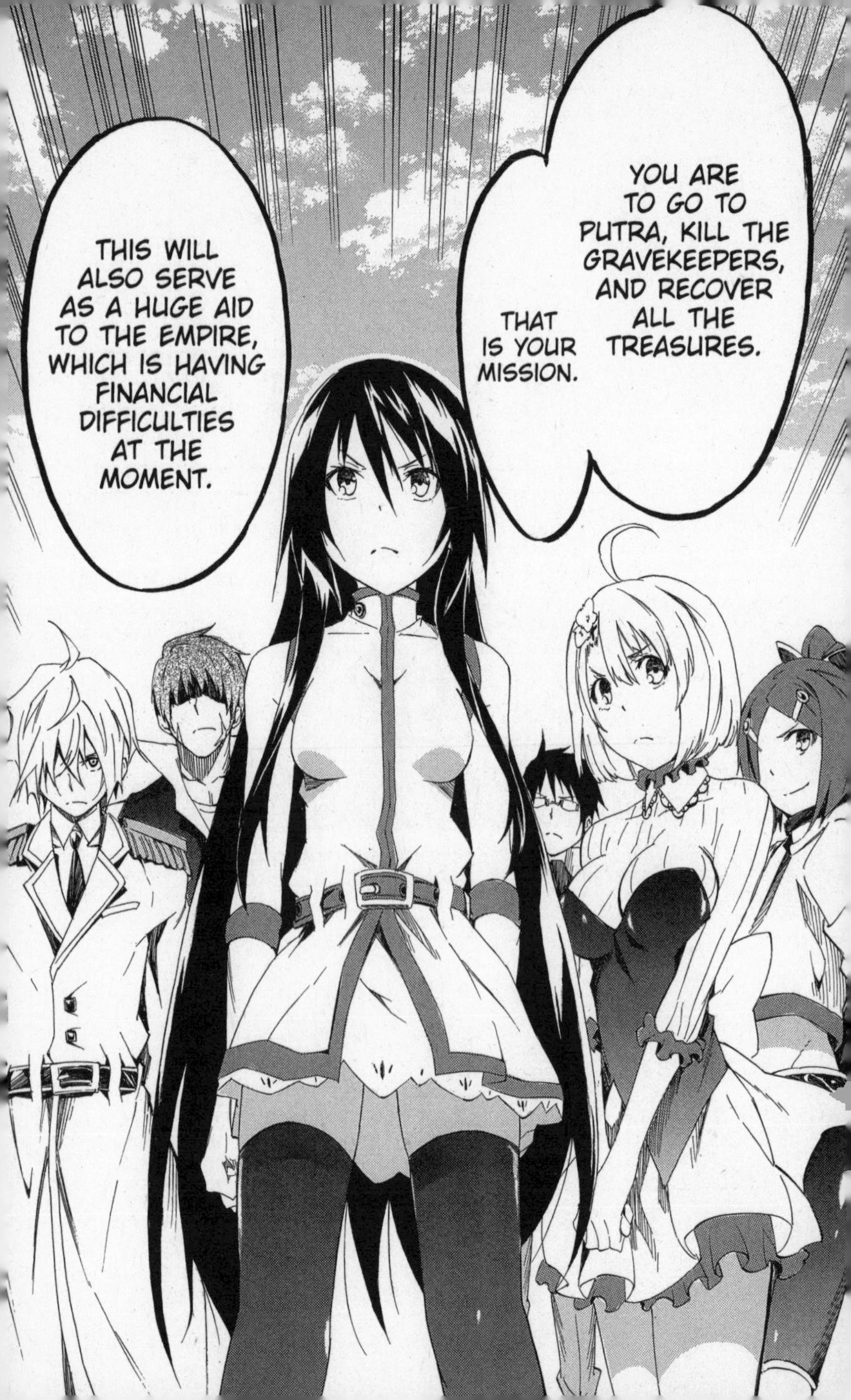
YOU ARE TO GO TO PUTRA, KILL THE GRAVEKEEPERS, AND RECOVER ALL THE TREASURES.
THAT IS YOUR MISSION.
THIS WILL ALSO SERVE AS A HUGE AID TO THE EMPIRE, WHICH IS HAVING FINANCIAL DIFFICULTIES AT THE MOMENT.

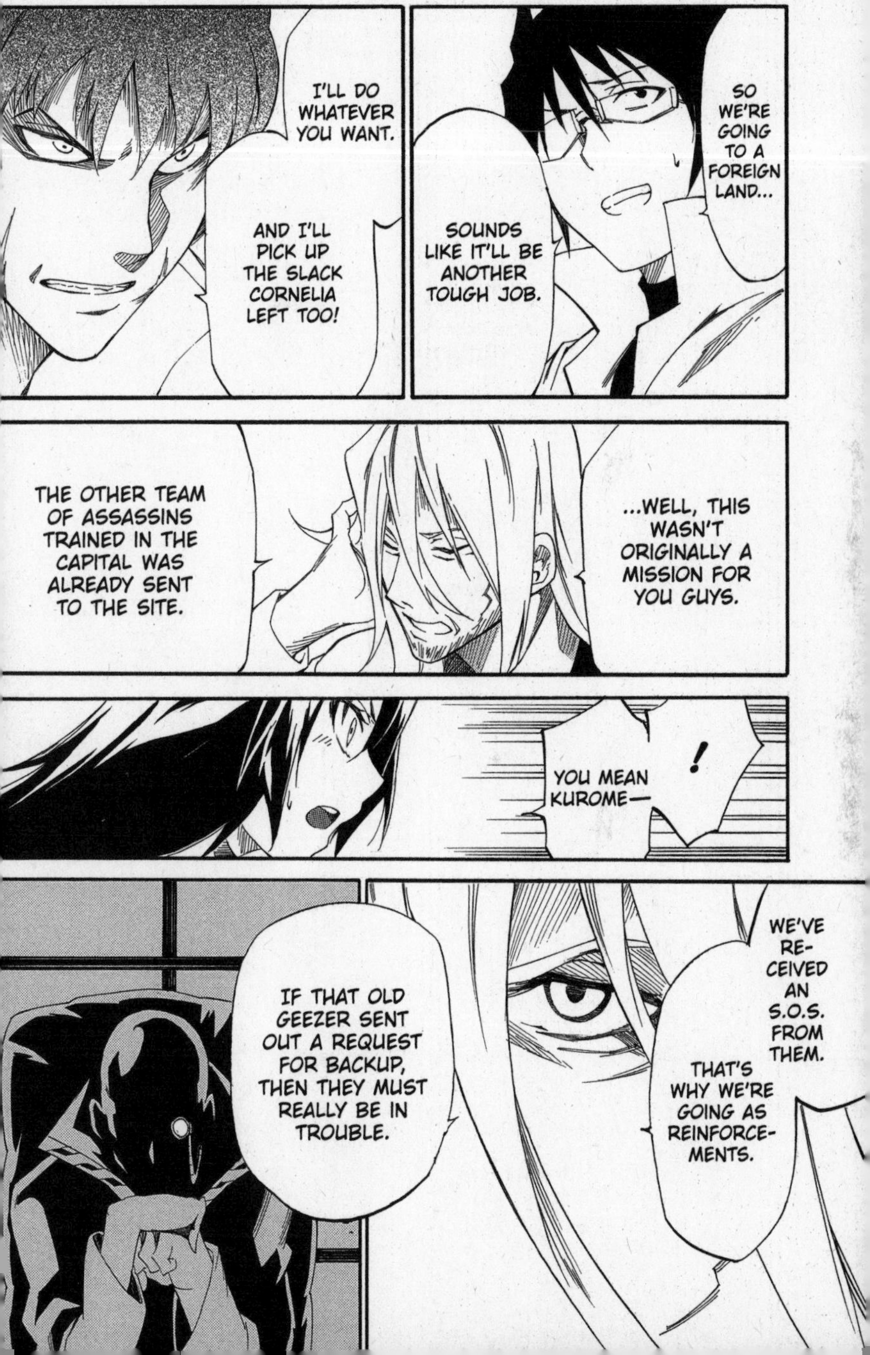
SO WE'RE GOING TO A FOREIGN LAND...
SOUNDS LIKE IT'LL BE ANOTHER TOUGH JOB.
I'LL DO WHATEVER YOU WANT.
AND I'LL PICK UP THE SLACK CORNELIA LEFT TOO!
...WELL, THIS WASN'T ORIGINALLY A MISSION FOR YOU GUYS.
THE OTHER TEAM OF ASSASSINS TRAINED IN THE CAPITAL WAS ALREADY SENT TO THE SITE.
!
YOU MEAN KUROME—
WE'VE RE-CEIVED AN S.O.S. FROM THEM.
THAT'S WHY WE'RE GOING AS REINFORCE-MENTS.
IF THAT OLD GEEZER SENT OUT A REQUEST FOR BACKUP, THEN THEY MUST REALLY BE IN TROUBLE.

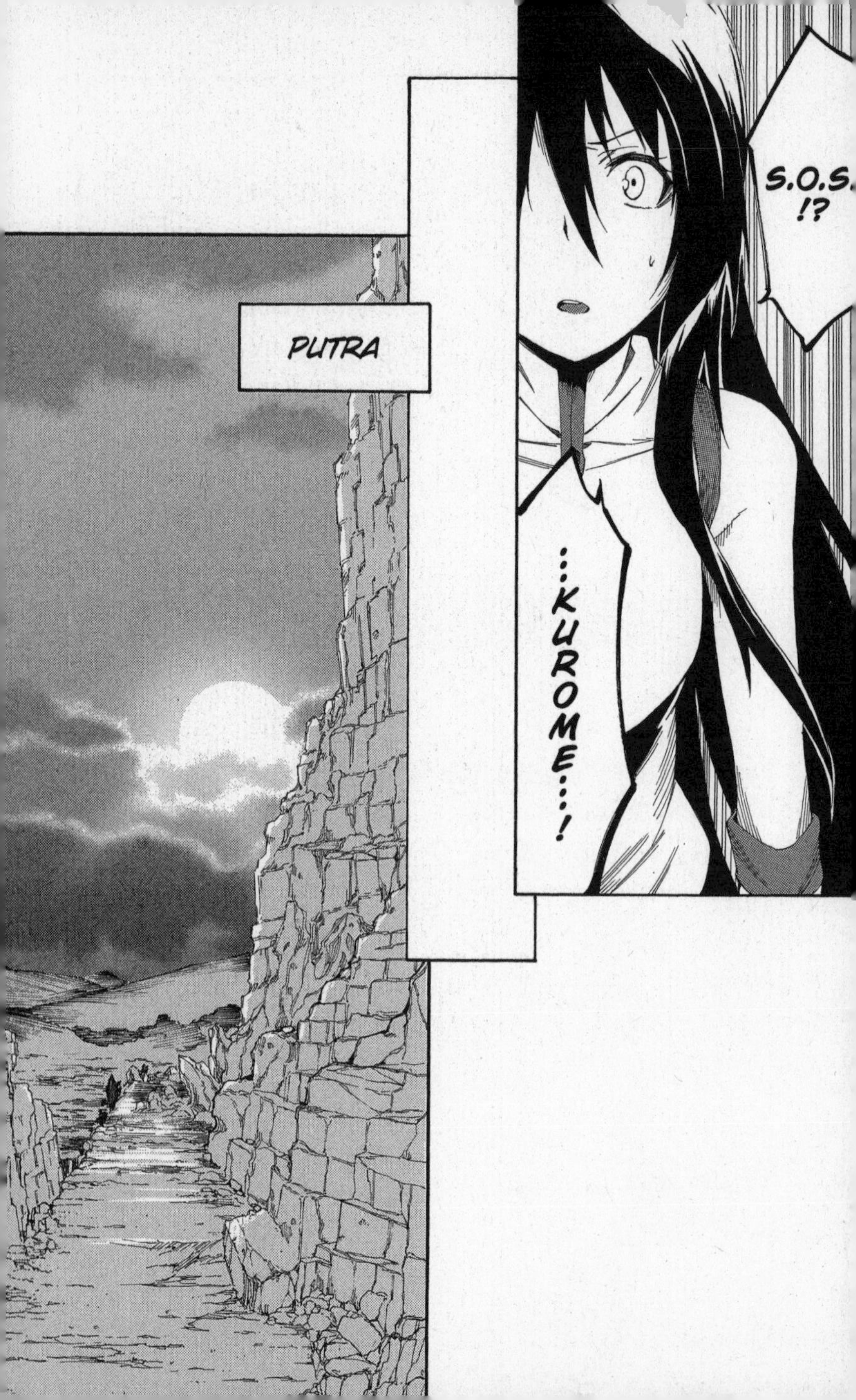
S.O.S. !?
...KUROME...!
PUTRA

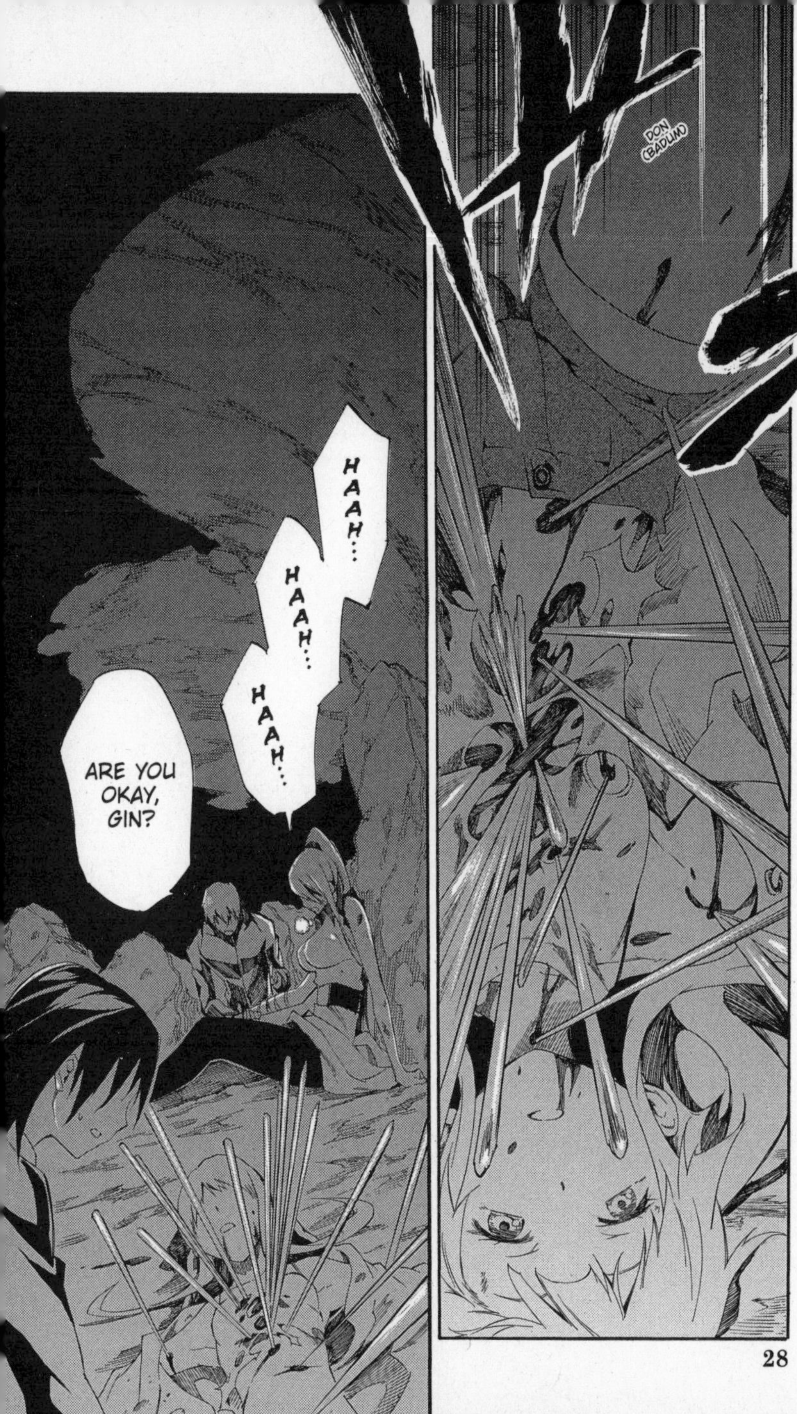
DON (BADUM)
HAAH...
HAAH...
HAAH...
ARE YOU OKAY, GIN?

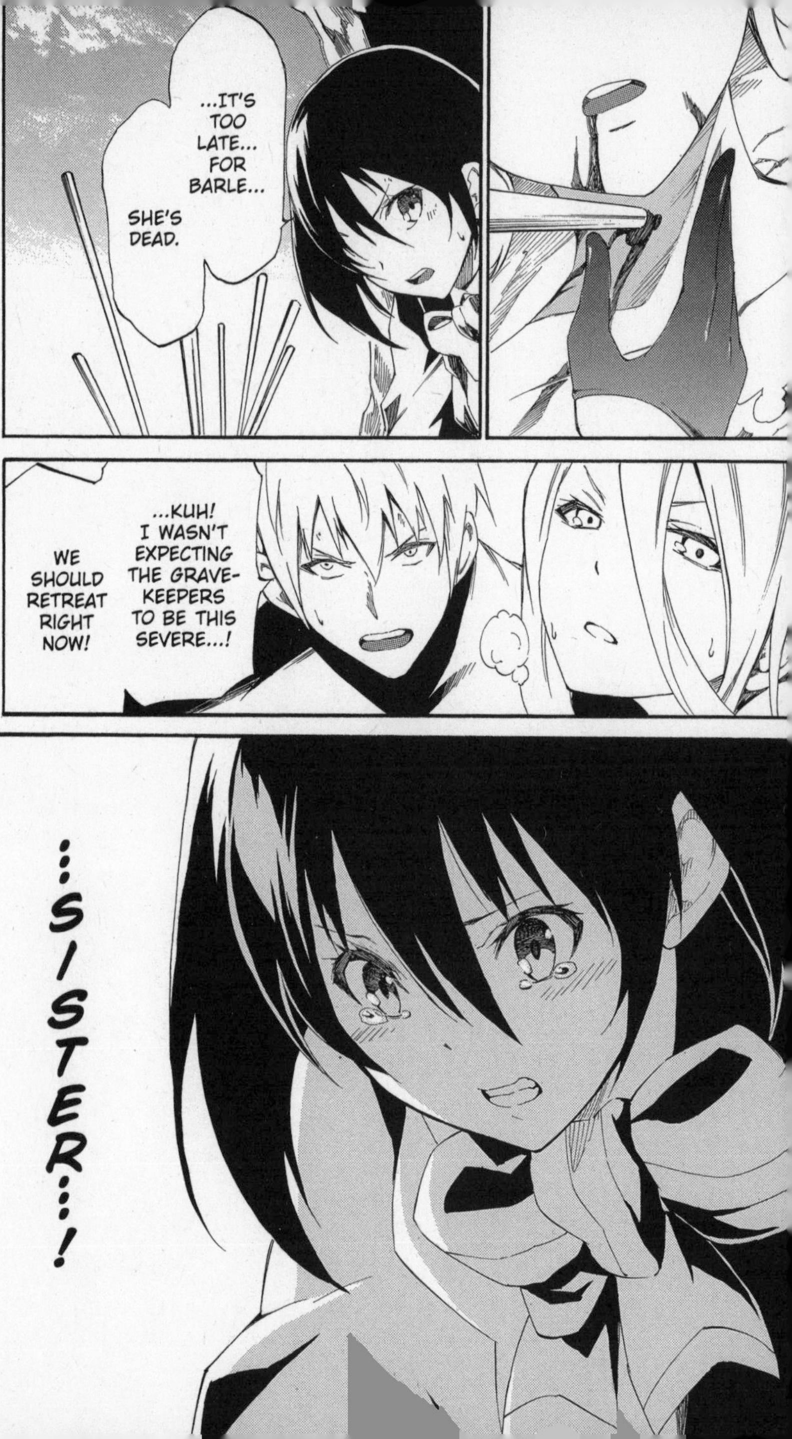
...IT'S TOO LATE... FOR BARLE...
SHE'S DEAD.
...KUH! I WASN'T EXPECTING THE GRAVE-KEEPERS TO BE THIS SEVERE...!
WE SHOULD RETREAT RIGHT NOW!
...SISTER...!

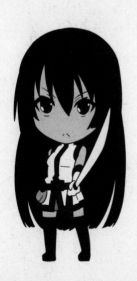

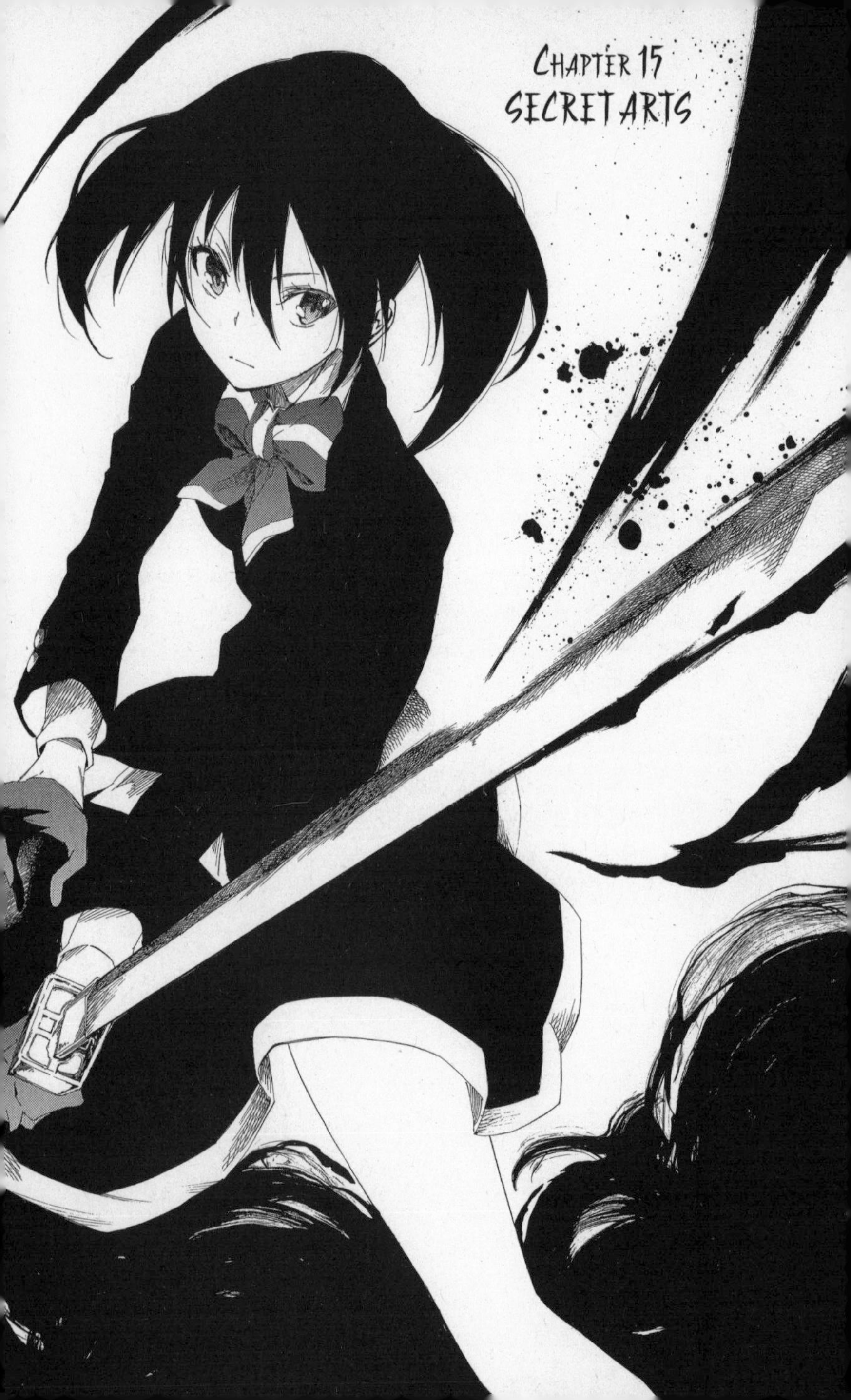
CHAPTER 15
SECRET ARTS

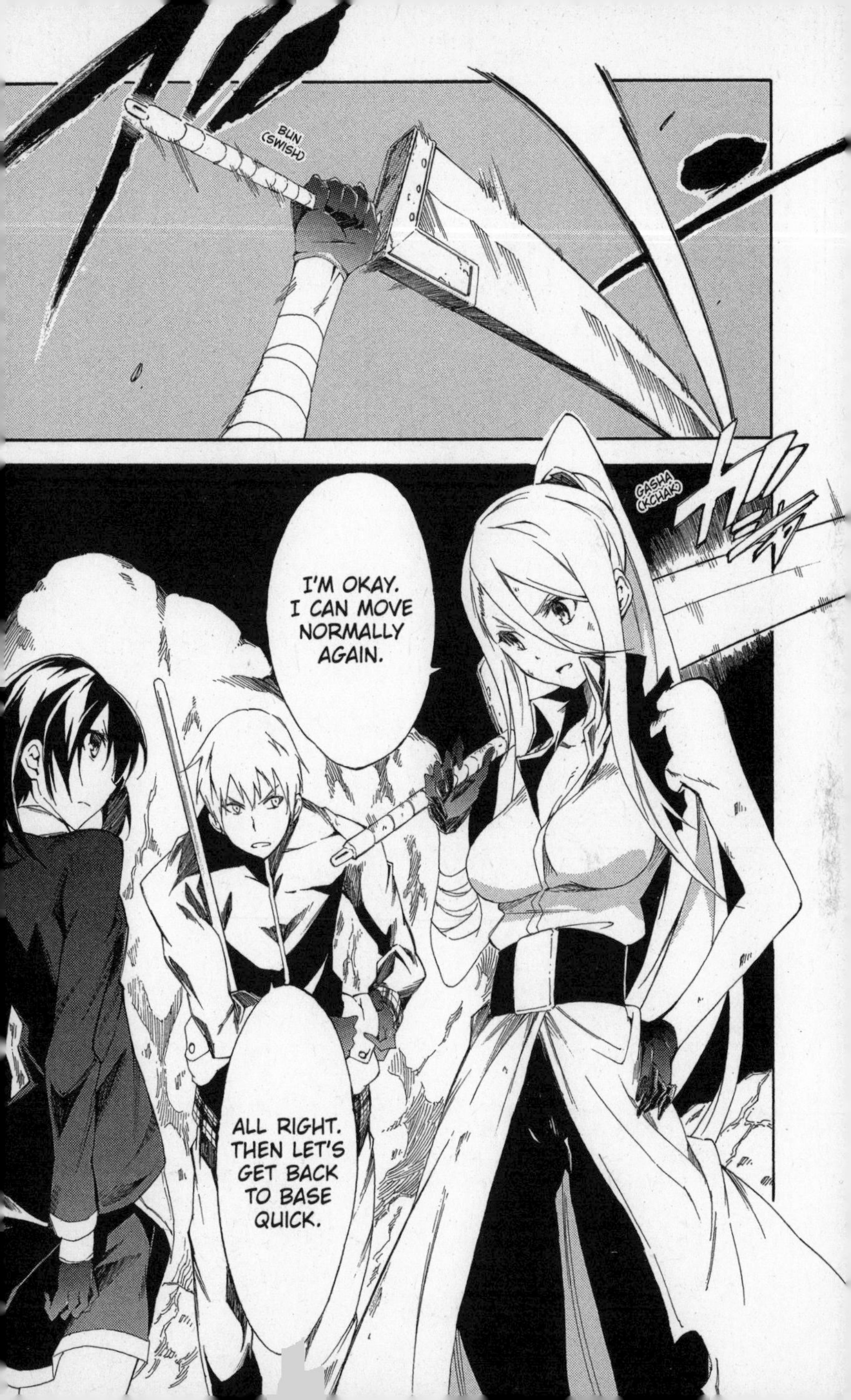
BUN (SWISH)
GASHA (KCHAK)
I'M OKAY. I CAN MOVE NORMALLY AGAIN.
ALL RIGHT. THEN LET'S GET BACK TO BASE QUICK.

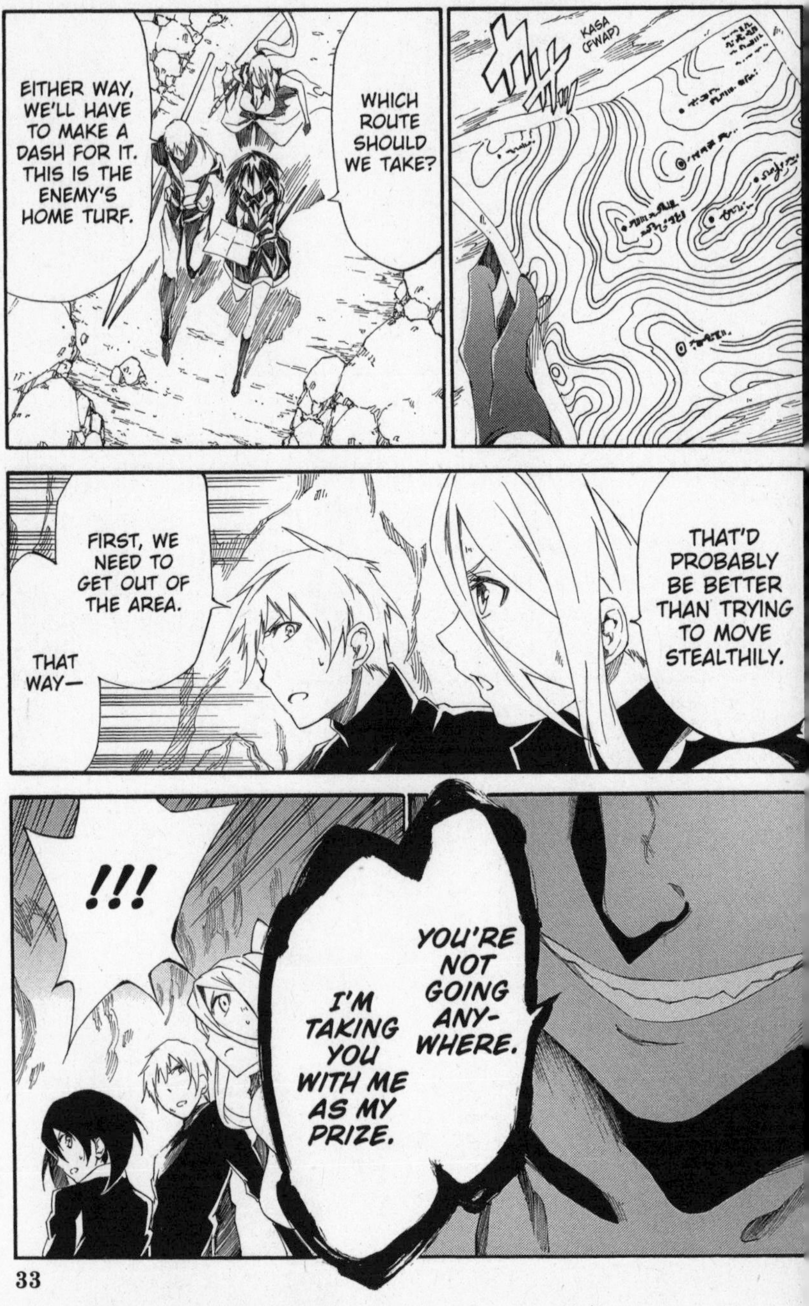
KASA (FWAP)
WHICH ROUTE SHOULD WE TAKE?
EITHER WAY, WE'LL HAVE TO MAKE A DASH FOR IT. THIS IS THE ENEMY'S HOME TURF.
THAT'D PROBABLY BE BETTER THAN TRYING TO MOVE STEALTHILY.
FIRST, WE NEED TO GET OUT OF THE AREA.
THAT WAY—
YOU'RE NOT GOING ANY-WHERE.
I'M TAKING YOU WITH ME AS MY PRIZE.
!!!

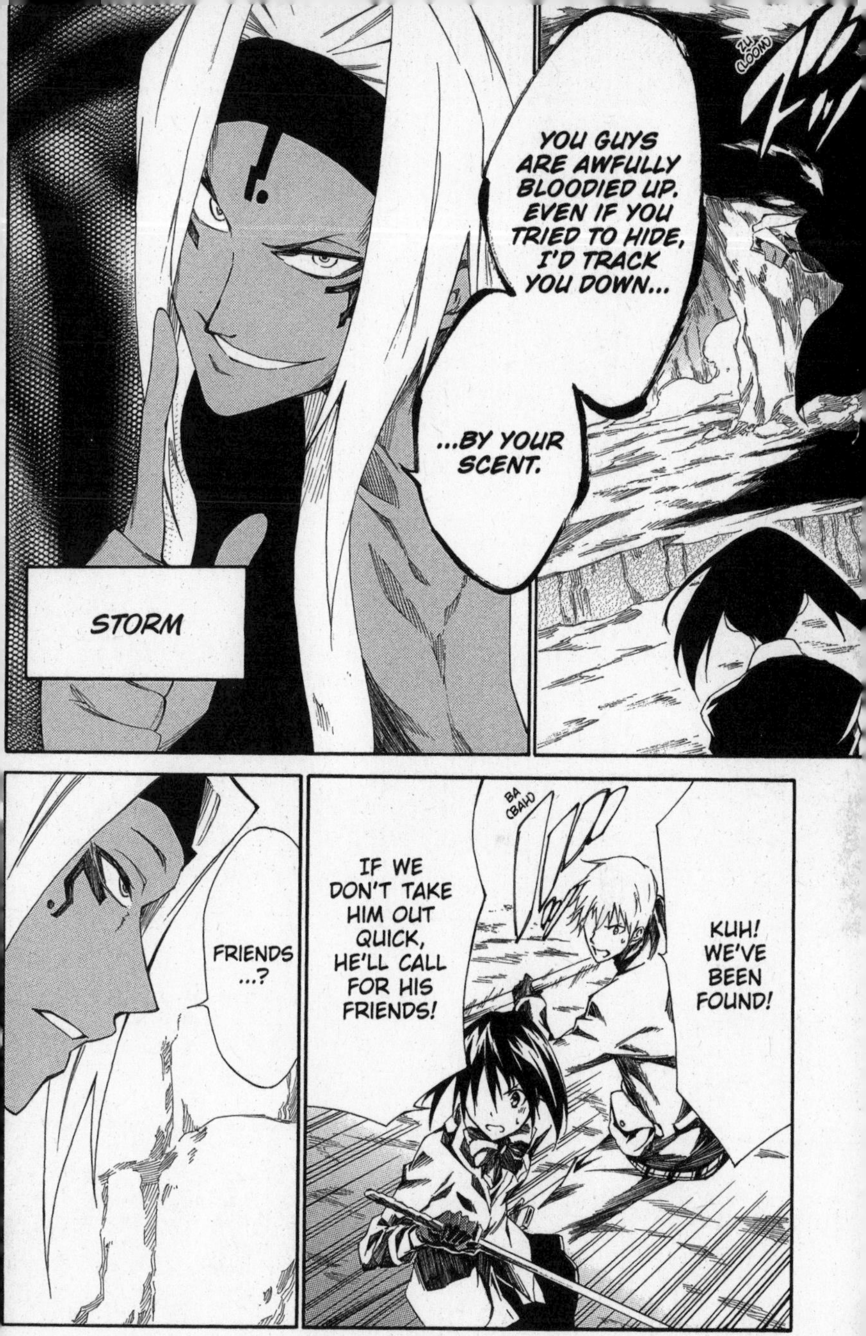
ZU (LOOM)
YOU GUYS ARE AWFULLY BLOODIED UP. EVEN IF YOU TRIED TO HIDE, I'D TRACK YOU DOWN...
...BY YOUR SCENT.
STORM
BA (BAH)
KUH! WE'VE BEEN FOUND!
IF WE DON'T TAKE HIM OUT QUICK, HE'LL CALL FOR HIS FRIENDS!
FRIENDS ...?

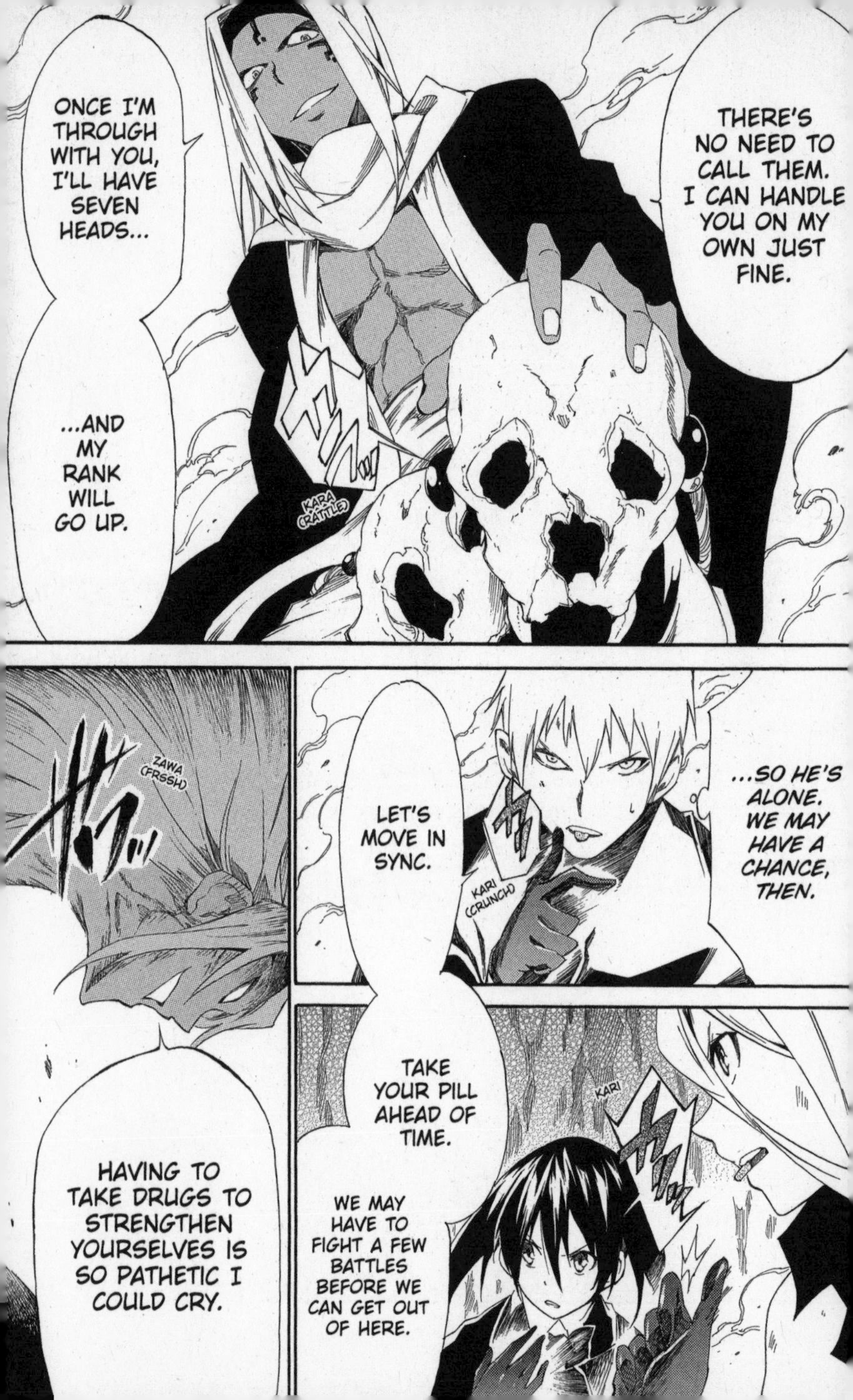
THERE'S NO NEED TO CALL THEM. I CAN HANDLE YOU ON MY OWN JUST FINE.
ONCE I'M THROUGH WITH YOU, I'LL HAVE SEVEN HEADS...
...AND MY RANK WILL GO UP.
KARA (RATTLE)
...SO HE'S ALONE. WE MAY HAVE A CHANCE, THEN.
LET'S MOVE IN SYNC.
KARI (CRUNCH)
TAKE YOUR PILL AHEAD OF TIME.
KARI
WE MAY HAVE TO FIGHT A FEW BATTLES BEFORE WE CAN GET OUT OF HERE.
ZAWA (FRSSH)
HAVING TO TAKE DRUGS TO STRENGTHEN YOURSELVES IS SO PATHETIC I COULD CRY.

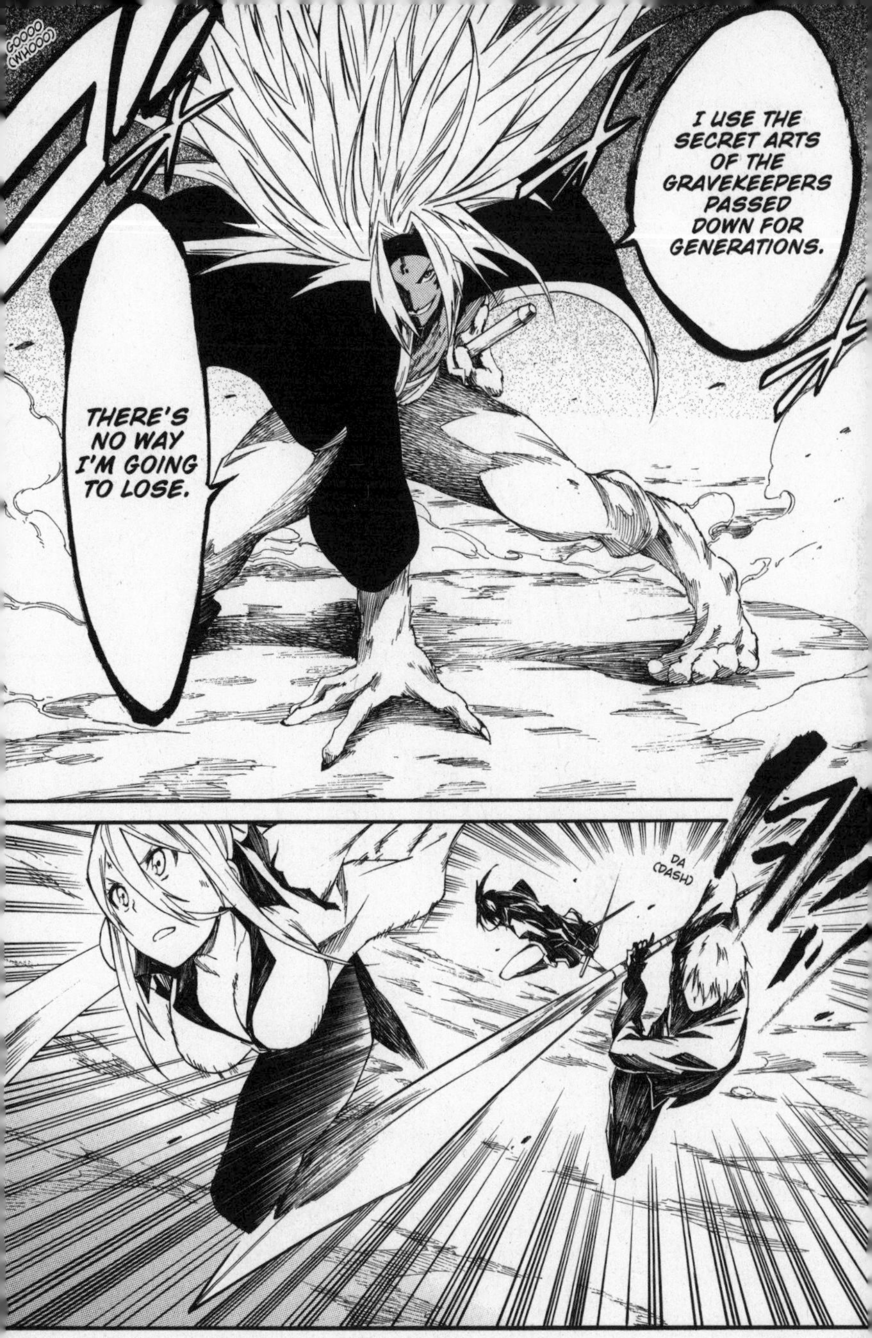

GOOOO (WHOOO)
I USE THE SECRET ARTS OF THE GRAVEKEEPERS PASSED DOWN FOR GENERATIONS.
THERE'S NO WAY I'M GOING TO LOSE.
DA (DASH)

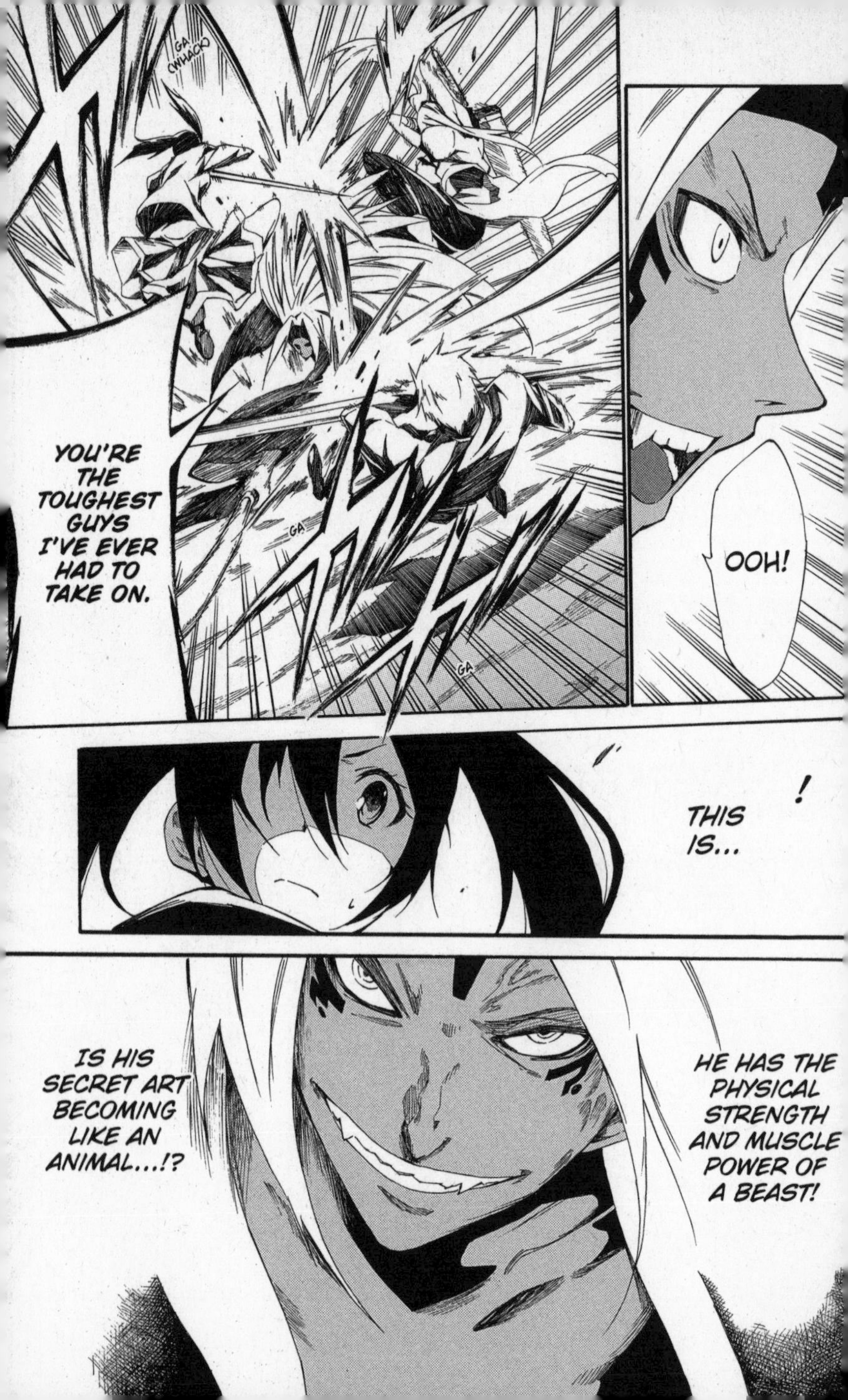
OOH!
GA (WHACK)
GA
GA
YOU'RE THE TOUGHEST GUYS I'VE EVER HAD TO TAKE ON.
!
THIS IS...
HE HAS THE PHYSICAL STRENGTH AND MUSCLE POWER OF A BEAST!
IS HIS SECRET ART BECOMING LIKE AN ANIMAL...!?

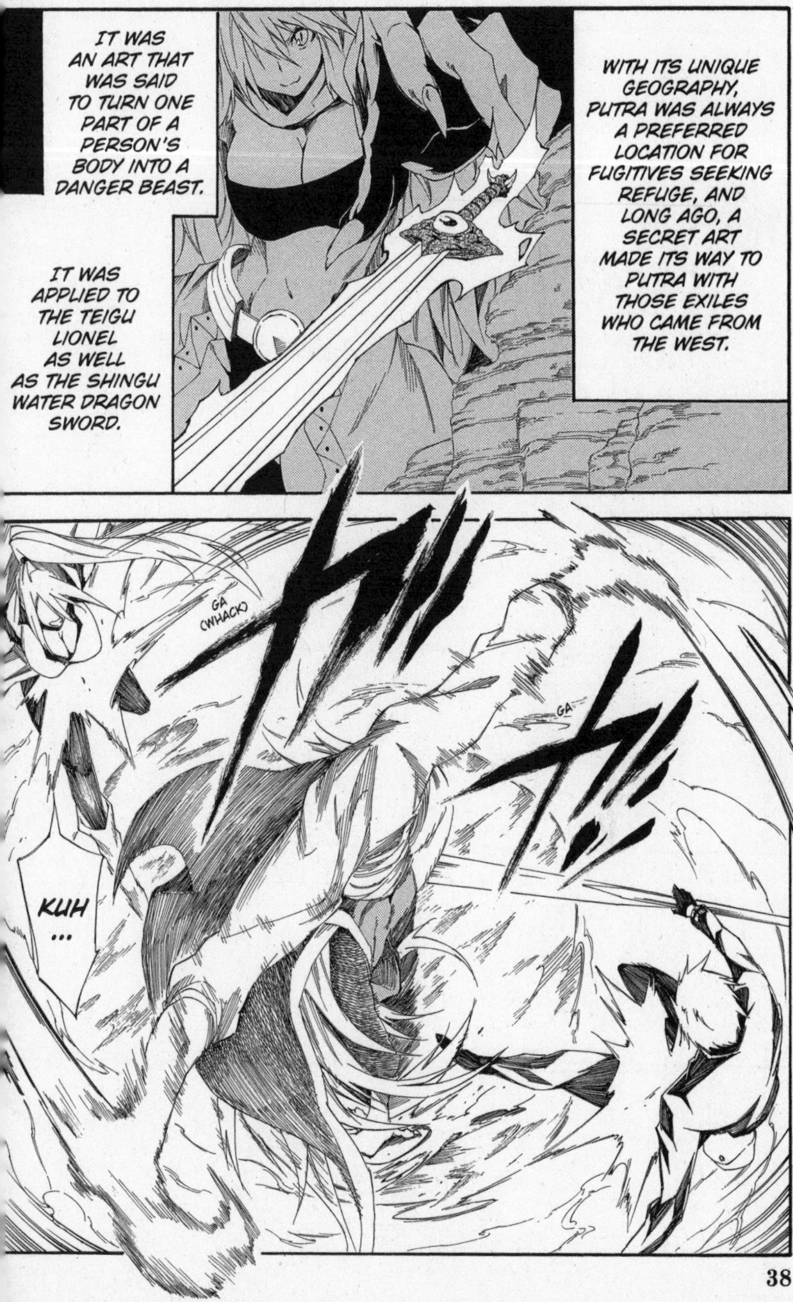
WITH ITS UNIQUE GEOGRAPHY, PUTRA WAS ALWAYS A PREFERRED LOCATION FOR FUGITIVES SEEKING REFUGE, AND LONG AGO, A SECRET ART MADE ITS WAY TO PUTRA WITH THOSE EXILES WHO CAME FROM THE WEST.
IT WAS AN ART THAT WAS SAID TO TURN ONE PART OF A PERSON'S BODY INTO A DANGER BEAST.
IT WAS APPLIED TO THE TEIGU LIONEL AS WELL AS THE SHINGU WATER DRAGON SWORD.
GA (WHACK)
GA
KUH ...

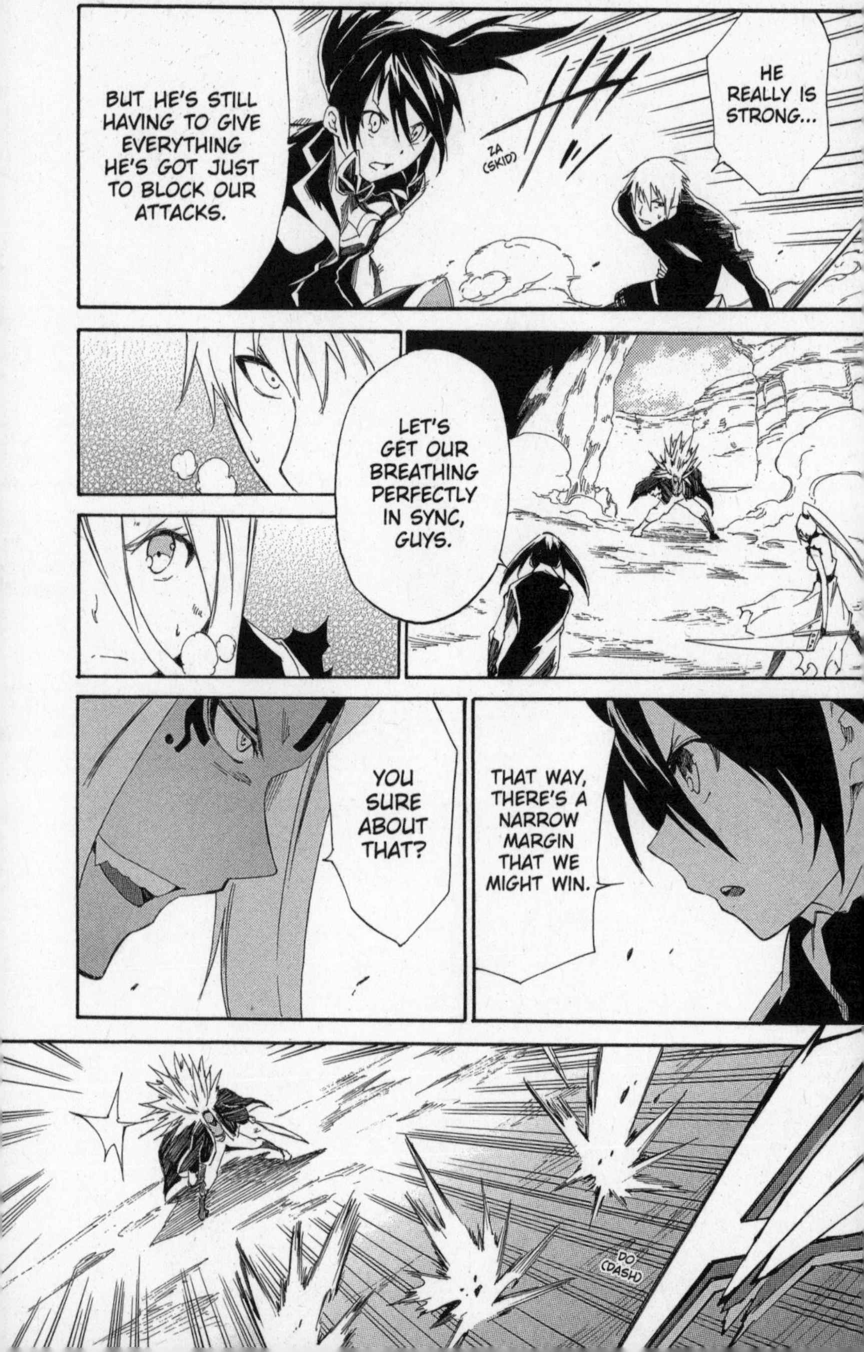
HE REALLY IS STRONG...
ZA (SKID)
BUT HE'S STILL HAVING TO GIVE EVERYTHING HE'S GOT JUST TO BLOCK OUR ATTACKS.
LET'S GET OUR BREATHING PERFECTLY IN SYNC, GUYS.
THAT WAY, THERE'S A NARROW MARGIN THAT WE MIGHT WIN.
YOU SURE ABOUT THAT?
DO (DASH)

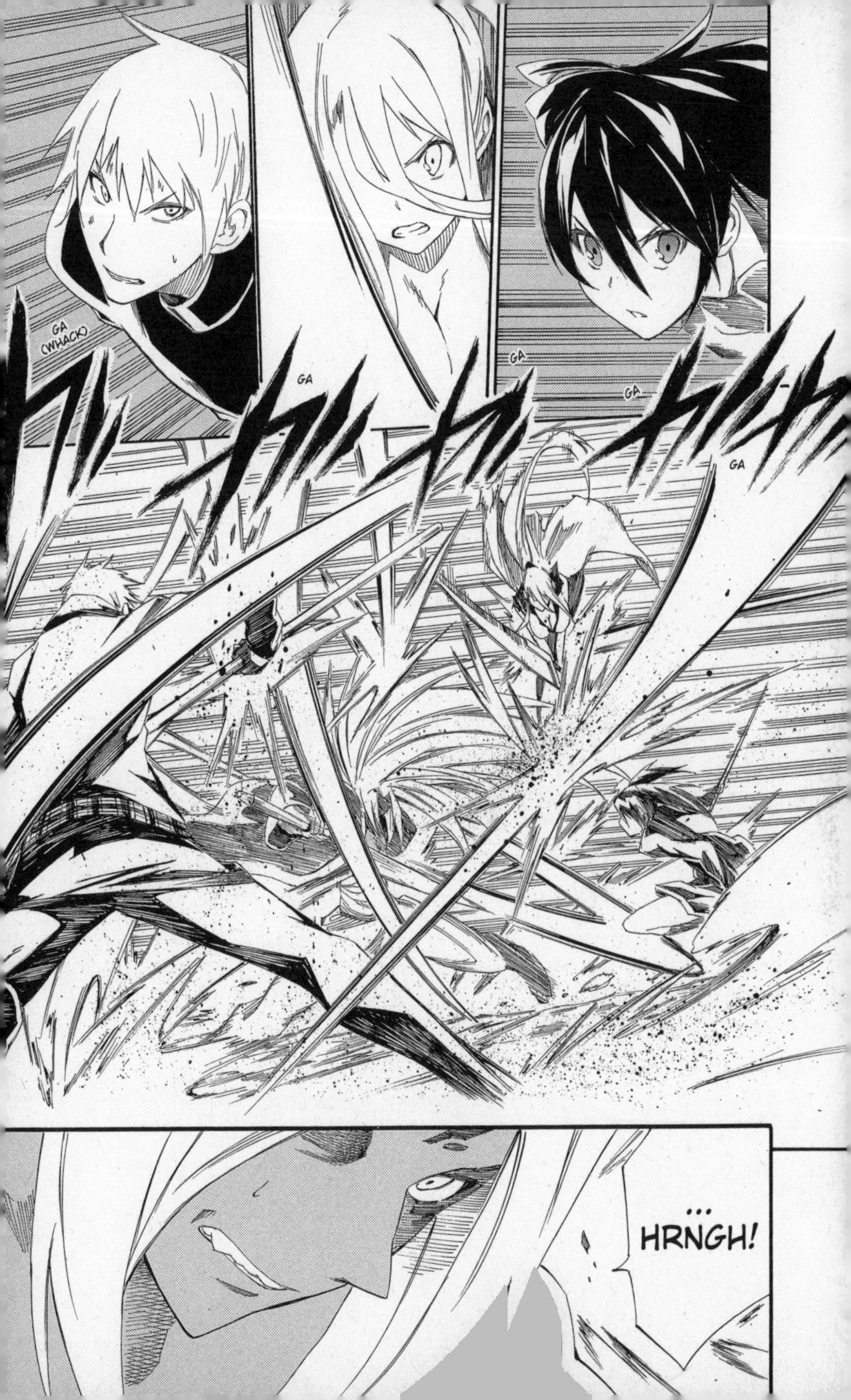
GA
GA
GA
GA
GA (WHACK)
... HRNGH!

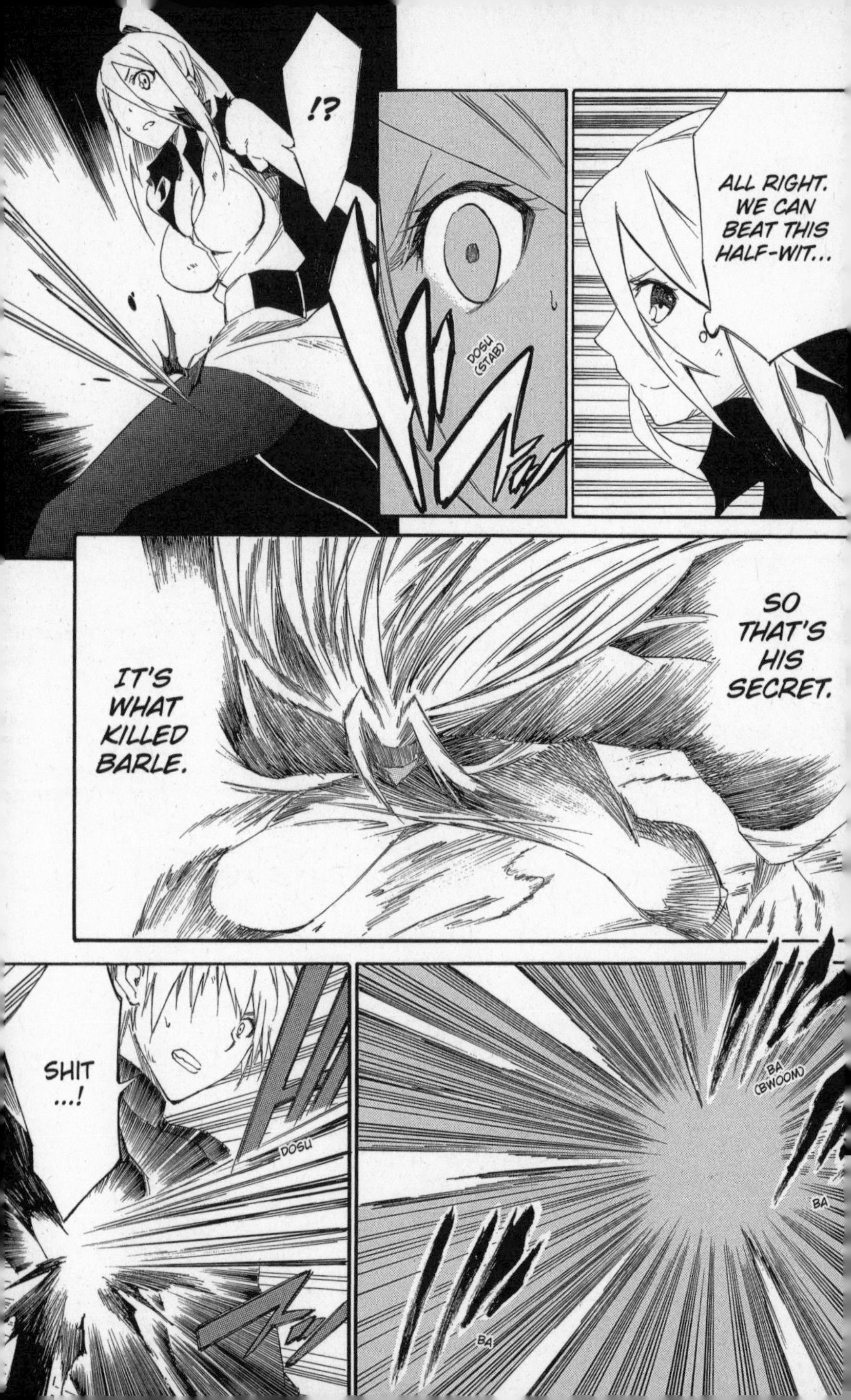
ALL RIGHT. WE CAN BEAT THIS HALF-WIT...
DOSU (STAB)
!?
SO THAT'S HIS SECRET.
IT'S WHAT KILLED BARLE.
BA (BWOOM)
BA
BA
SHIT ...!
DOSU

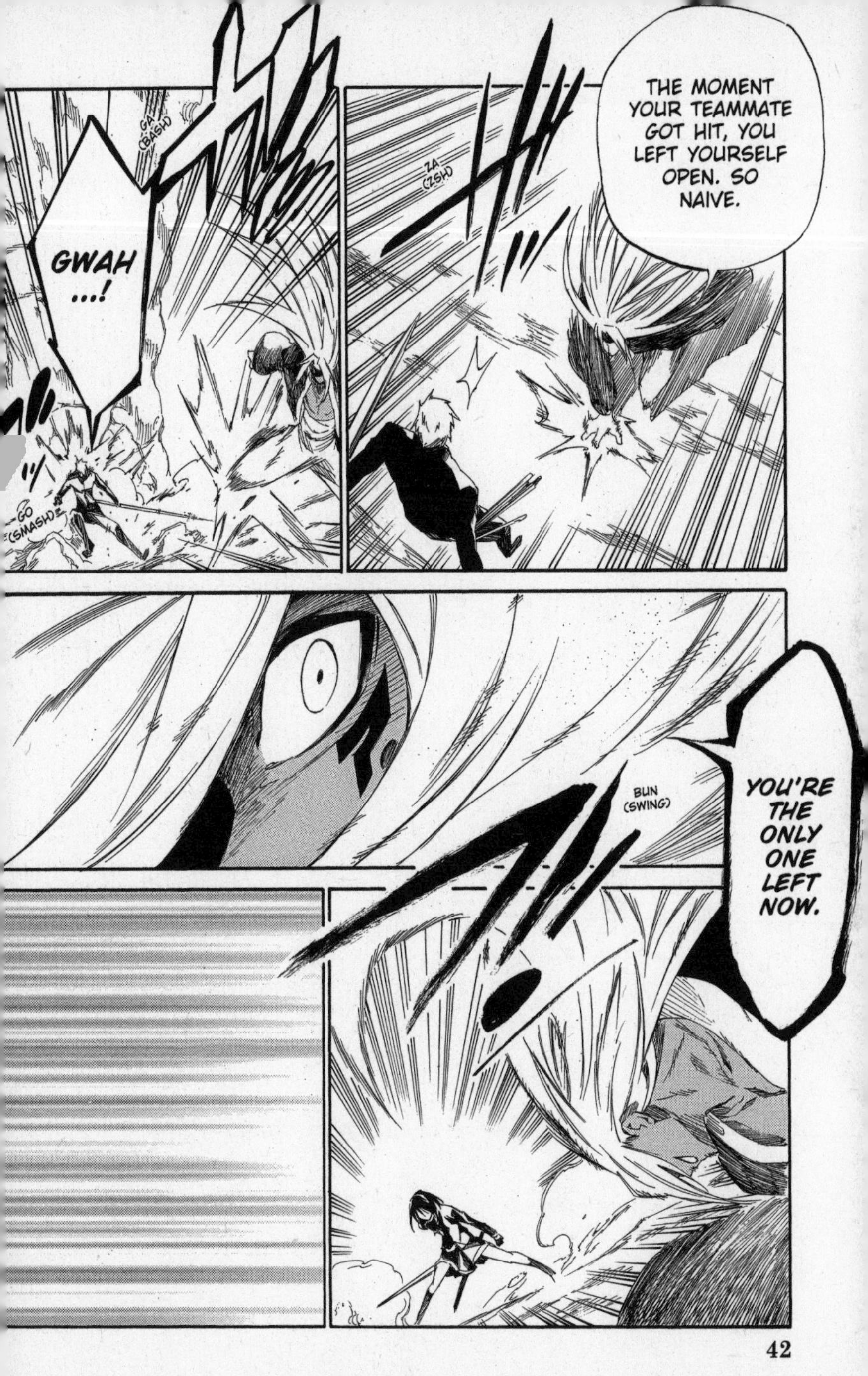
THE MOMENT YOUR TEAMMATE GOT HIT, YOU LEFT YOURSELF OPEN. SO NAIVE.
ZA (ZSH)
GA (BASH)
GWAH ...!
GO (SMASH)
YOU'RE THE ONLY ONE LEFT NOW.
BUN (SWING)

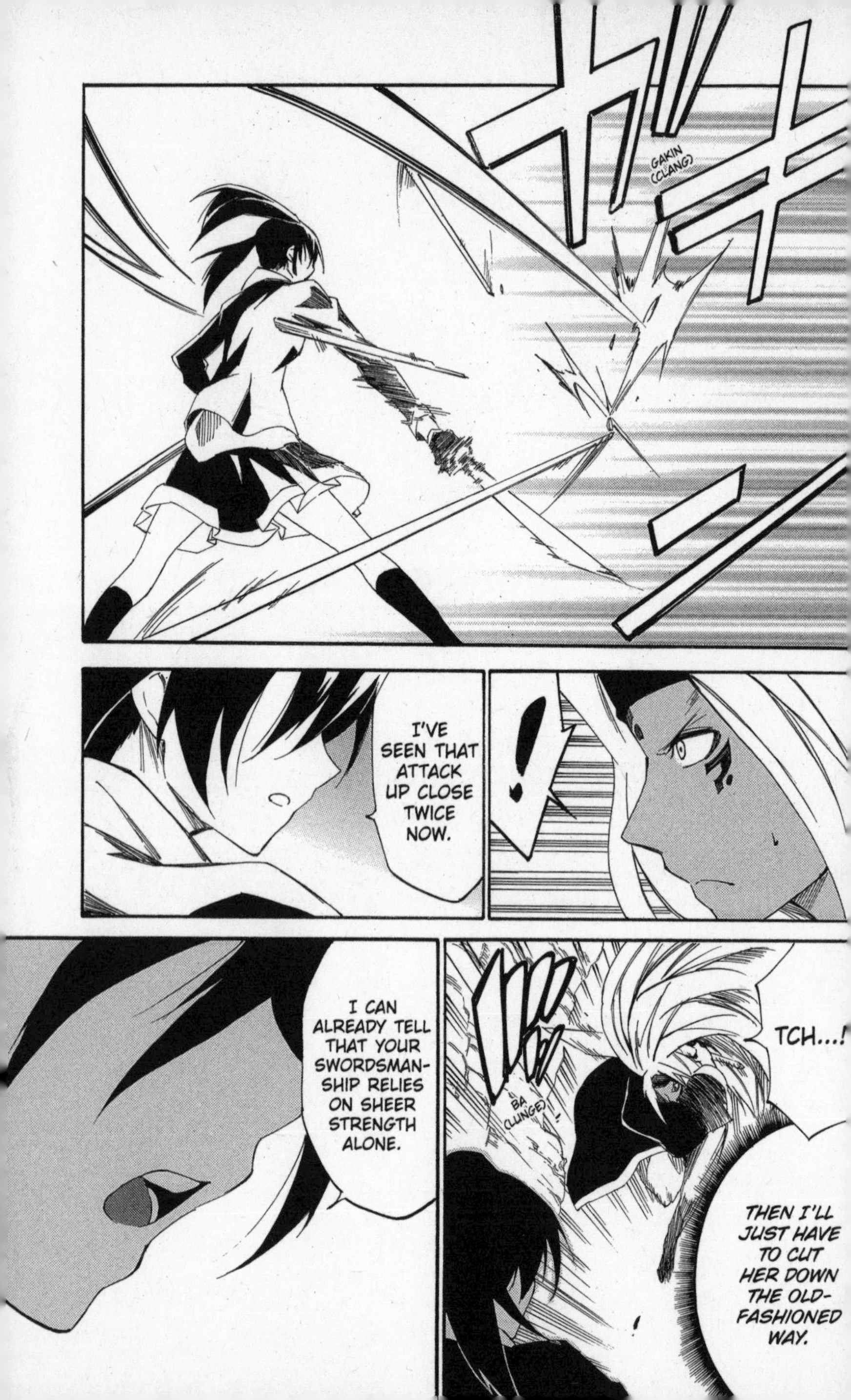
GAKIN (CLANG)
!
I'VE SEEN THAT ATTACK UP CLOSE TWICE NOW.
BA (LUNGE)
TCH...!
THEN I'LL JUST HAVE TO CUT HER DOWN THE OLD-FASHIONED WAY.
I CAN ALREADY TELL THAT YOUR SWORDSMANSHIP RELIES ON SHEER STRENGTH ALONE.

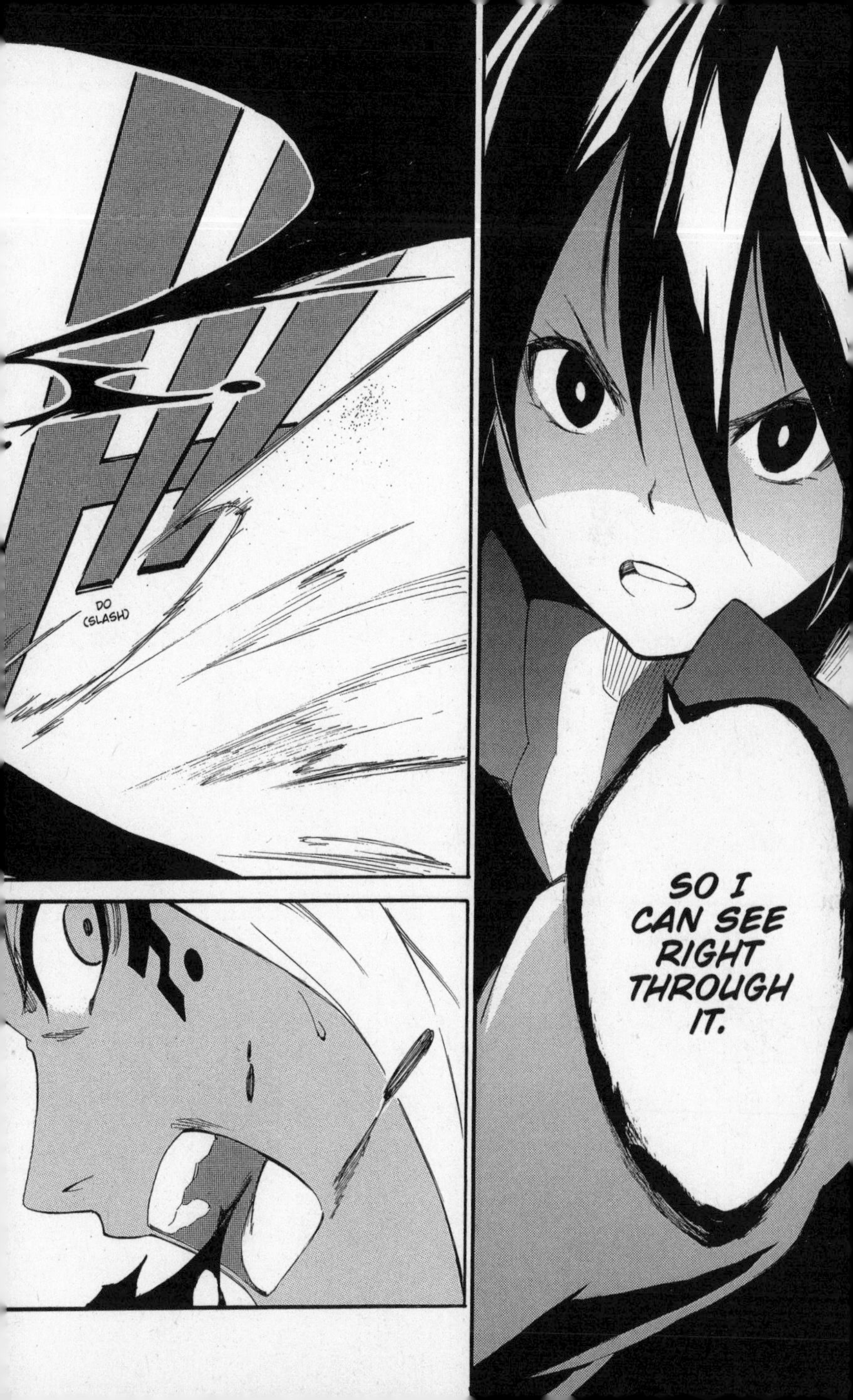
SO I CAN SEE RIGHT THROUGH IT.
DO (SLASH)

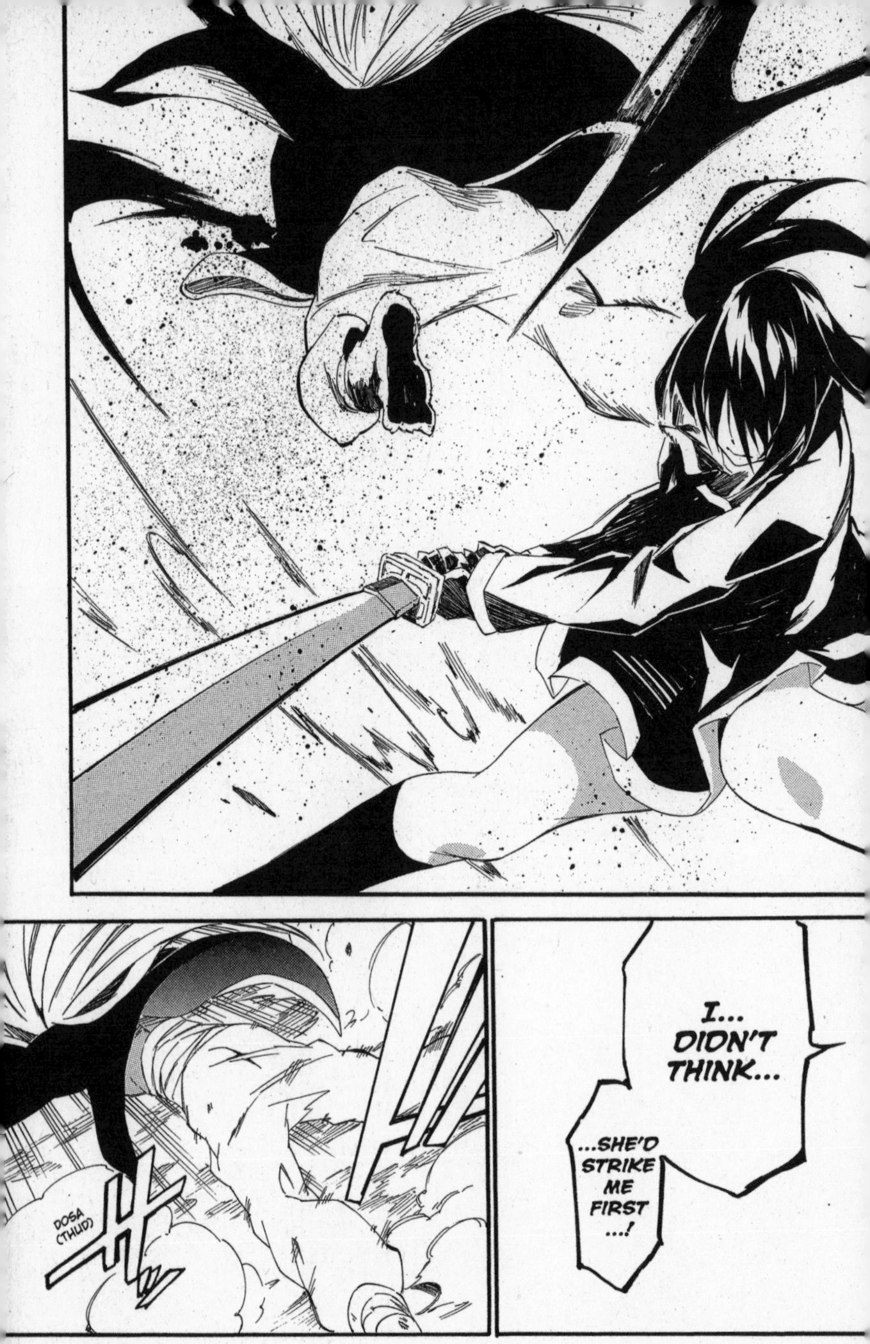
I... DIDN'T THINK...
...SHE'D STRIKE ME FIRST ...!
DOSA (THUD)

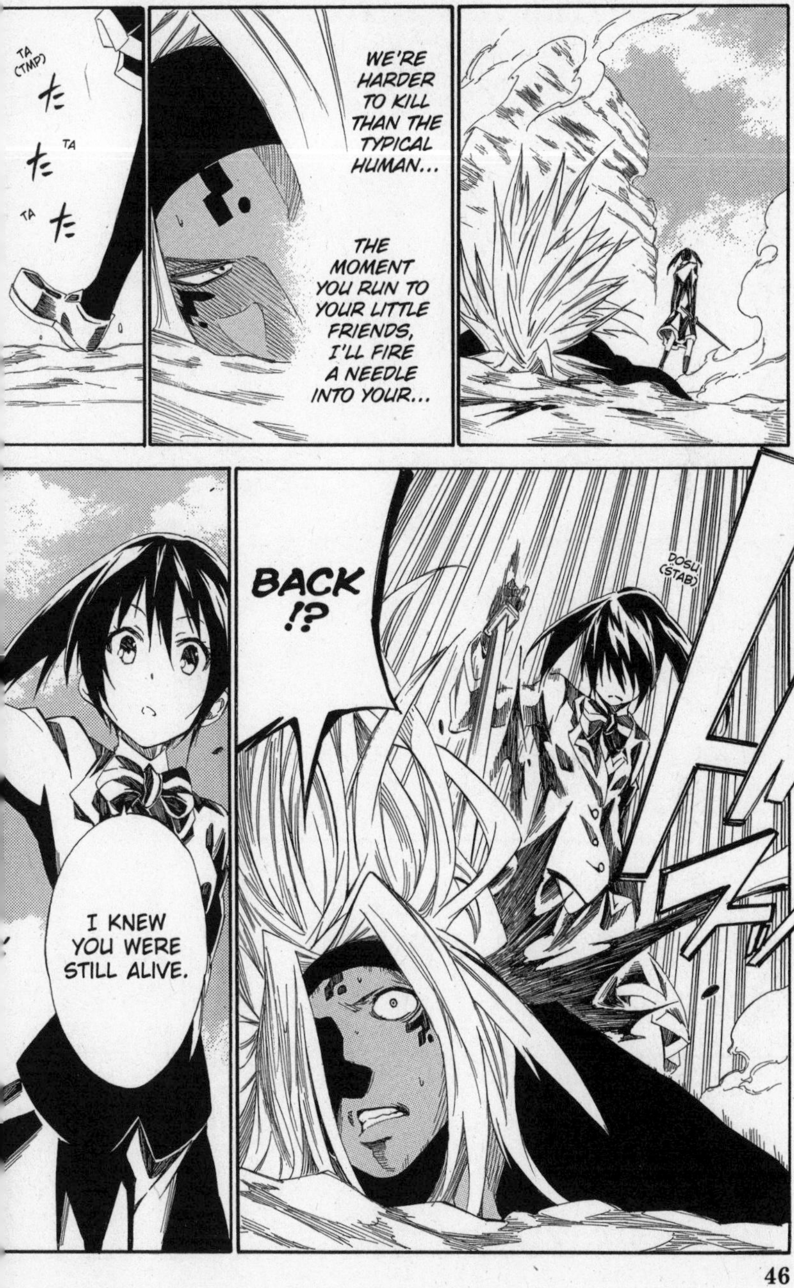
WE'RE HARDER TO KILL THAN THE TYPICAL HUMAN...
THE MOMENT YOU RUN TO YOUR LITTLE FRIENDS, I'LL FIRE A NEEDLE INTO YOUR...
TA (TMP) た
TA た
TA た
DOSU (STAB)
BACK !?
I KNEW YOU WERE STILL ALIVE.

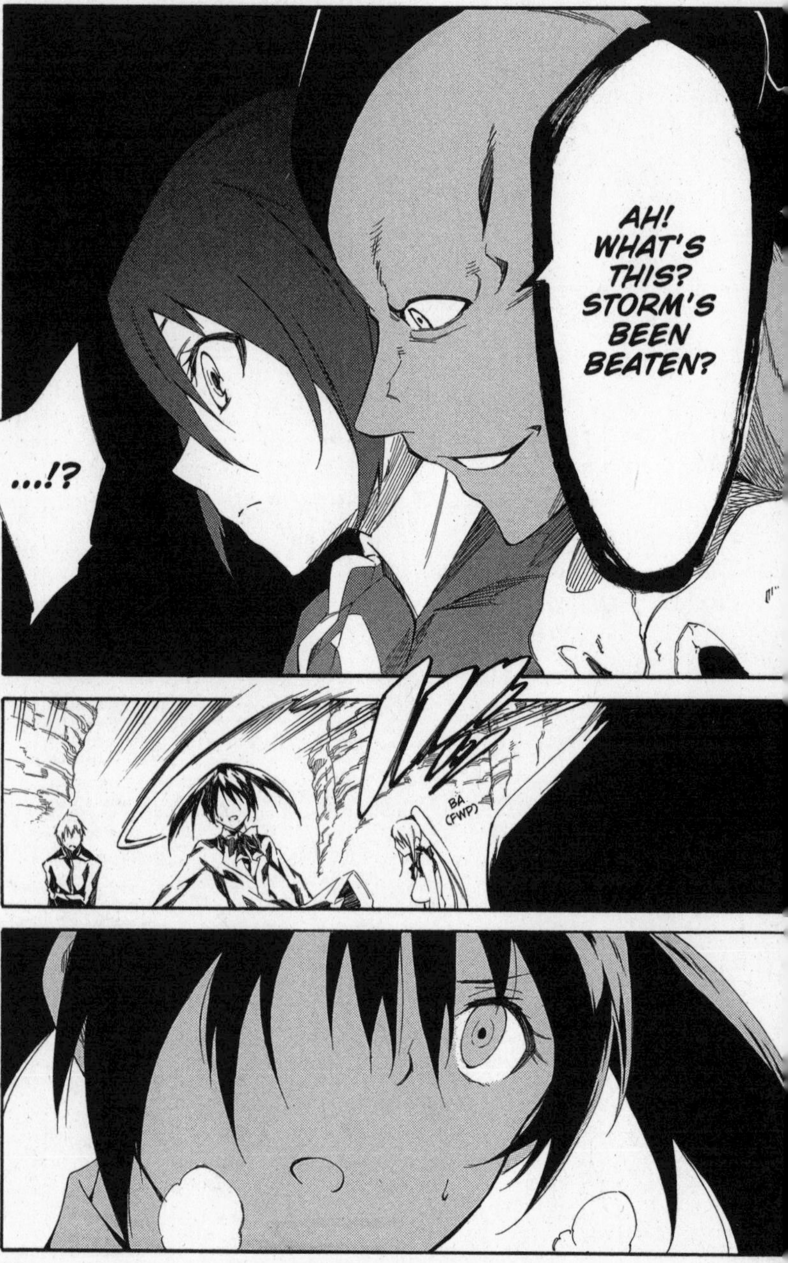
AH! WHAT'S THIS? STORM'S BEEN BEATEN?
...!?
BA (FWP)

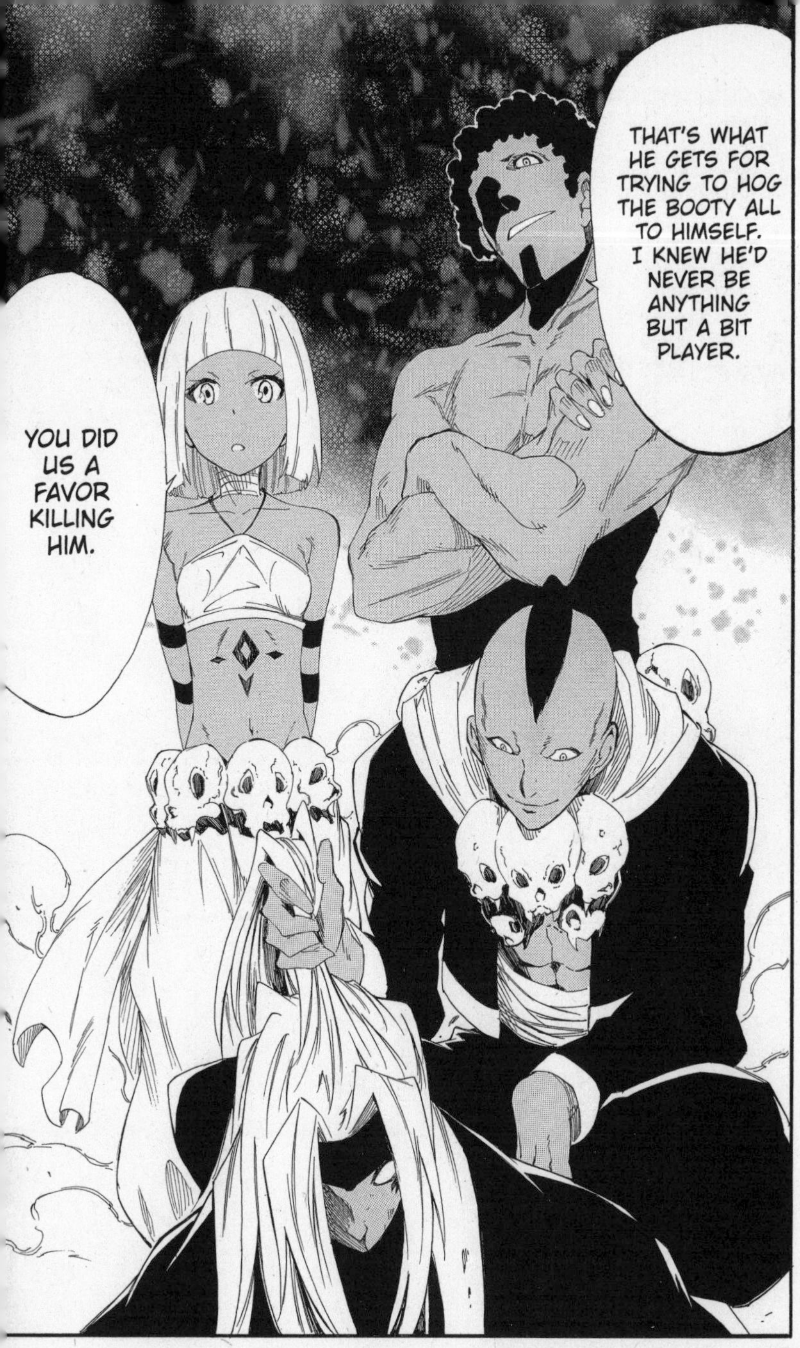
THAT'S WHAT HE GETS FOR TRYING TO HOG THE BOOTY ALL TO HIMSELF. I KNEW HE'D NEVER BE ANYTHING BUT A BIT PLAYER.
YOU DID US A FAVOR KILLING HIM.

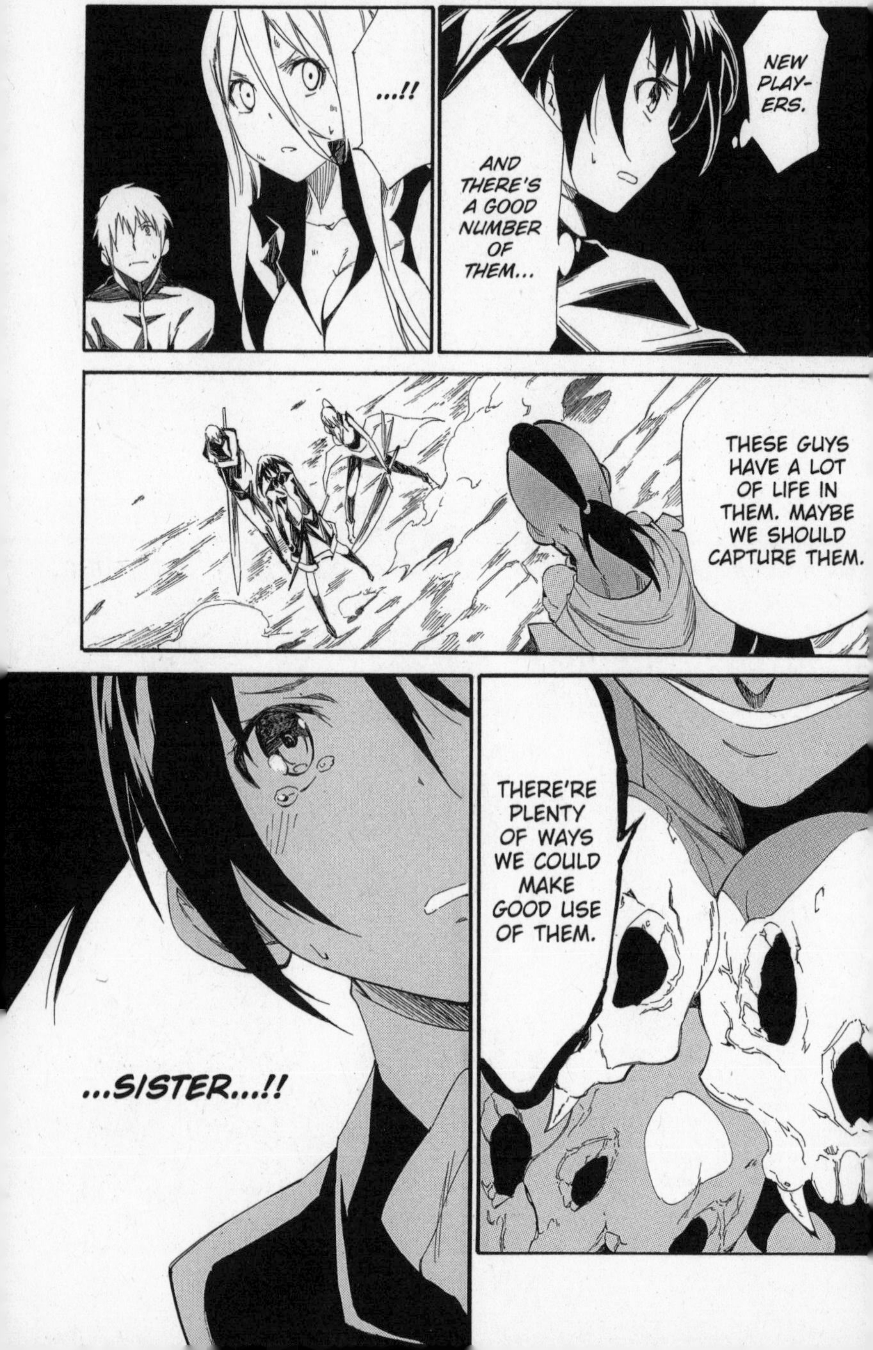
NEW PLAYERS.
AND THERE'S A GOOD NUMBER OF THEM...
...!!
THESE GUYS HAVE A LOT OF LIFE IN THEM. MAYBE WE SHOULD CAPTURE THEM.
THERE'RE PLENTY OF WAYS WE COULD MAKE GOOD USE OF THEM.
...SISTER...!!

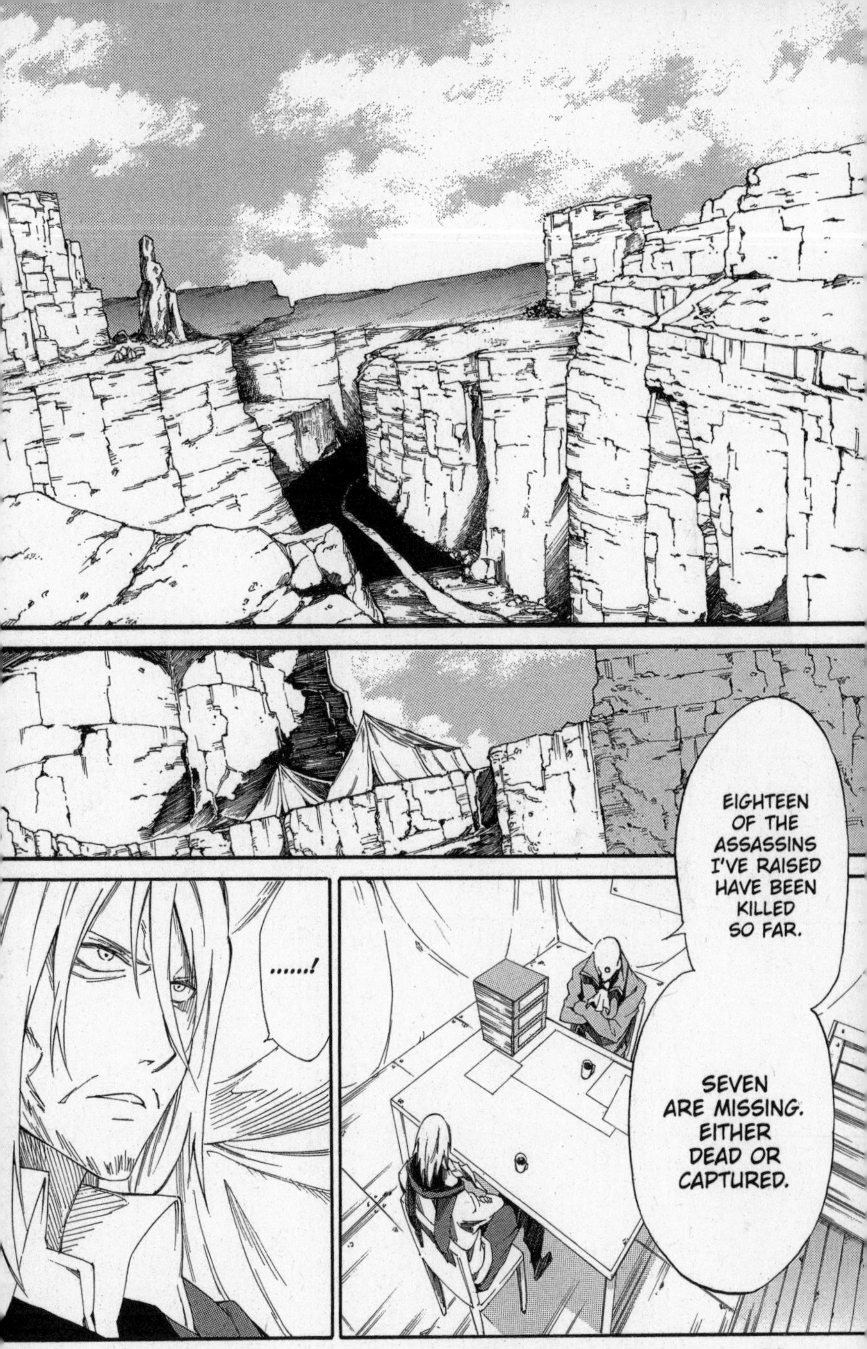
EIGHTEEN OF THE ASSASSINS I'VE RAISED HAVE BEEN KILLED SO FAR.
SEVEN ARE MISSING. EITHER DEAD OR CAPTURED.
......!

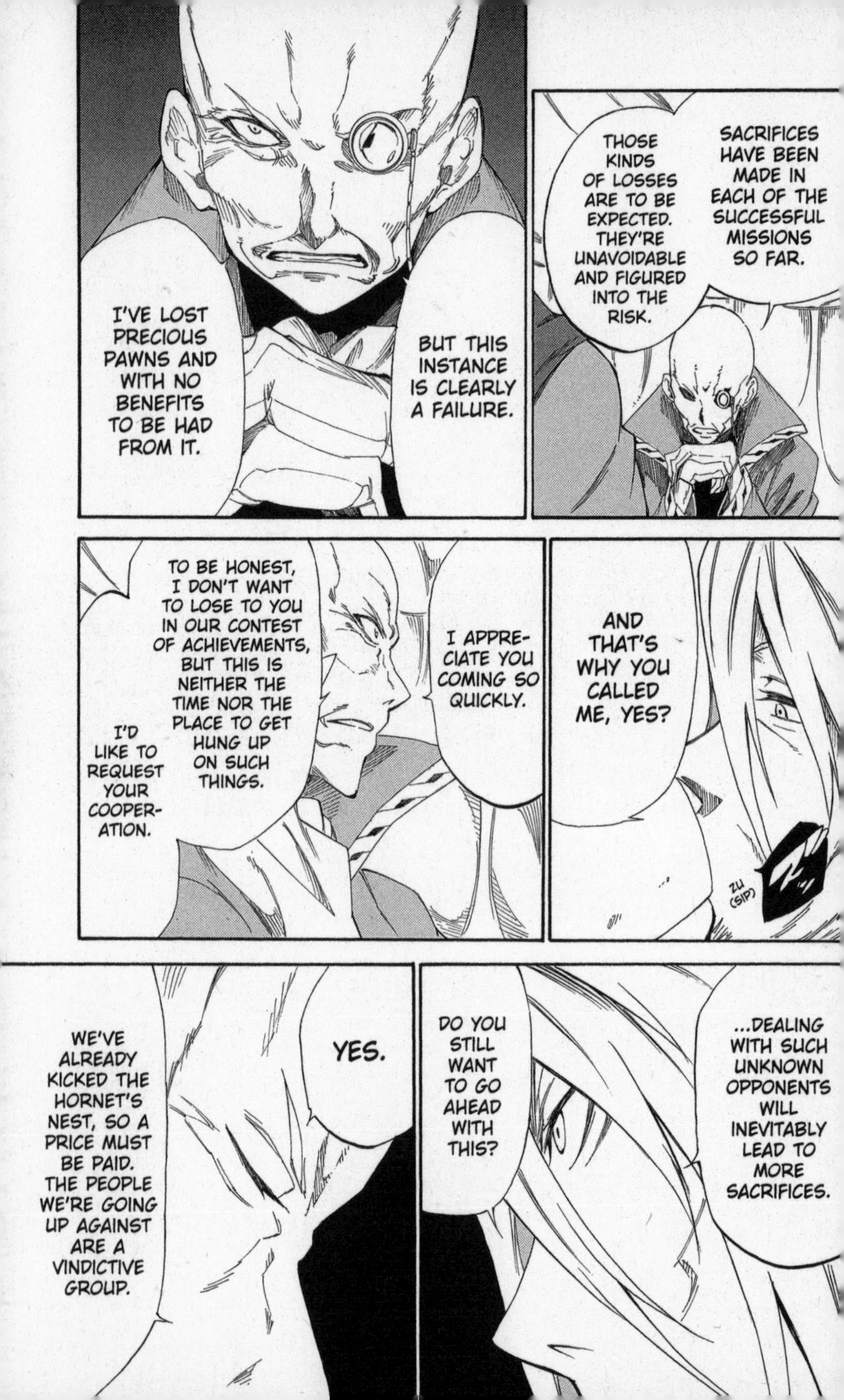
SACRIFICES HAVE BEEN MADE IN EACH OF THE SUCCESSFUL MISSIONS SO FAR.
THOSE KINDS OF LOSSES ARE TO BE EXPECTED. THEY'RE UNAVOIDABLE AND FIGURED INTO THE RISK.
BUT THIS INSTANCE IS CLEARLY A FAILURE.
I'VE LOST PRECIOUS PAWNS AND WITH NO BENEFITS TO BE HAD FROM IT.
AND THAT'S WHY YOU CALLED ME, YES?
ZU (SIP)
I APPRE-CIATE YOU COMING SO QUICKLY.
TO BE HONEST, I DON'T WANT TO LOSE TO YOU IN OUR CONTEST OF ACHIEVEMENTS, BUT THIS IS NEITHER THE TIME NOR THE PLACE TO GET HUNG UP ON SUCH THINGS.
I'D LIKE TO REQUEST YOUR COOPER-ATION.
...DEALING WITH SUCH UNKNOWN OPPONENTS WILL INEVITABLY LEAD TO MORE SACRIFICES.
DO YOU STILL WANT TO GO AHEAD WITH THIS?
YES.
WE'VE ALREADY KICKED THE HORNET'S NEST, SO A PRICE MUST BE PAID. THE PEOPLE WE'RE GOING UP AGAINST ARE A VINDICTIVE GROUP.

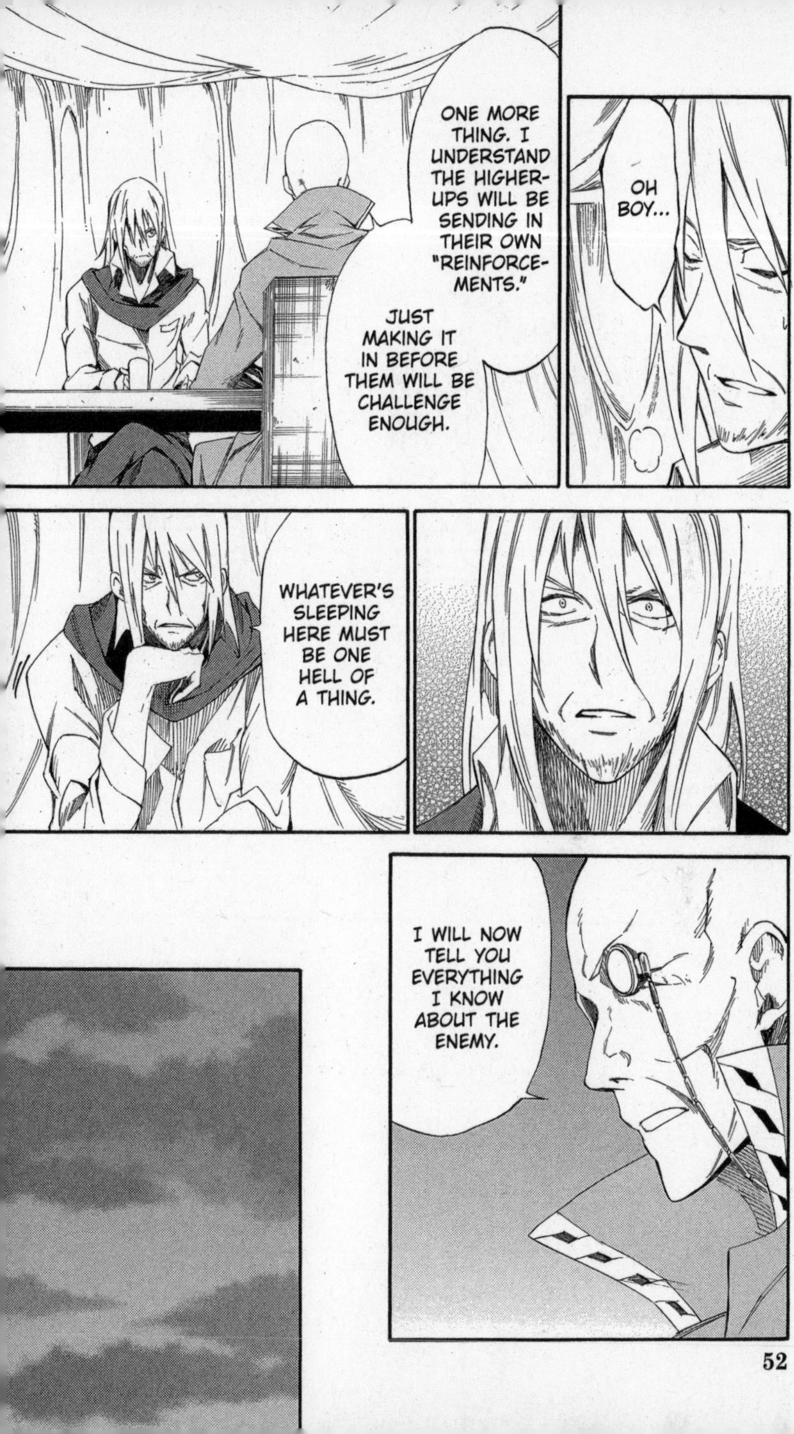
OH BOY...
ONE MORE THING. I UNDERSTAND THE HIGHER-UPS WILL BE SENDING IN THEIR OWN "REINFORCEMENTS."
JUST MAKING IT IN BEFORE THEM WILL BE CHALLENGE ENOUGH.
WHATEVER'S SLEEPING HERE MUST BE ONE HELL OF A THING.
I WILL NOW TELL YOU EVERYTHING I KNOW ABOUT THE ENEMY.

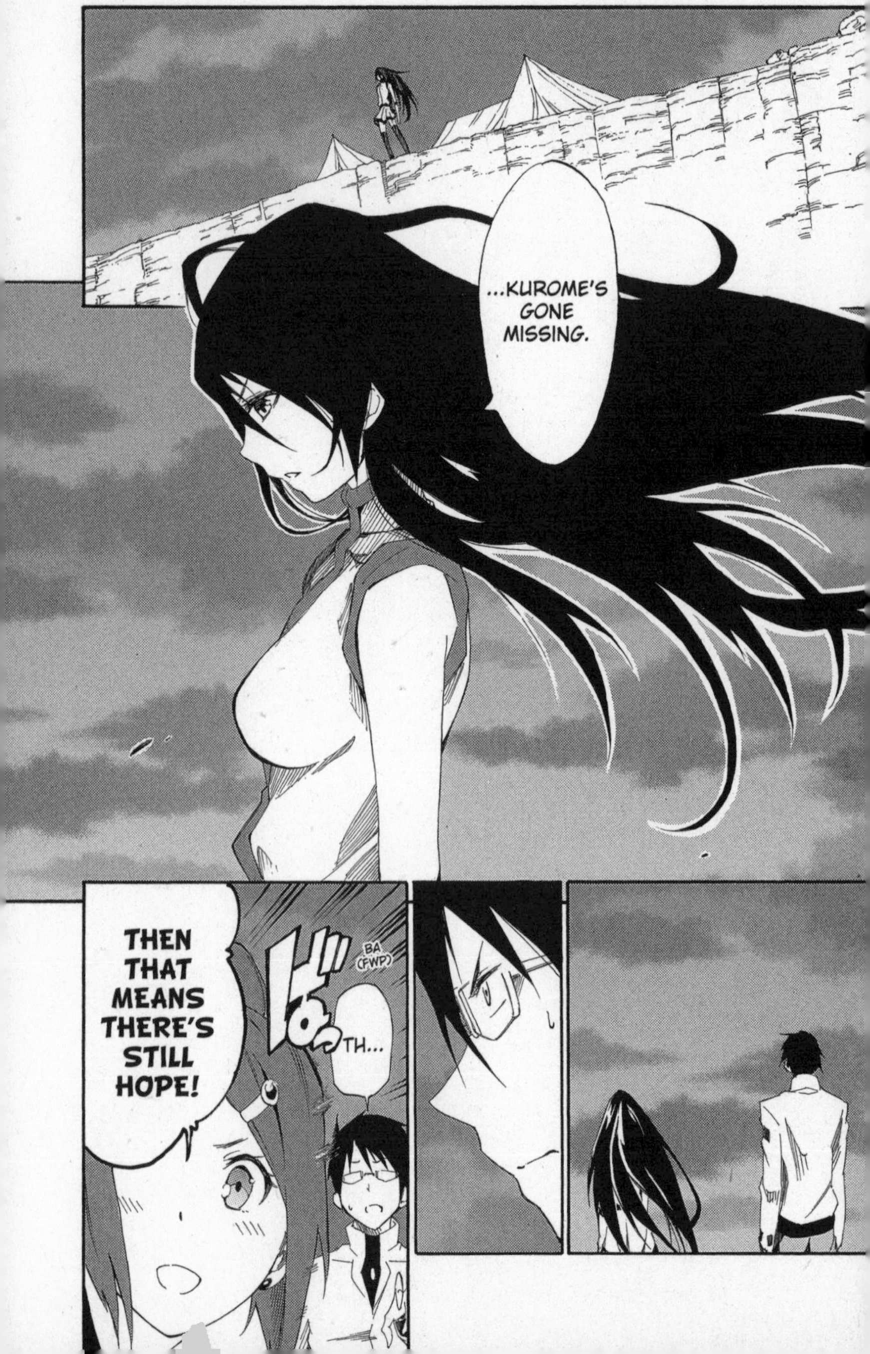
...KUROME'S GONE MISSING.
BA (FWP)
TH...
THEN THAT MEANS THERE'S STILL HOPE!

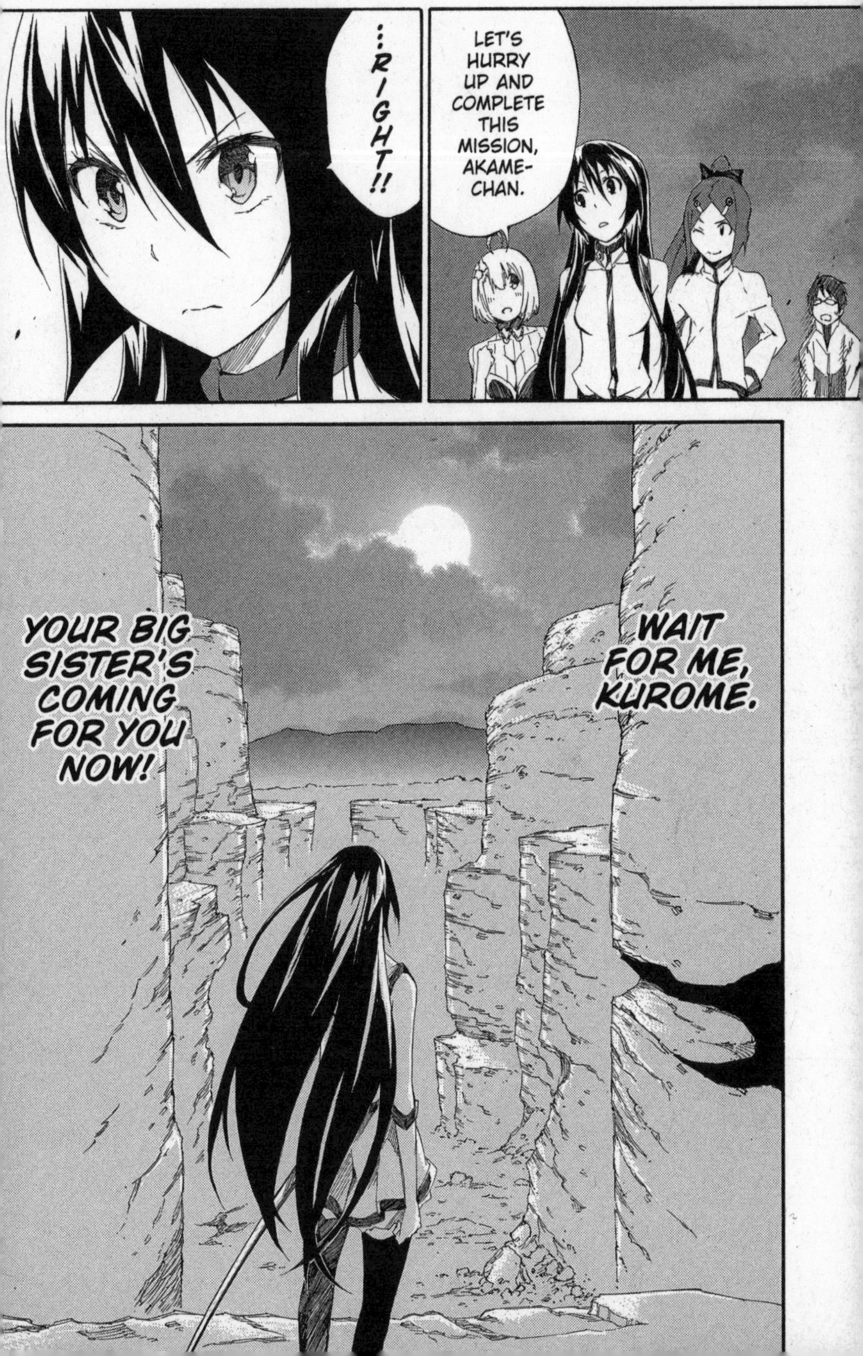
LET'S HURRY UP AND COMPLETE THIS MISSION, AKAME-CHAN.
...RIGHT!!
WAIT FOR ME, KUROME.
YOUR BIG SISTER'S COMING FOR YOU NOW!

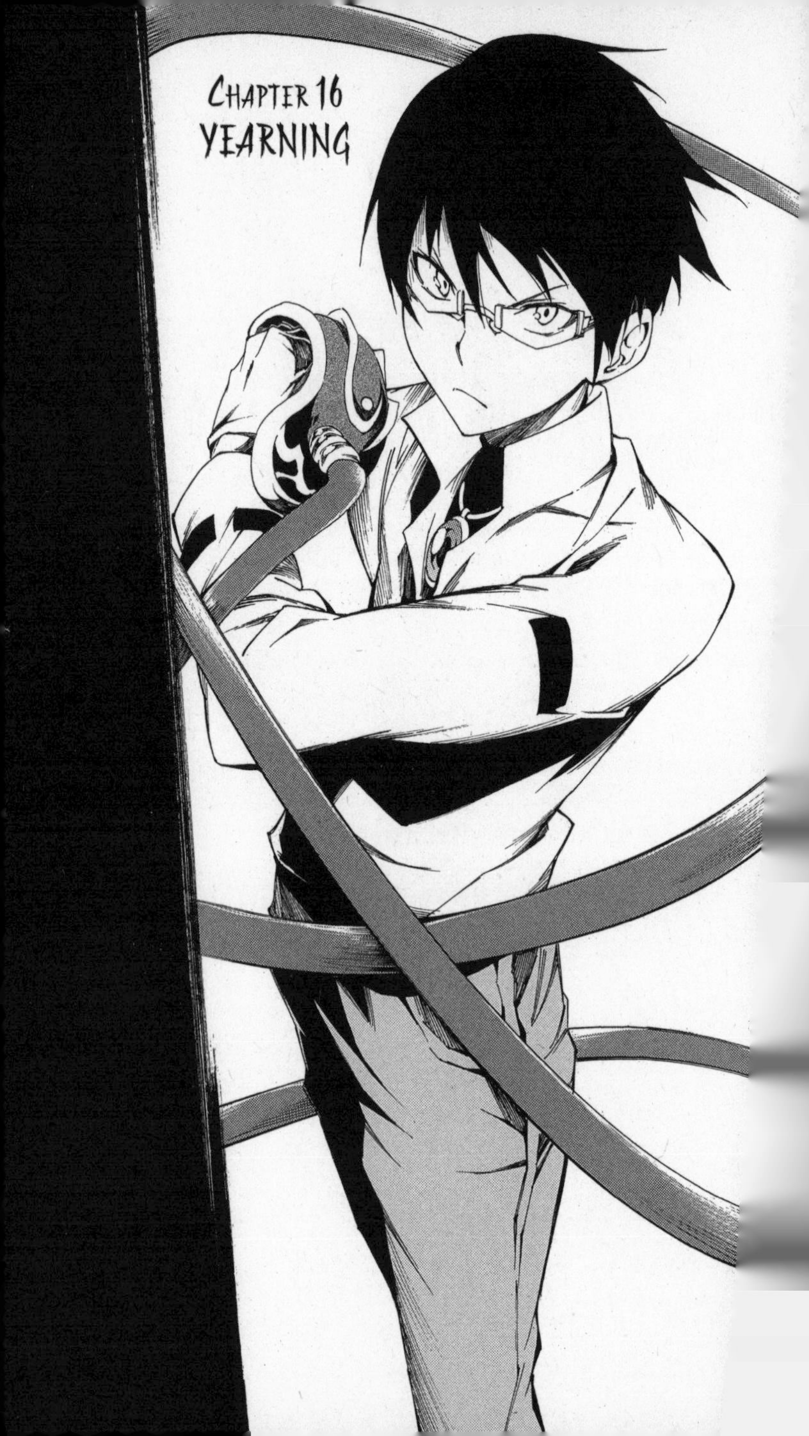
Chapter 16
Yearning

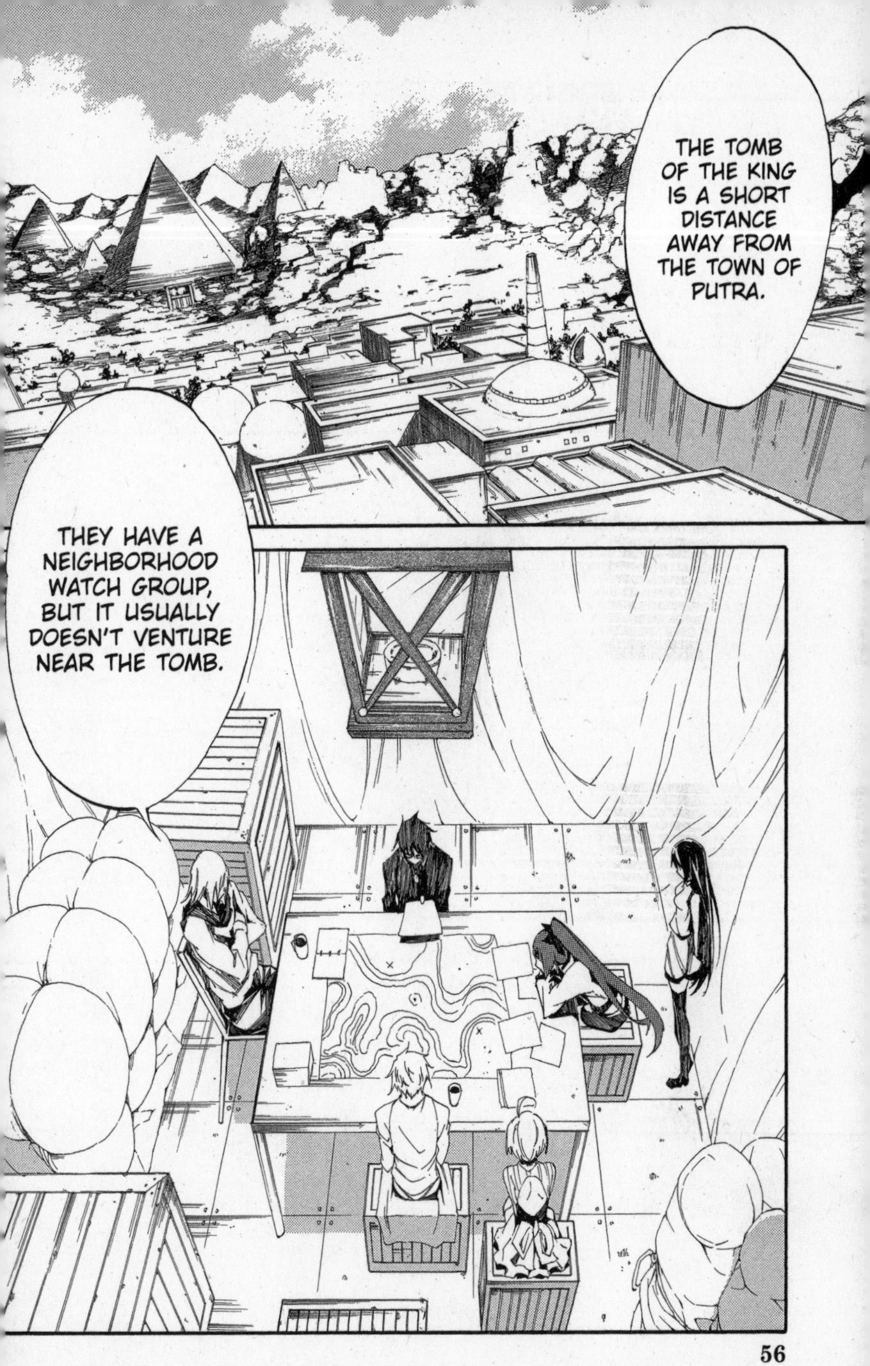
THE TOMB OF THE KING IS A SHORT DISTANCE AWAY FROM THE TOWN OF PUTRA.
THEY HAVE A NEIGHBORHOOD WATCH GROUP, BUT IT USUALLY DOESN'T VENTURE NEAR THE TOMB.

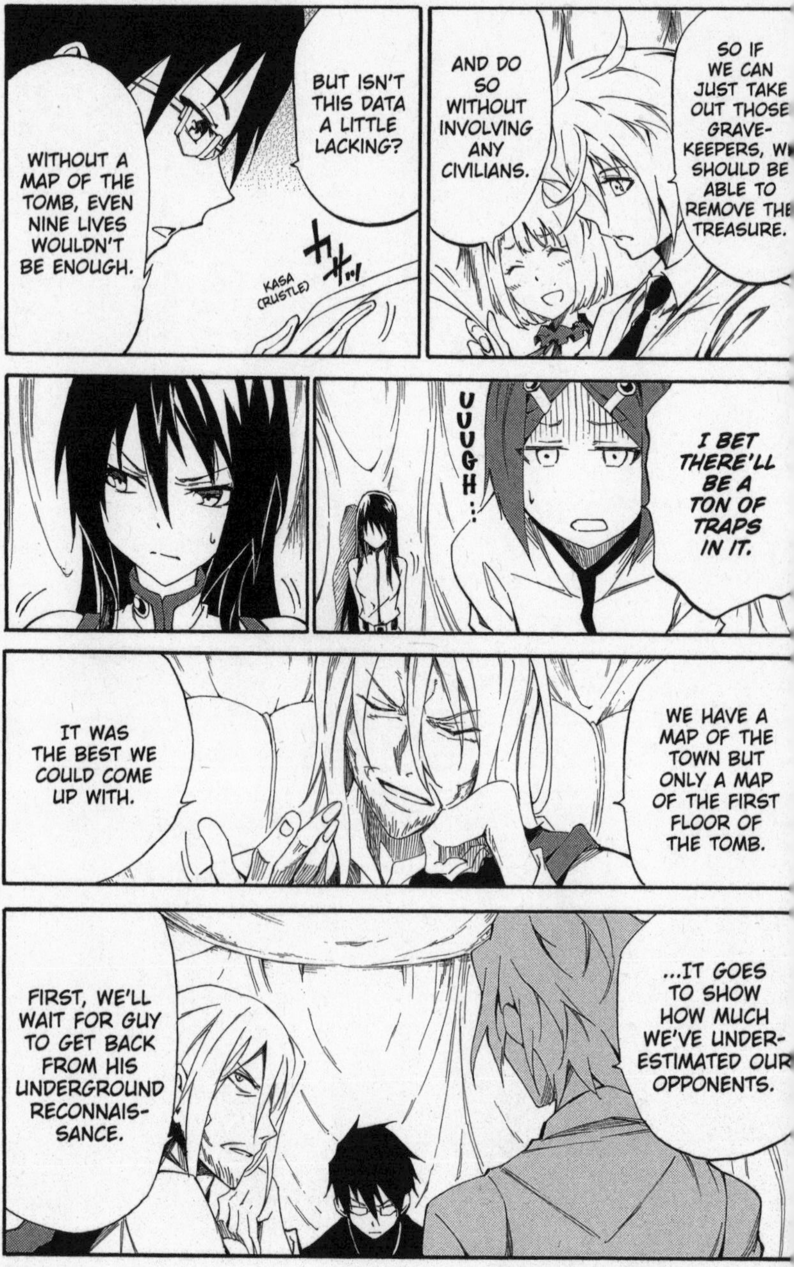
SO IF WE CAN JUST TAKE OUT THOSE GRAVE-KEEPERS, WE SHOULD BE ABLE TO REMOVE THE TREASURE.
AND DO SO WITHOUT INVOLVING ANY CIVILIANS.
BUT ISN'T THIS DATA A LITTLE LACKING?
カサッ
KASA (RUSTLE)
WITHOUT A MAP OF THE TOMB, EVEN NINE LIVES WOULDN'T BE ENOUGH.
UUUGH...
I BET THERE'LL BE A TON OF TRAPS IN IT.
WE HAVE A MAP OF THE TOWN BUT ONLY A MAP OF THE FIRST FLOOR OF THE TOMB.
IT WAS THE BEST WE COULD COME UP WITH.
...IT GOES TO SHOW HOW MUCH WE'VE UNDER-ESTIMATED OUR OPPONENTS.
FIRST, WE'LL WAIT FOR GUY TO GET BACK FROM HIS UNDERGROUND RECONNAIS-SANCE.

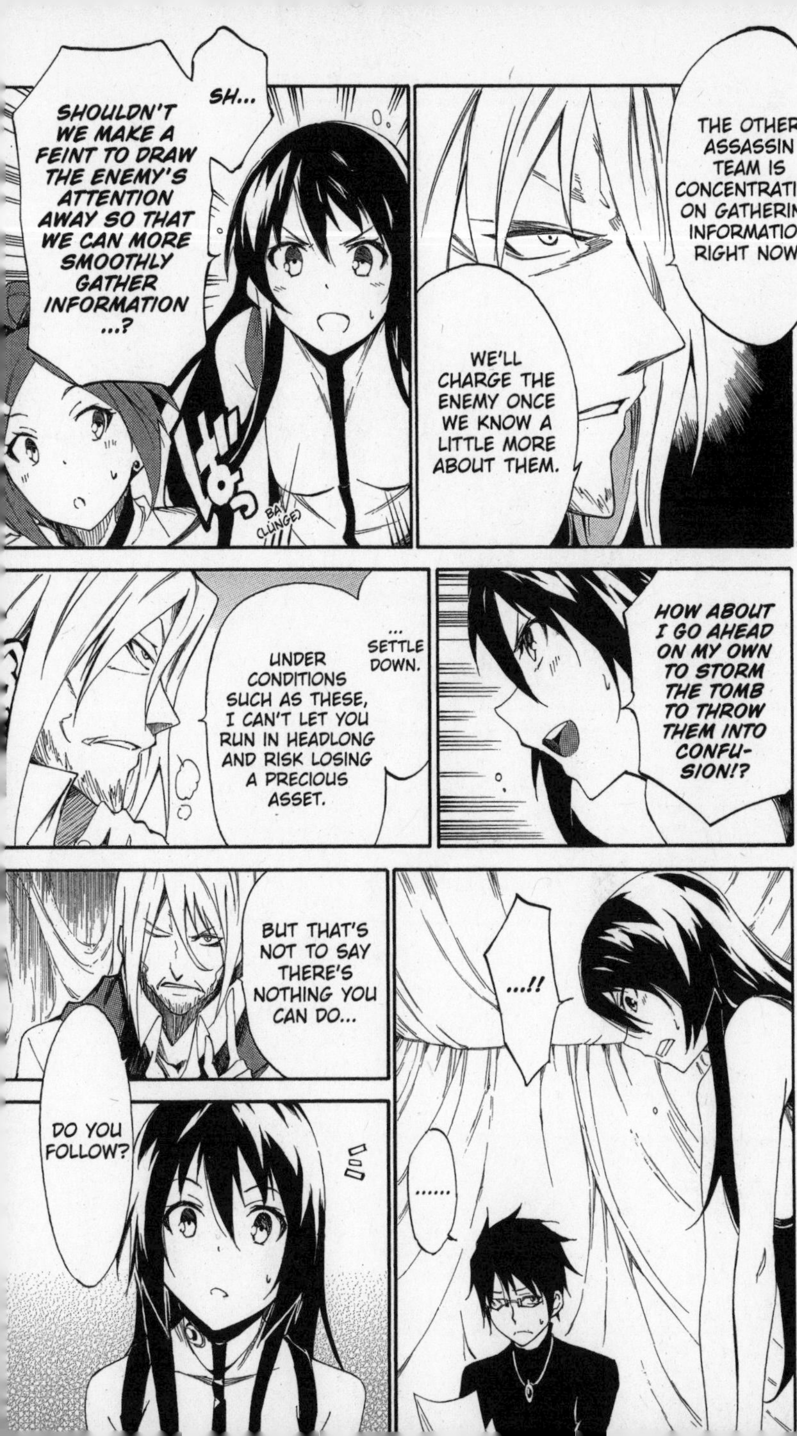
THE OTHER ASSASSIN TEAM IS CONCENTRATING ON GATHERING INFORMATION RIGHT NOW.
WE'LL CHARGE THE ENEMY ONCE WE KNOW A LITTLE MORE ABOUT THEM.
SH...
SHOULDN'T WE MAKE A FEINT TO DRAW THE ENEMY'S ATTENTION AWAY SO THAT WE CAN MORE SMOOTHLY GATHER INFORMATION ...?
BA (LUNGE)
HOW ABOUT I GO AHEAD ON MY OWN TO STORM THE TOMB TO THROW THEM INTO CONFUSION!?
... SETTLE DOWN.
UNDER CONDITIONS SUCH AS THESE, I CAN'T LET YOU RUN IN HEADLONG AND RISK LOSING A PRECIOUS ASSET.
...!!
......
BUT THAT'S NOT TO SAY THERE'S NOTHING YOU CAN DO...
DO YOU FOLLOW?

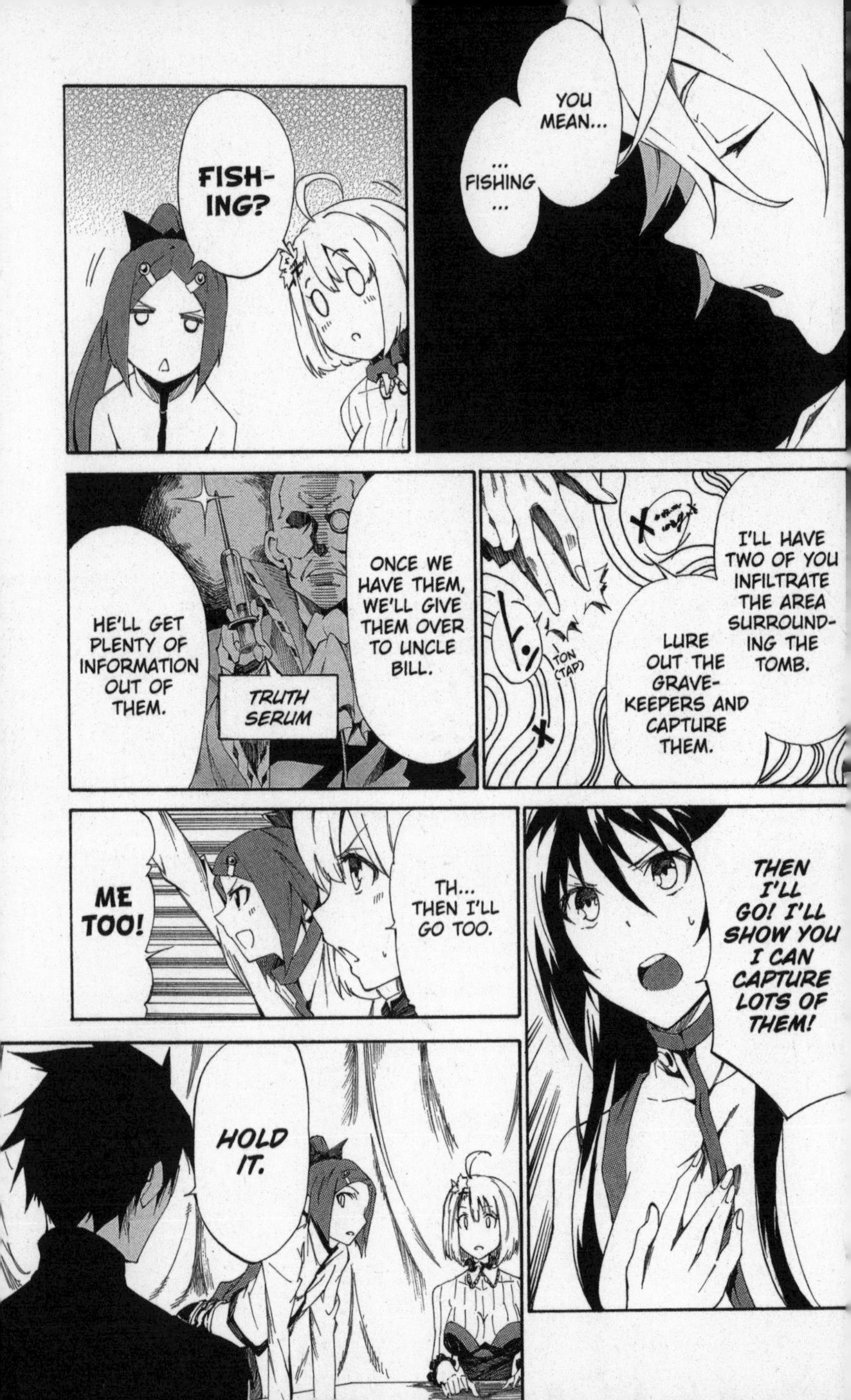
YOU MEAN...
...FISHING...
FISH-ING?
I'LL HAVE TWO OF YOU INFILTRATE THE AREA SURROUNDING THE TOMB.
LURE OUT THE GRAVE-KEEPERS AND CAPTURE THEM.
TON (TAP)
ONCE WE HAVE THEM, WE'LL GIVE THEM OVER TO UNCLE BILL.
TRUTH SERUM
HE'LL GET PLENTY OF INFORMATION OUT OF THEM.
THEN I'LL GO! I'LL SHOW YOU I CAN CAPTURE LOTS OF THEM!
TH... THEN I'LL GO TOO.
ME TOO!
HOLD IT.

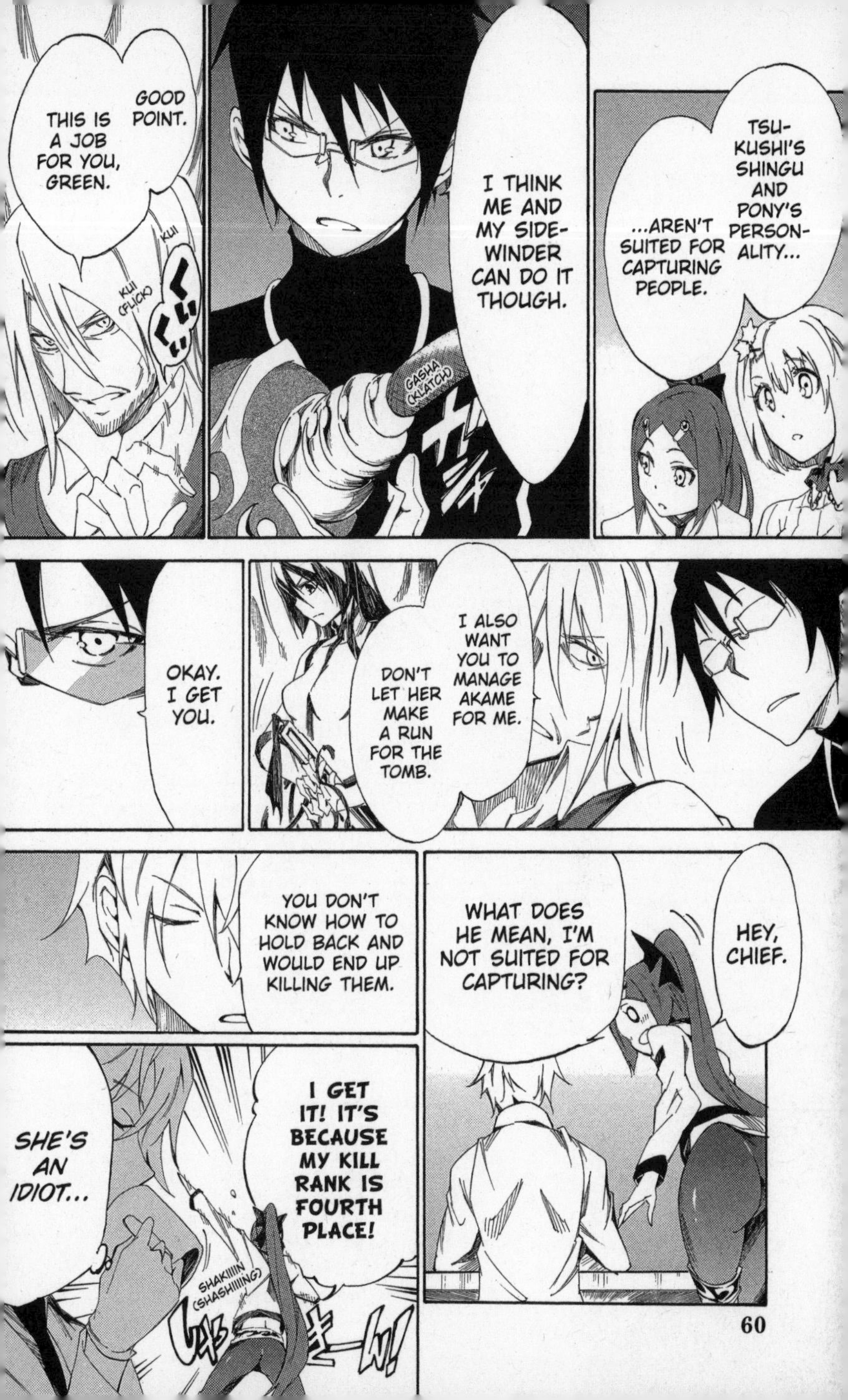
TSU-KUSHI'S SHINGU AND PONY'S PERSON-ALITY... ...AREN'T SUITED FOR CAPTURING PEOPLE.
I THINK ME AND MY SIDE-WINDER CAN DO IT THOUGH.
GASHA (KLATCH)
GOOD POINT. THIS IS A JOB FOR YOU, GREEN.
KUI KUI (FLICK)
I ALSO WANT YOU TO MANAGE AKAME FOR ME. DON'T LET HER MAKE A RUN FOR THE TOMB.
OKAY. I GET YOU.
HEY, CHIEF.
WHAT DOES HE MEAN, I'M NOT SUITED FOR CAPTURING?
YOU DON'T KNOW HOW TO HOLD BACK AND WOULD END UP KILLING THEM.
I GET IT! IT'S BECAUSE MY KILL RANK IS FOURTH PLACE!
SHAKIIIIN (SHASHIIIING)
SHE'S AN IDIOT...

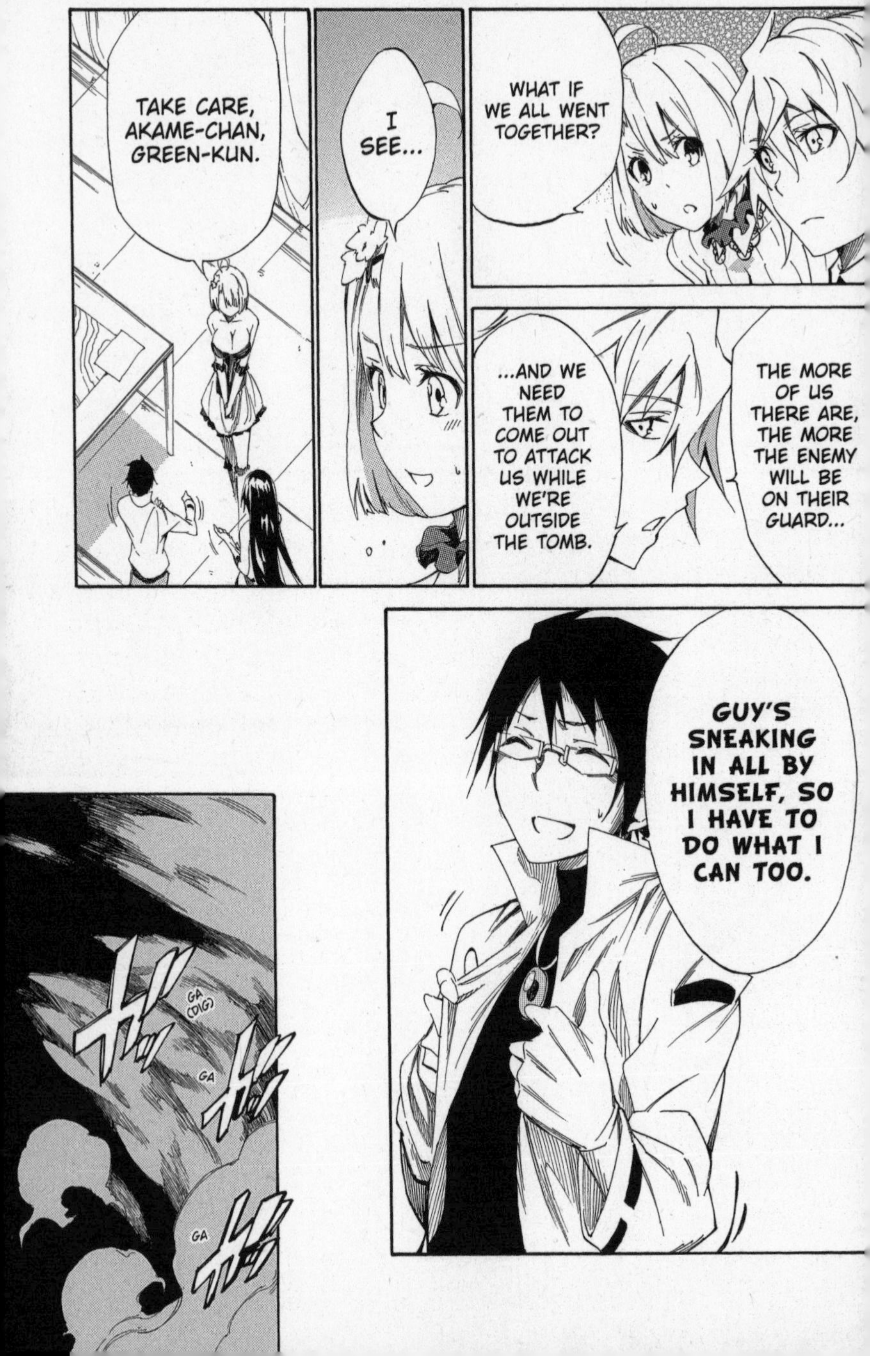
WHAT IF WE ALL WENT TOGETHER?
THE MORE OF US THERE ARE, THE MORE THE ENEMY WILL BE ON THEIR GUARD...
...AND WE NEED THEM TO COME OUT TO ATTACK US WHILE WE'RE OUTSIDE THE TOMB.
I SEE...
TAKE CARE, AKAME-CHAN, GREEN-KUN.
GUY'S SNEAKING IN ALL BY HIMSELF, SO I HAVE TO DO WHAT I CAN TOO.
GA (DIG)
GA
GA

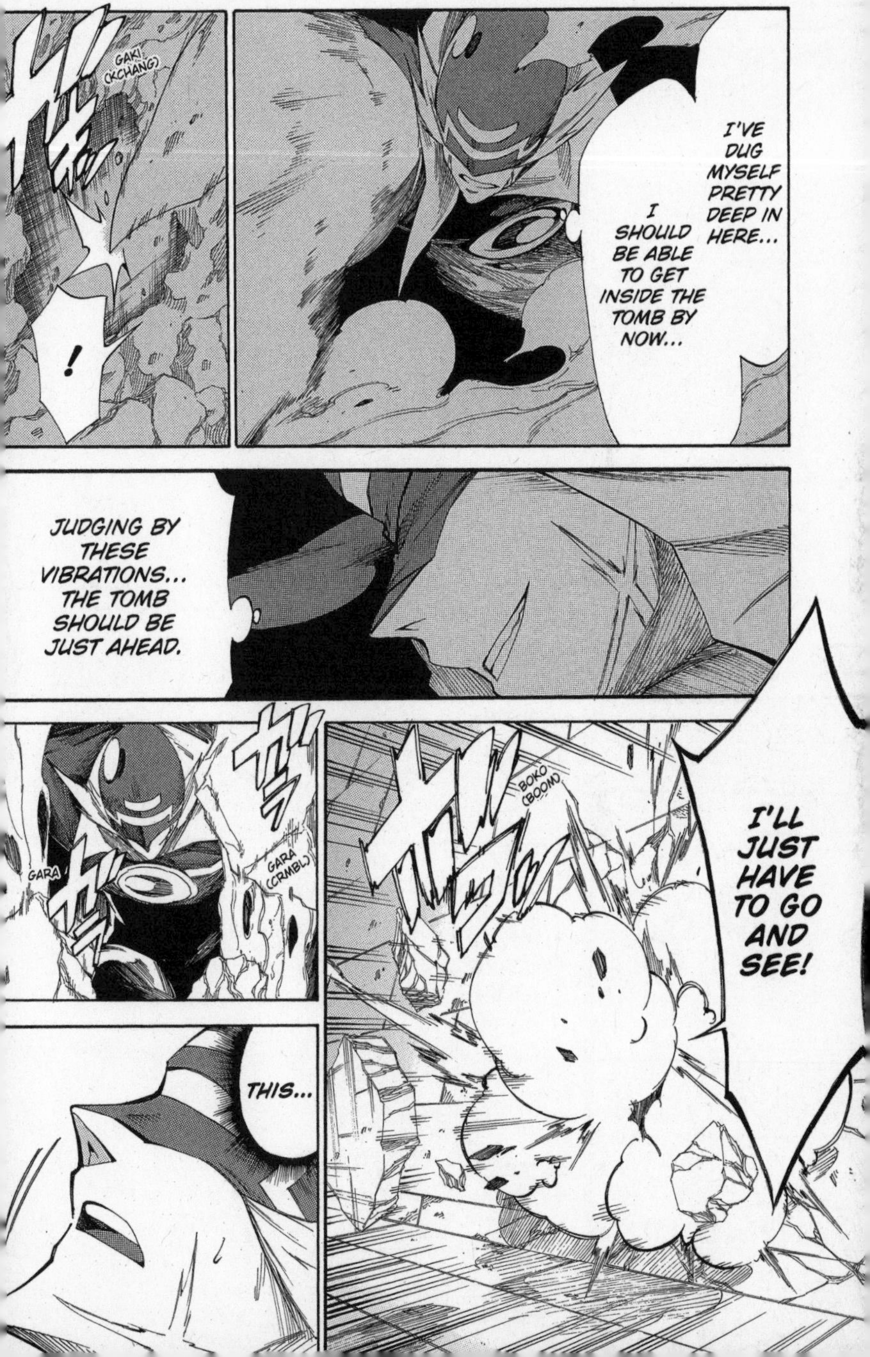
I'VE DUG MYSELF PRETTY DEEP IN HERE...
I SHOULD BE ABLE TO GET INSIDE THE TOMB BY NOW...
GAKI (KCHANG)
!
JUDGING BY THESE VIBRATIONS... THE TOMB SHOULD BE JUST AHEAD.
BOKO (BOOM)
I'LL JUST HAVE TO GO AND SEE!
GARA (CRMBL)
GARA
THIS...

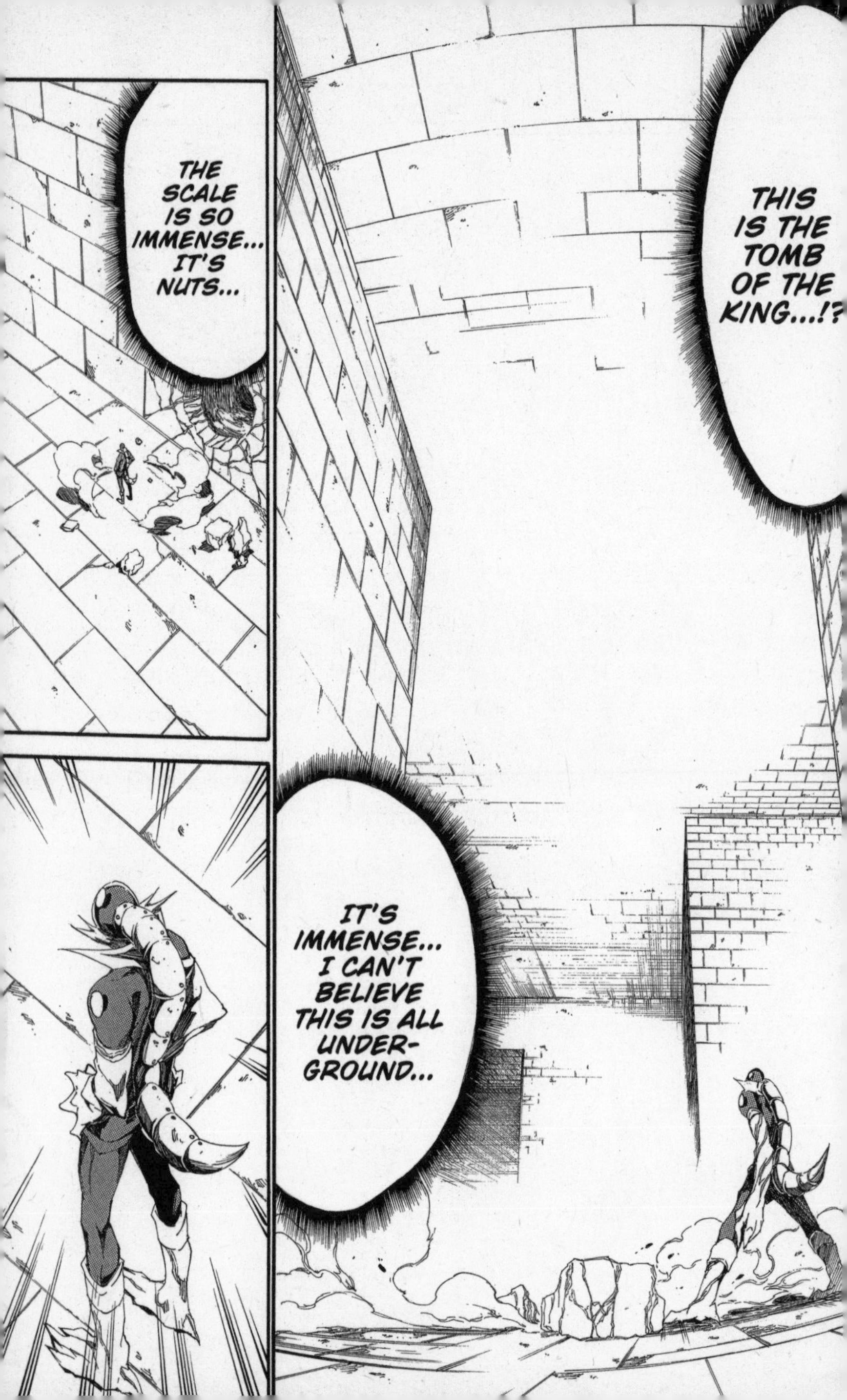
THIS IS THE TOMB OF THE KING...!?
IT'S IMMENSE... I CAN'T BELIEVE THIS IS ALL UNDER-GROUND...
THE SCALE IS SO IMMENSE... IT'S NUTS...

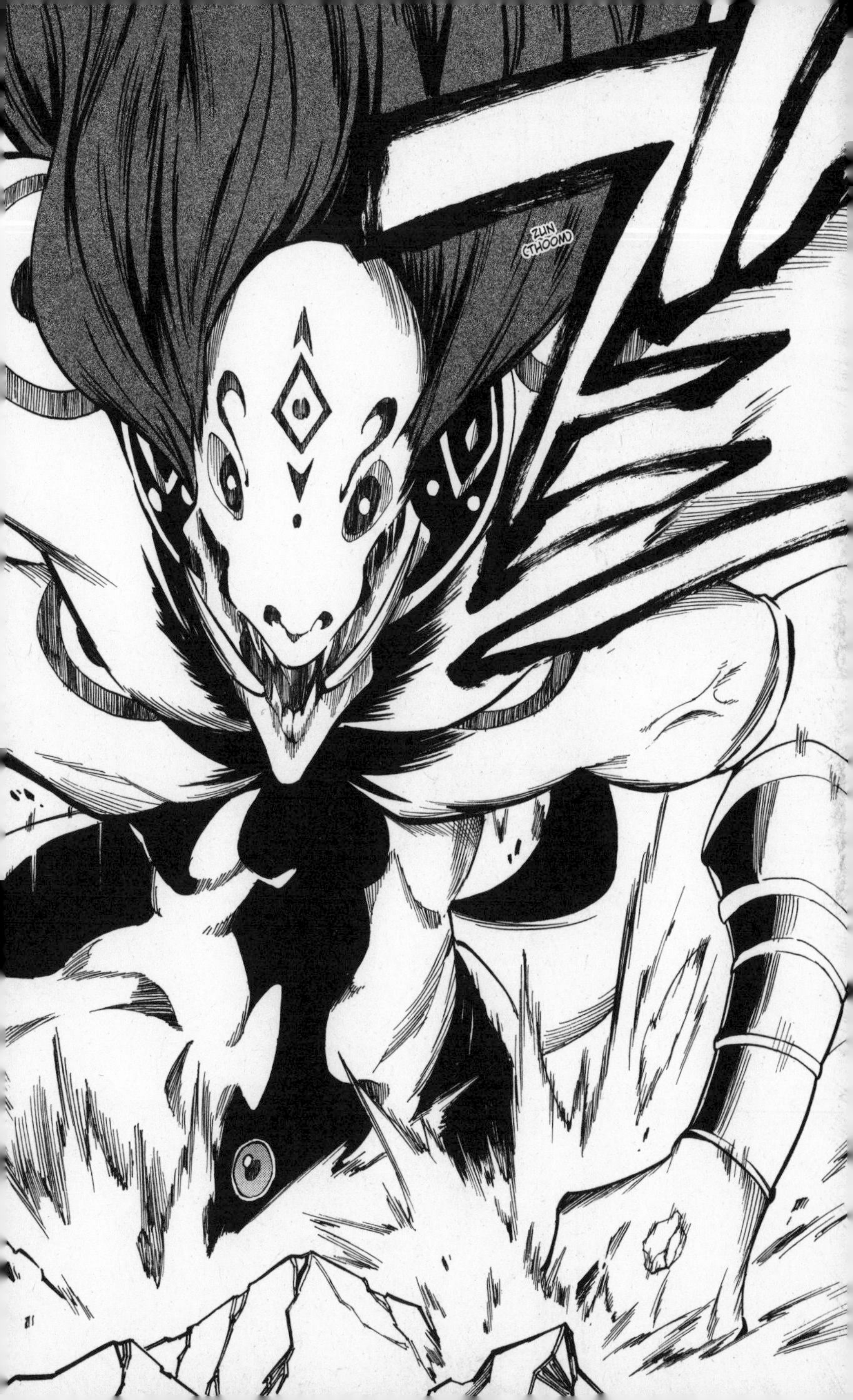
ZUN
(THOOM)

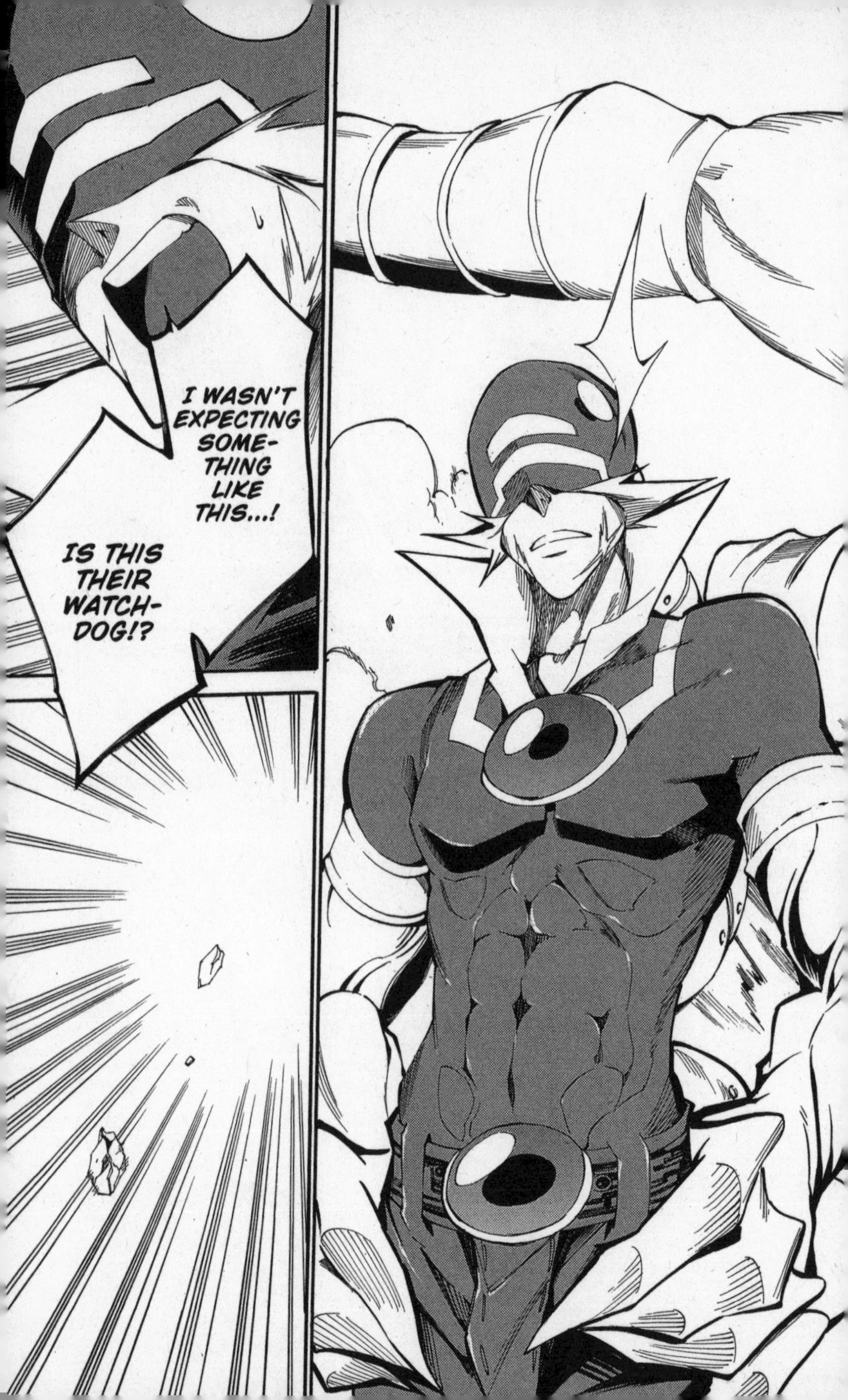
I WASN'T EXPECTING SOME-THING LIKE THIS...!
IS THIS THEIR WATCH-DOG!?

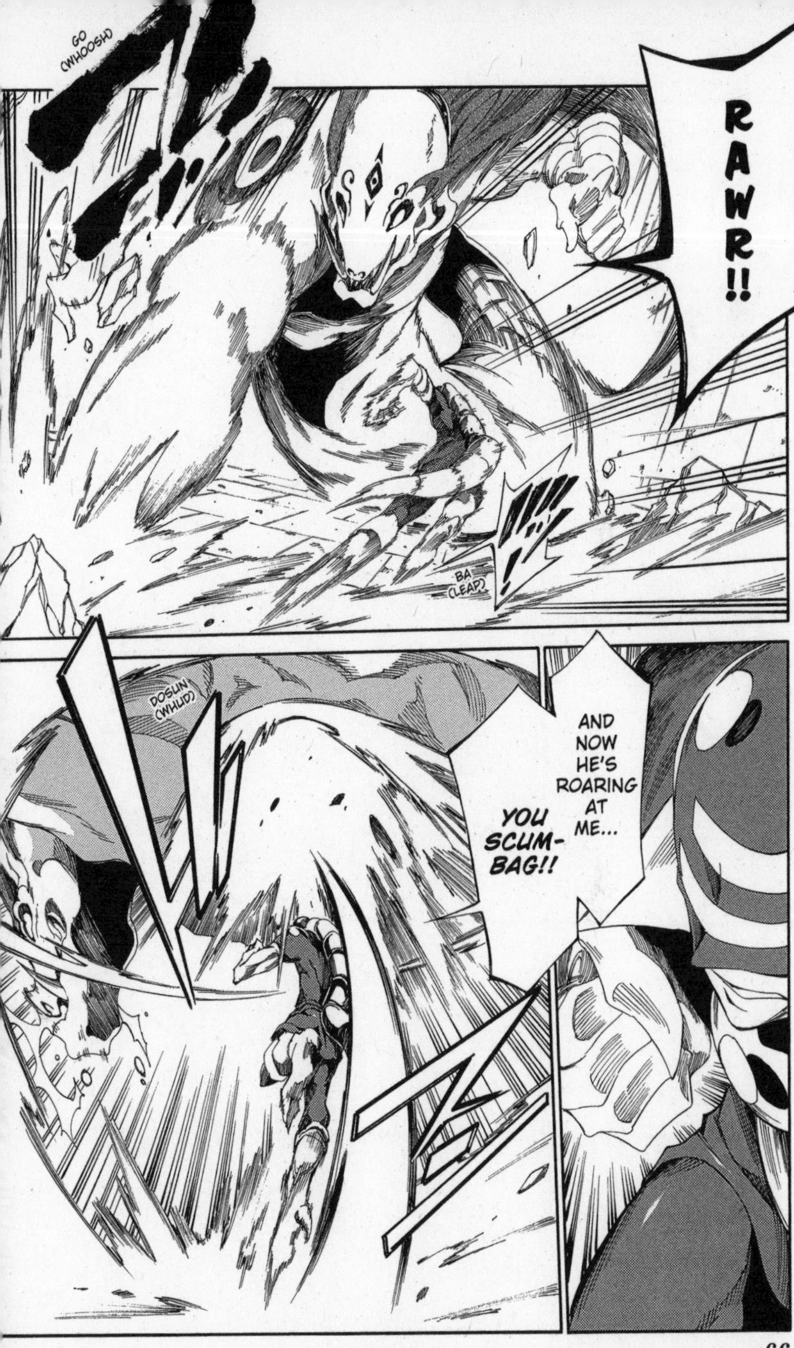
RAWR!!
BA (LEAP)
GO (WHOOSH)
AND NOW HE'S ROARING AT ME...
YOU SCUM-BAG!!
DOSUN (WHUD)

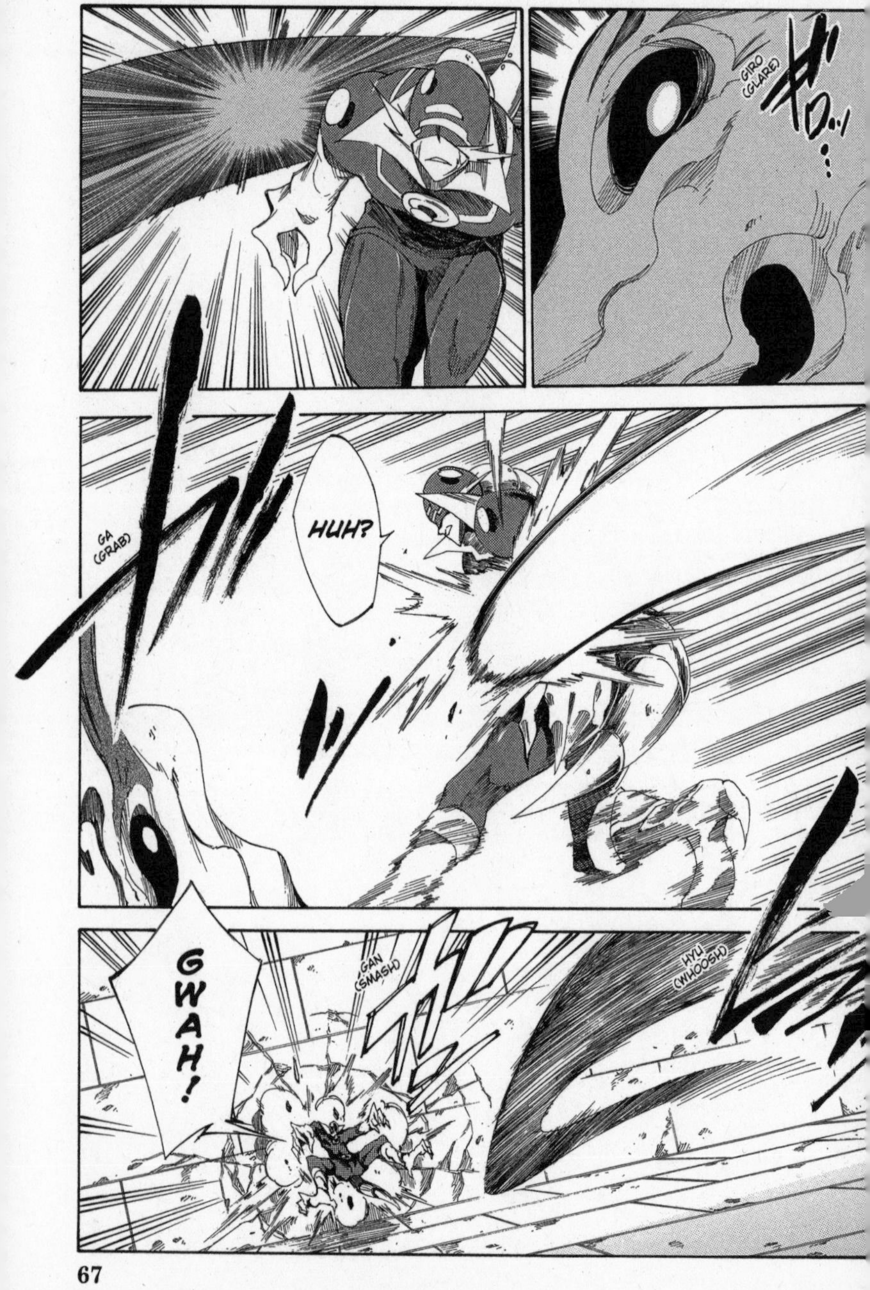
GIRO (GLARE)
HUH?
GA (GRAB)
HYU (WHOOSH)
GAN (SMASH)
GWAH!

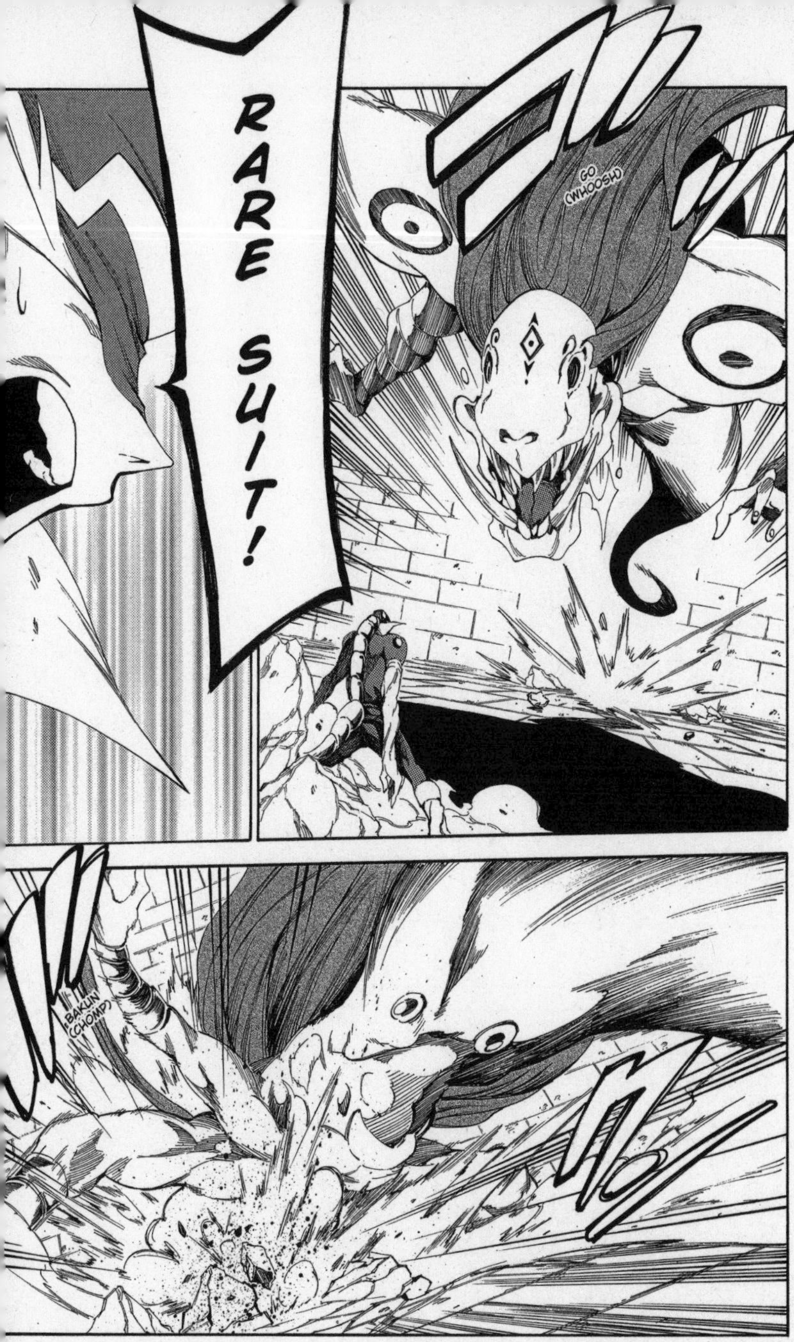
GO (WHOOSH)
RARE SUIT!
BAKUN (CHOMP)

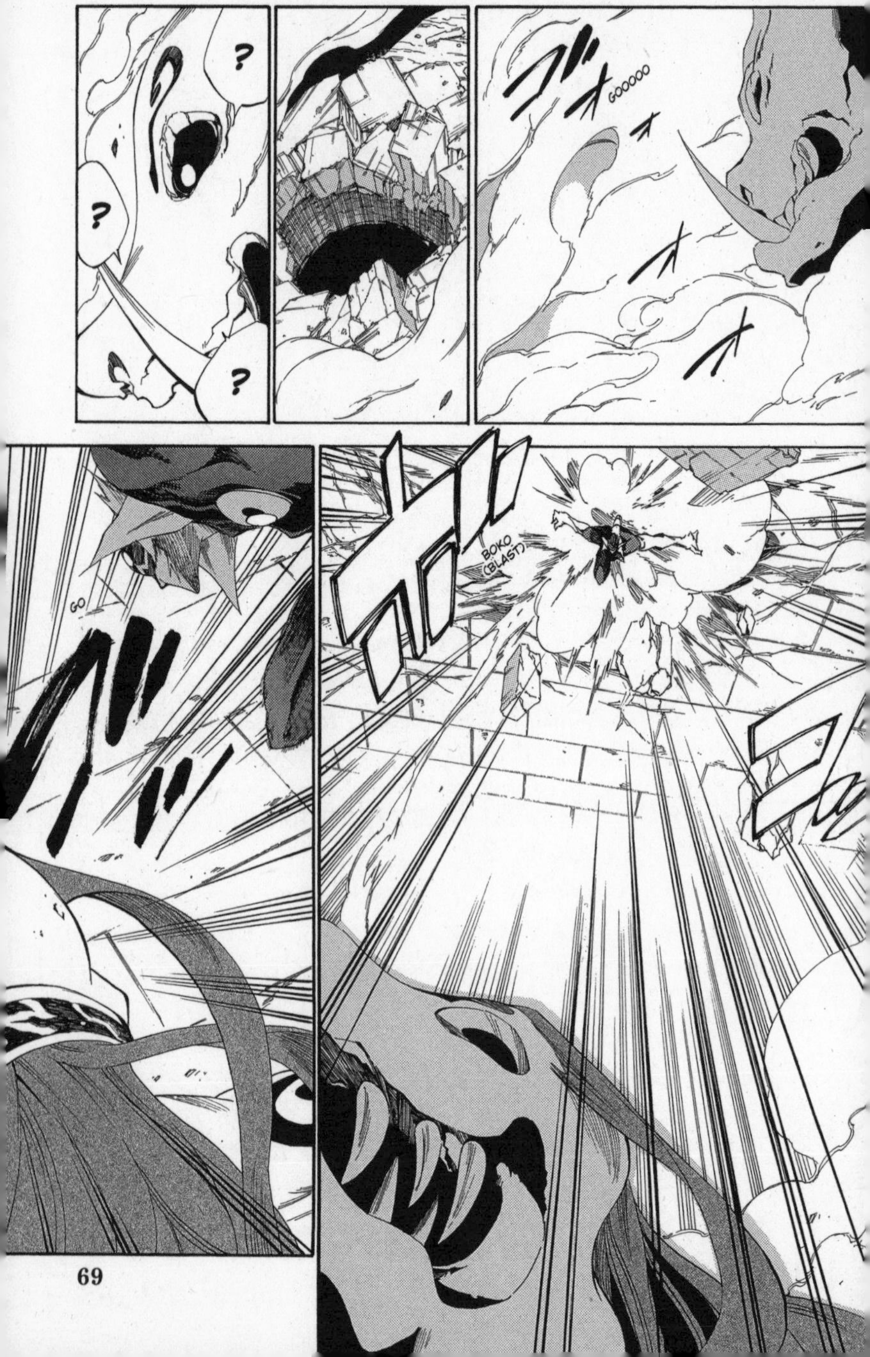
GOOOOO
?
?
?
BOKO (BLAST)
GO

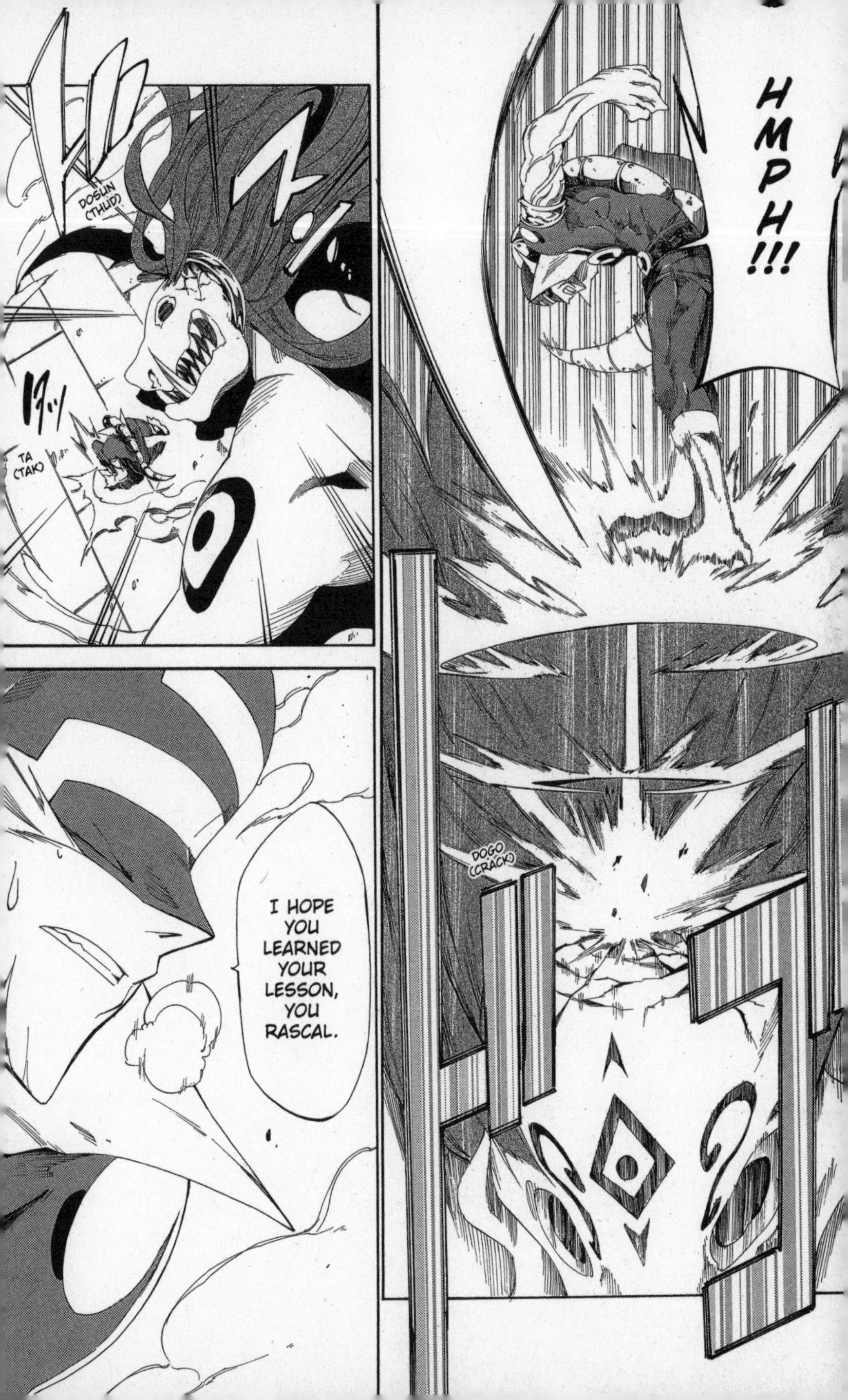
HMPH!!!
DOSUN (THUD)
TA (TAK)
DOGO (CRACK)
I HOPE YOU LEARNED YOUR LESSON, YOU RASCAL.

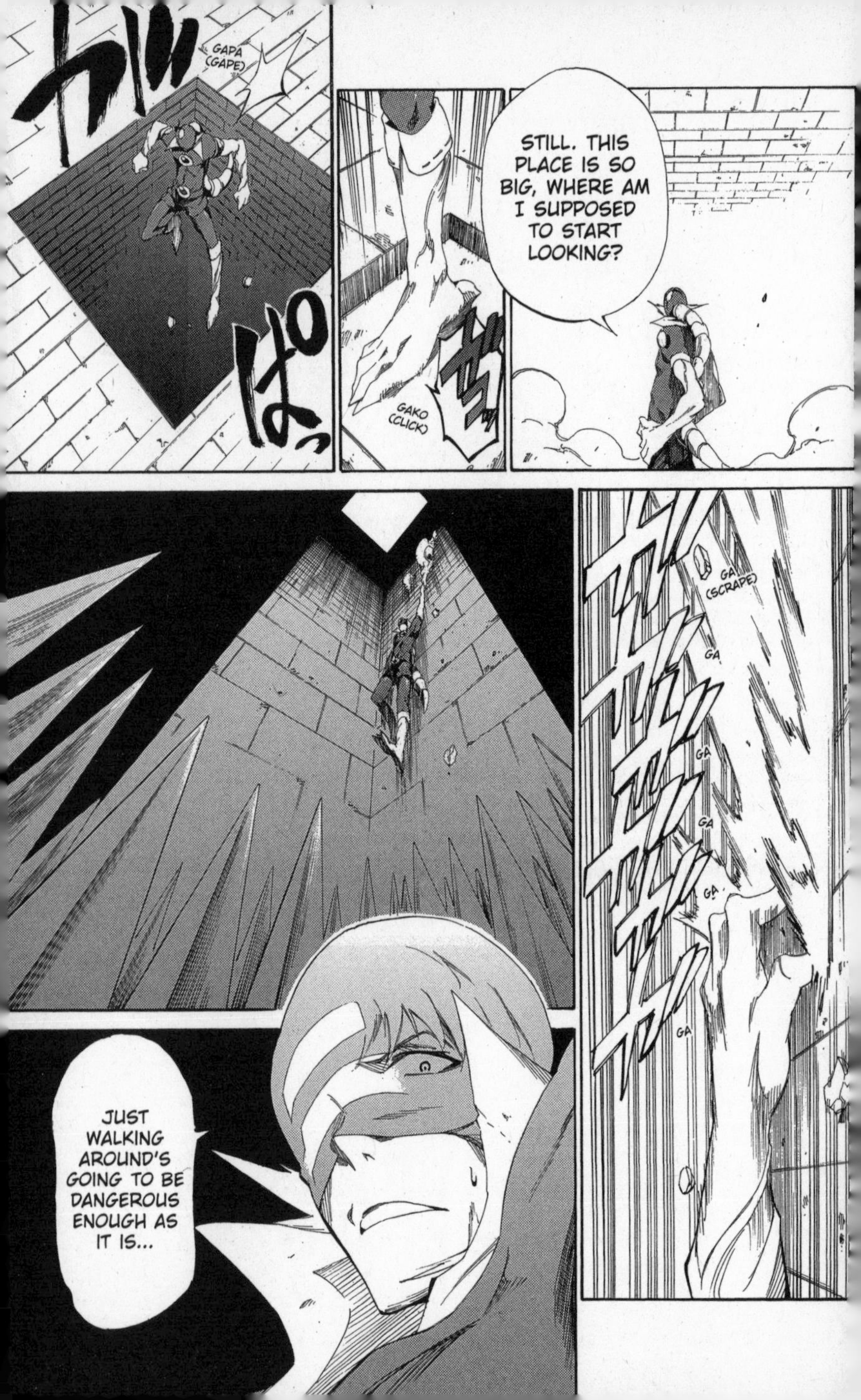
STILL. THIS PLACE IS SO BIG, WHERE AM I SUPPOSED TO START LOOKING?
GAKO (CLICK)
GAPA (GAPE)
ぱっ
GA (SCRAPE)
GA
GA
GA
GA
GA
JUST WALKING AROUND'S GOING TO BE DANGEROUS ENOUGH AS IT IS...

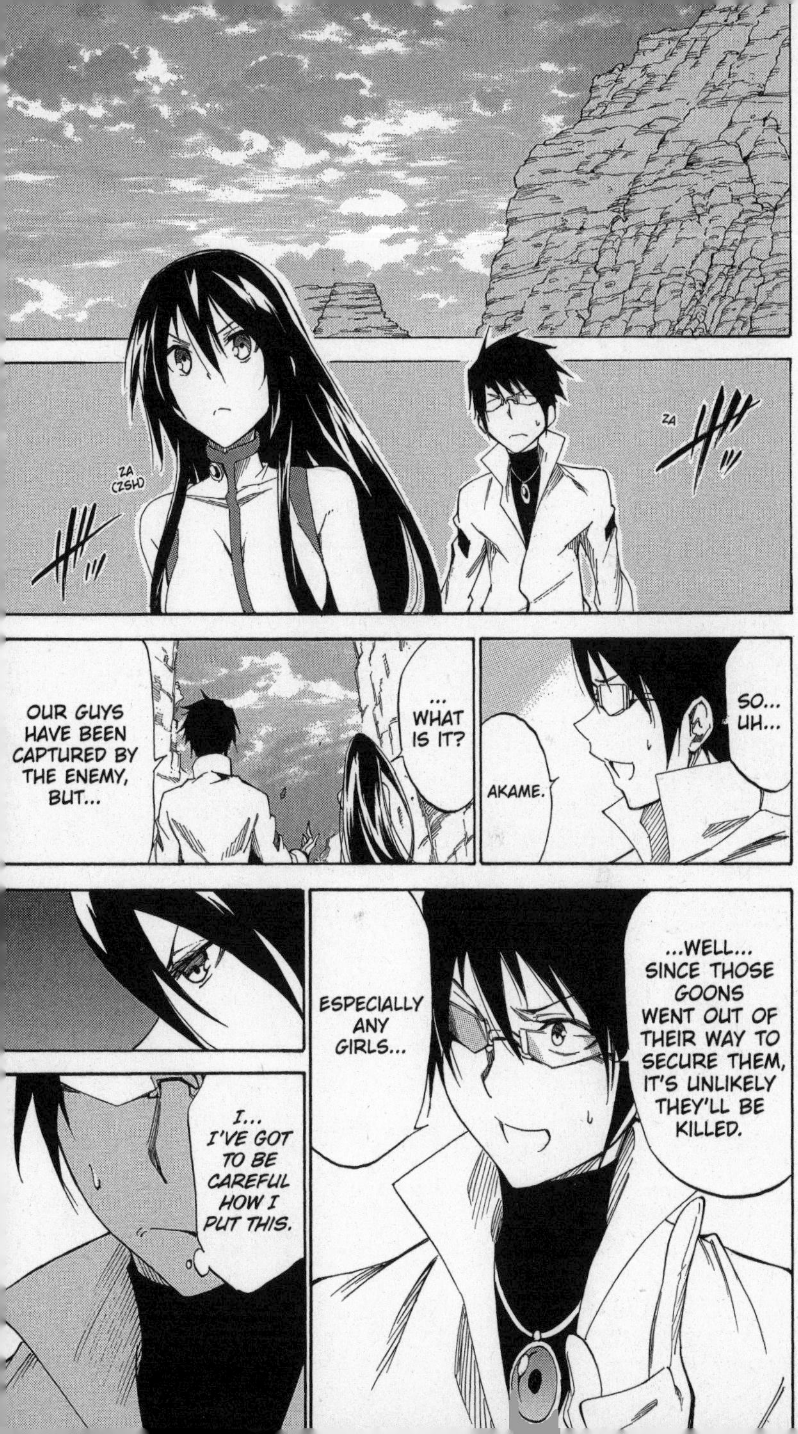
ZA
ZA (ZSH)
SO... UH...
AKAME.
... WHAT IS IT?
OUR GUYS HAVE BEEN CAPTURED BY THE ENEMY, BUT...
...WELL... SINCE THOSE GOONS WENT OUT OF THEIR WAY TO SECURE THEM, IT'S UNLIKELY THEY'LL BE KILLED.
ESPECIALLY ANY GIRLS...
I... I'VE GOT TO BE CAREFUL HOW I PUT THIS.

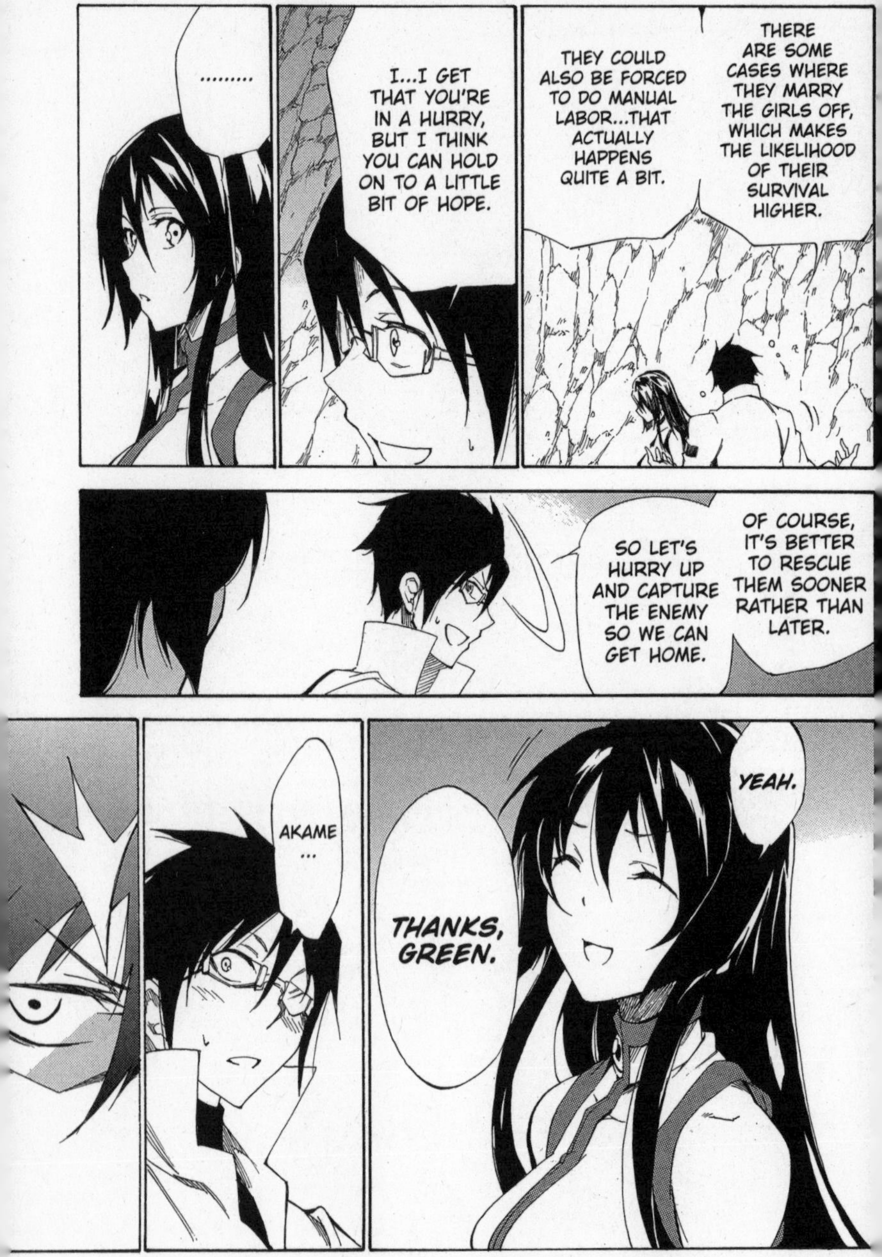
THERE ARE SOME CASES WHERE THEY MARRY THE GIRLS OFF, WHICH MAKES THE LIKELIHOOD OF THEIR SURVIVAL HIGHER.
THEY COULD ALSO BE FORCED TO DO MANUAL LABOR...THAT ACTUALLY HAPPENS QUITE A BIT.
I...I GET THAT YOU'RE IN A HURRY, BUT I THINK YOU CAN HOLD ON TO A LITTLE BIT OF HOPE.
....
OF COURSE, IT'S BETTER TO RESCUE THEM SOONER RATHER THAN LATER.
SO LET'S HURRY UP AND CAPTURE THE ENEMY SO WE CAN GET HOME.
YEAH.
THANKS, GREEN.
AKAME ...

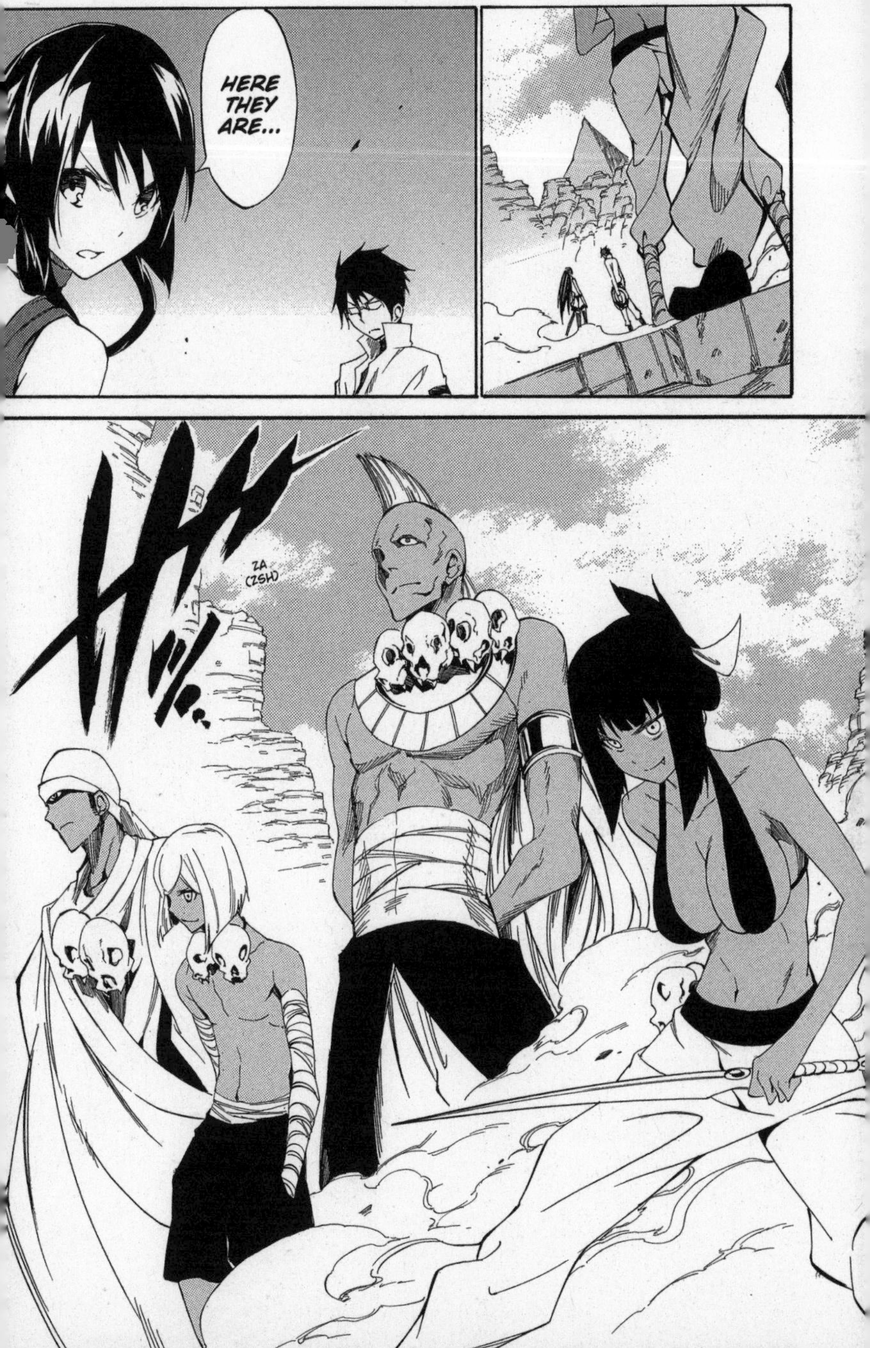
HERE THEY ARE...
ZA (ZSH)

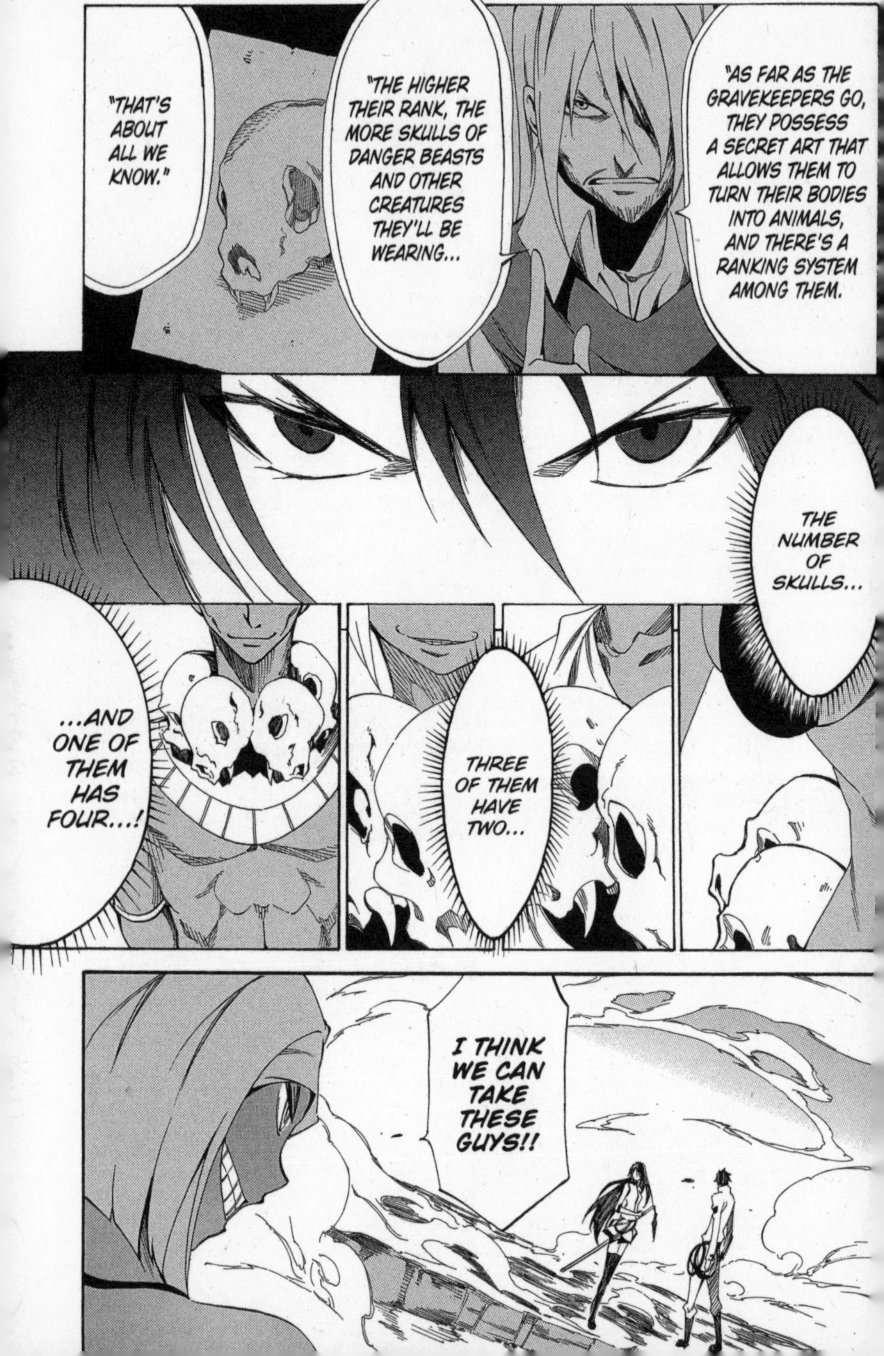
"AS FAR AS THE GRAVEKEEPERS GO, THEY POSSESS A SECRET ART THAT ALLOWS THEM TO TURN THEIR BODIES INTO ANIMALS, AND THERE'S A RANKING SYSTEM AMONG THEM.
"THE HIGHER THEIR RANK, THE MORE SKULLS OF DANGER BEASTS AND OTHER CREATURES THEY'LL BE WEARING...
"THAT'S ABOUT ALL WE KNOW."
THE NUMBER OF SKULLS...
THREE OF THEM HAVE TWO...
...AND ONE OF THEM HAS FOUR...!
I THINK WE CAN TAKE THESE GUYS!!

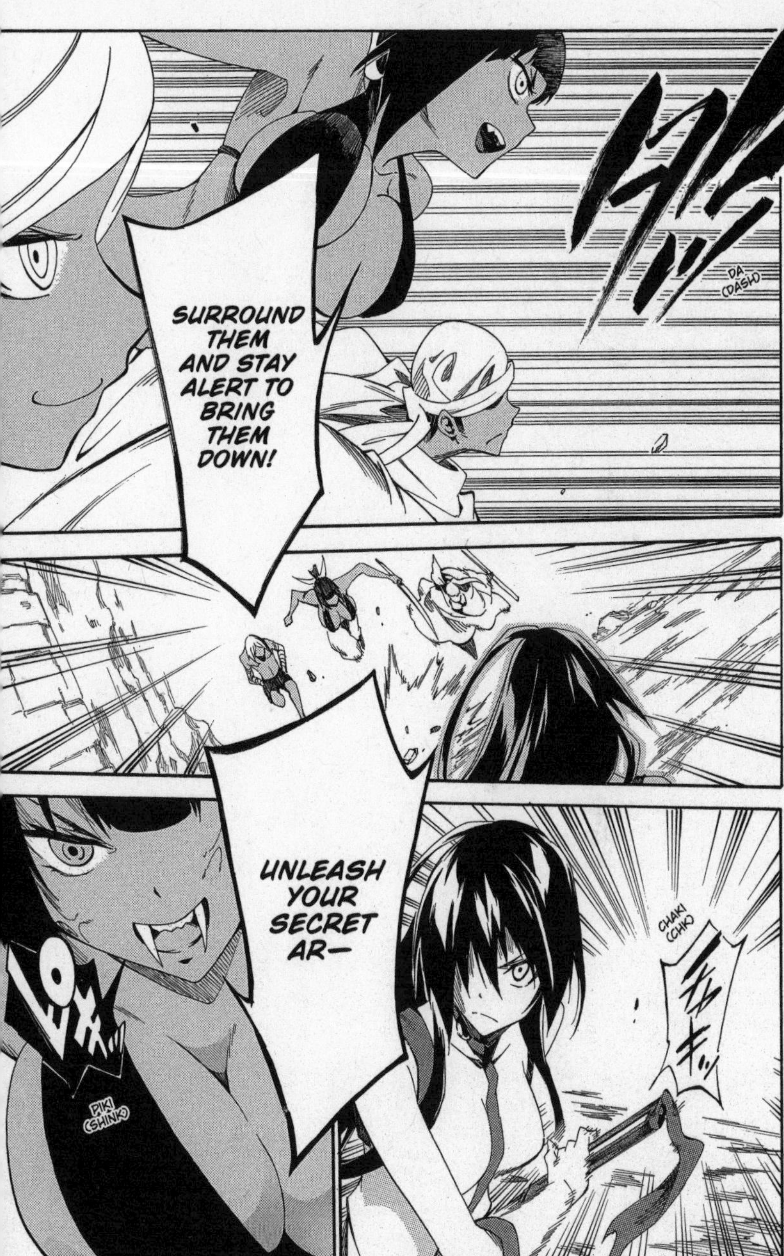
DA (DASH)
SURROUND THEM AND STAY ALERT TO BRING THEM DOWN!
CHAKI (CHK)
UNLEASH YOUR SECRET AR—
PIKI (SHINK)

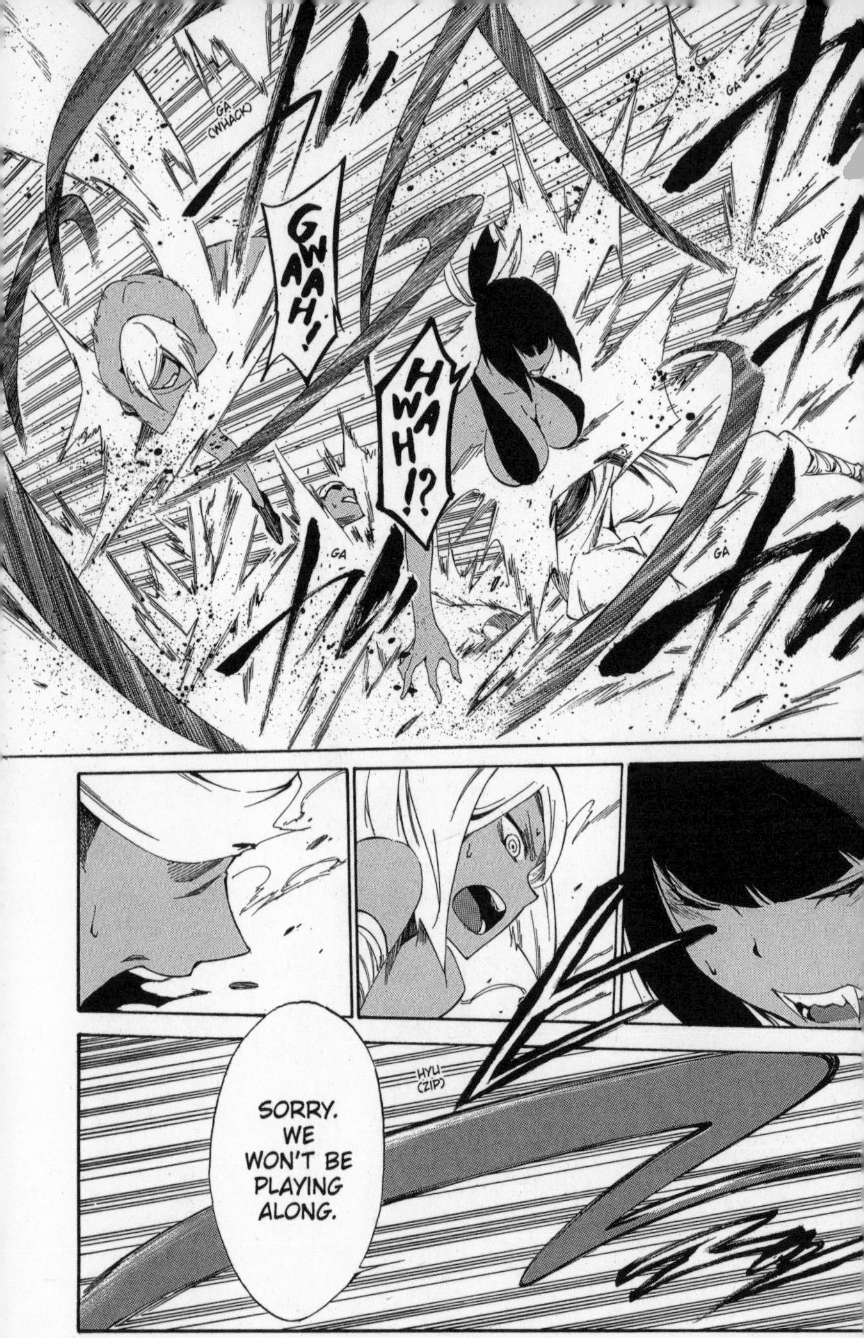
GA
GA
GA
GA
GA (WHACK)
GWAAH!
HWAAH!?
GA
HYU (ZIP)
SORRY. WE WON'T BE PLAYING ALONG.

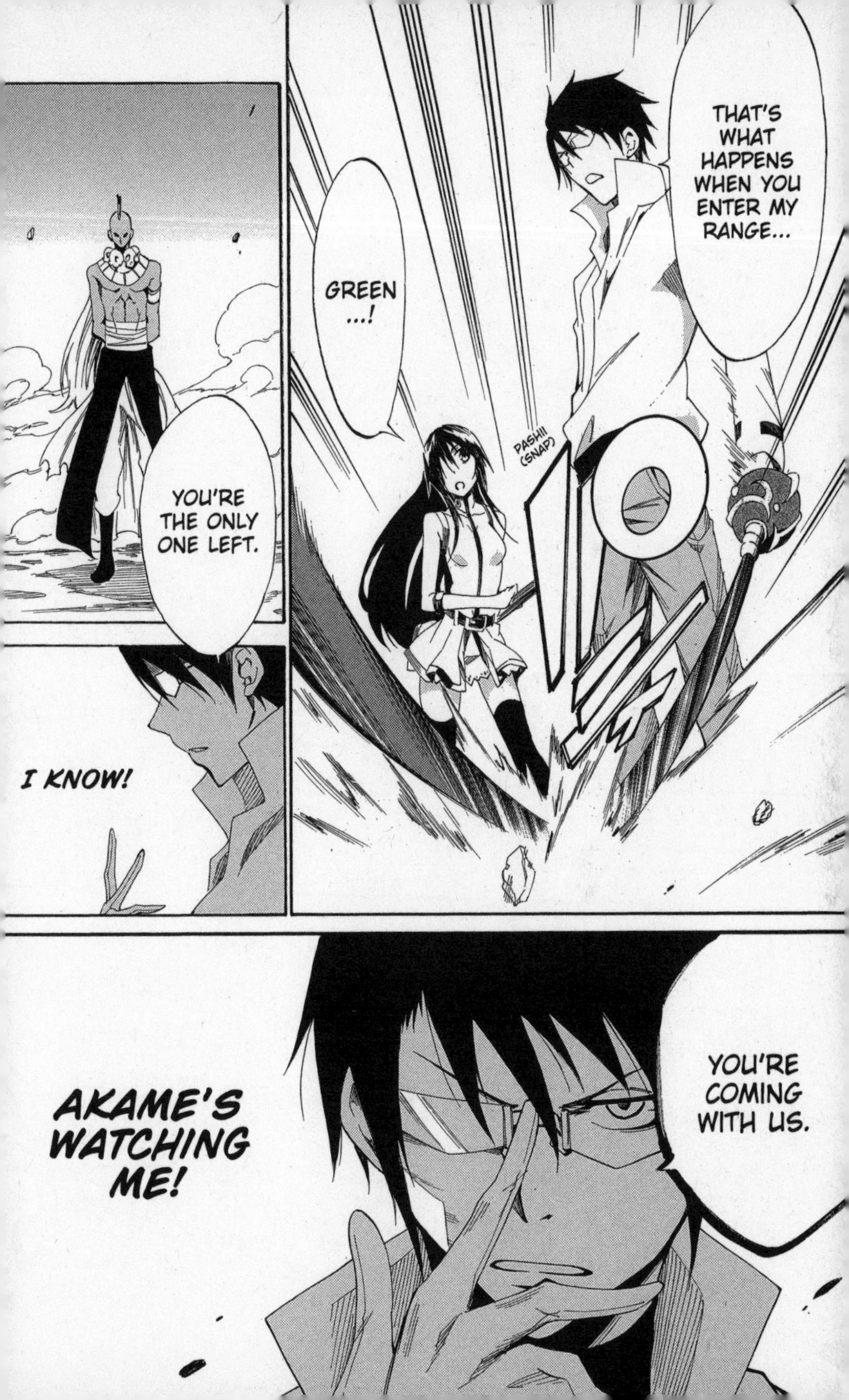
THAT'S WHAT HAPPENS WHEN YOU ENTER MY RANGE...
GREEN ...!
PASHII (SNAP)
YOU'RE THE ONLY ONE LEFT.
I KNOW!
YOU'RE COMING WITH US.
AKAME'S WATCHING ME!

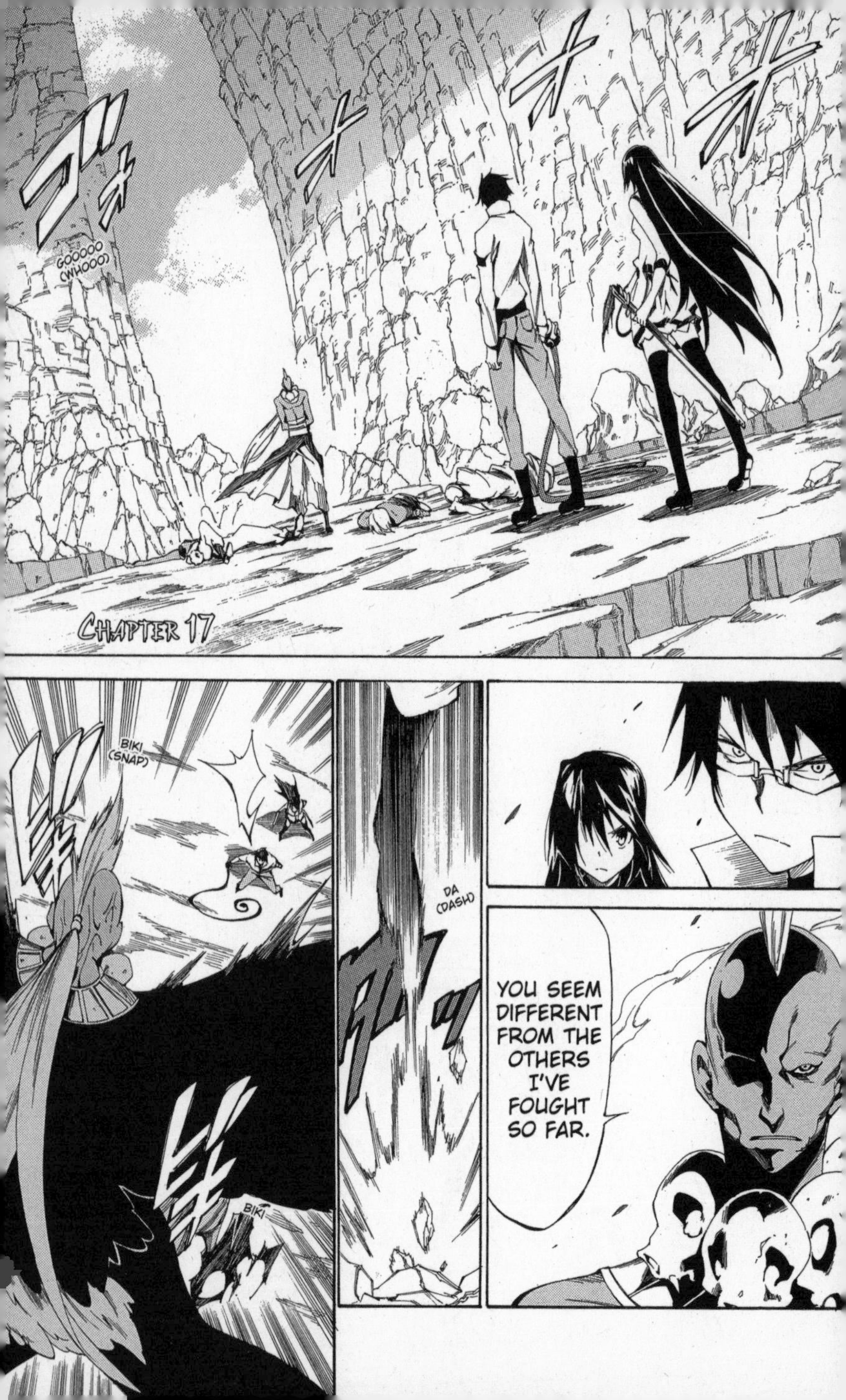
GOOOOO (WHOOO)
CHAPTER 17
YOU SEEM DIFFERENT FROM THE OTHERS I'VE FOUGHT SO FAR.
DA (DASH)
BIKI (SNAP)
BIKI

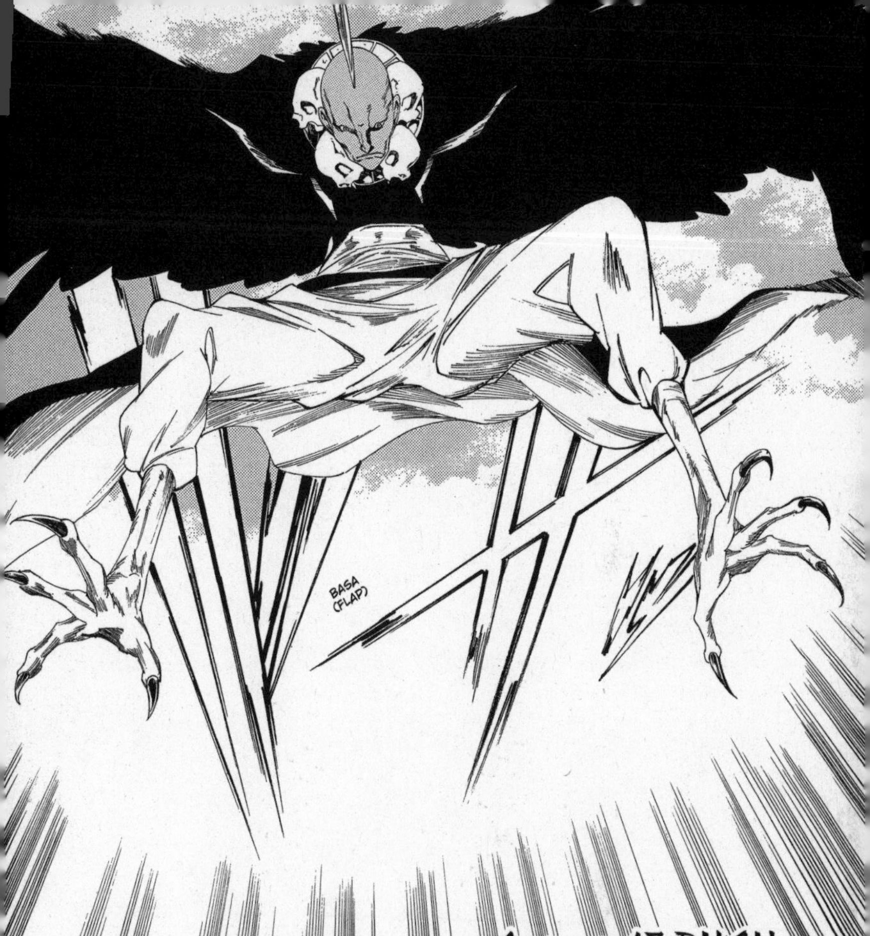
BASA (FLAP)

Chapter 17 Rush

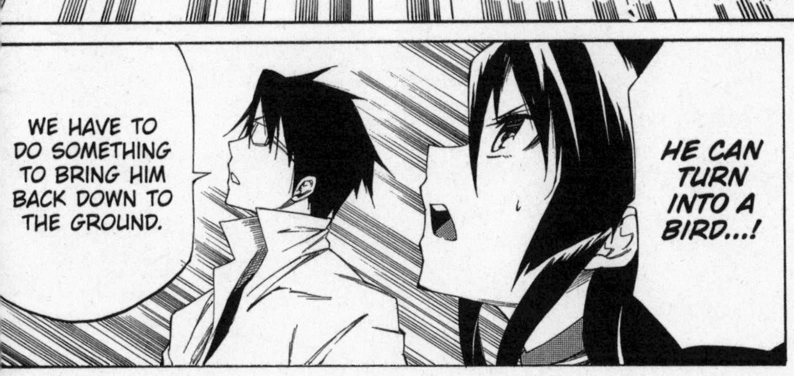
HE CAN TURN INTO A BIRD...!
WE HAVE TO DO SOMETHING TO BRING HIM BACK DOWN TO THE GROUND.

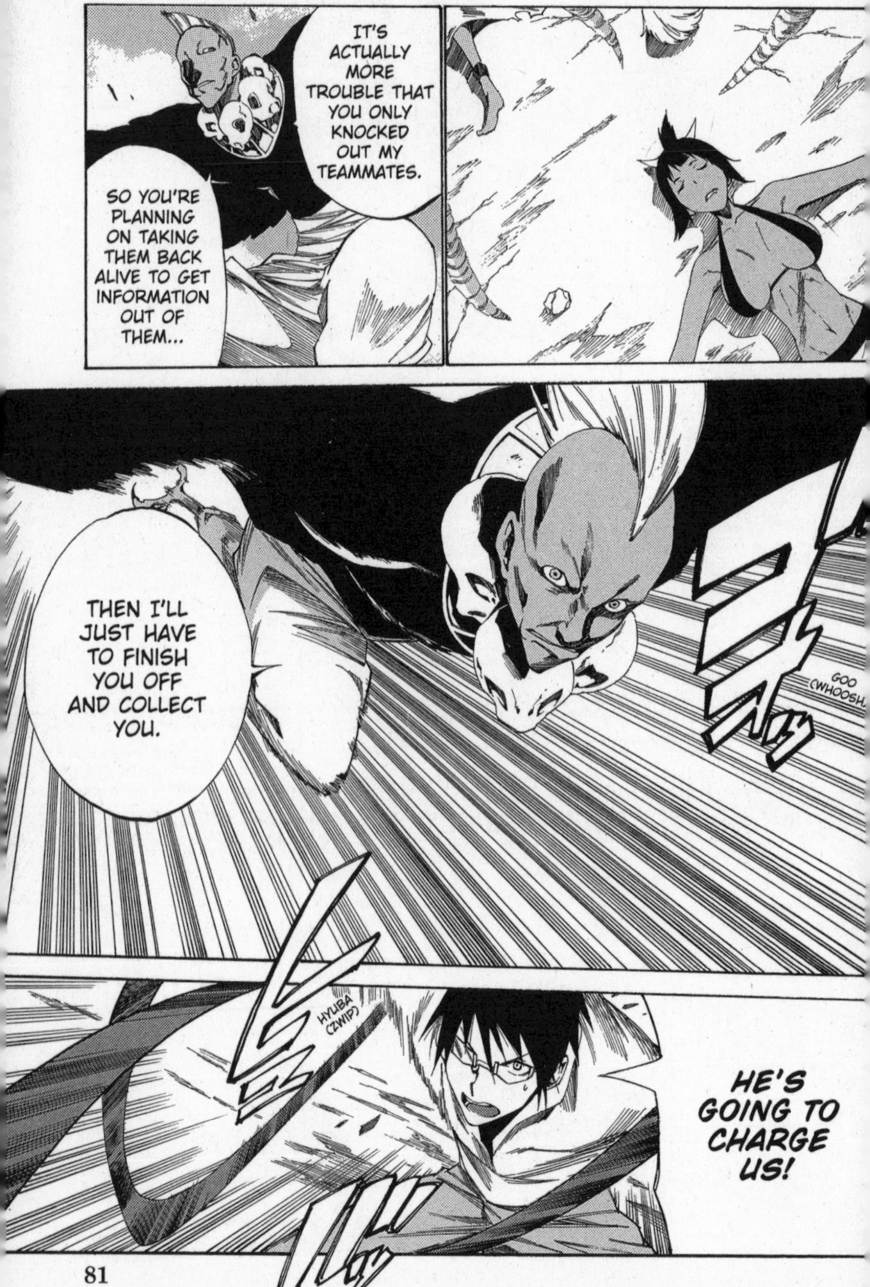
IT'S ACTUALLY MORE TROUBLE THAT YOU ONLY KNOCKED OUT MY TEAMMATES.
SO YOU'RE PLANNING ON TAKING THEM BACK ALIVE TO GET INFORMATION OUT OF THEM...
THEN I'LL JUST HAVE TO FINISH YOU OFF AND COLLECT YOU.
GOO (WHOOSH)
HYUBA (ZWIP)
HE'S GOING TO CHARGE US!

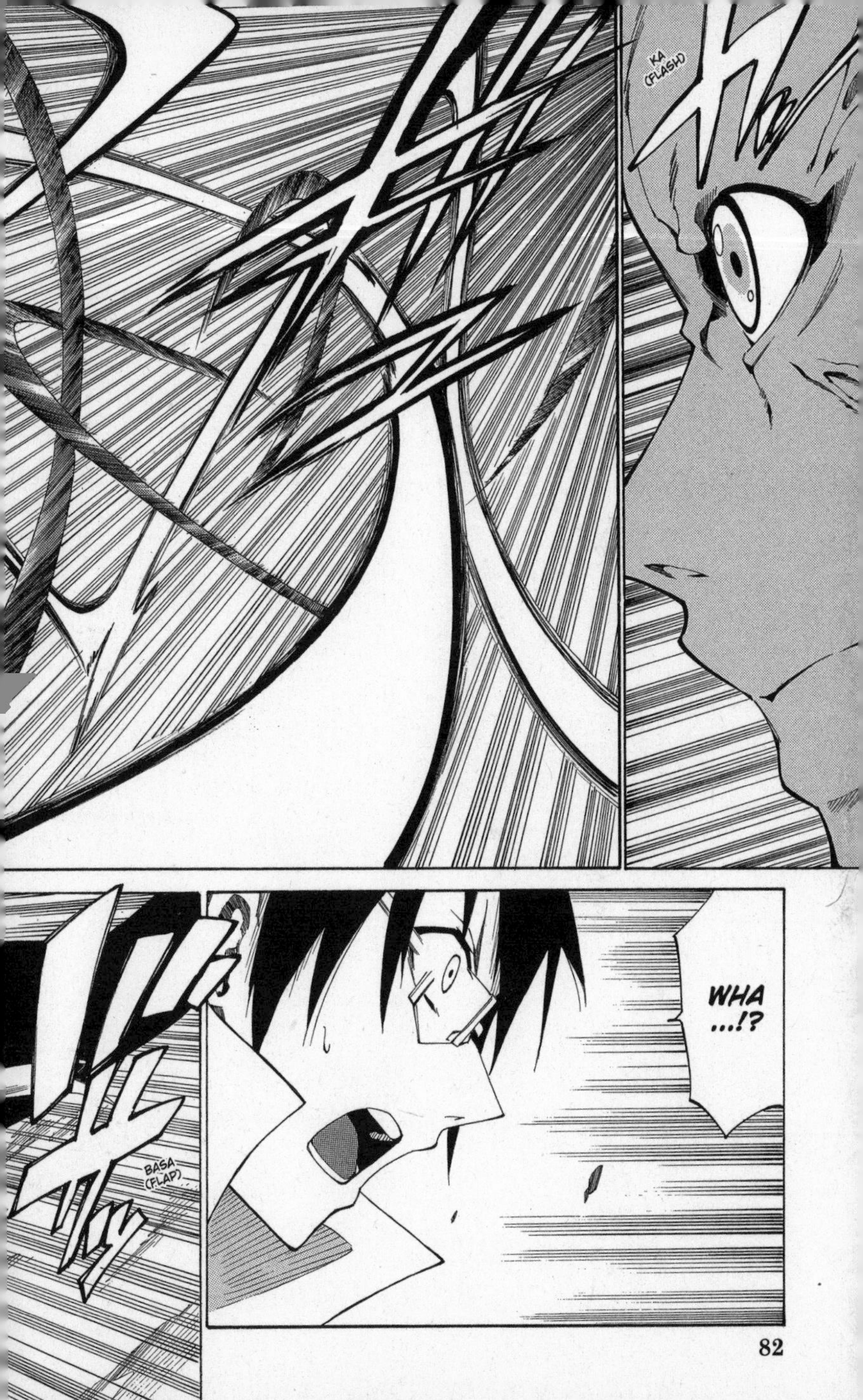
KA
(FLASH)
WHA
...!?
BASA
(FLAP)

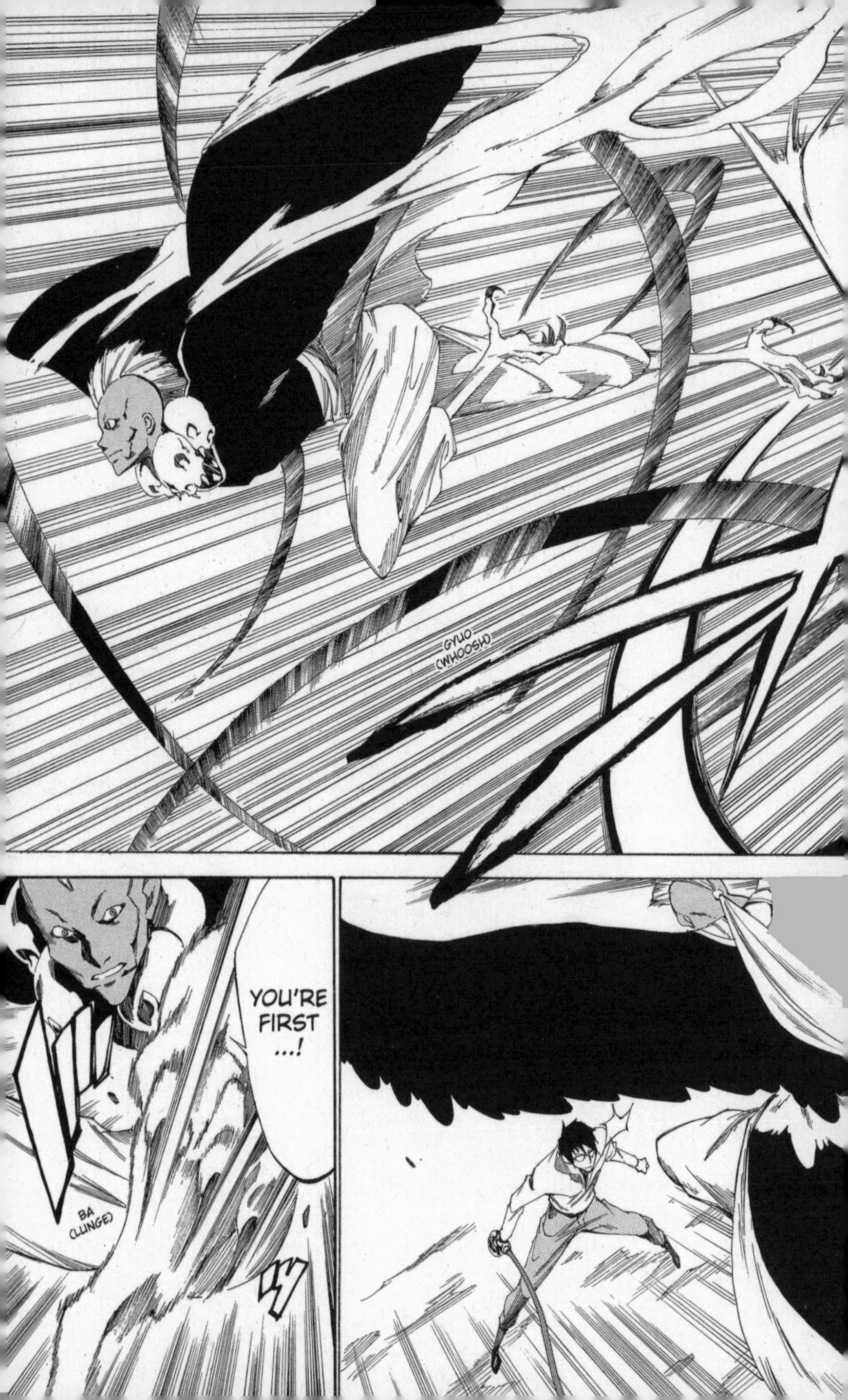
GYUO (WHOOSH)
YOU'RE FIRST ...!
BA (LUNGE)

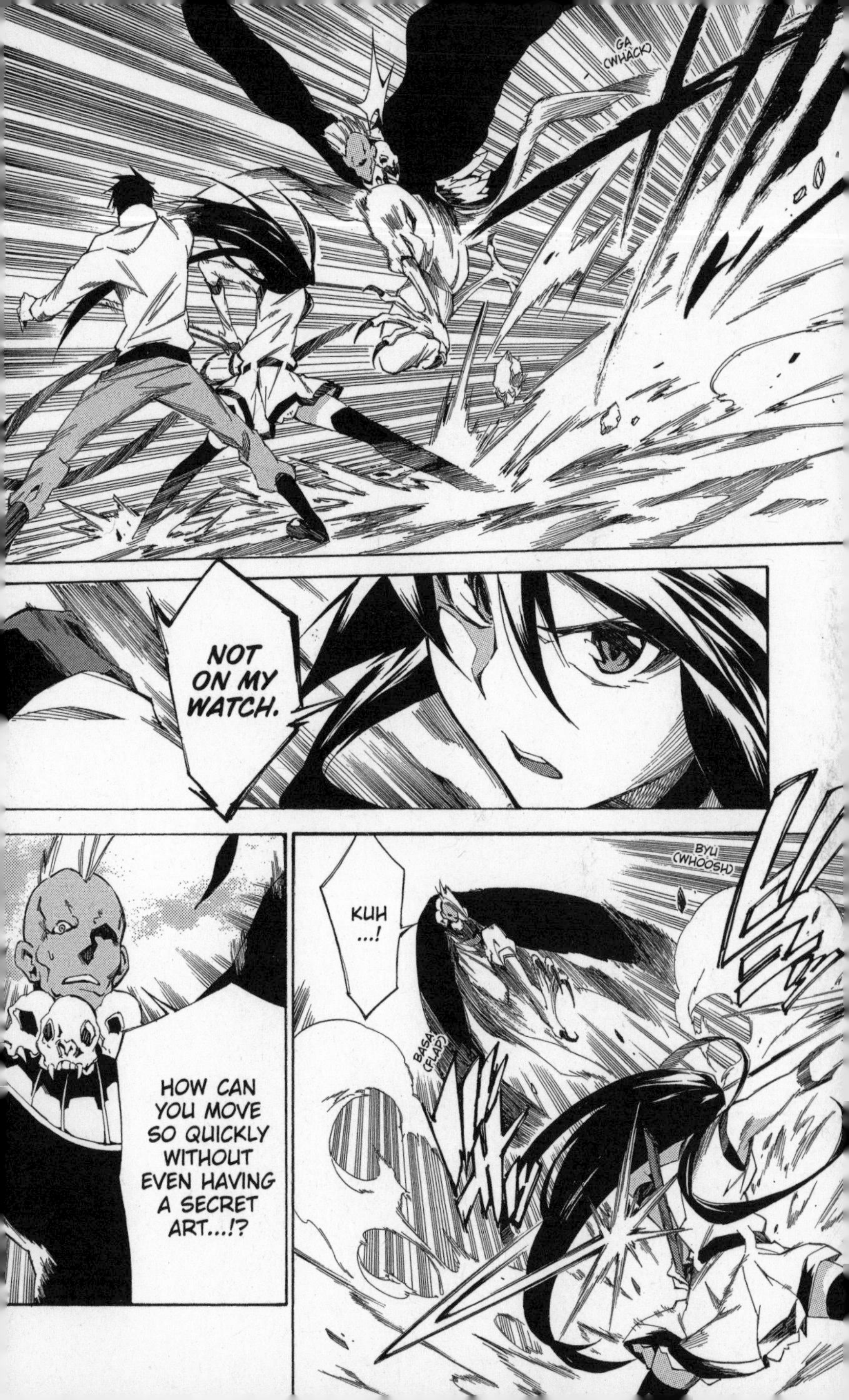
GA (WHACK)
NOT ON MY WATCH.
BYU (WHOOSH)
KUH ...!
BASA (FLAP)
HOW CAN YOU MOVE SO QUICKLY WITHOUT EVEN HAVING A SECRET ART...!?

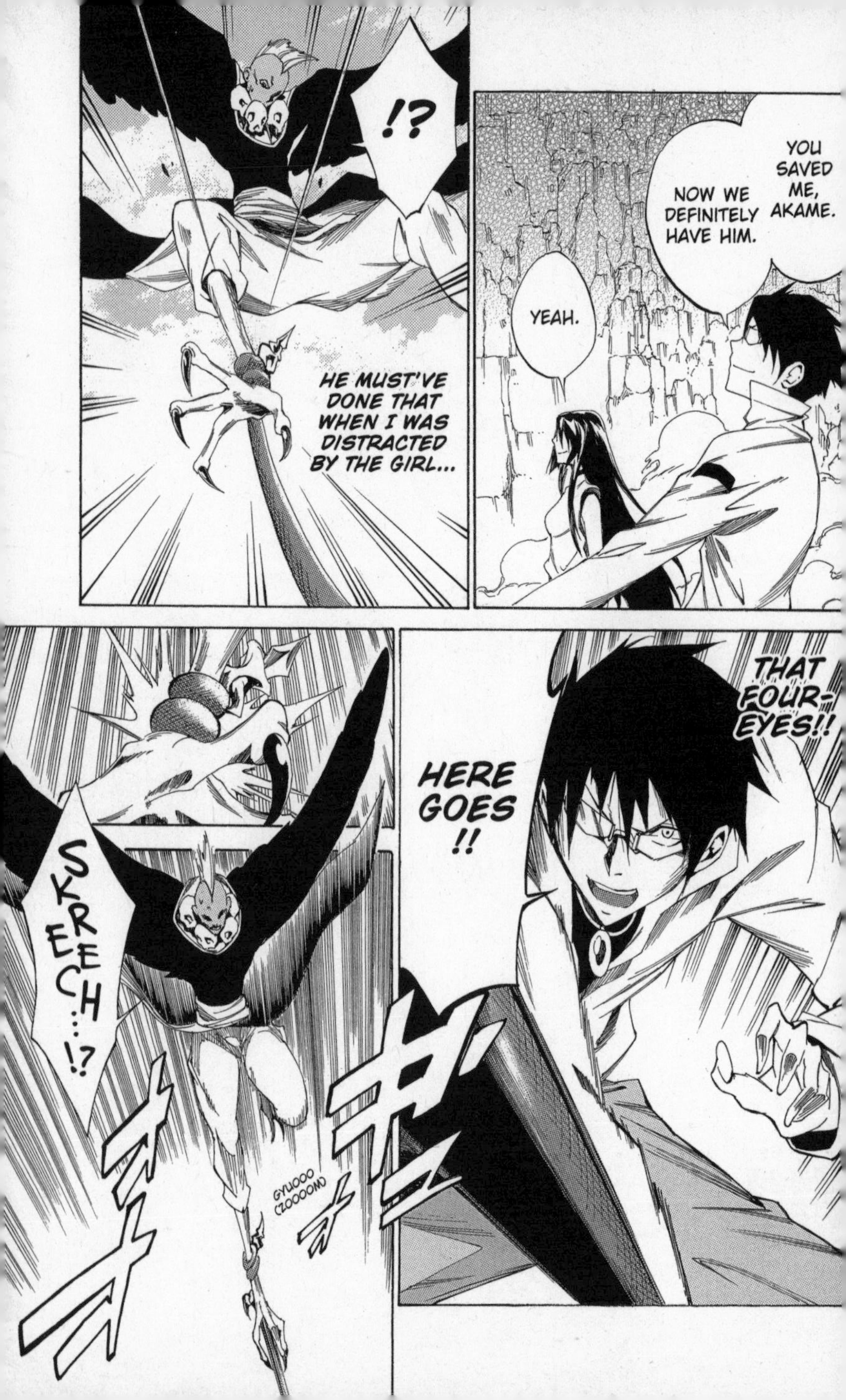
YOU SAVED ME, AKAME.
NOW WE DEFINITELY HAVE HIM.
YEAH.
!?
HE MUST'VE DONE THAT WHEN I WAS DISTRACTED BY THE GIRL...
THAT FOUR-EYES!!
HERE GOES!!
SKRECH...!?
GYUOOO (ZOOOOM)

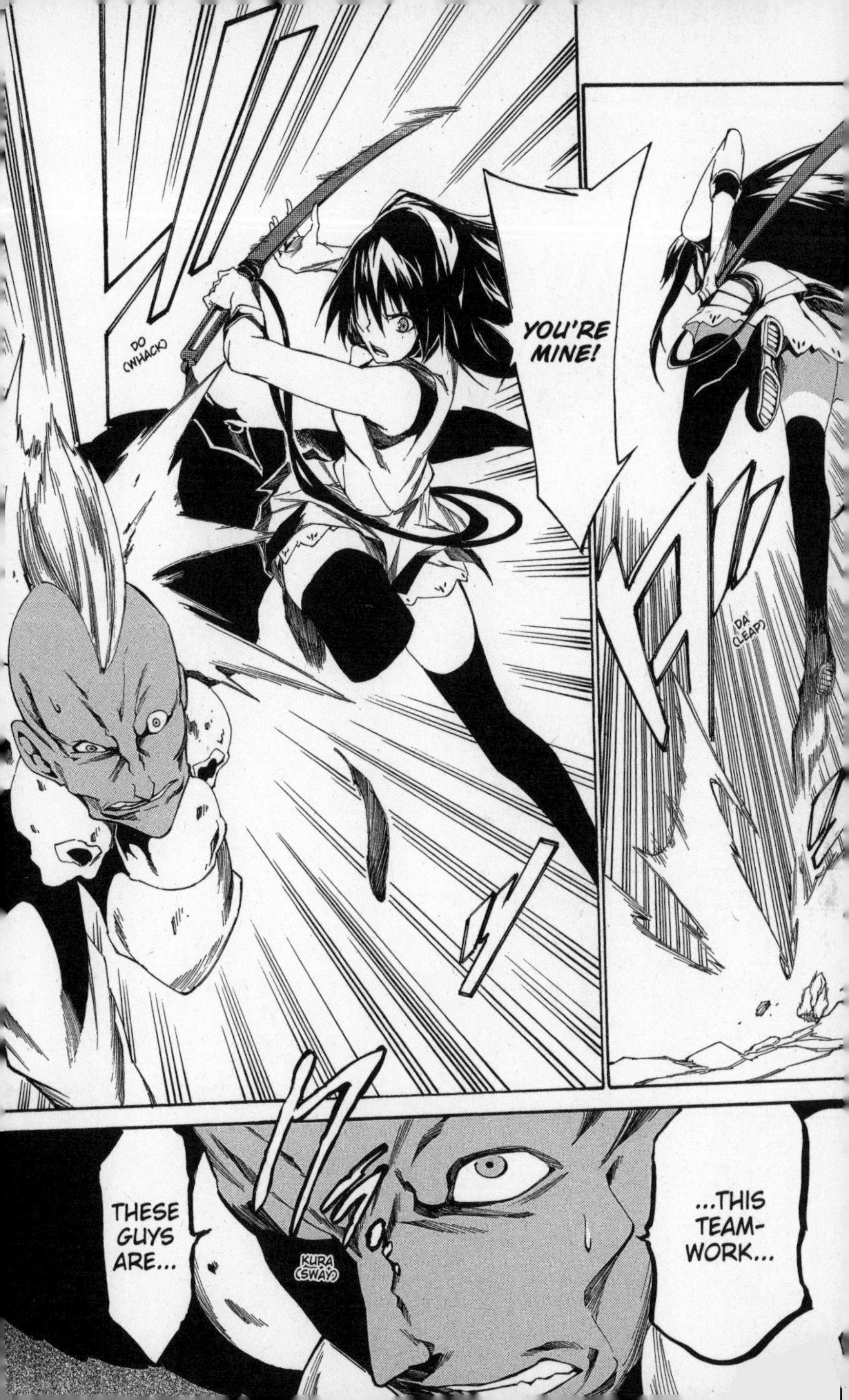
DA' (LEAP)
YOU'RE MINE!
DO (WHACK)
...THIS TEAM-WORK...
KURA (SWAY)
THESE GUYS ARE...

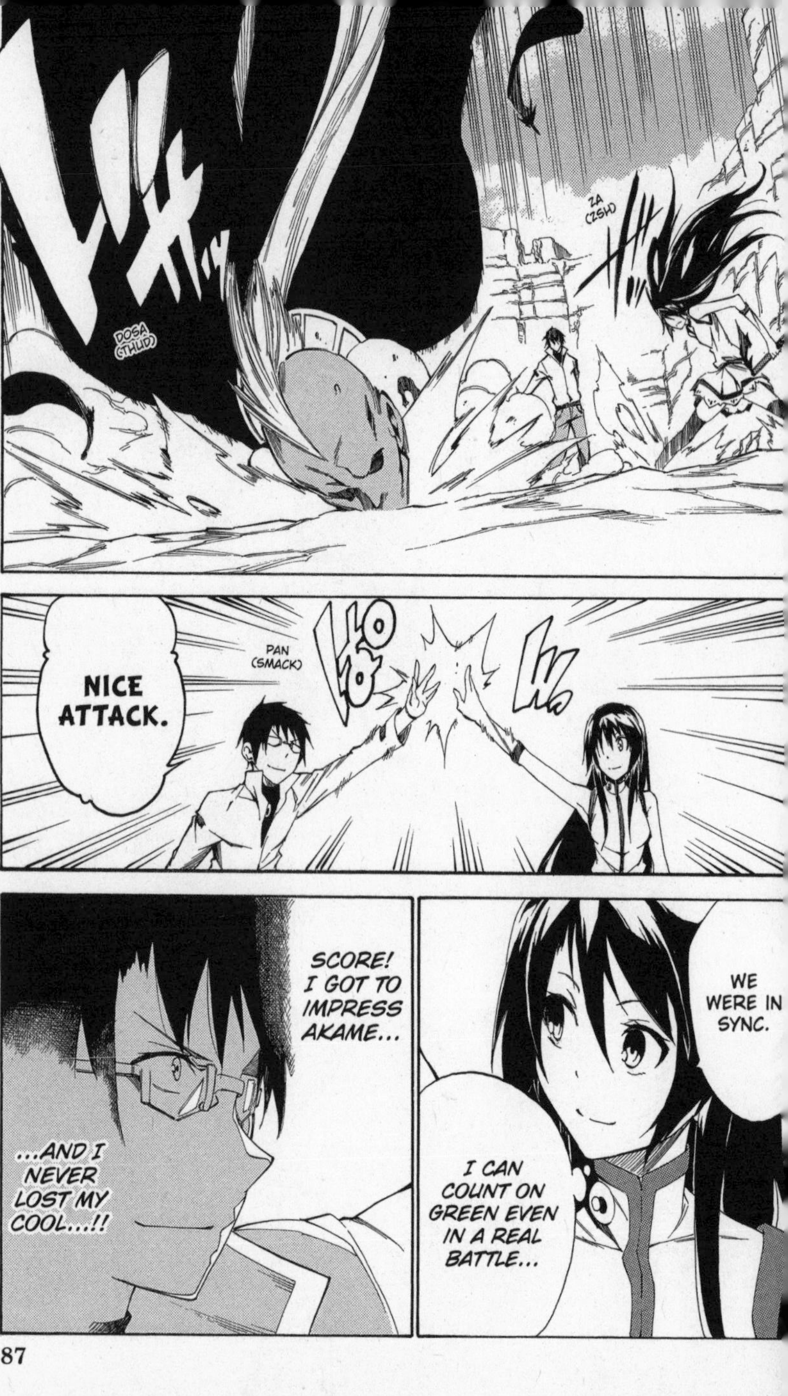
ZA (ZSH)
DOSA (THUD)
PAN (SMACK)
NICE ATTACK.
WE WERE IN SYNC.
I CAN COUNT ON GREEN EVEN IN A REAL BATTLE...
SCORE! I GOT TO IMPRESS AKAME...
...AND I NEVER LOST MY COOL...!!

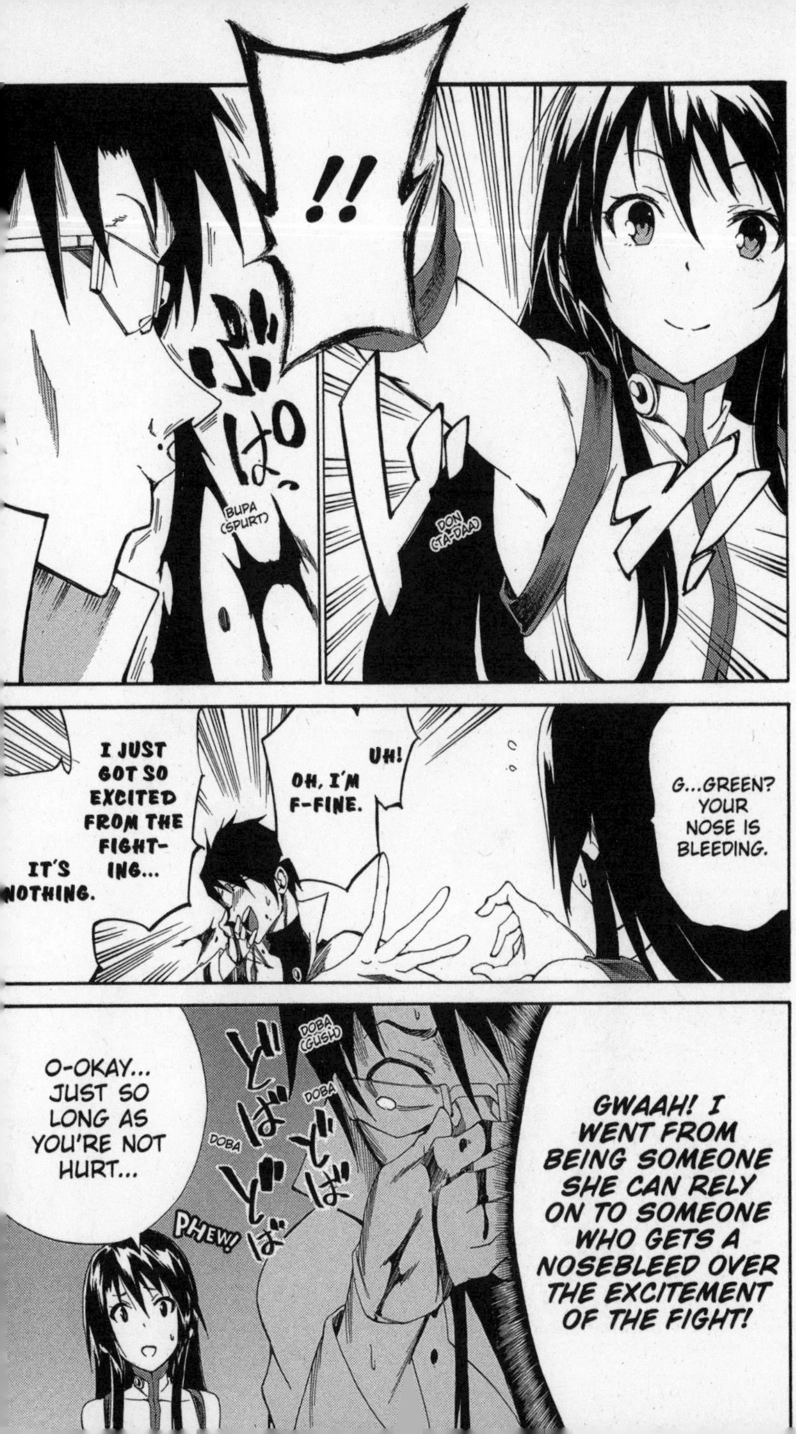
DON (TA-DAA)
!!
BUPA (SPURT)
G...GREEN? YOUR NOSE IS BLEEDING.
UH!
OH, I'M F-FINE.
I JUST GOT SO EXCITED FROM THE FIGHTING...
IT'S NOTHING.
GWAAH! I WENT FROM BEING SOMEONE SHE CAN RELY ON TO SOMEONE WHO GETS A NOSEBLEED OVER THE EXCITEMENT OF THE FIGHT!
DOBA (GUSH)
DOBA
DOBA
O-OKAY... JUST SO LONG AS YOU'RE NOT HURT...
PHEW!

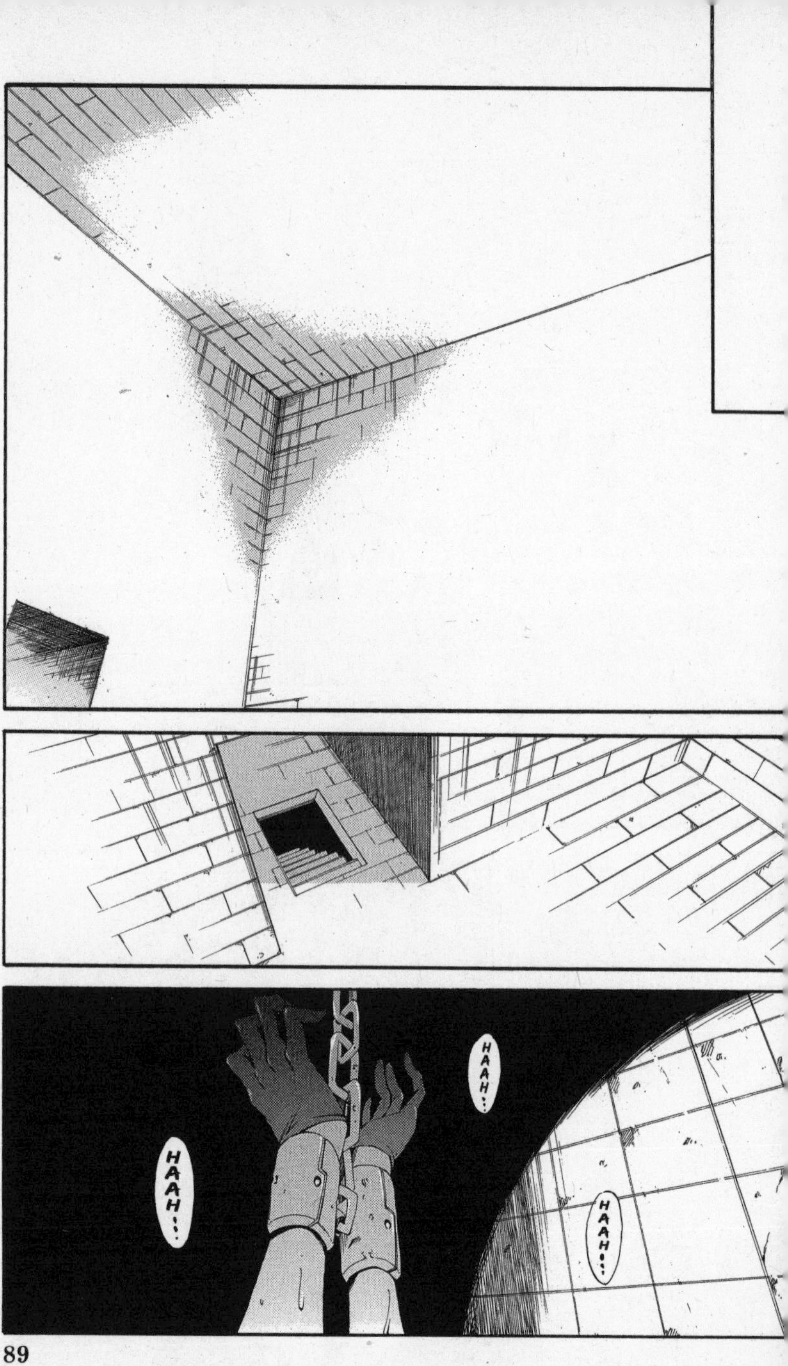
HAAH...
HAAH...
HAAH...

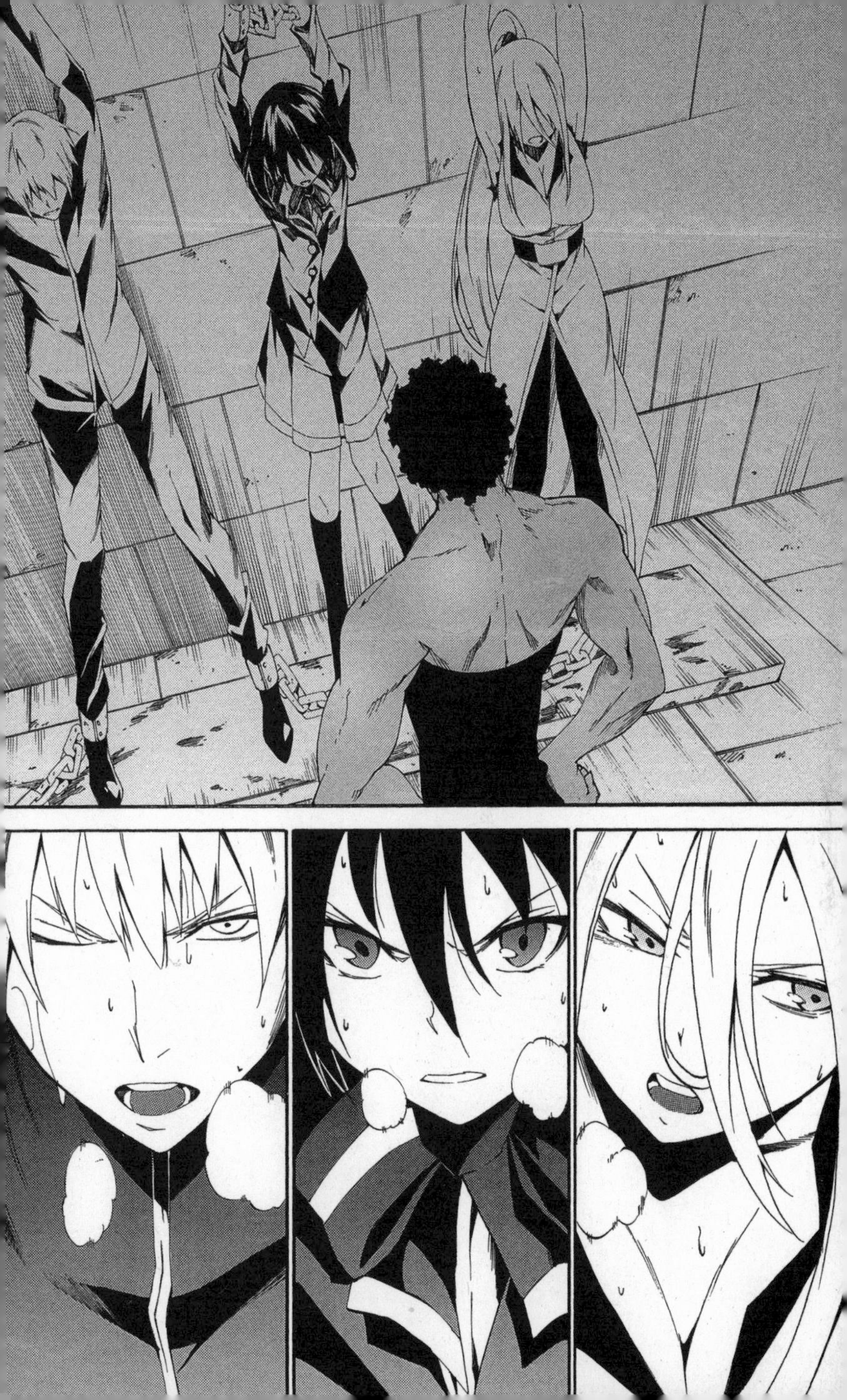

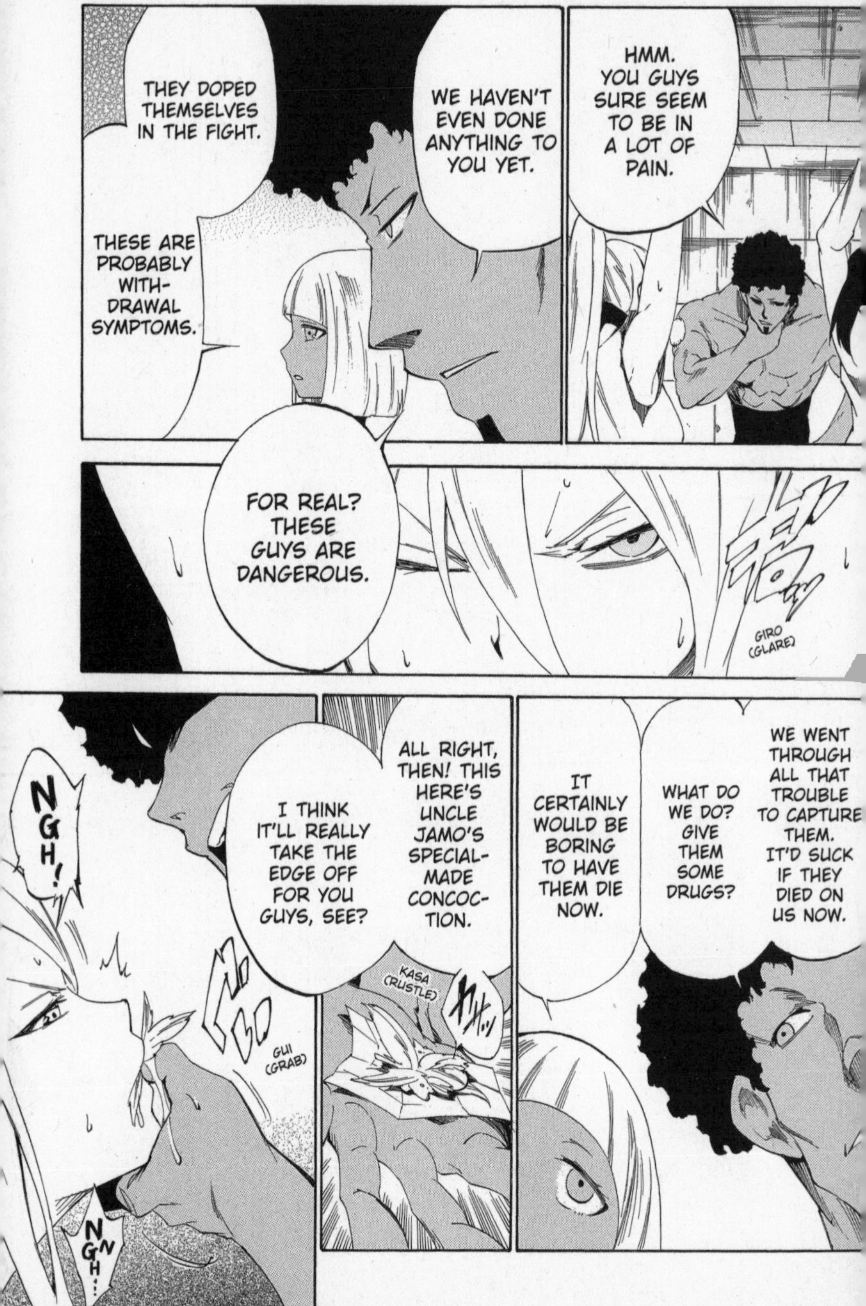
HMM. YOU GUYS SURE SEEM TO BE IN A LOT OF PAIN.
WE HAVEN'T EVEN DONE ANYTHING TO YOU YET.
THEY DOPED THEMSELVES IN THE FIGHT.
THESE ARE PROBABLY WITH-DRAWAL SYMPTOMS.
GIRO (GLARE)
FOR REAL? THESE GUYS ARE DANGEROUS.
WE WENT THROUGH ALL THAT TROUBLE TO CAPTURE THEM. IT'D SUCK IF THEY DIED ON US NOW.
WHAT DO WE DO? GIVE THEM SOME DRUGS?
IT CERTAINLY WOULD BE BORING TO HAVE THEM DIE NOW.
ALL RIGHT, THEN! THIS HERE'S UNCLE JAMO'S SPECIAL-MADE CONCOC-TION.
I THINK IT'LL REALLY TAKE THE EDGE OFF FOR YOU GUYS, SEE?
KASA (RUSTLE)
NGH!
GUI (GRAB)
NGNGH...!

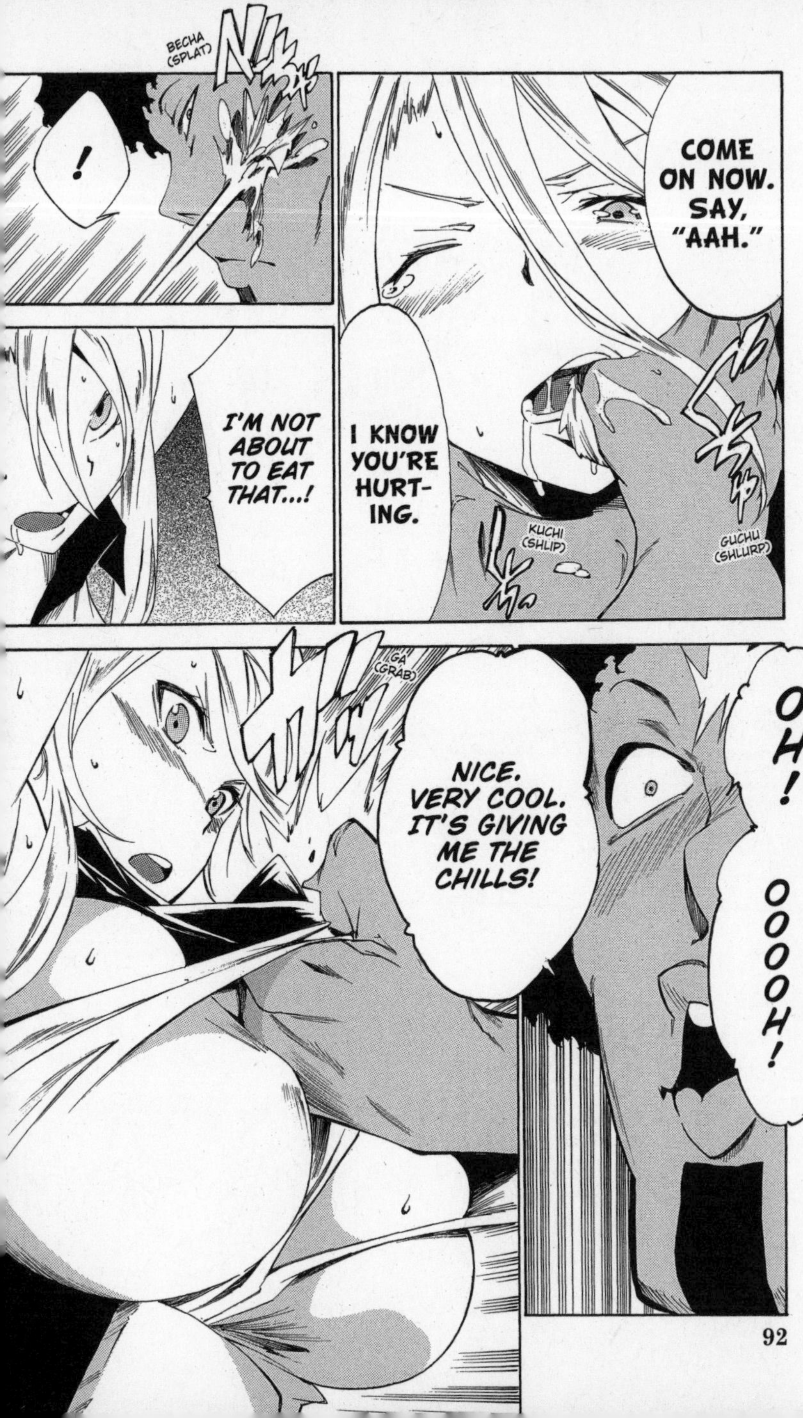
COME ON NOW. SAY, "AAH."
GUCHU (SHLURP)
I KNOW YOU'RE HURT-ING.
KUCHI (SHLIP)
BECHA (SPLAT)
!
I'M NOT ABOUT TO EAT THAT...!
OH! OOOOOH!
NICE. VERY COOL. IT'S GIVING ME THE CHILLS!
GA (GRAB)

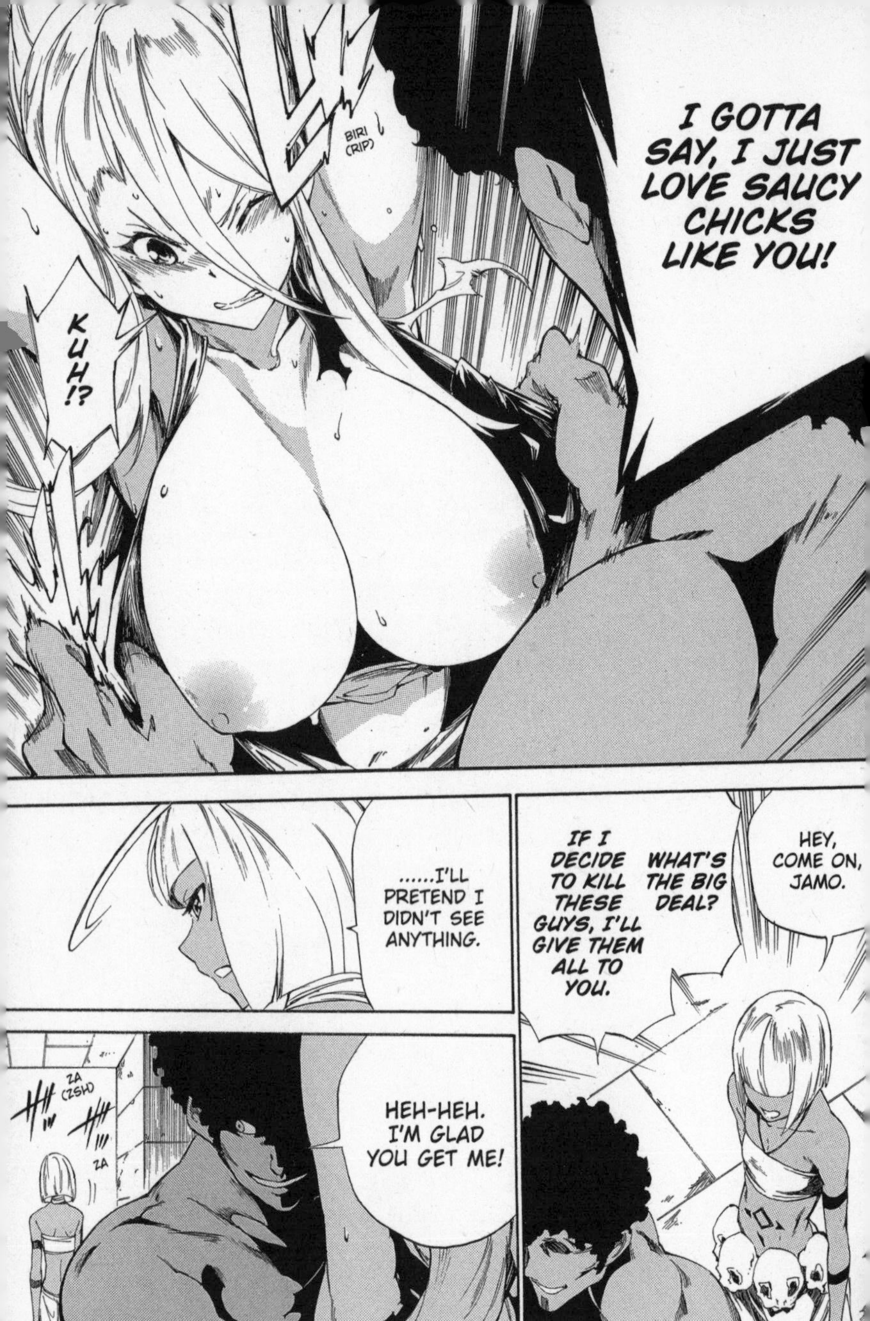
I GOTTA SAY, I JUST LOVE SAUCY CHICKS LIKE YOU!
BIRI (RIP)
KUH!?
HEY, COME ON, JAMO.
WHAT'S THE BIG DEAL?
IF I DECIDE TO KILL THESE GUYS, I'LL GIVE THEM ALL TO YOU.
......I'LL PRETEND I DIDN'T SEE ANYTHING.
HEH-HEH. I'M GLAD YOU GET ME!
ZA (ZSH)
ZA

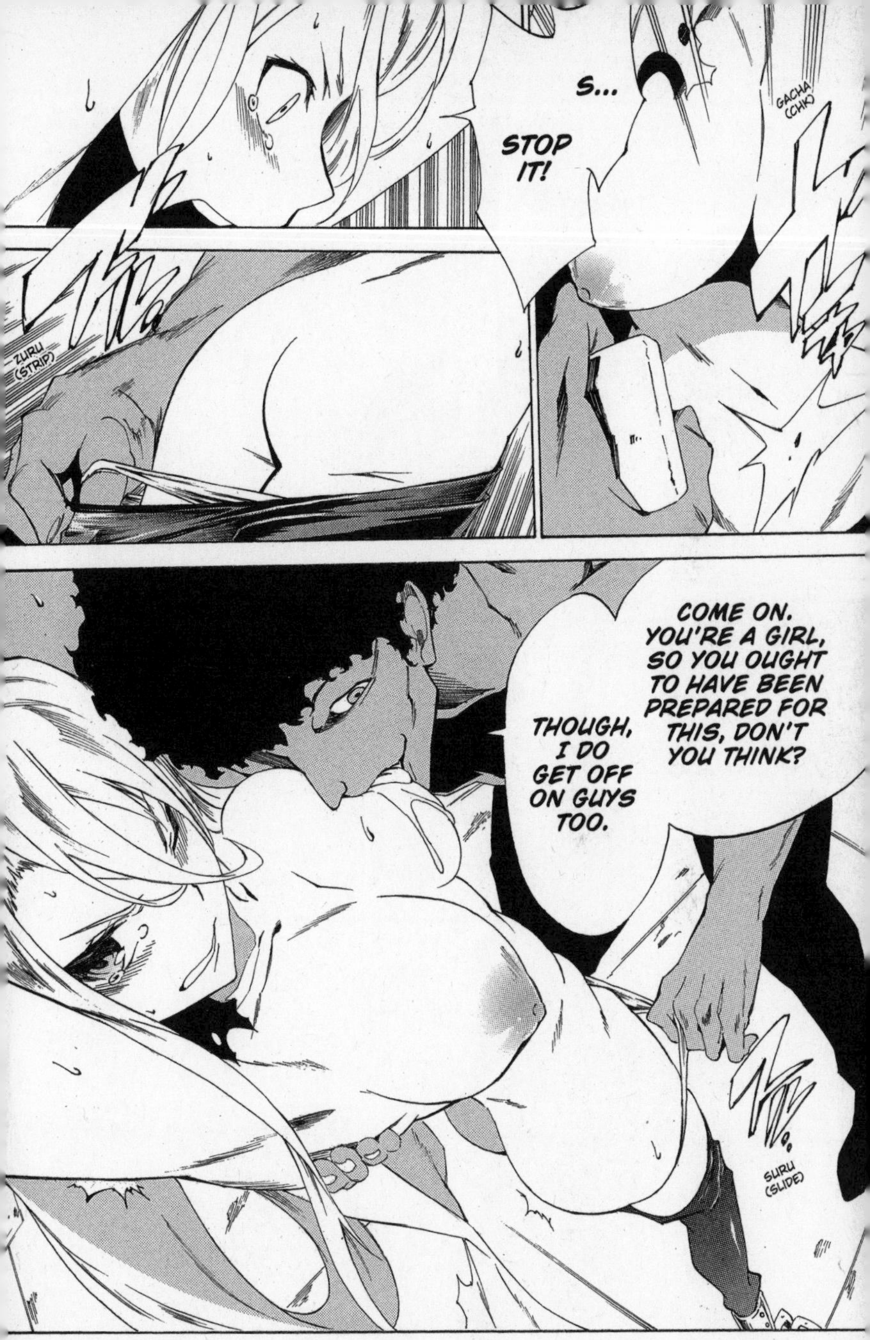
GACHA (CHK)
S...
STOP IT!
ZURU (STRIP)
COME ON. YOU'RE A GIRL, SO YOU OUGHT TO HAVE BEEN PREPARED FOR THIS, DON'T YOU THINK?
THOUGH, I DO GET OFF ON GUYS TOO.
SURU (SLIDE)

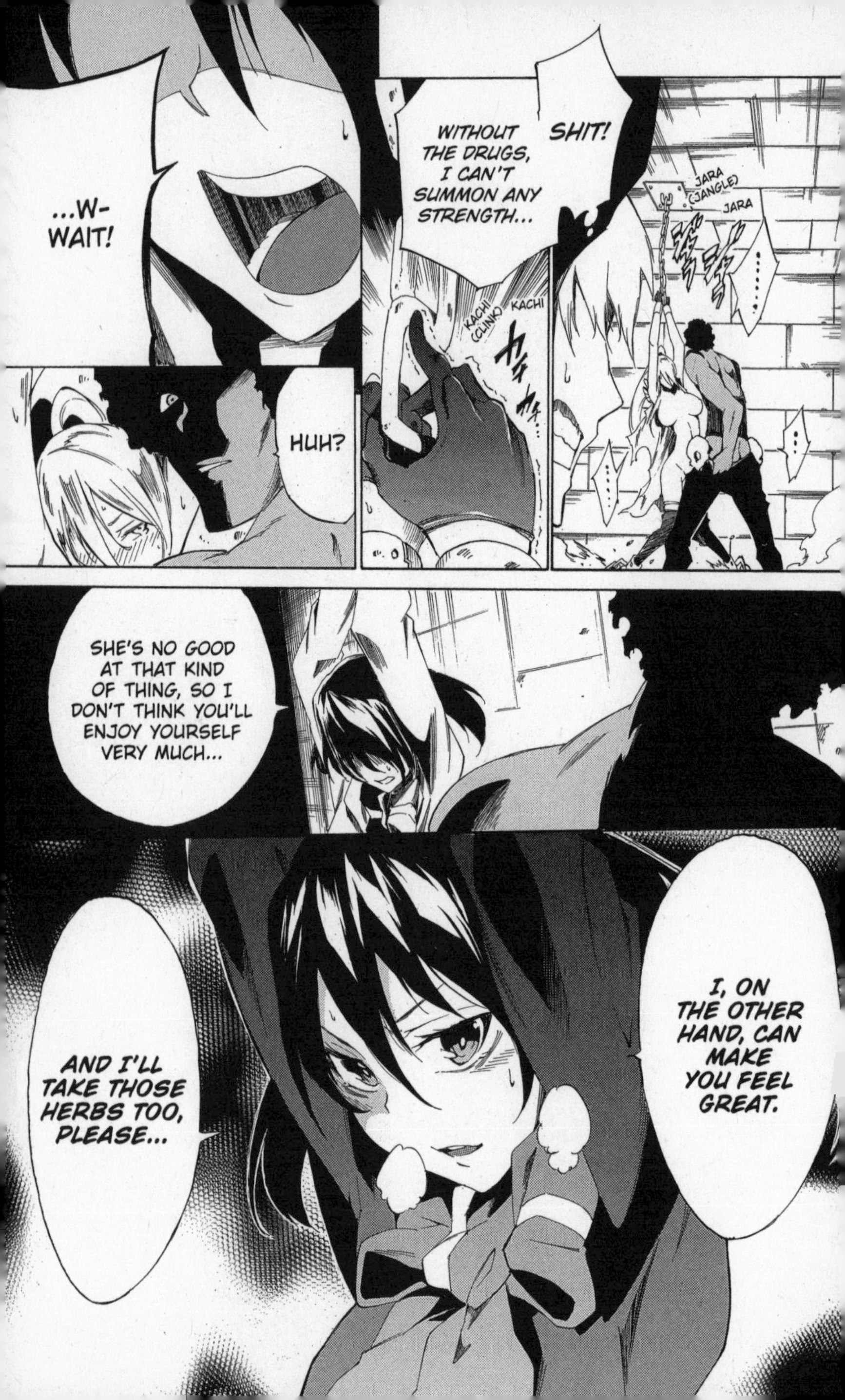
SHIT!
JARA (JANGLE)
JARA
......
...
...
WITHOUT THE DRUGS, I CAN'T SUMMON ANY STRENGTH...
KACHI (CLINK)
KACHI
...W-WAIT!
HUH?
SHE'S NO GOOD AT THAT KIND OF THING, SO I DON'T THINK YOU'LL ENJOY YOURSELF VERY MUCH...
I, ON THE OTHER HAND, CAN MAKE YOU FEEL GREAT.
AND I'LL TAKE THOSE HERBS TOO, PLEASE...

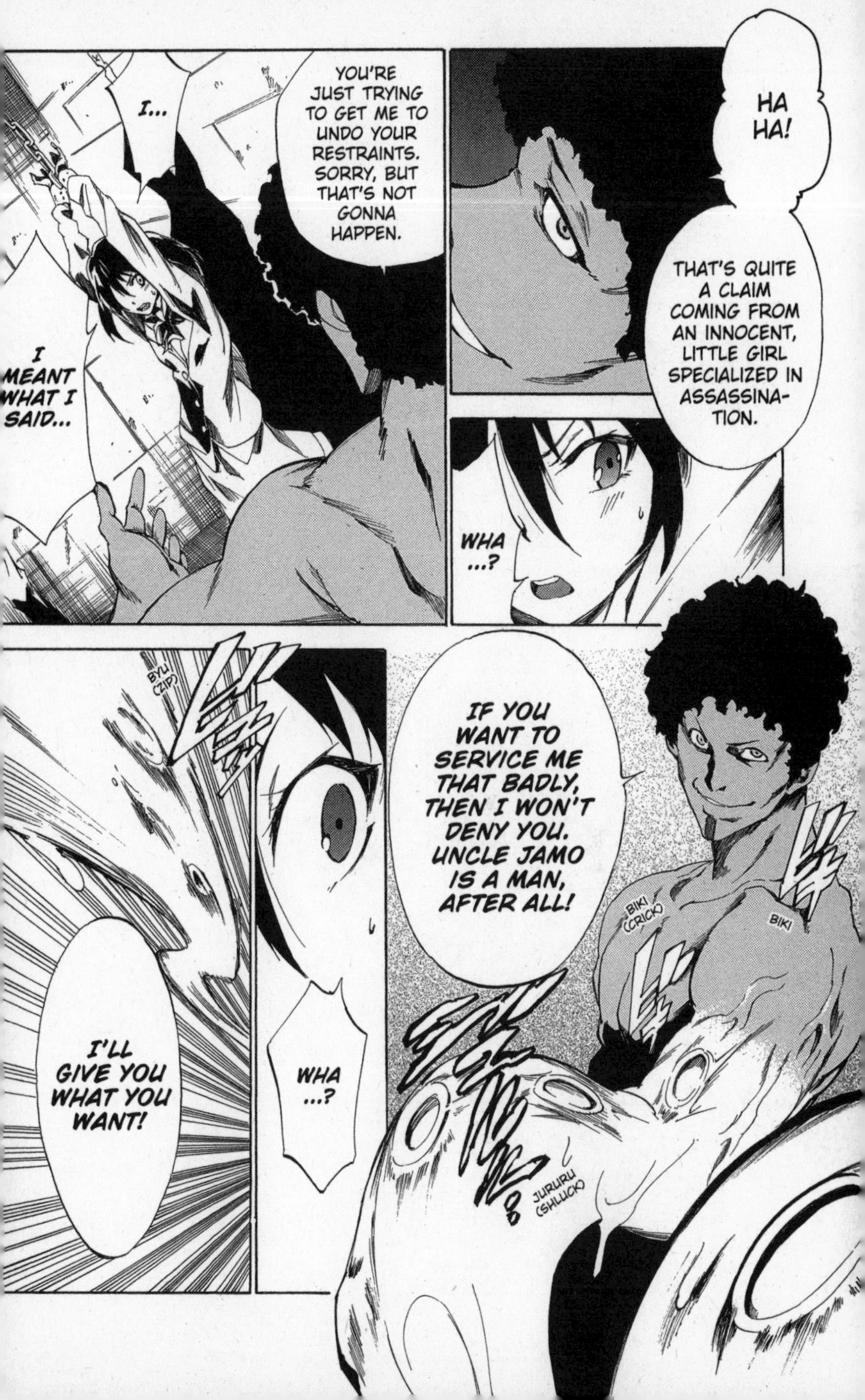
HA HA!
THAT'S QUITE A CLAIM COMING FROM AN INNOCENT, LITTLE GIRL SPECIALIZED IN ASSASSINA-TION.
WHA ...?
YOU'RE JUST TRYING TO GET ME TO UNDO YOUR RESTRAINTS. SORRY, BUT THAT'S NOT GONNA HAPPEN.
I...
I MEANT WHAT I SAID...
IF YOU WANT TO SERVICE ME THAT BADLY, THEN I WON'T DENY YOU. UNCLE JAMO IS A MAN, AFTER ALL!
BIKI (CRICK)
BIKI
JURURU (SHLUCK)
BYU (ZIP)
WHA ...?
I'LL GIVE YOU WHAT YOU WANT!

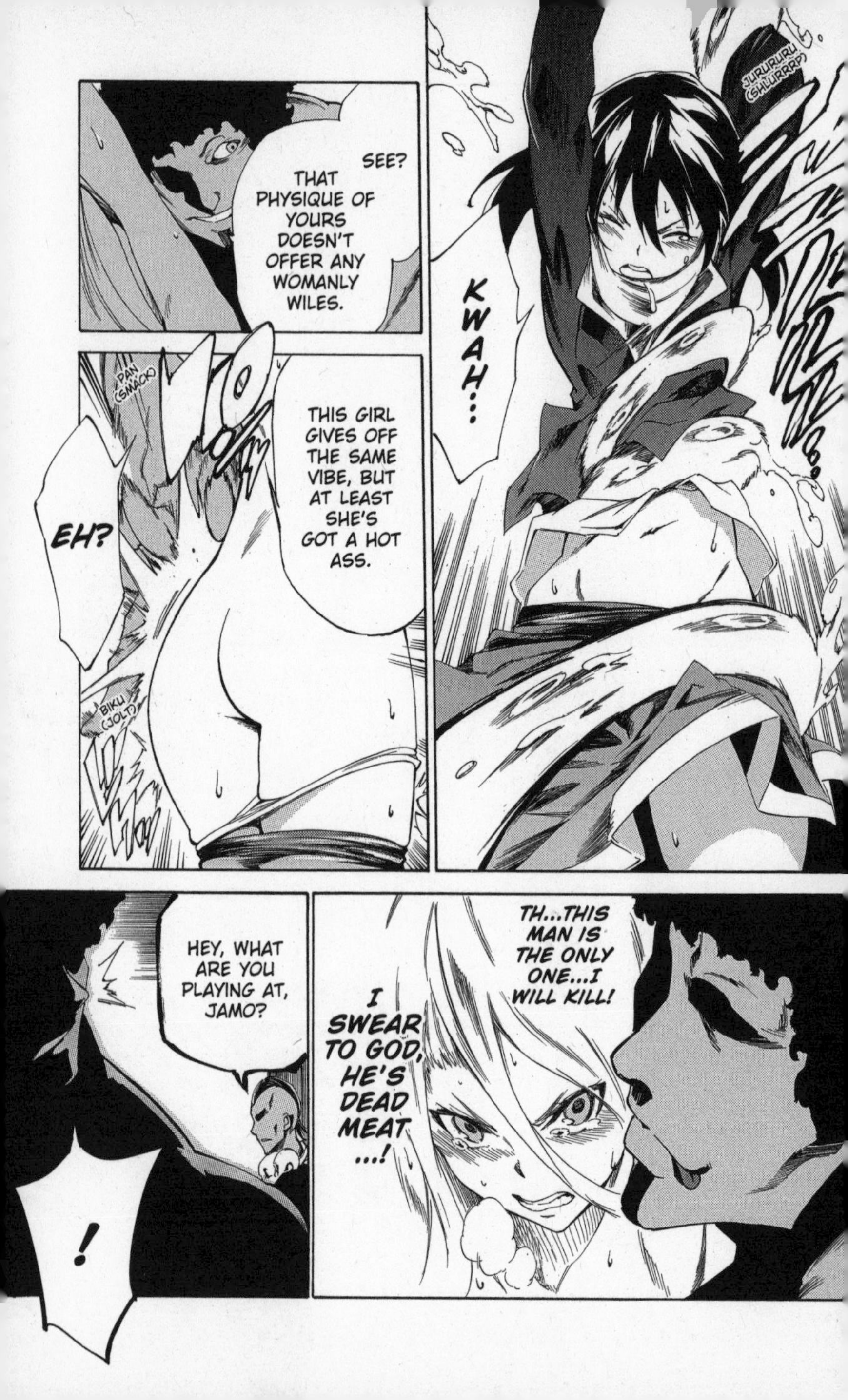
JURURURU (SHLURRRP)
KWAH...
SEE? THAT PHYSIQUE OF YOURS DOESN'T OFFER ANY WOMANLY WILES.
PAN (SMACK)
THIS GIRL GIVES OFF THE SAME VIBE, BUT AT LEAST SHE'S GOT A HOT ASS.
EH?
BIKU (JOLT)
TH...THIS MAN IS THE ONLY ONE...I WILL KILL!
I SWEAR TO GOD, HE'S DEAD MEAT...!
HEY, WHAT ARE YOU PLAYING AT, JAMO?
!

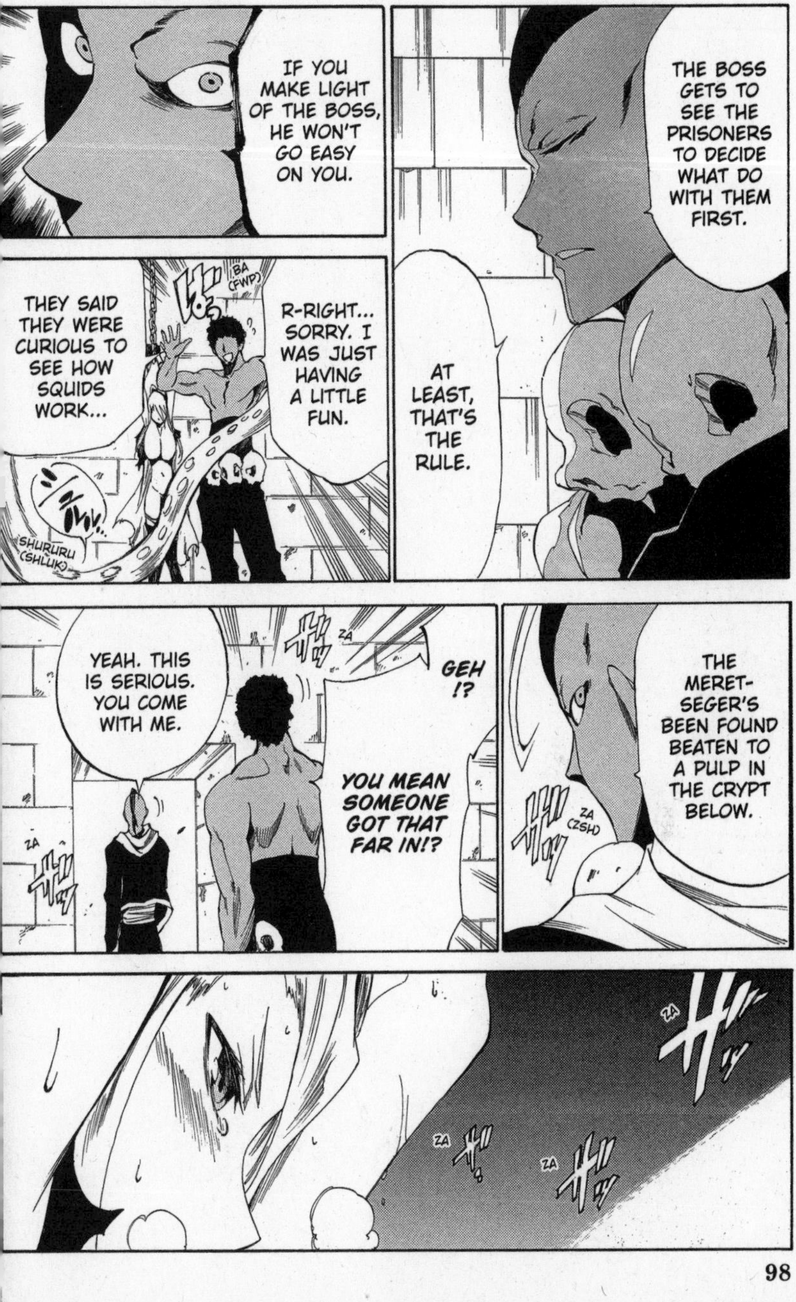
THE BOSS GETS TO SEE THE PRISONERS TO DECIDE WHAT DO WITH THEM FIRST.
AT LEAST, THAT'S THE RULE.
IF YOU MAKE LIGHT OF THE BOSS, HE WON'T GO EASY ON YOU.
BA (FWP)
R-RIGHT... SORRY. I WAS JUST HAVING A LITTLE FUN.
THEY SAID THEY WERE CURIOUS TO SEE HOW SQUIDS WORK...
SHURURU (SHLUK)
ZA (ZSH)
THE MERET-SEGER'S BEEN FOUND BEATEN TO A PULP IN THE CRYPT BELOW.
ZA
GEH !?
YOU MEAN SOMEONE GOT THAT FAR IN!?
YEAH. THIS IS SERIOUS. YOU COME WITH ME.
ZA
ZA
ZA
ZA

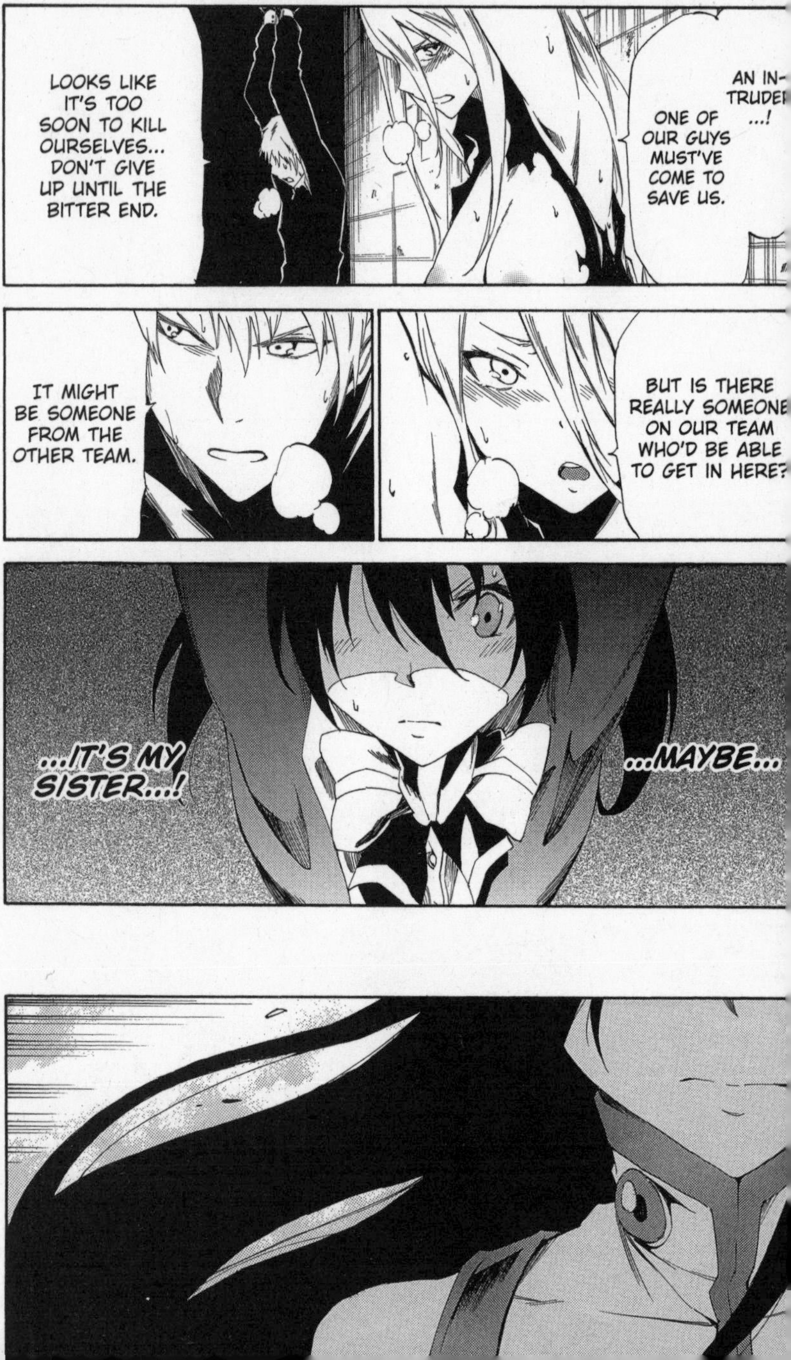
AN IN-TRUDER ...!
ONE OF OUR GUYS MUST'VE COME TO SAVE US.
LOOKS LIKE IT'S TOO SOON TO KILL OURSELVES... DON'T GIVE UP UNTIL THE BITTER END.
BUT IS THERE REALLY SOMEONE ON OUR TEAM WHO'D BE ABLE TO GET IN HERE?
IT MIGHT BE SOMEONE FROM THE OTHER TEAM.
...MAYBE...
...IT'S MY SISTER...!

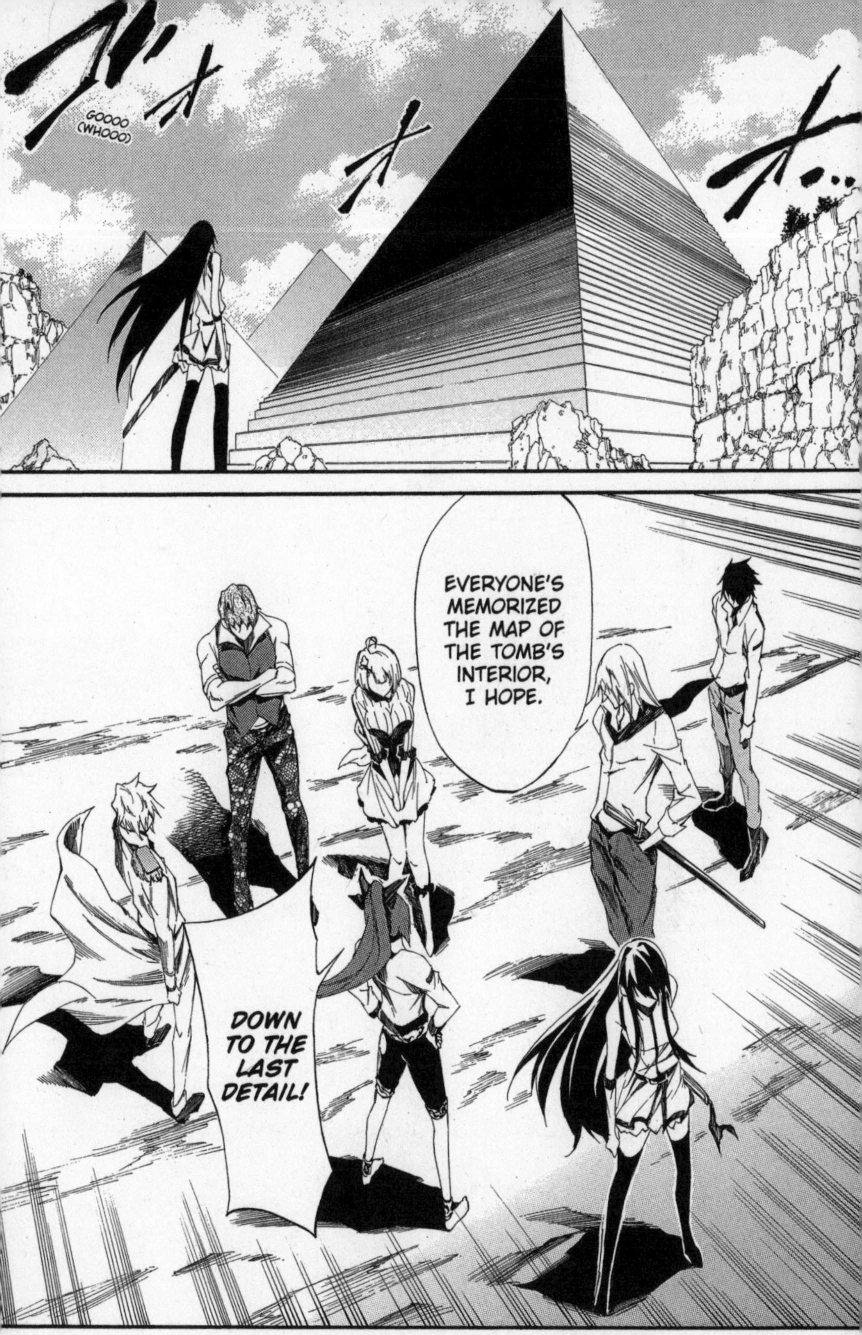
GOOOO (WHOOO)
EVERYONE'S MEMORIZED THE MAP OF THE TOMB'S INTERIOR, I HOPE.
DOWN TO THE LAST DETAIL!

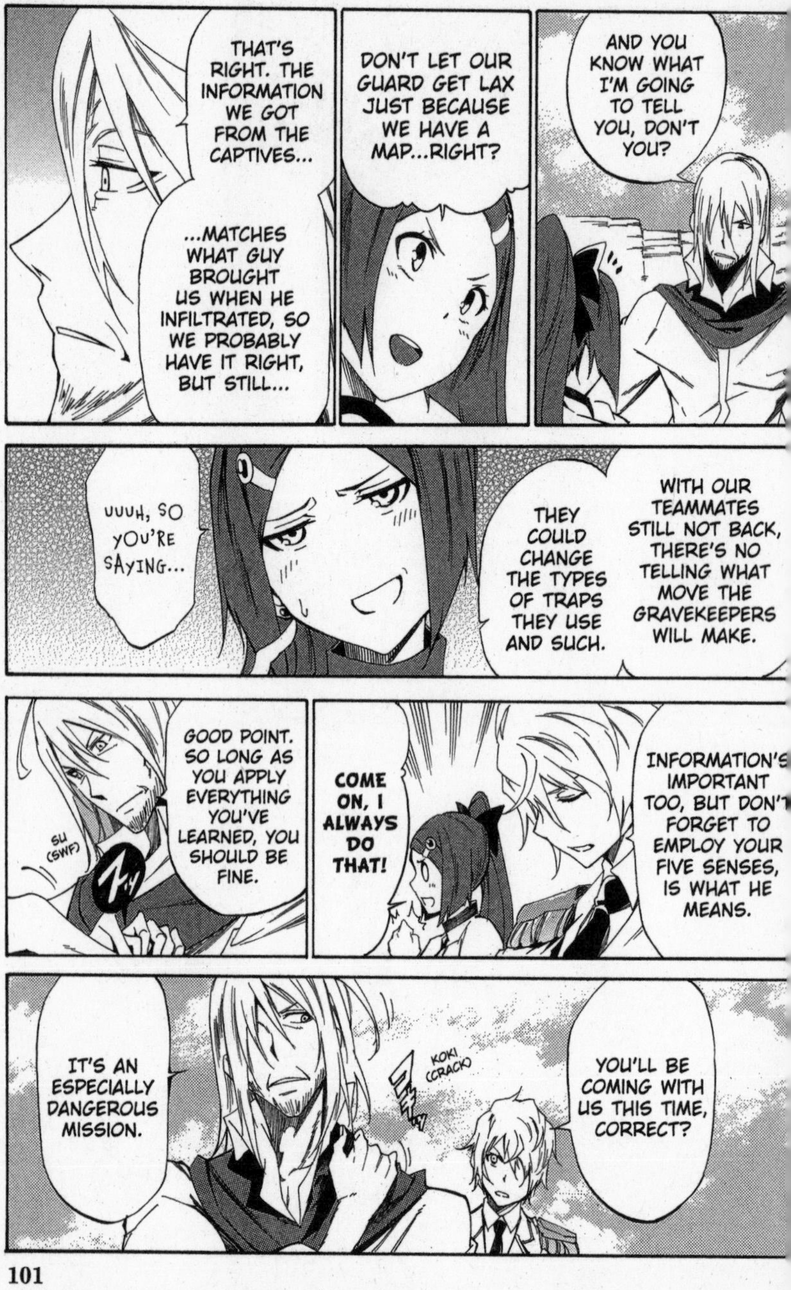
AND YOU KNOW WHAT I'M GOING TO TELL YOU, DON'T YOU?
DON'T LET OUR GUARD GET LAX JUST BECAUSE WE HAVE A MAP...RIGHT?
THAT'S RIGHT. THE INFORMATION WE GOT FROM THE CAPTIVES...
...MATCHES WHAT GUY BROUGHT US WHEN HE INFILTRATED, SO WE PROBABLY HAVE IT RIGHT, BUT STILL...
WITH OUR TEAMMATES STILL NOT BACK, THERE'S NO TELLING WHAT MOVE THE GRAVEKEEPERS WILL MAKE.
THEY COULD CHANGE THE TYPES OF TRAPS THEY USE AND SUCH.
UUUH, SO YOU'RE SAYING...
INFORMATION'S IMPORTANT TOO, BUT DON'T FORGET TO EMPLOY YOUR FIVE SENSES, IS WHAT HE MEANS.
COME ON, I ALWAYS DO THAT!
GOOD POINT. SO LONG AS YOU APPLY EVERYTHING YOU'VE LEARNED, YOU SHOULD BE FINE.
SU (SWF)
YOU'LL BE COMING WITH US THIS TIME, CORRECT?
KOKI (CRACK)
IT'S AN ESPECIALLY DANGEROUS MISSION.

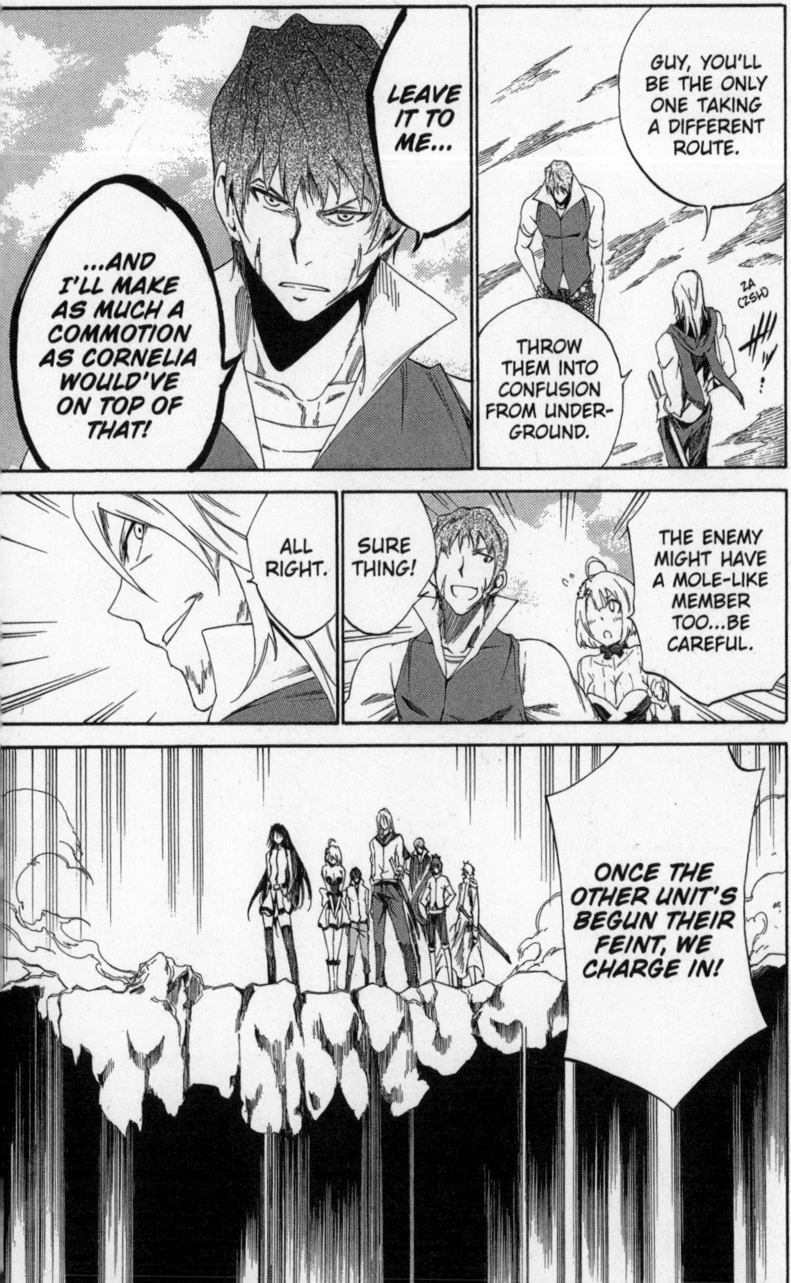
GUY, YOU'LL BE THE ONLY ONE TAKING A DIFFERENT ROUTE.
THROW THEM INTO CONFUSION FROM UNDER-GROUND.
ZA CZSH
LEAVE IT TO ME...
...AND I'LL MAKE AS MUCH A COMMOTION AS CORNELIA WOULD'VE ON TOP OF THAT!
THE ENEMY MIGHT HAVE A MOLE-LIKE MEMBER TOO...BE CAREFUL.
SURE THING!
ALL RIGHT.
ONCE THE OTHER UNIT'S BEGUN THEIR FEINT, WE CHARGE IN!

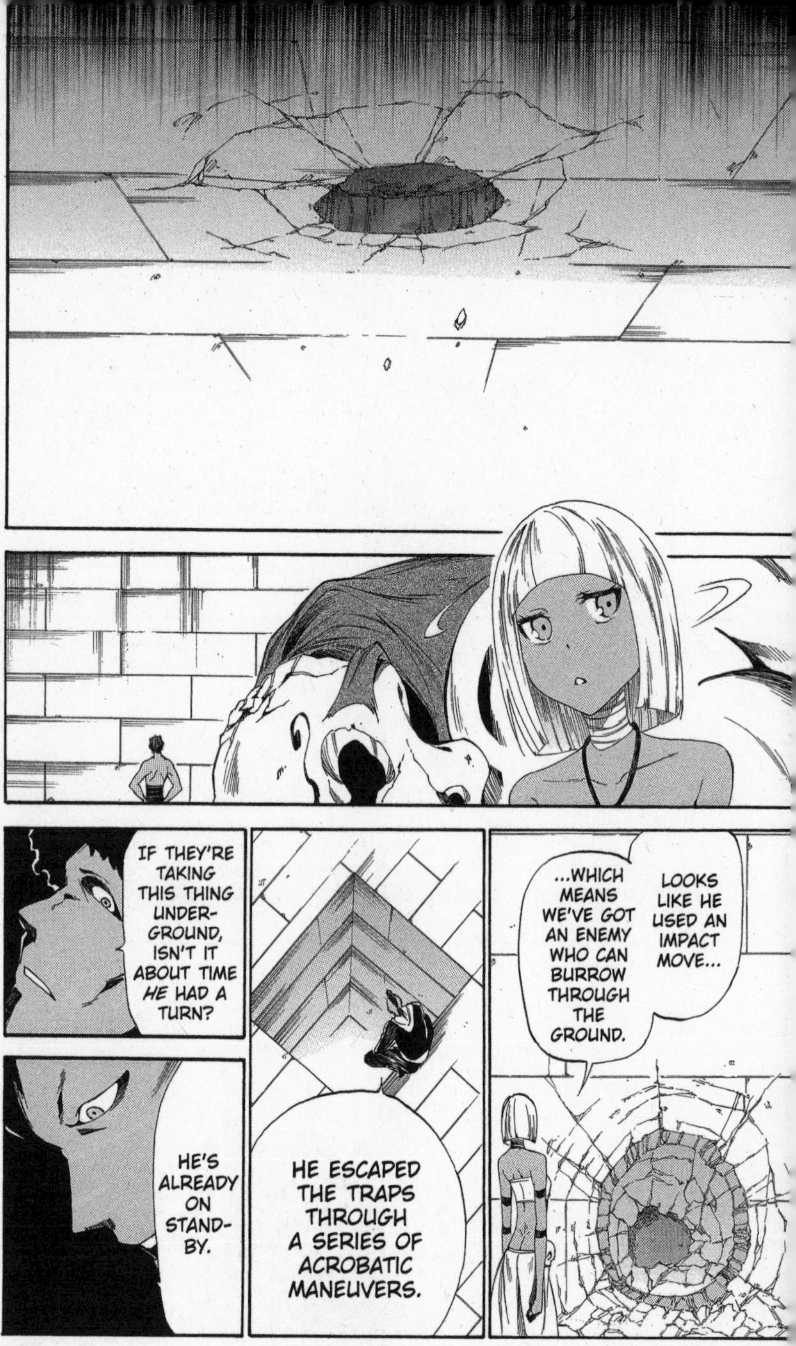
LOOKS LIKE HE USED AN IMPACT MOVE...
...WHICH MEANS WE'VE GOT AN ENEMY WHO CAN BURROW THROUGH THE GROUND.
HE ESCAPED THE TRAPS THROUGH A SERIES OF ACROBATIC MANEUVERS.
IF THEY'RE TAKING THIS THING UNDER-GROUND, ISN'T IT ABOUT TIME HE HAD A TURN?
HE'S ALREADY ON STAND-BY.

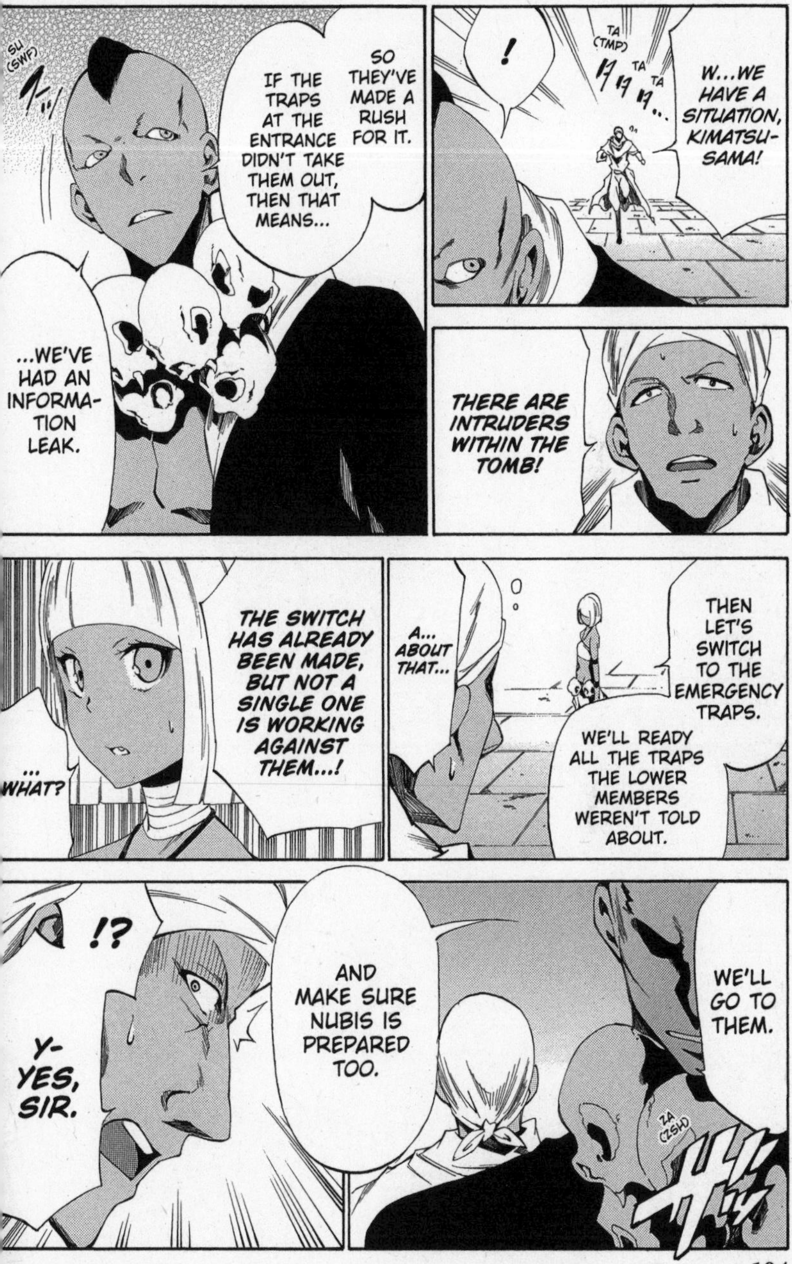
!
TA (TMP) TA TA TA...
W...WE HAVE A SITUATION, KIMATSU-SAMA!
THERE ARE INTRUDERS WITHIN THE TOMB!
SU (SWF)
SO THEY'VE MADE A RUSH FOR IT.
IF THE TRAPS AT THE ENTRANCE DIDN'T TAKE THEM OUT, THEN THAT MEANS...
...WE'VE HAD AN INFORMATION LEAK.
THEN LET'S SWITCH TO THE EMERGENCY TRAPS.
WE'LL READY ALL THE TRAPS THE LOWER MEMBERS WEREN'T TOLD ABOUT.
A... ABOUT THAT...
THE SWITCH HAS ALREADY BEEN MADE, BUT NOT A SINGLE ONE IS WORKING AGAINST THEM...!
...WHAT?
WE'LL GO TO THEM.
ZA (ZSHD)
AND MAKE SURE NUBIS IS PREPARED TOO.
!?
Y-YES, SIR.

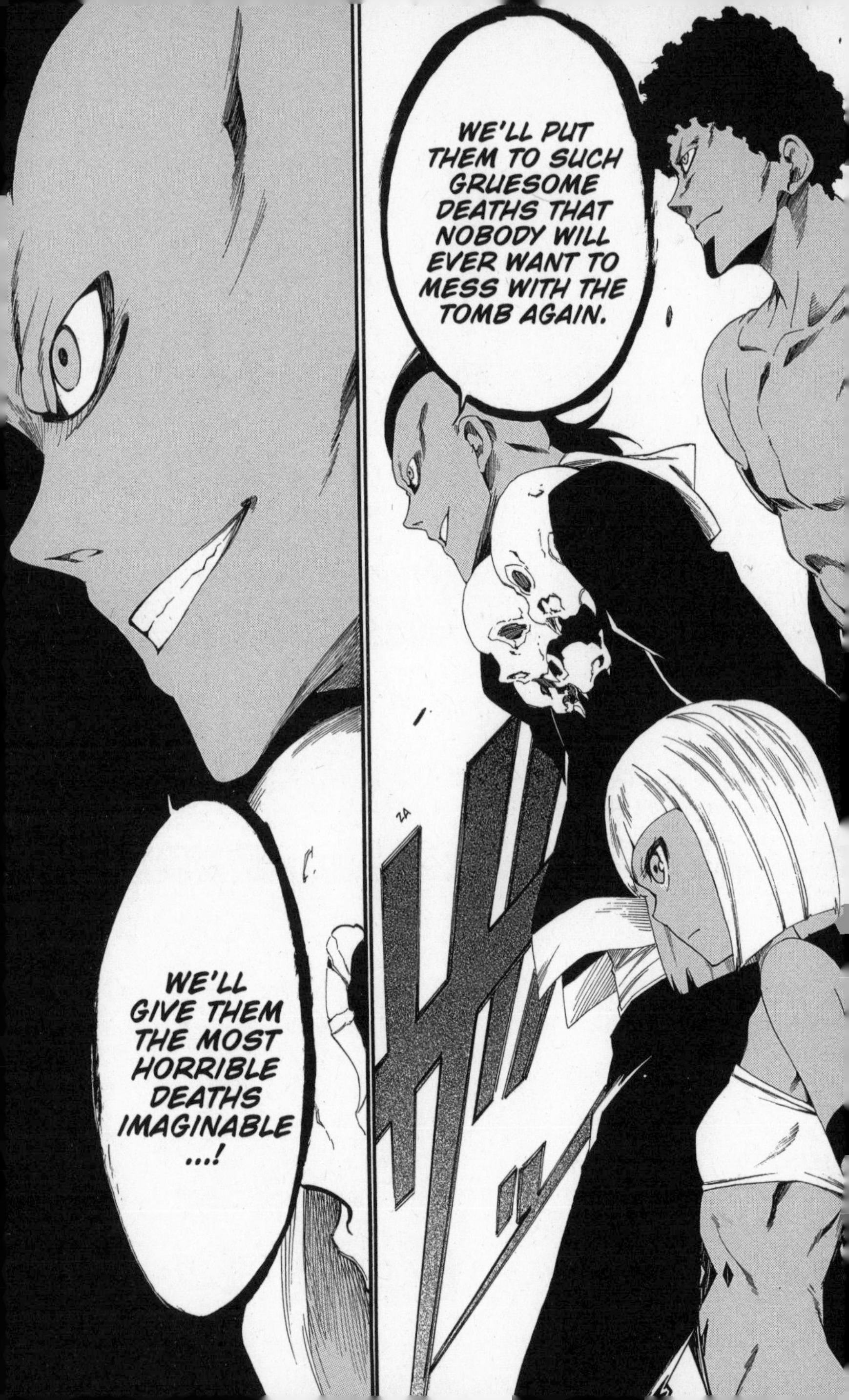
WE'LL PUT THEM TO SUCH GRUESOME DEATHS THAT NOBODY WILL EVER WANT TO MESS WITH THE TOMB AGAIN.
ZA
WE'LL GIVE THEM THE MOST HORRIBLE DEATHS IMAGINABLE ...!

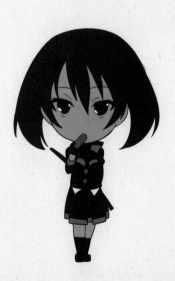

Chapter 18
MELEE

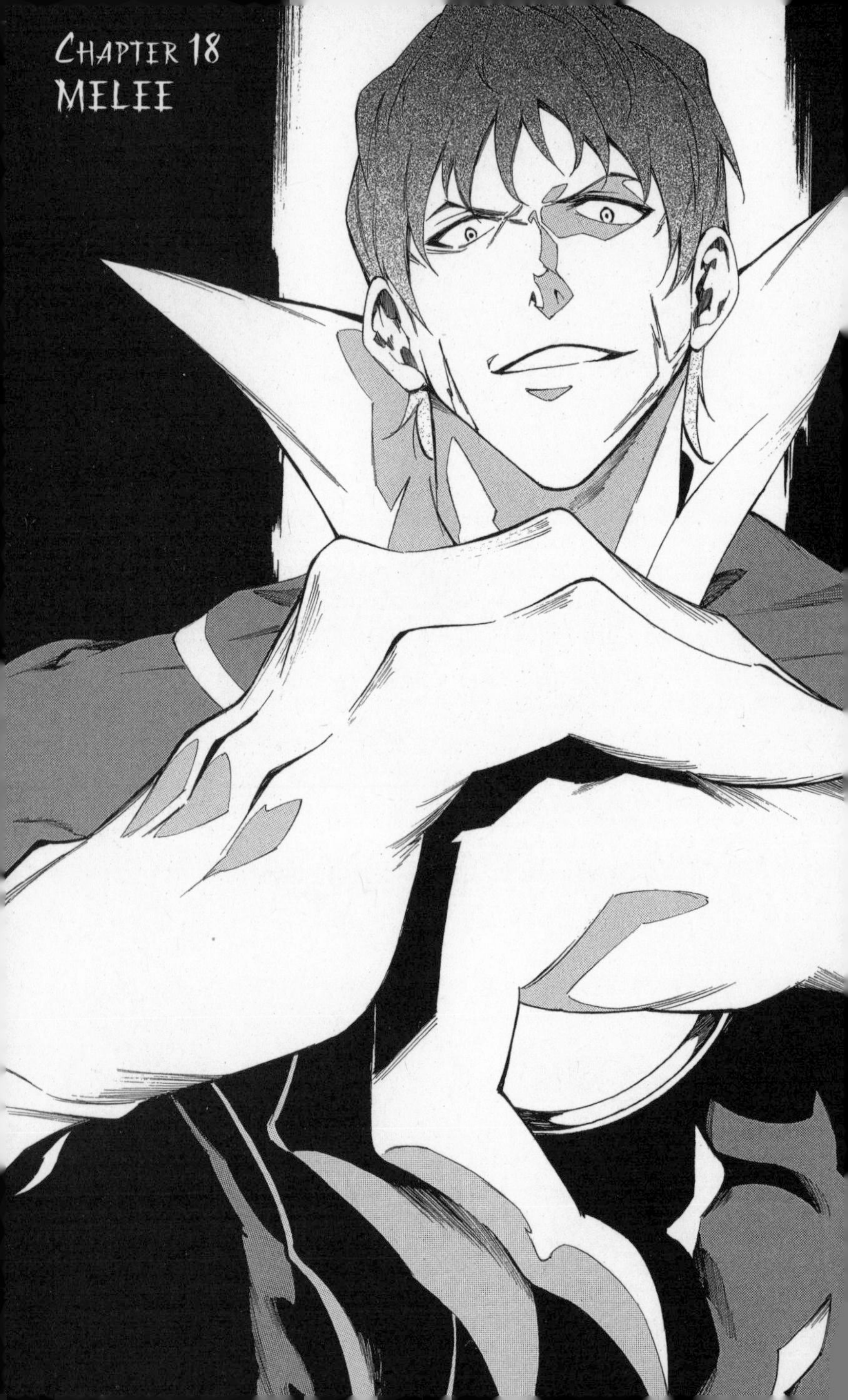

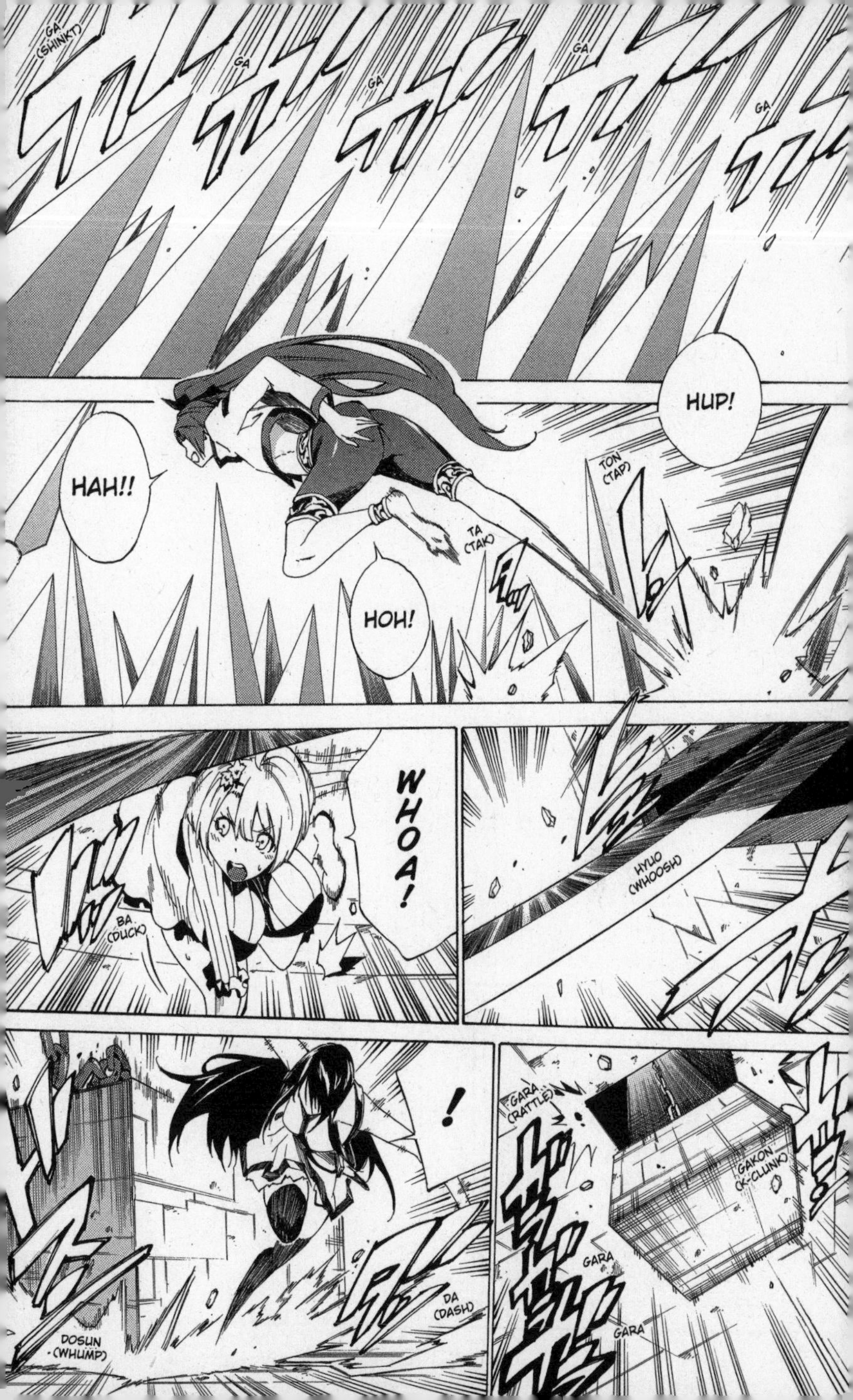
GA (SHINKT)
GA
GA
GA
GA
HUP!
TON (TAP)
HAH!!
TA (TAK)
HOH!
HYUO (WHOOSH)
WHOA!
BA (DUCK)
GARA (RATTLE)
GAKON (K-CLUNK)
GARA
GARA
!
DA (DASH)
DOSUN (WHUMP)

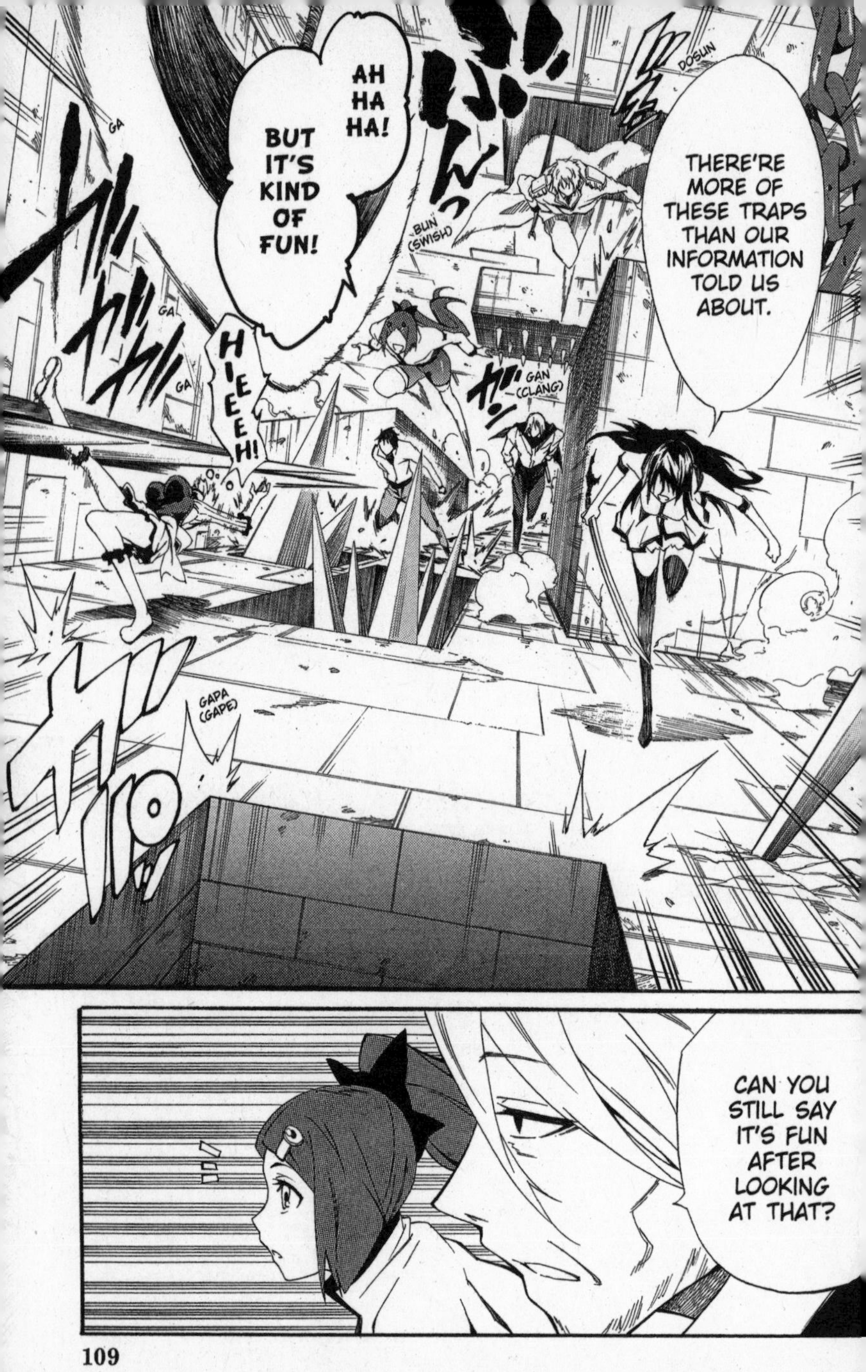
DOSUN
THERE'RE MORE OF THESE TRAPS THAN OUR INFORMATION TOLD US ABOUT.
BUN (SWISH)
AH HA HA!
BUT IT'S KIND OF FUN!
GAN (CLANG)
HIEEEEH!
GA
GA
GA
GAPA (GAPE)
CAN YOU STILL SAY IT'S FUN AFTER LOOKING AT THAT?

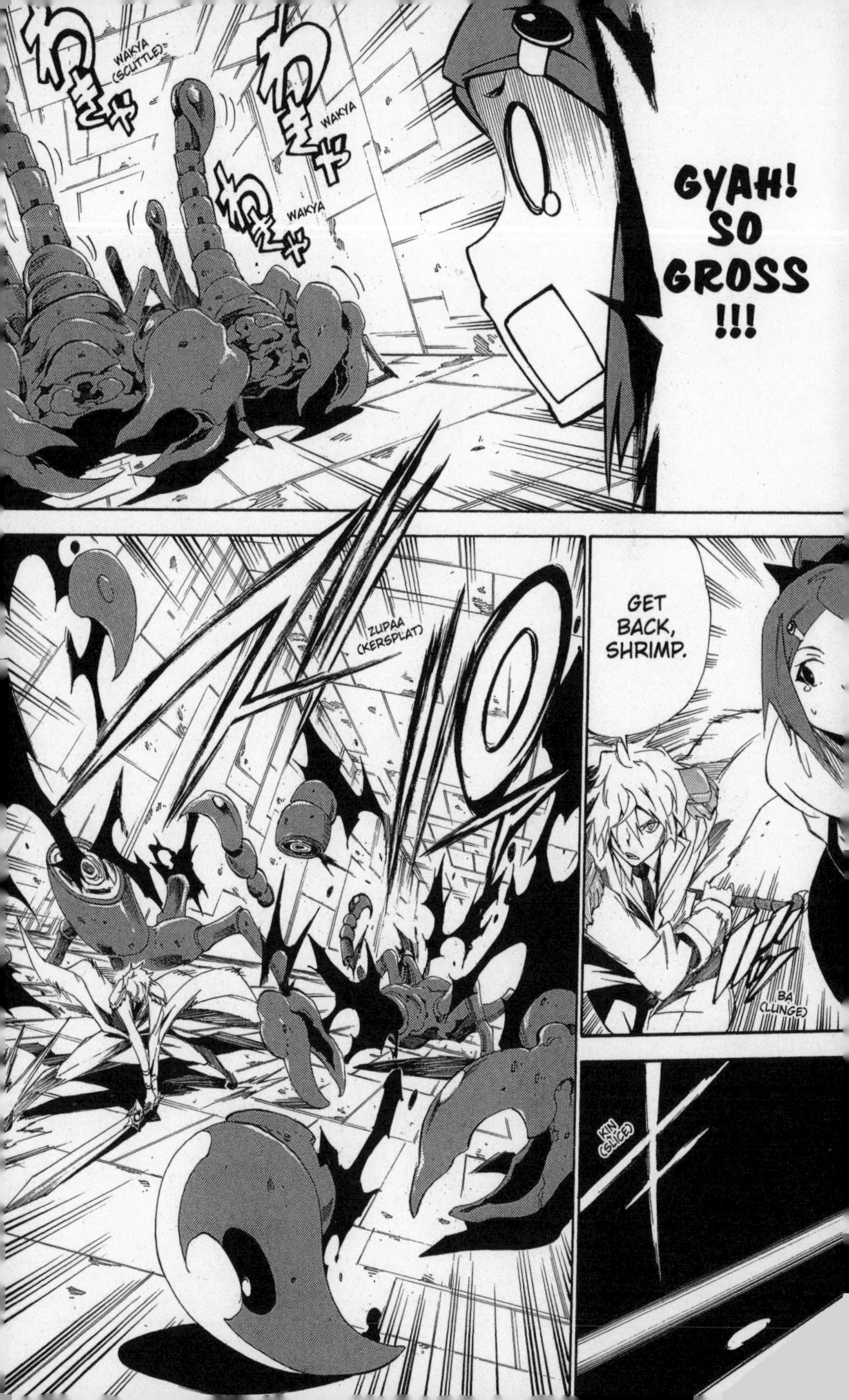

GYAH! SO GROSS!!!
WAKYA
WAKYA
WAKYA (SCUTTLE)
GET BACK, SHRIMP.
BA (LUNGE)
KIN (SLICE)
ZUPAA (KERSPLAT)

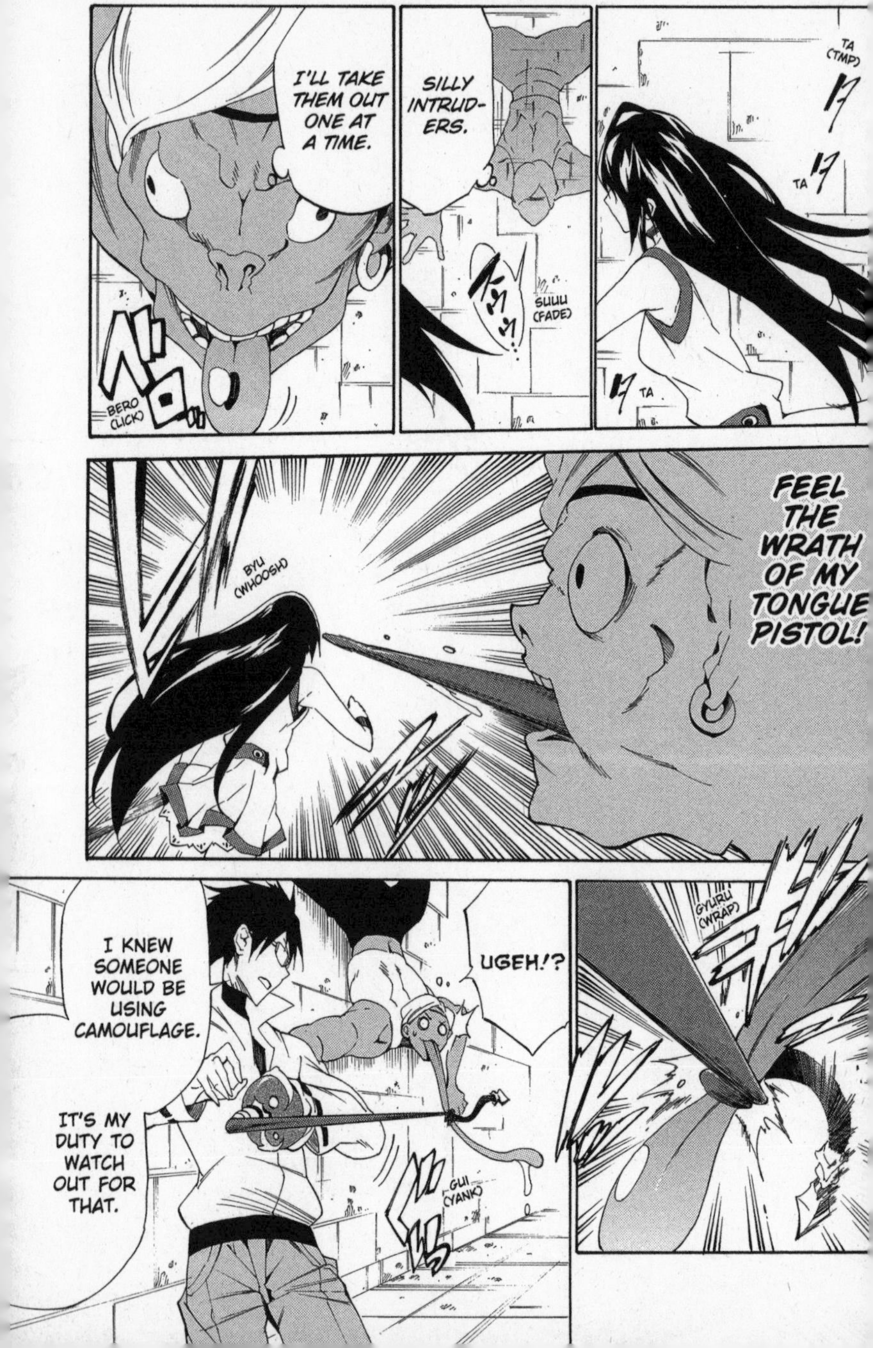
TA
(TMP)
TA
TA
SILLY INTRUD-ERS.
SUUU
(FADE)
I'LL TAKE THEM OUT ONE AT A TIME.
BERO
(LICK)
FEEL THE WRATH OF MY TONGUE PISTOL!
BYU
(WHOOSH)
GYURU
(WRAP)
UGEH!?
I KNEW SOMEONE WOULD BE USING CAMOUFLAGE.
IT'S MY DUTY TO WATCH OUT FOR THAT.
GUI
(YANK)

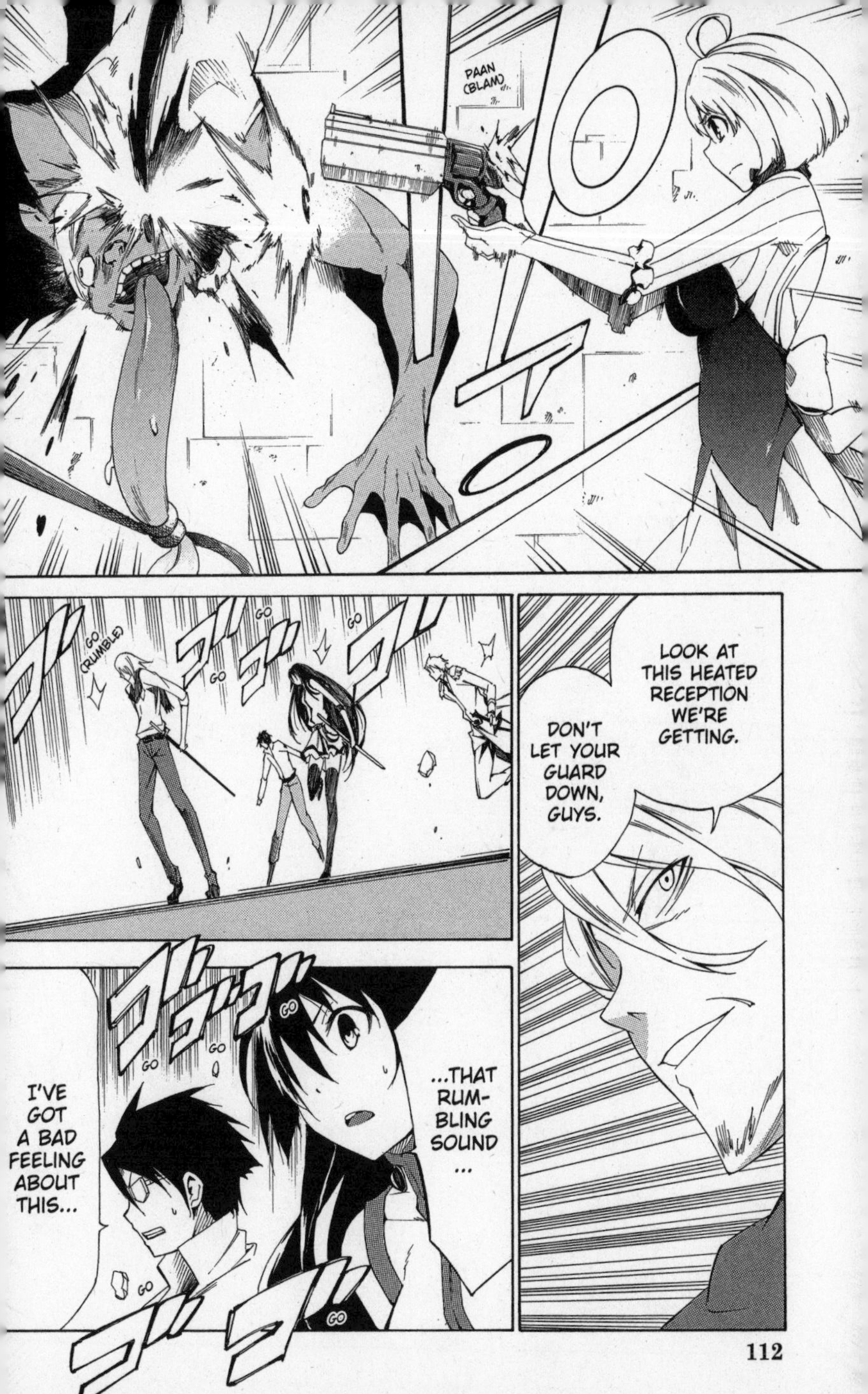
PAAN (BLAM)
LOOK AT THIS HEATED RECEPTION WE'RE GETTING.
DON'T LET YOUR GUARD DOWN, GUYS.
GO
GO (RUMBLE)
GO
GO
GO
GO
...THAT RUMBLING SOUND...
I'VE GOT A BAD FEELING ABOUT THIS...
GO
GO

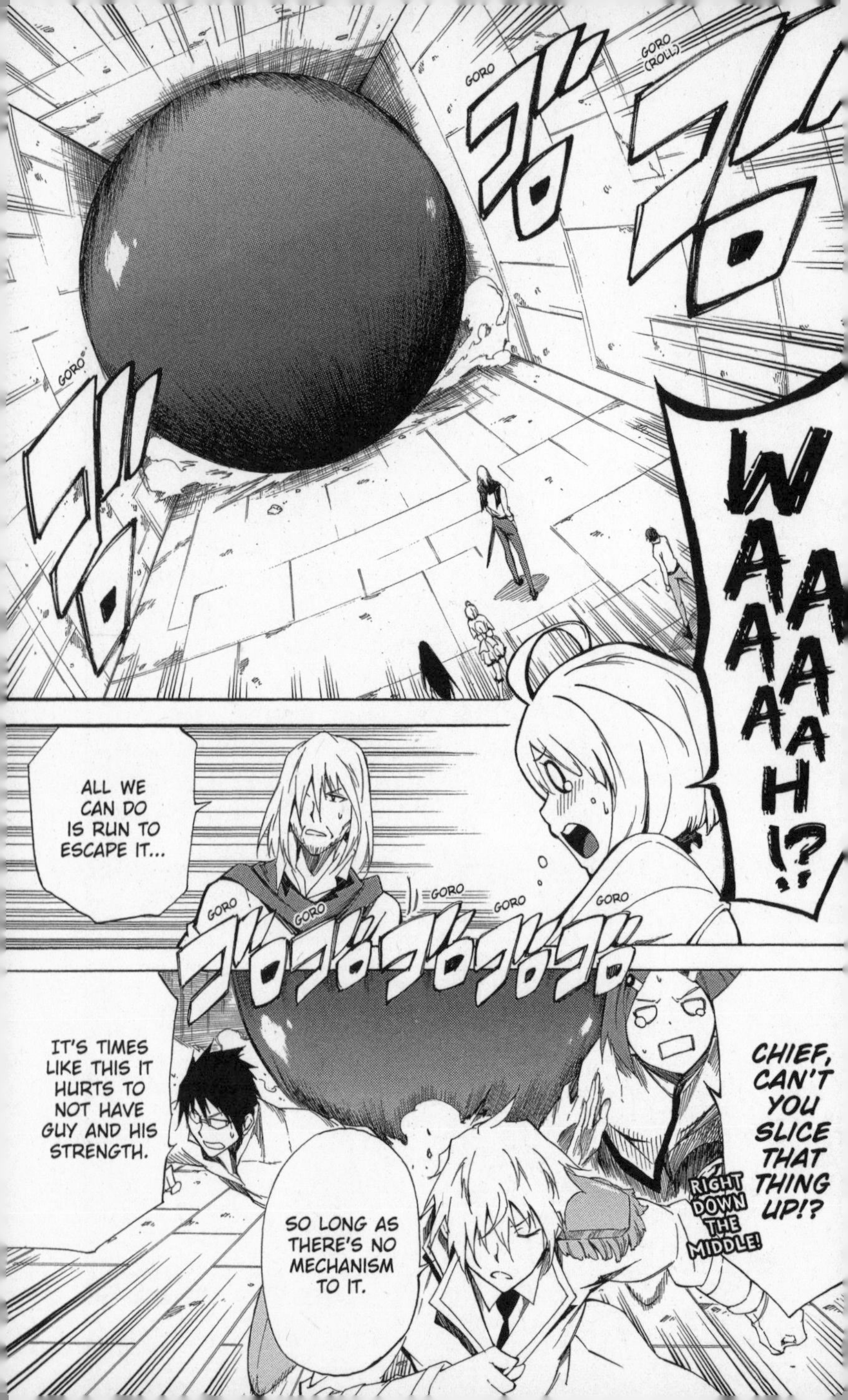
GORO (ROLL)
GORO
GORO
WAAAAAAAH!?
ALL WE CAN DO IS RUN TO ESCAPE IT...
GORO
GORO
GORO
GORO
CHIEF, CAN'T YOU SLICE THAT THING UP!?
RIGHT DOWN THE MIDDLE!
IT'S TIMES LIKE THIS IT HURTS TO NOT HAVE GUY AND HIS STRENGTH.
SO LONG AS THERE'S NO MECHANISM TO IT.

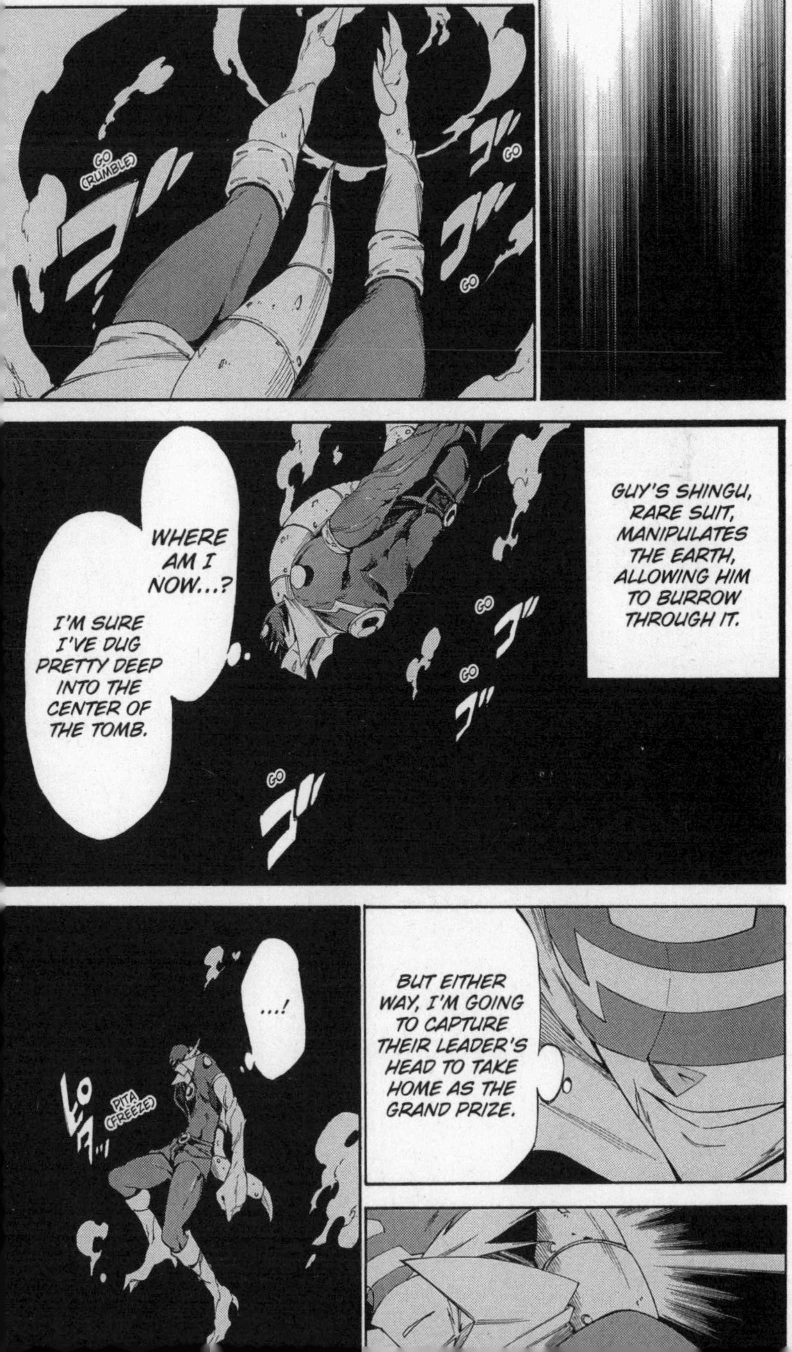
GO
GO (RUMBLE)
GO
GUY'S SHINGU, RARE SUIT, MANIPULATES THE EARTH, ALLOWING HIM TO BURROW THROUGH IT.
WHERE AM I NOW...?
I'M SURE I'VE DUG PRETTY DEEP INTO THE CENTER OF THE TOMB.
GO
GO
GO
BUT EITHER WAY, I'M GOING TO CAPTURE THEIR LEADER'S HEAD TO TAKE HOME AS THE GRAND PRIZE.
...!
PITA (FREEZE)

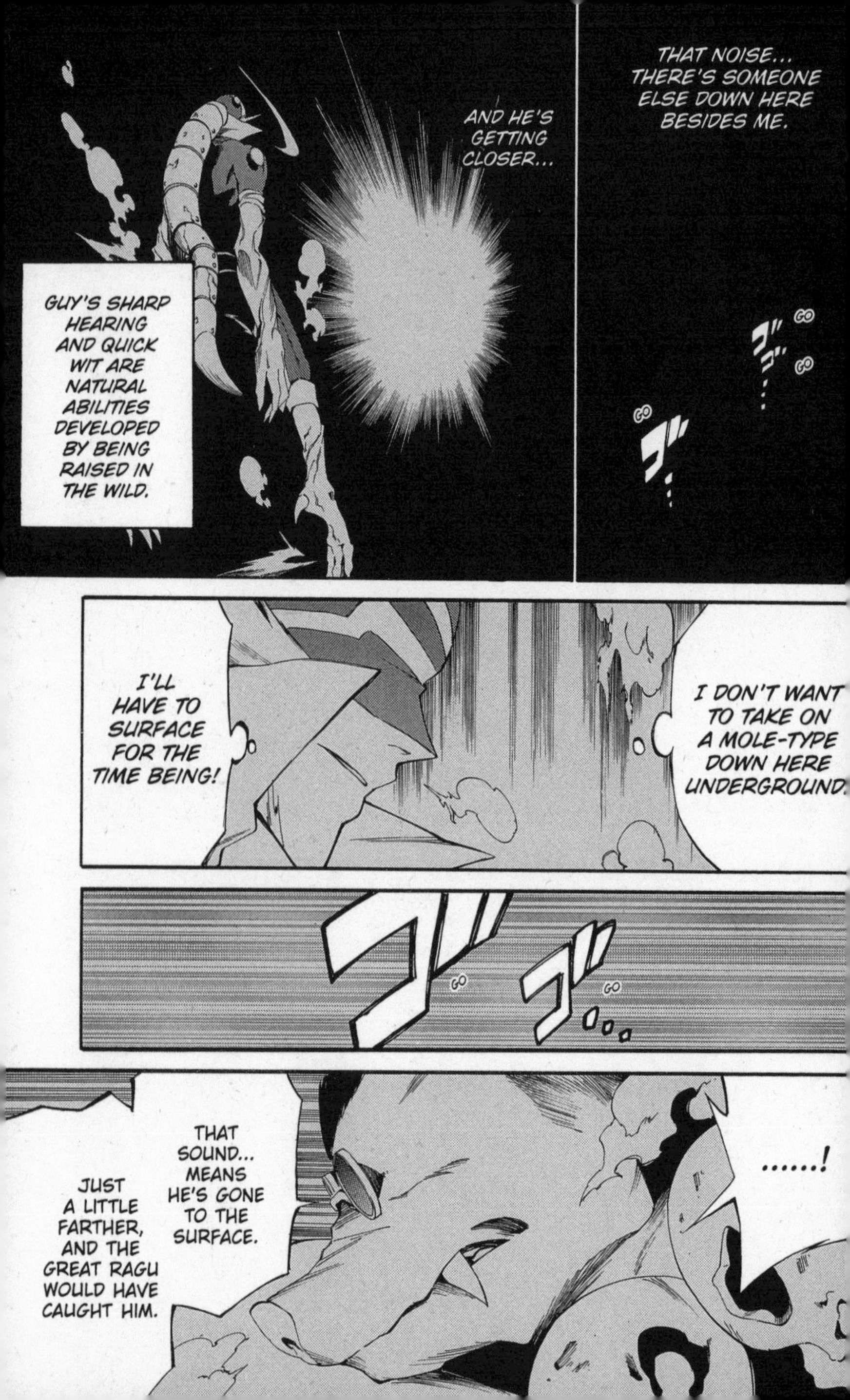
THAT NOISE... THERE'S SOMEONE ELSE DOWN HERE BESIDES ME.
GO
GO
GO
AND HE'S GETTING CLOSER...
GUY'S SHARP HEARING AND QUICK WIT ARE NATURAL ABILITIES DEVELOPED BY BEING RAISED IN THE WILD.
I DON'T WANT TO TAKE ON A MOLE-TYPE DOWN HERE UNDERGROUND.
I'LL HAVE TO SURFACE FOR THE TIME BEING!
GO
GO
......!
THAT SOUND... MEANS HE'S GONE TO THE SURFACE.
JUST A LITTLE FARTHER, AND THE GREAT RAGU WOULD HAVE CAUGHT HIM.

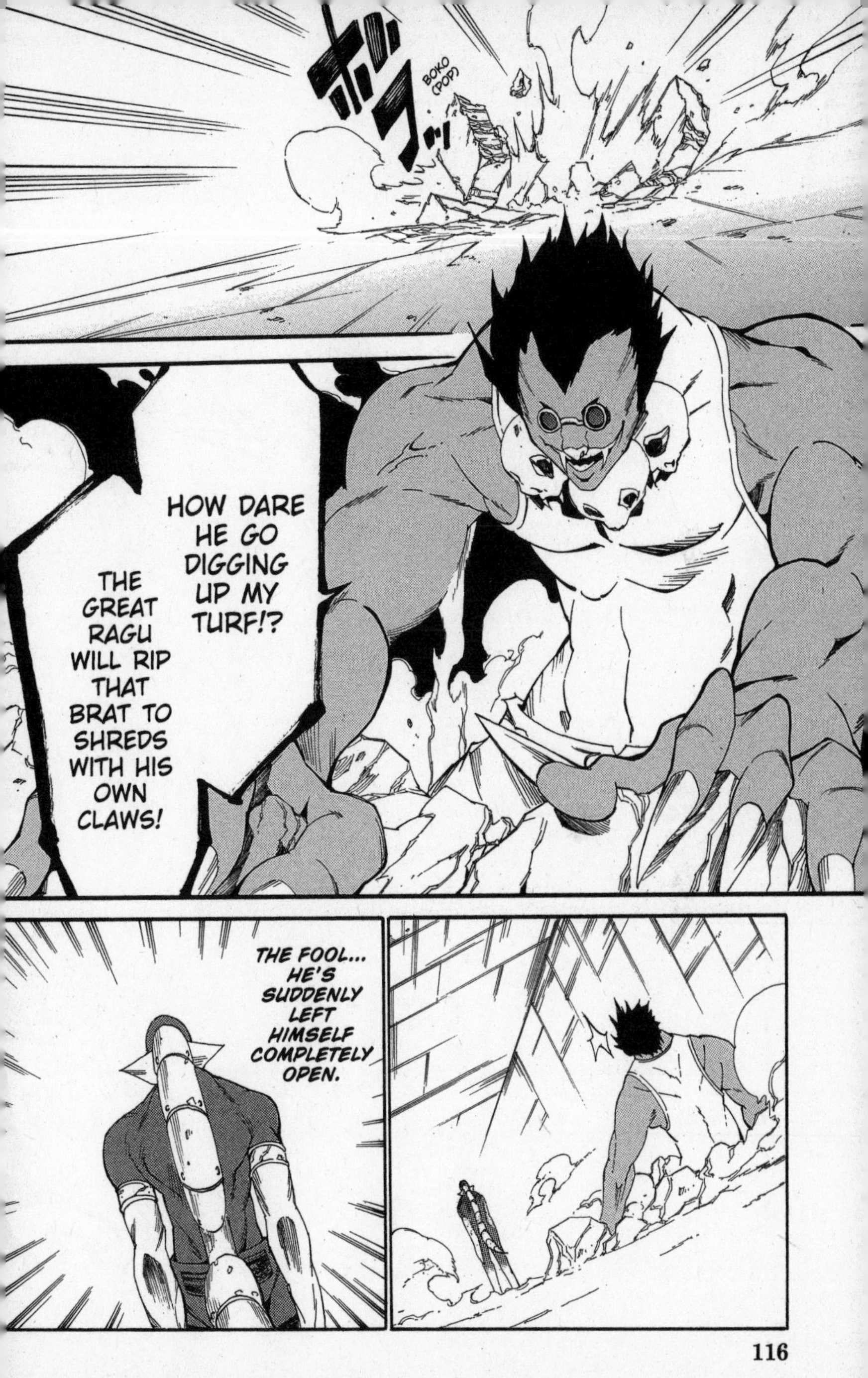
BOKO (POP)
HOW DARE HE GO DIGGING UP MY TURF!?
THE GREAT RAGU WILL RIP THAT BRAT TO SHREDS WITH HIS OWN CLAWS!
THE FOOL... HE'S SUDDENLY LEFT HIMSELF COMPLETELY OPEN.

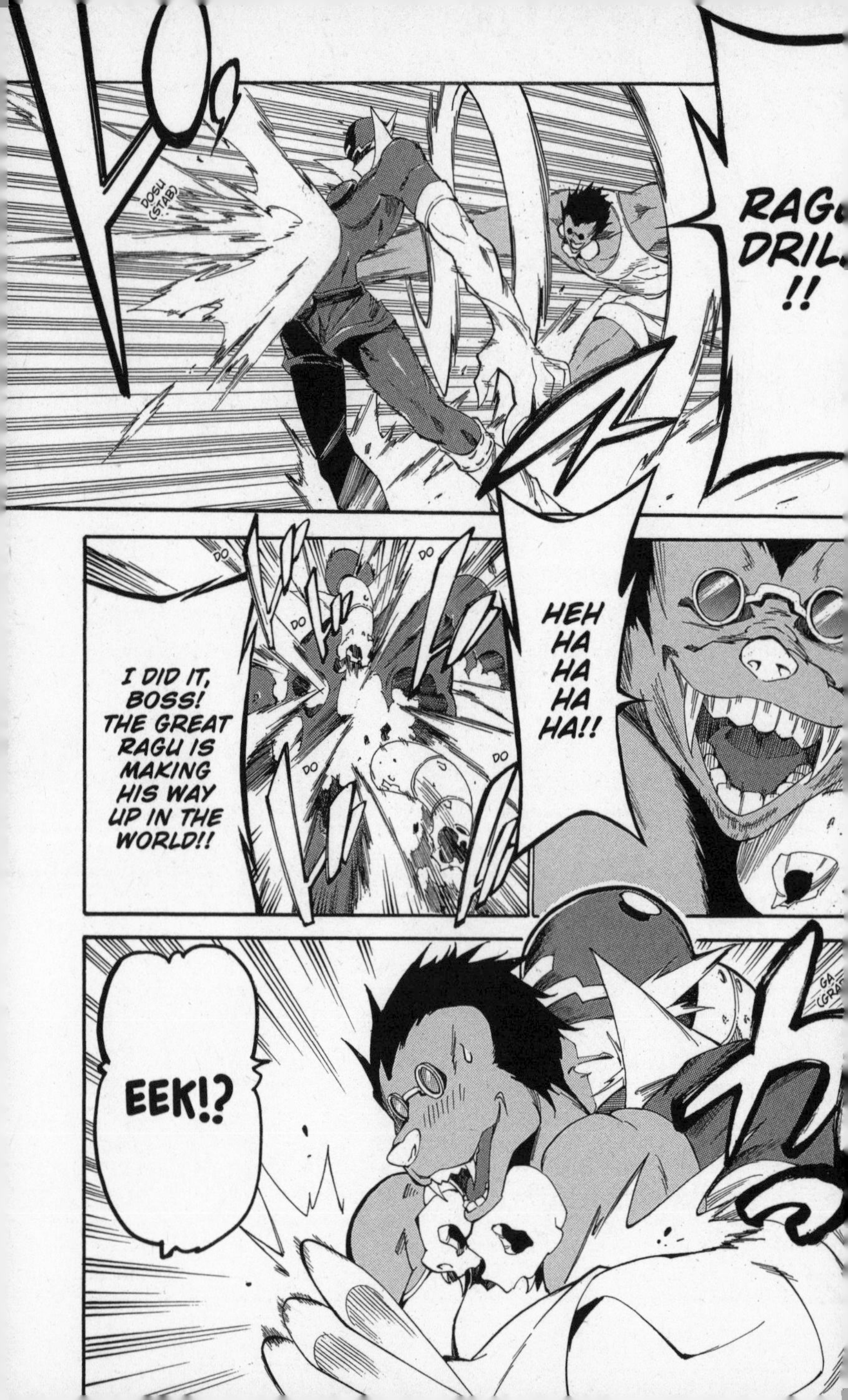

RAG
DRIL
!!
DOSU (STAB)
HEH HA HA HA HA!!
I DID IT, BOSS! THE GREAT RAGU IS MAKING HIS WAY UP IN THE WORLD!!
DO
DO
DO
DO
DO
GA
EEK!?

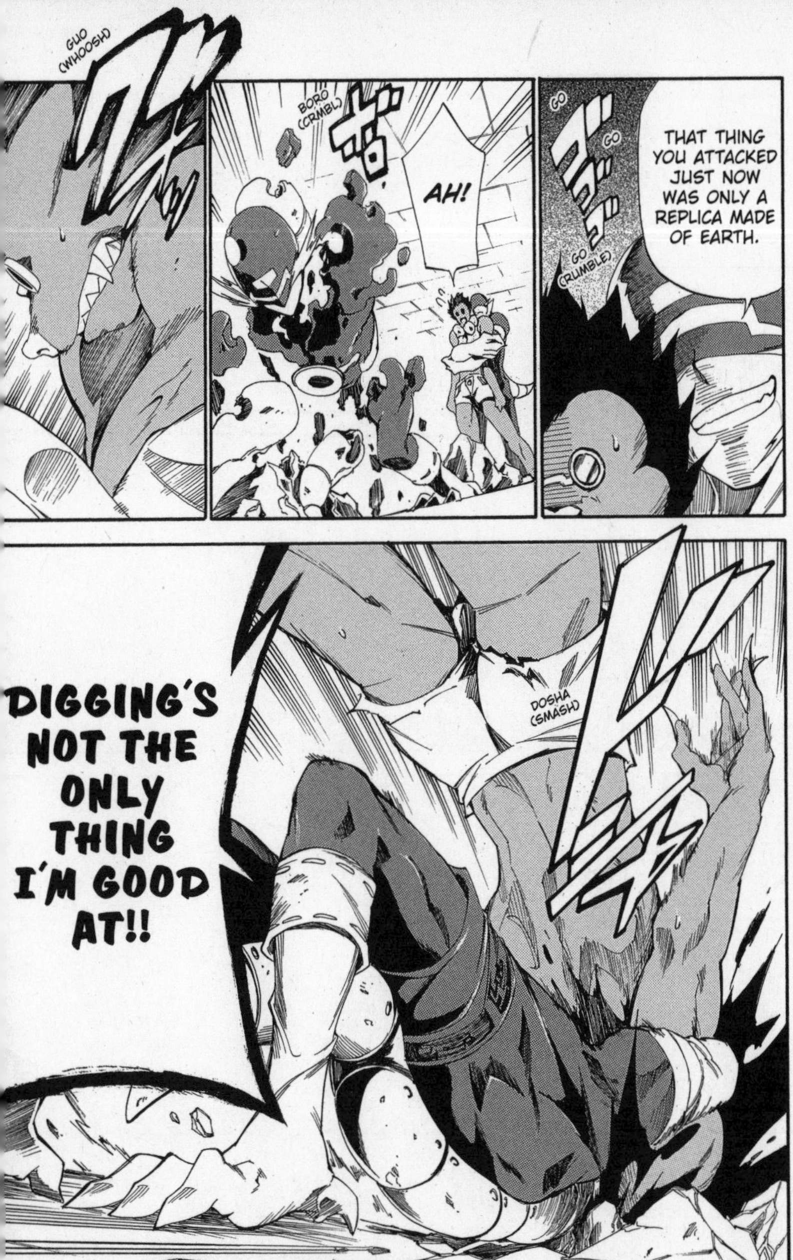
GO
GO
GO (RUMBLE)
THAT THING YOU ATTACKED JUST NOW WAS ONLY A REPLICA MADE OF EARTH.
BORO (CRMBL)
AH!
GUO (WHOOSH)
DOSHA (SMASH)
DIGGING'S NOT THE ONLY THING I'M GOOD AT!!

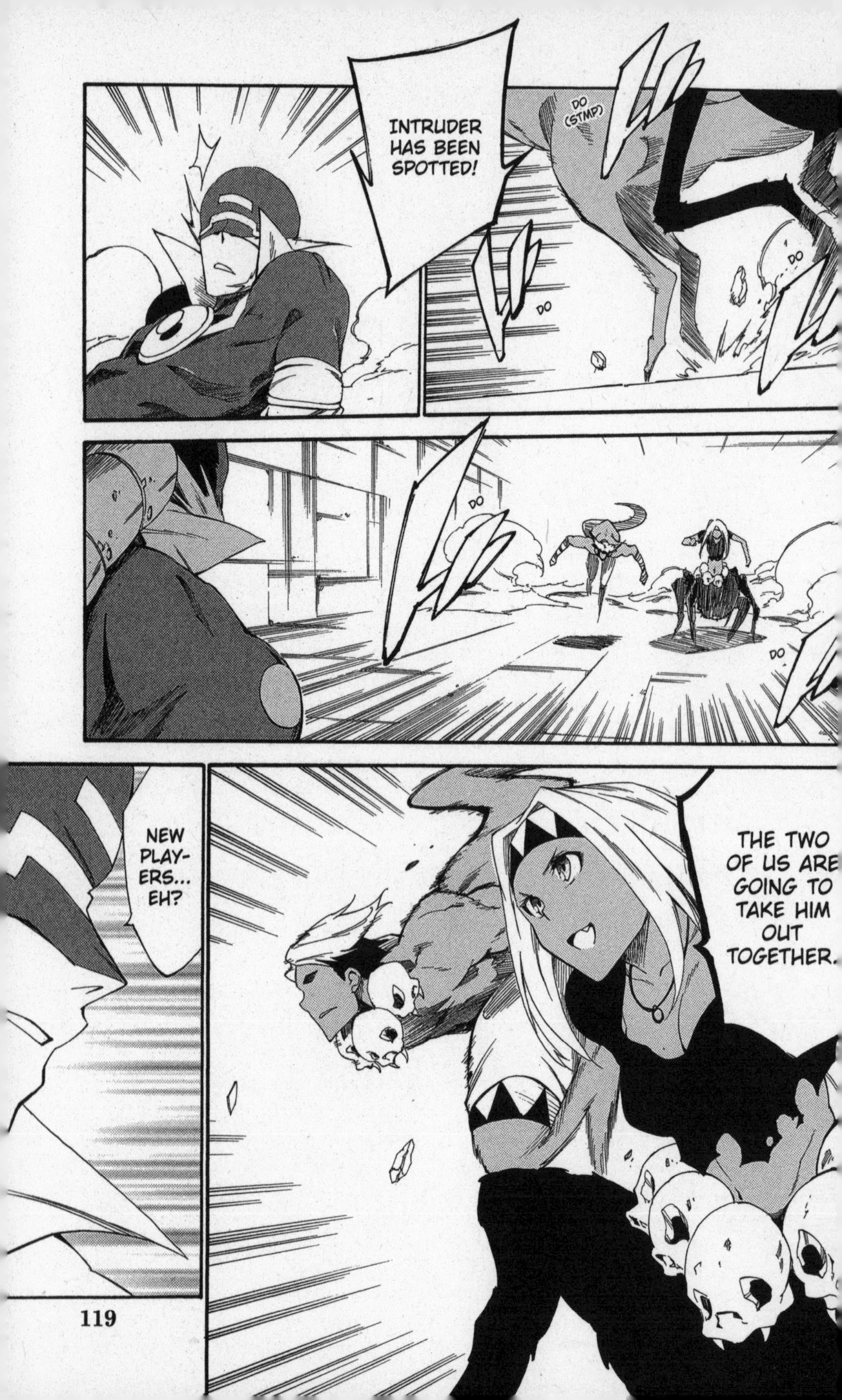
DO (STMP)
DO
DO
INTRUDER HAS BEEN SPOTTED!
DO
DO
THE TWO OF US ARE GOING TO TAKE HIM OUT TOGETHER.
NEW PLAY-ERS... EH?

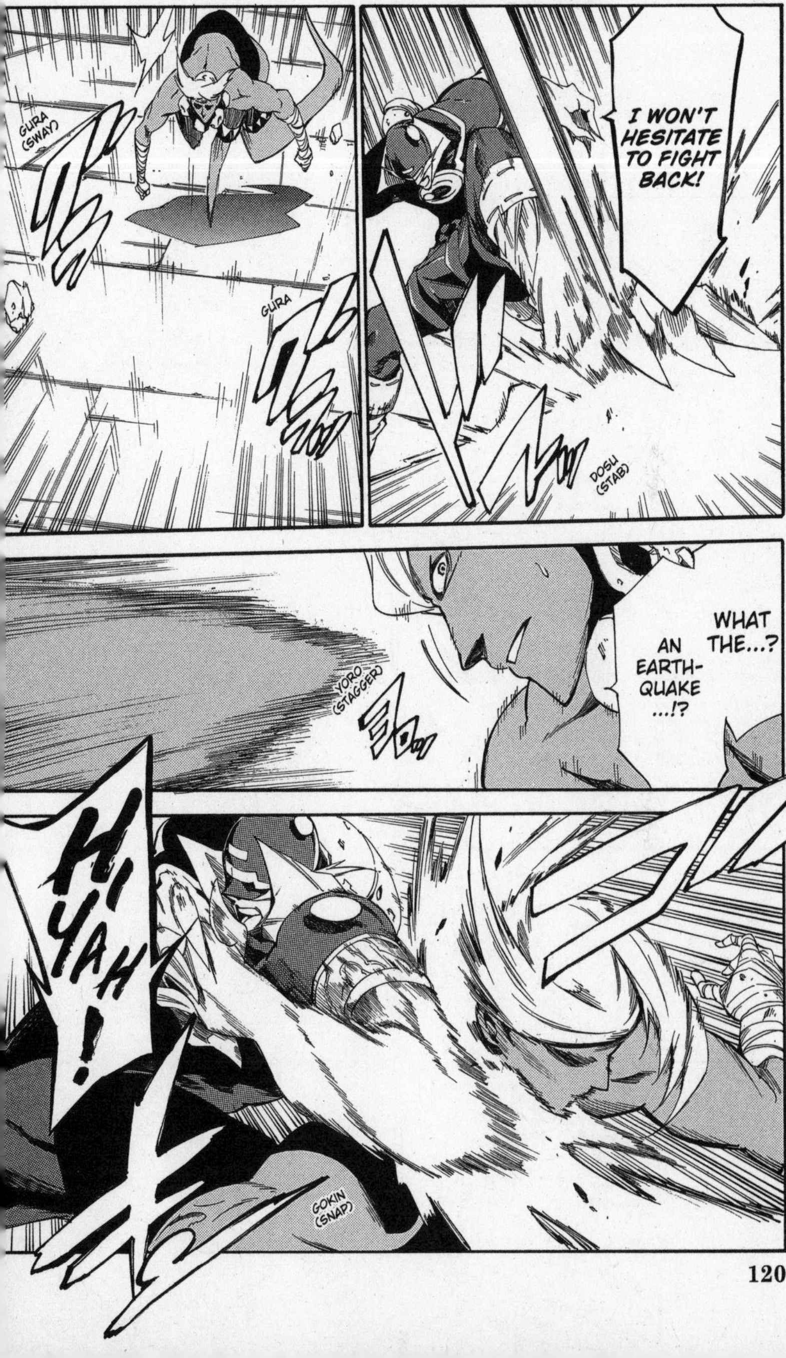
I WON'T HESITATE TO FIGHT BACK!
DOSU (STAB)
GURA (SWAY)
GURA
WHAT THE...?
AN EARTH-QUAKE ...!?
YORO (STAGGER)
HIYAH!
GOKIN (SNAP)

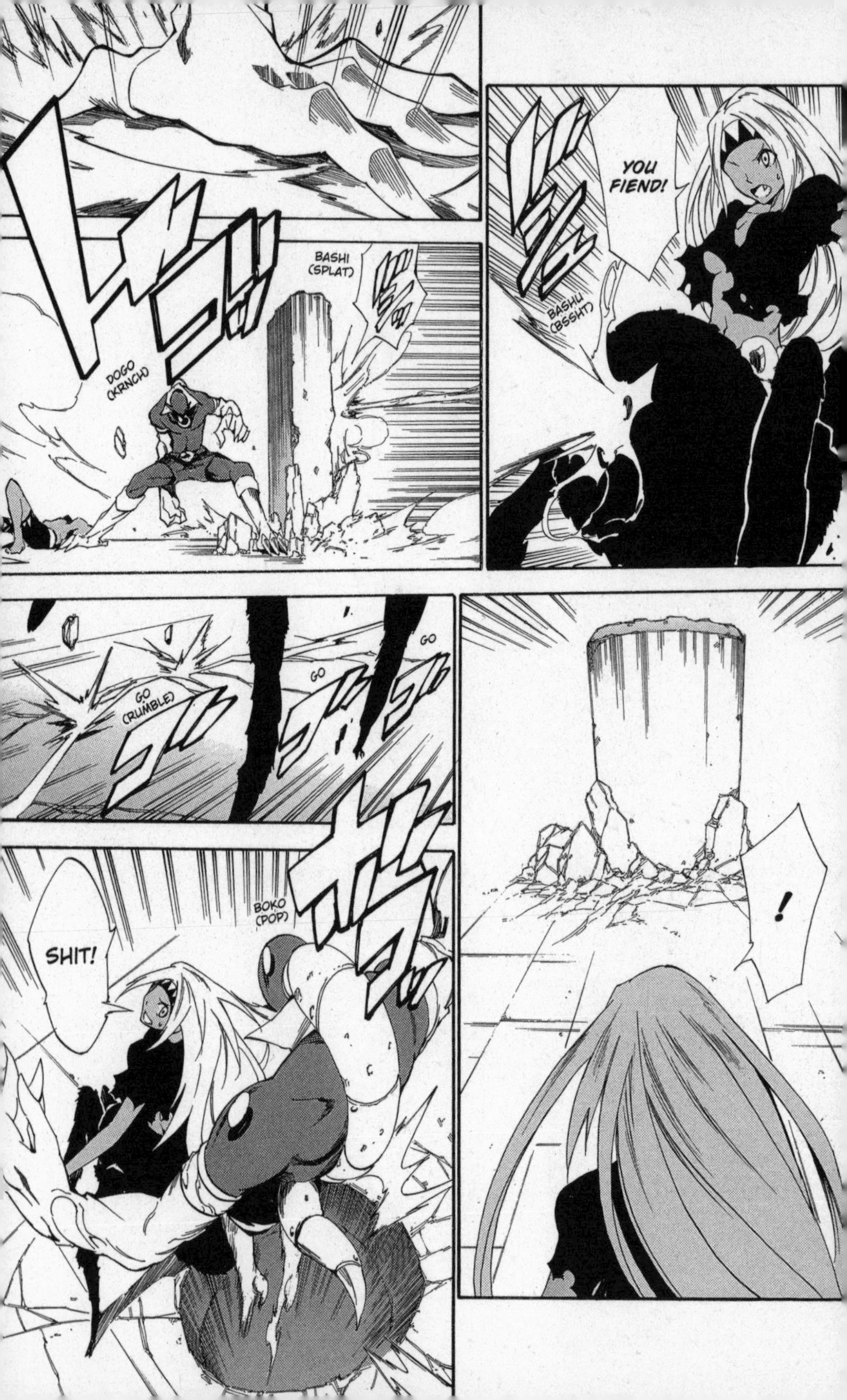
YOU FIEND!
BASHU (BSSHT)
BASHI (SPLAT)
DOGO (KRNCH)
!
GO
GO
GO (RUMBLE)
BOKO (POP)
SHIT!

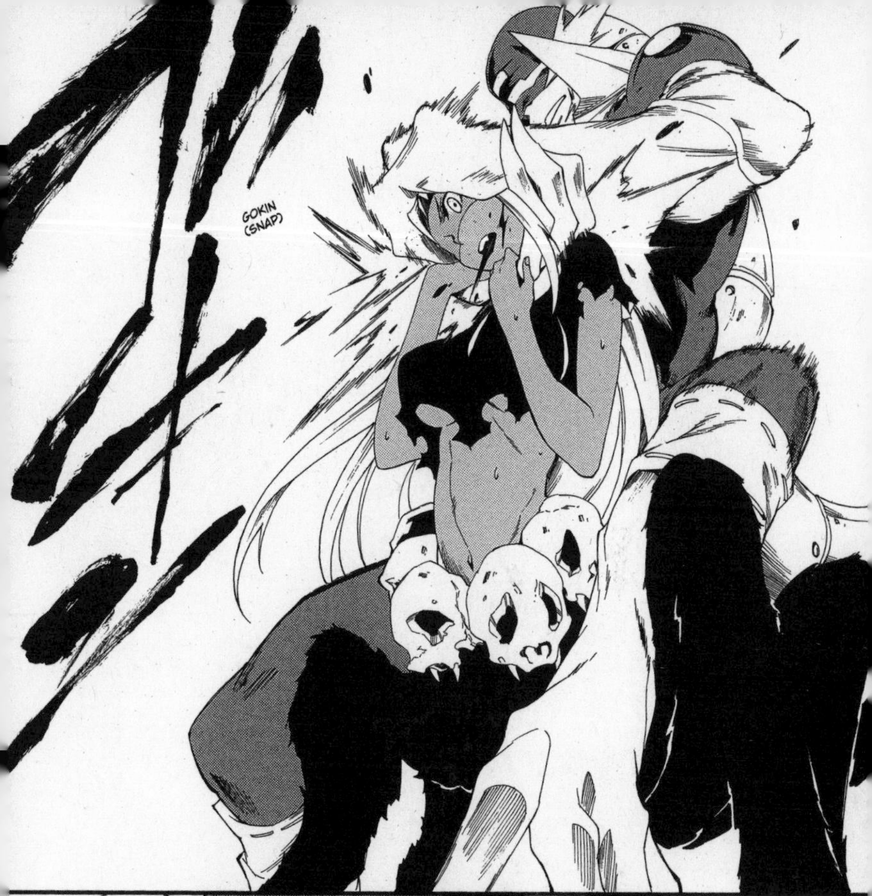
GOKIN (SNAP)

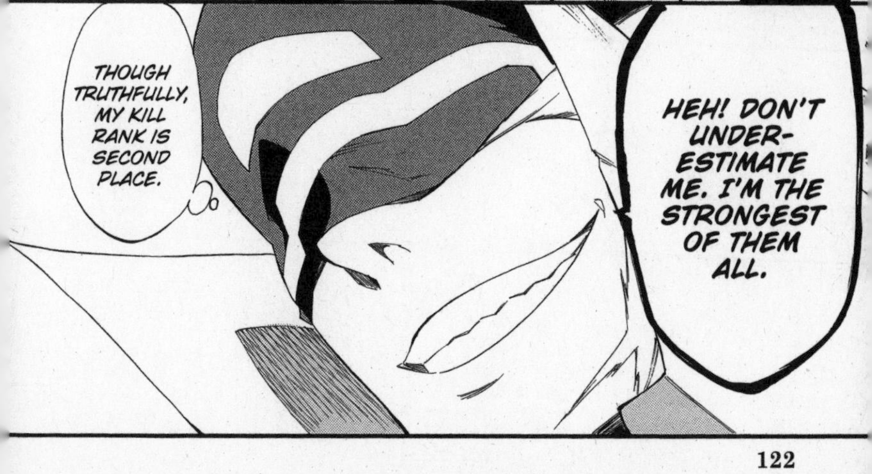
HEH! DON'T UNDER-ESTIMATE ME. I'M THE STRONGEST OF THEM ALL.
THOUGH TRUTHFULLY, MY KILL RANK IS SECOND PLACE.

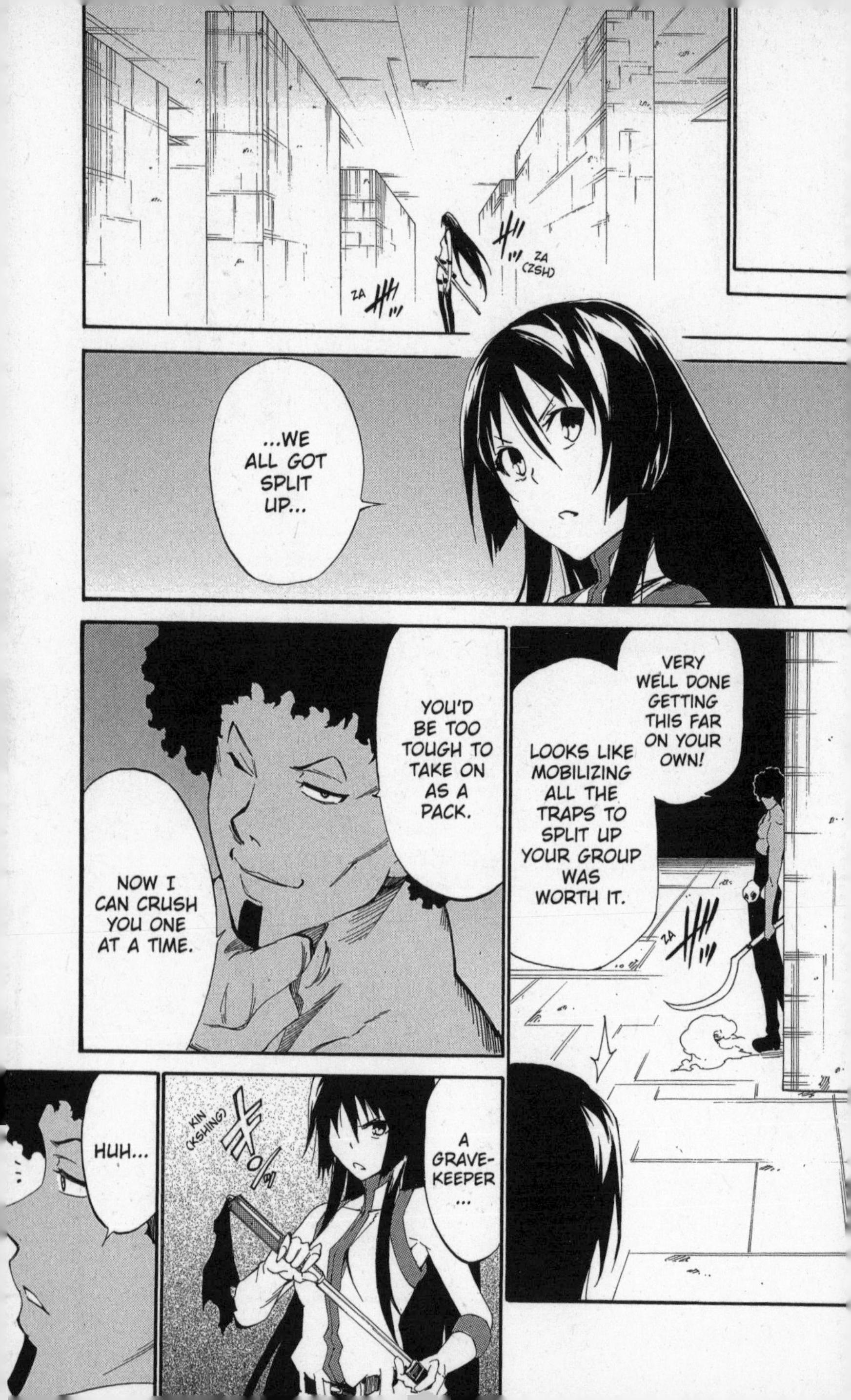
ZA (ZSH)
ZA
...WE ALL GOT SPLIT UP...
VERY WELL DONE GETTING THIS FAR ON YOUR OWN!
LOOKS LIKE MOBILIZING ALL THE TRAPS TO SPLIT UP YOUR GROUP WAS WORTH IT.
ZA
YOU'D BE TOO TOUGH TO TAKE ON AS A PACK.
NOW I CAN CRUSH YOU ONE AT A TIME.
A GRAVE-KEEPER...
KIN (KSHING)
HUH...

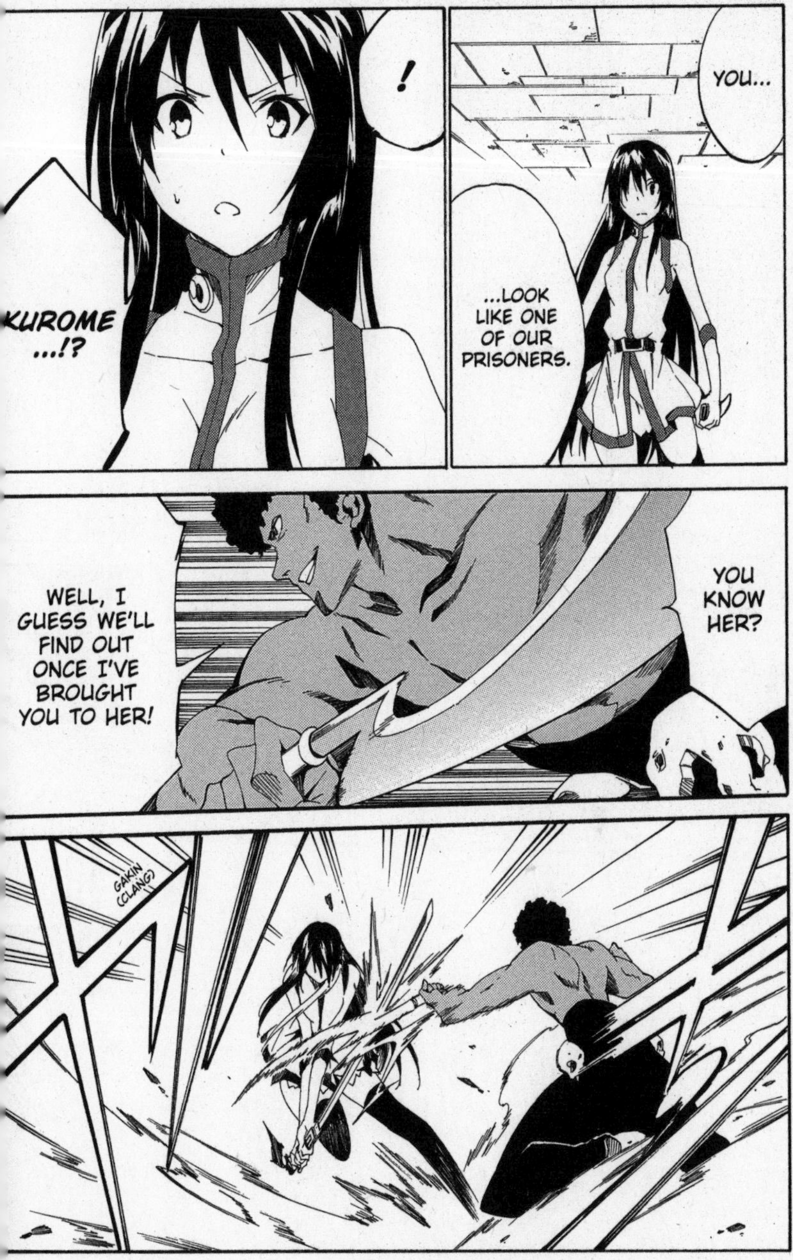

YOU...
...LOOK LIKE ONE OF OUR PRISONERS.
!
KUROME ...!?
YOU KNOW HER?
WELL, I GUESS WE'LL FIND OUT ONCE I'VE BROUGHT YOU TO HER!
GAKIN (CLANG)

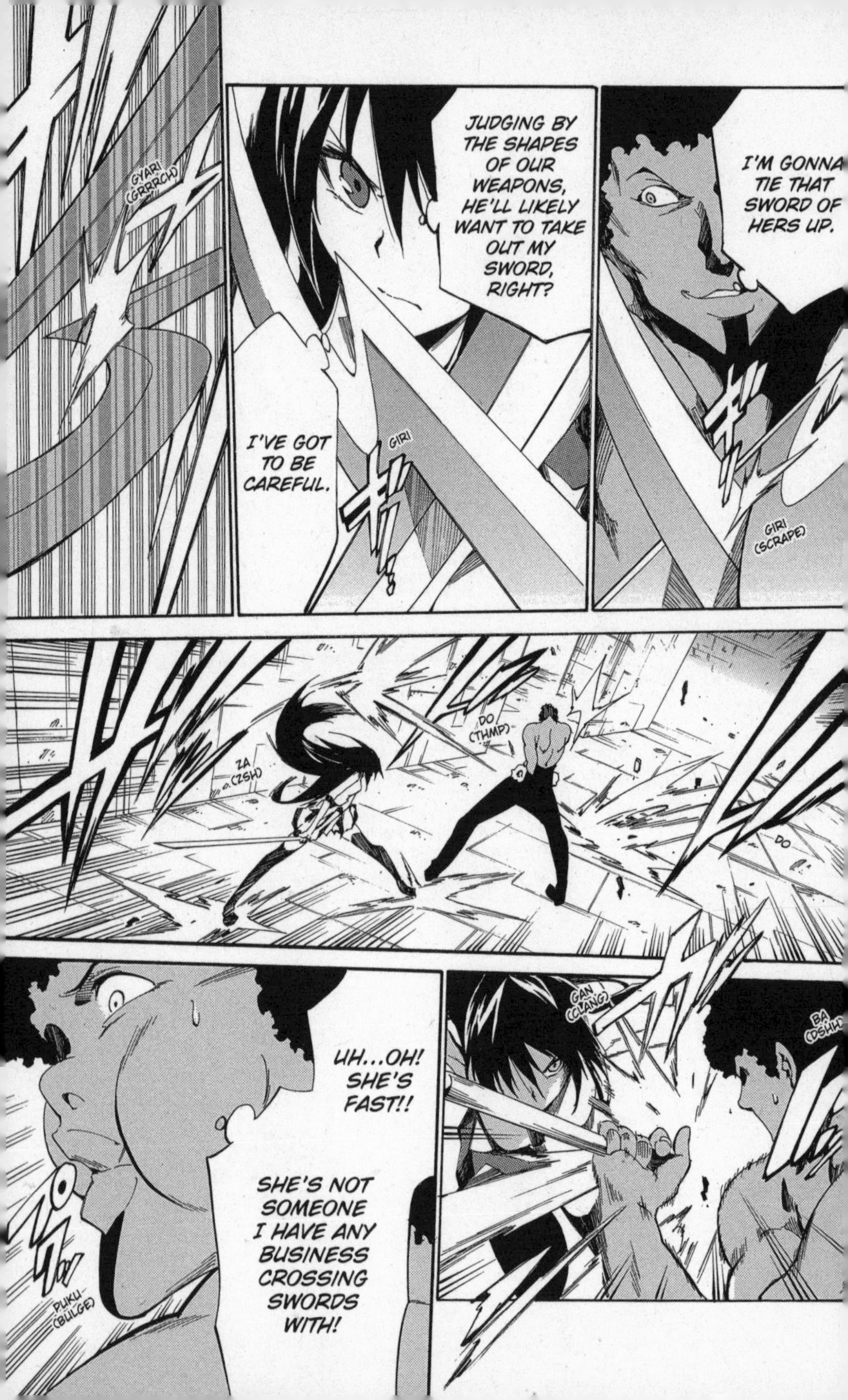
I'M GONNA TIE THAT SWORD OF HERS UP.
GIRI (SCRAPE)
JUDGING BY THE SHAPES OF OUR WEAPONS, HE'LL LIKELY WANT TO TAKE OUT MY SWORD, RIGHT?
GIRI
I'VE GOT TO BE CAREFUL.
GYARI (GRRRCH)
DO
DO (THMP)
ZA (ZSH)
BA (DSHH)
GAN (CLANG)
UH...OH! SHE'S FAST!!
SHE'S NOT SOMEONE I HAVE ANY BUSINESS CROSSING SWORDS WITH!
PUKU (BULGE)

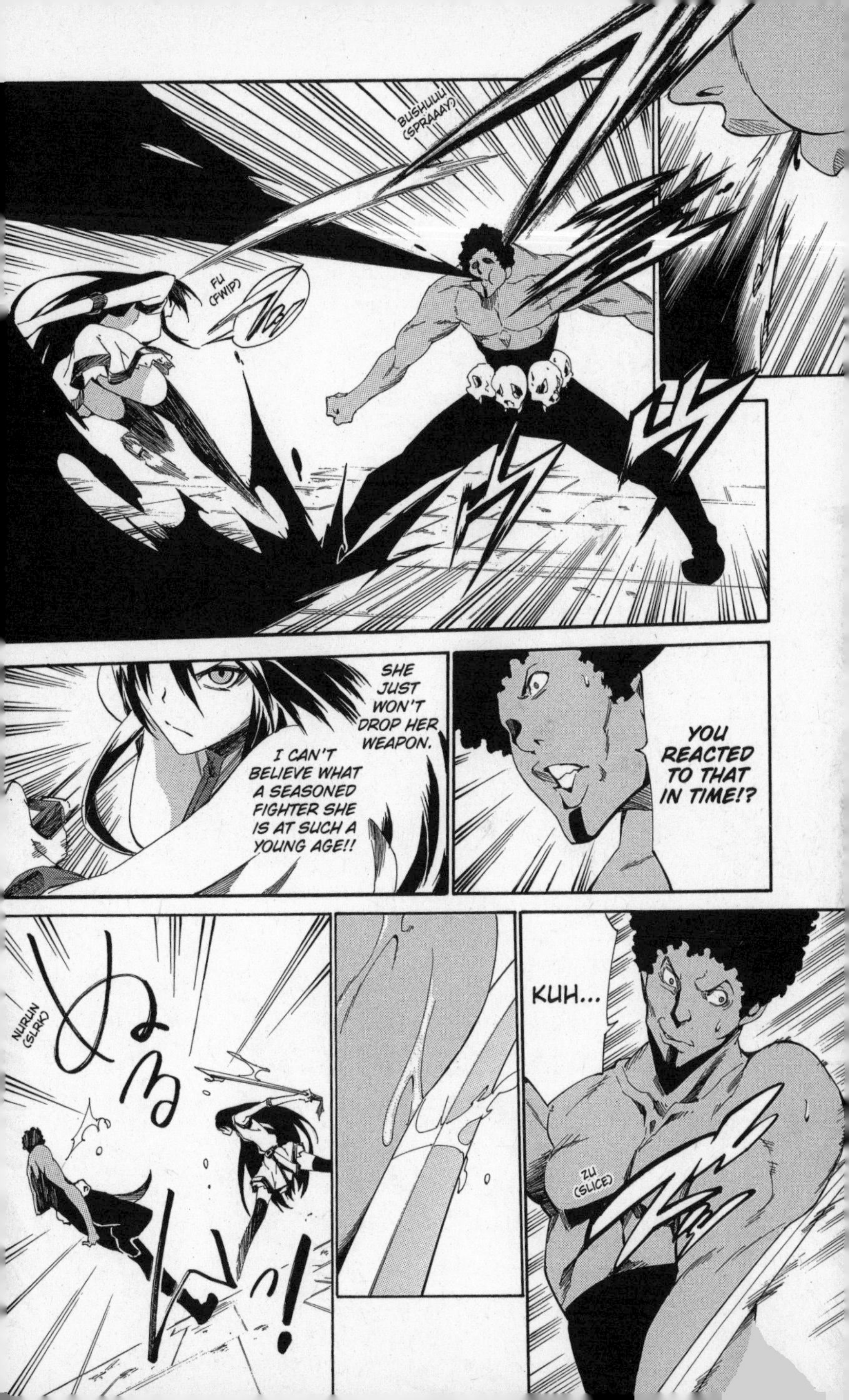
BUSHUUU (SPRAAAY)
FU (FWIP)
YOU REACTED TO THAT IN TIME!?
SHE JUST WON'T DROP HER WEAPON.
I CAN'T BELIEVE WHAT A SEASONED FIGHTER SHE IS AT SUCH A YOUNG AGE!!
KUH...
ZU (SLICE)
NURUN (SLRK)

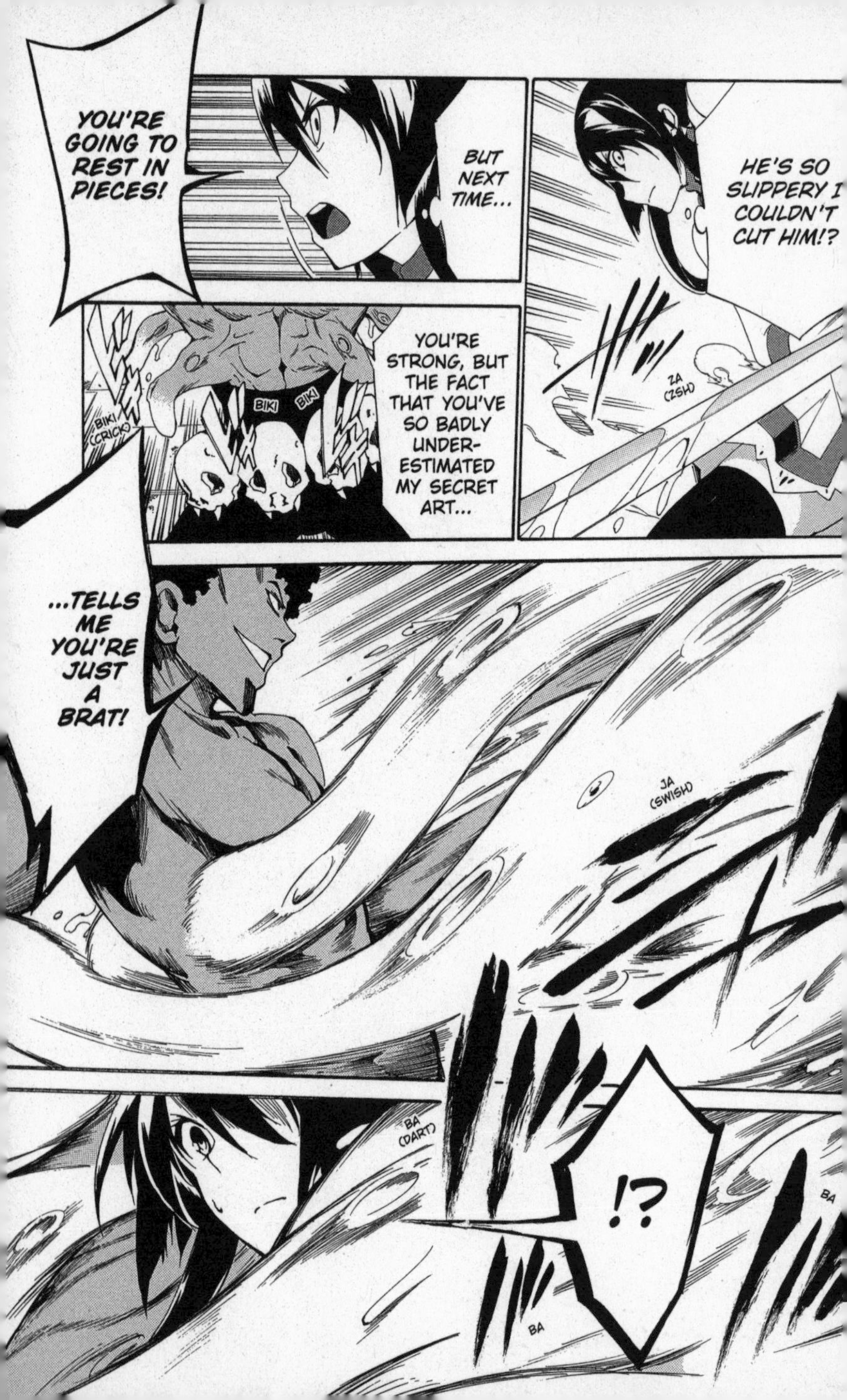
HE'S SO SLIPPERY I COULDN'T CUT HIM!?
ZA (ZSH)
BUT NEXT TIME...
YOU'RE GOING TO REST IN PIECES!
YOU'RE STRONG, BUT THE FACT THAT YOU'VE SO BADLY UNDER-ESTIMATED MY SECRET ART...
BIKI
BIKI
BIKI (CRICK)
...TELLS ME YOU'RE JUST A BRAT!
JA (SWISH)
BA
!?
BA (DART)
BA

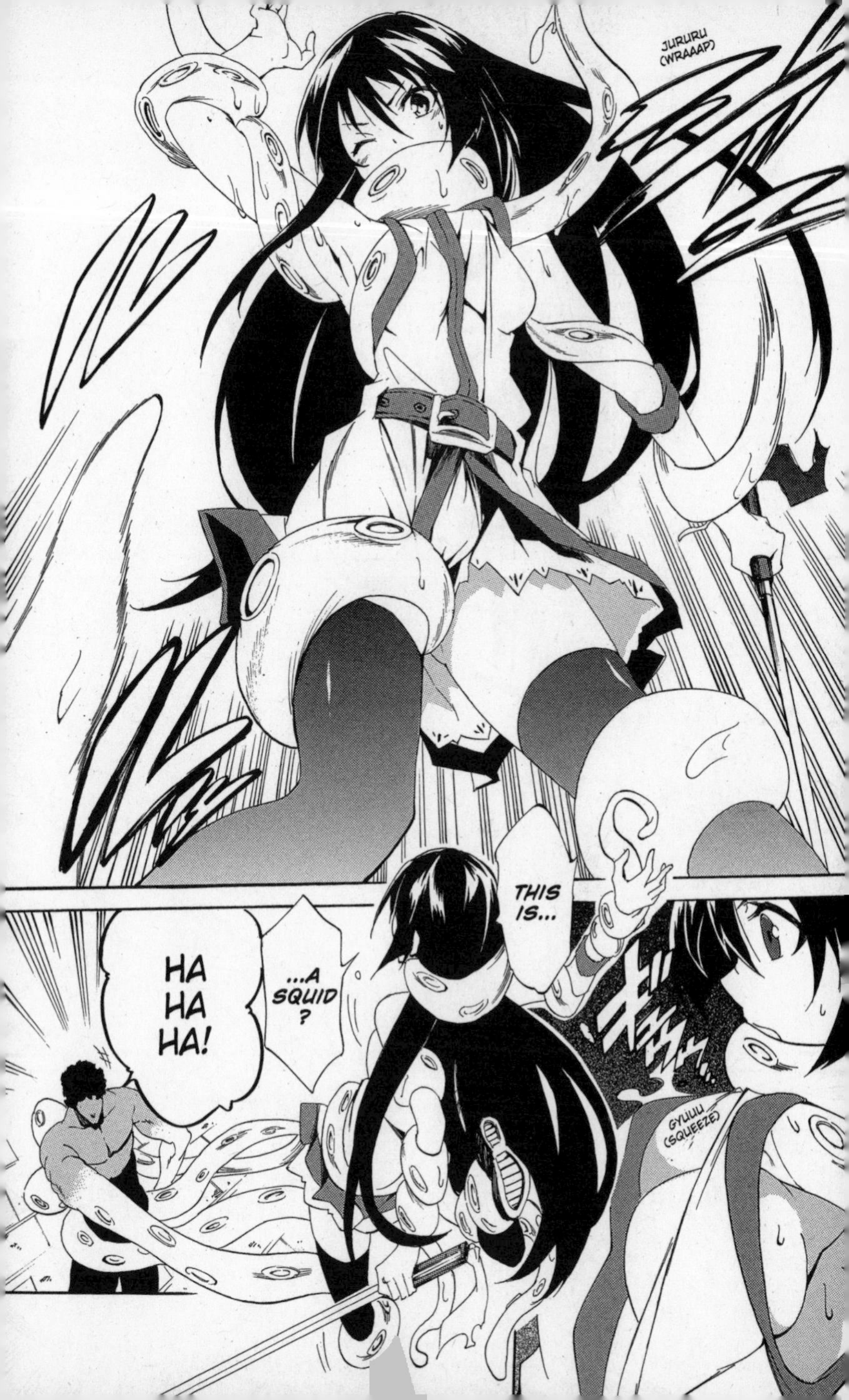
JURURU
(WRAAAP)
THIS IS...
GYUUU
(SQUEEZE)
...A SQUID?
HA HA HA!

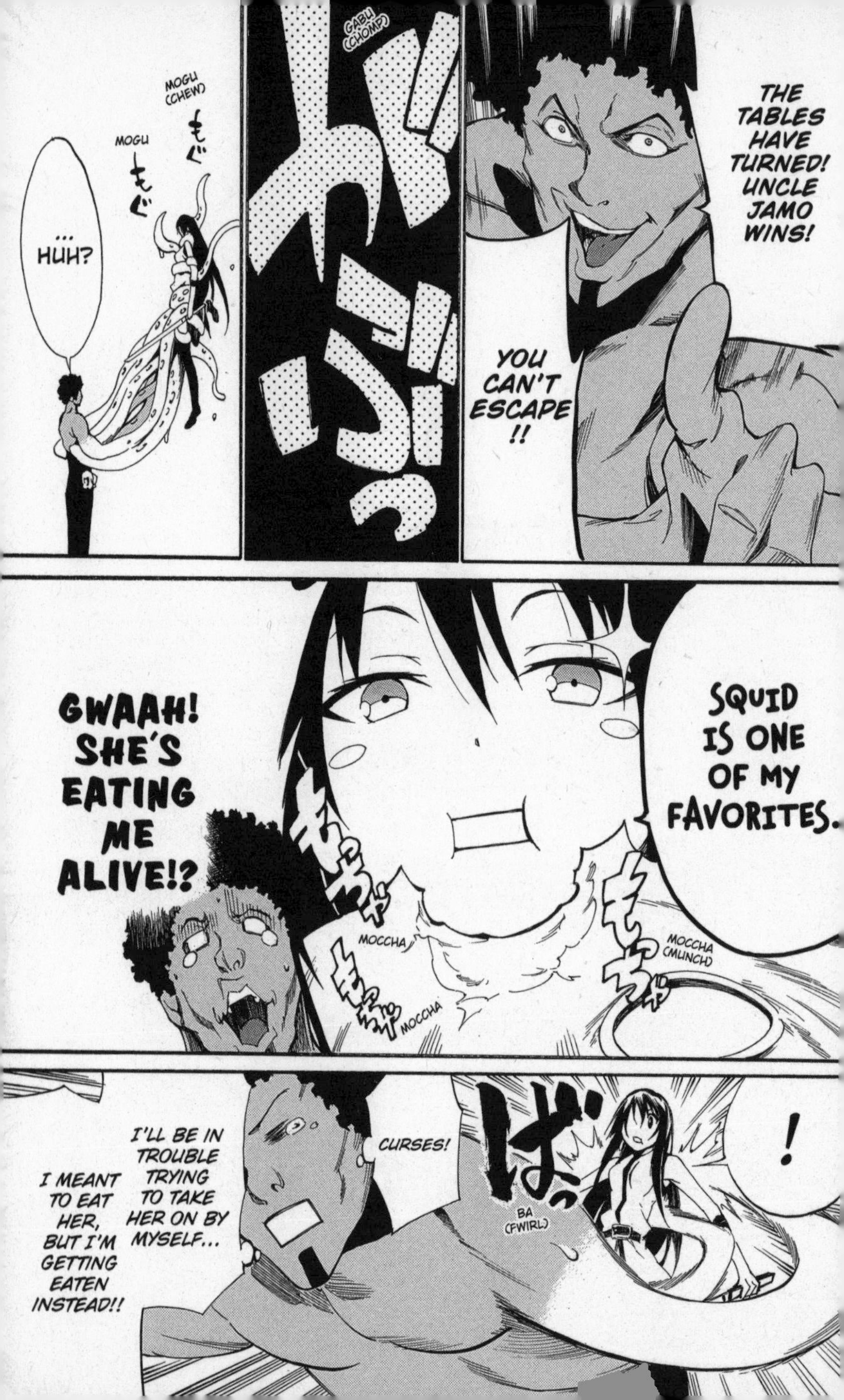
THE TABLES HAVE TURNED! UNCLE JAMO WINS!
YOU CAN'T ESCAPE!!
GABU (CHOMP)
MOGU (CHEW)
もぐ
MOGU
もぐ
... HUH?
SQUID IS ONE OF MY FAVORITES.
MOCCHA (MUNCH)
MOCCHA
MOCCHA
GWAAH! SHE'S EATING ME ALIVE!?
!
BA (FWIRL)
CURSES!
I'LL BE IN TROUBLE TRYING TO TAKE HER ON BY MYSELF...
I MEANT TO EAT HER, BUT I'M GETTING EATEN INSTEAD!!

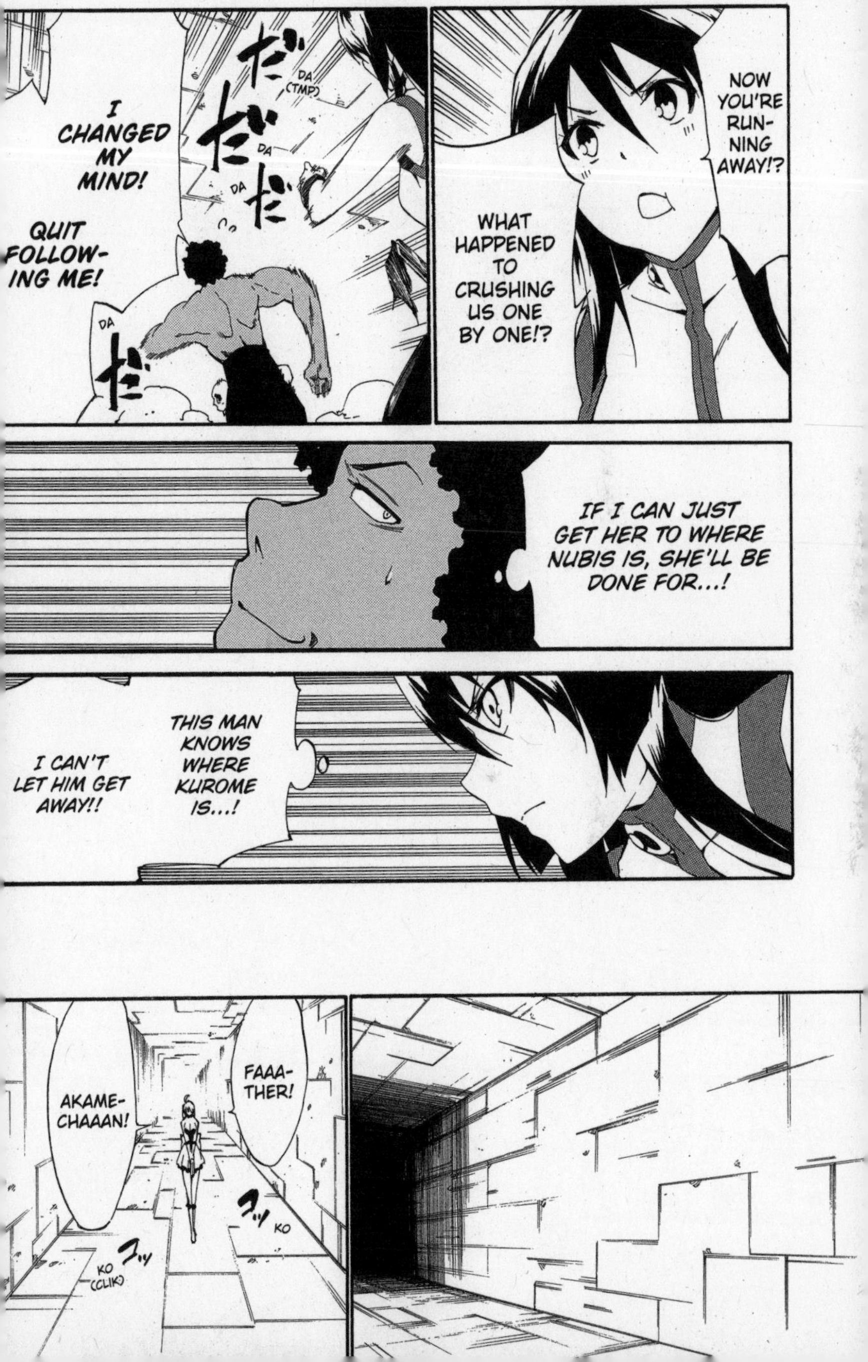
NOW YOU'RE RUN-NING AWAY!?
WHAT HAPPENED TO CRUSHING US ONE BY ONE!?
だだだだ
DA (TMP)
DA
DA
I CHANGED MY MIND!
QUIT FOLLOW-ING ME!
DA
IF I CAN JUST GET HER TO WHERE NUBIS IS, SHE'LL BE DONE FOR...!
THIS MAN KNOWS WHERE KUROME IS...!
I CAN'T LET HIM GET AWAY!!
FAAA-THER!
AKAME-CHAAAN!
KO
KO (CLIK)

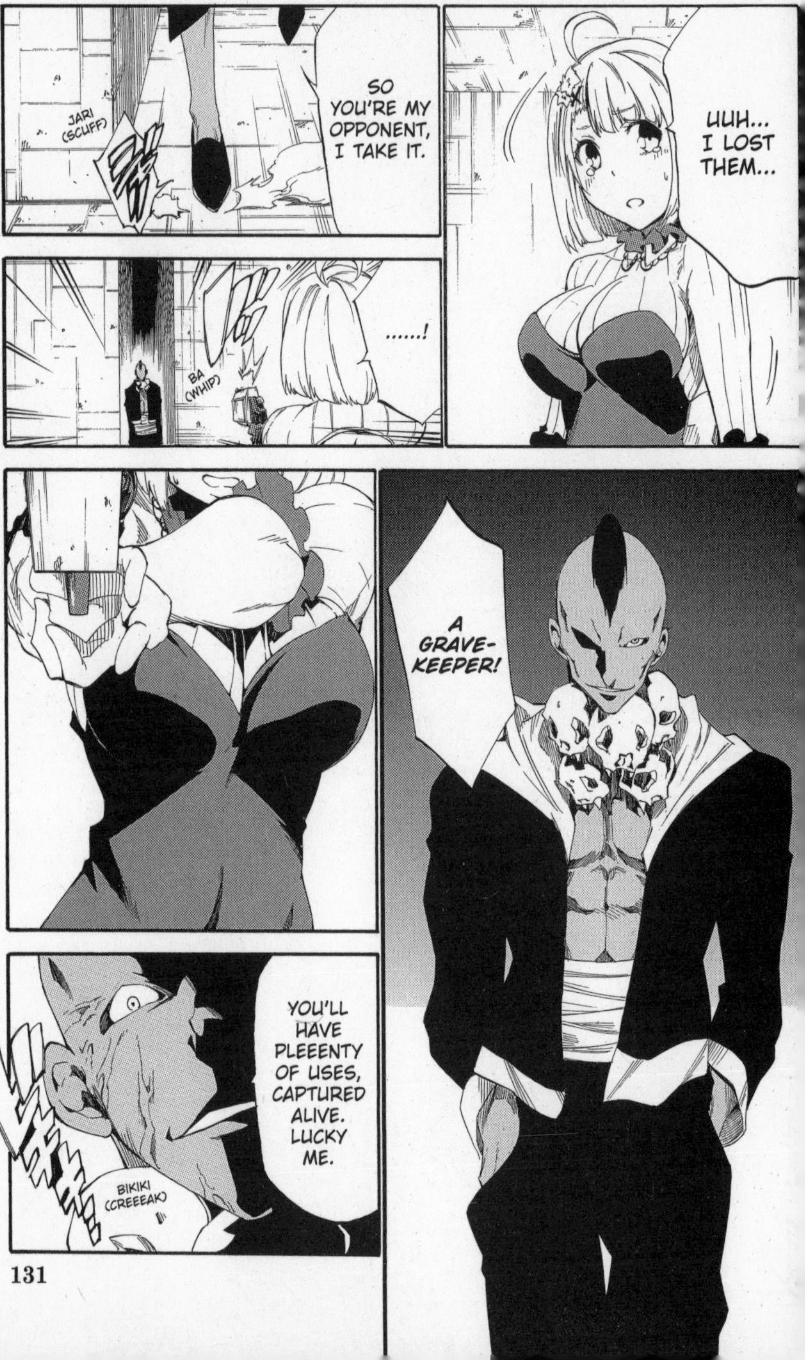
UUH... I LOST THEM...
SO YOU'RE MY OPPONENT, I TAKE IT.
JARI (SCUFF)
......!
BA (WHIP)
A GRAVE-KEEPER!
YOU'LL HAVE PLEEENTY OF USES, CAPTURED ALIVE. LUCKY ME.
BIKIKI (CREEEAK)

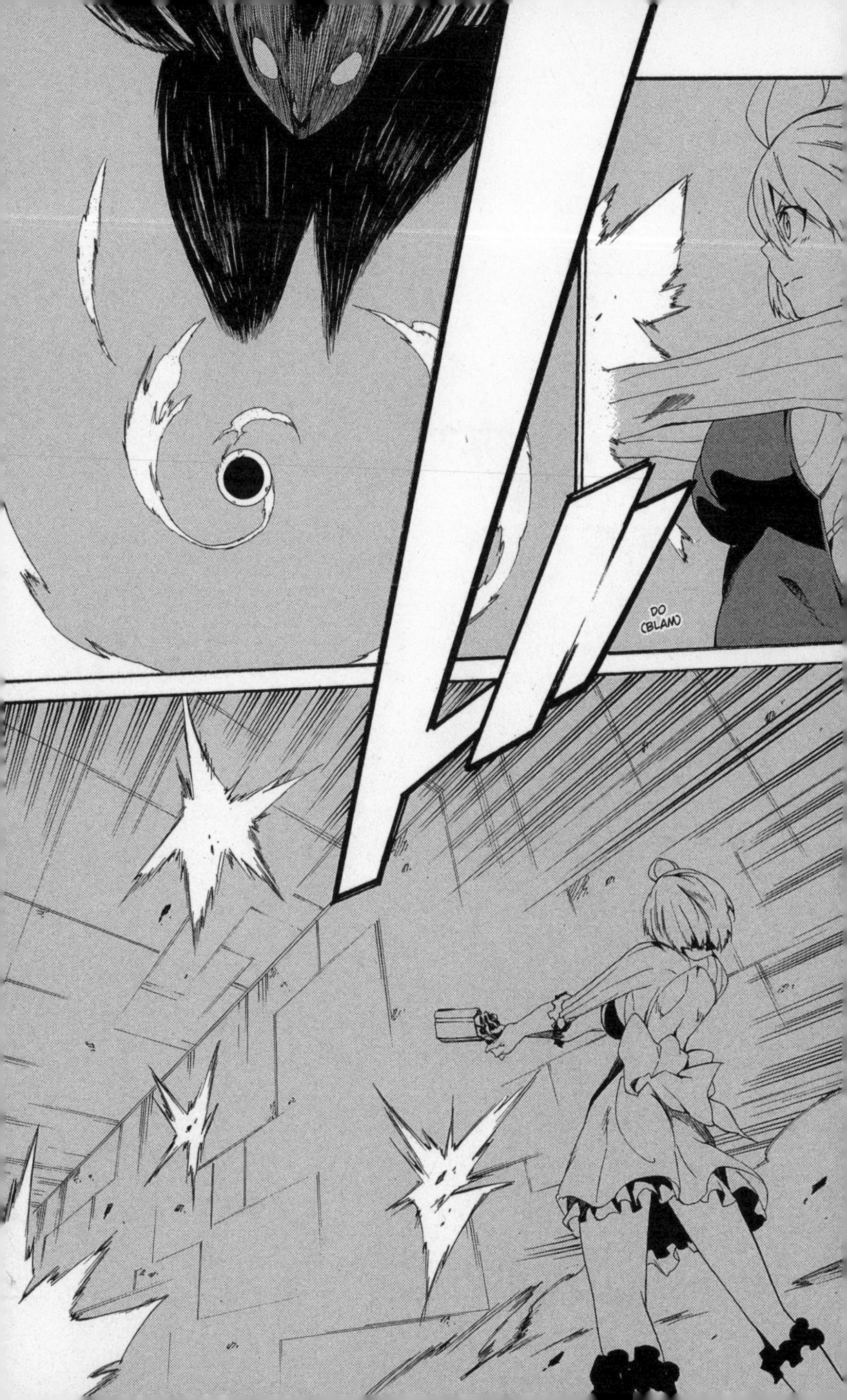
DO
(BLAM)

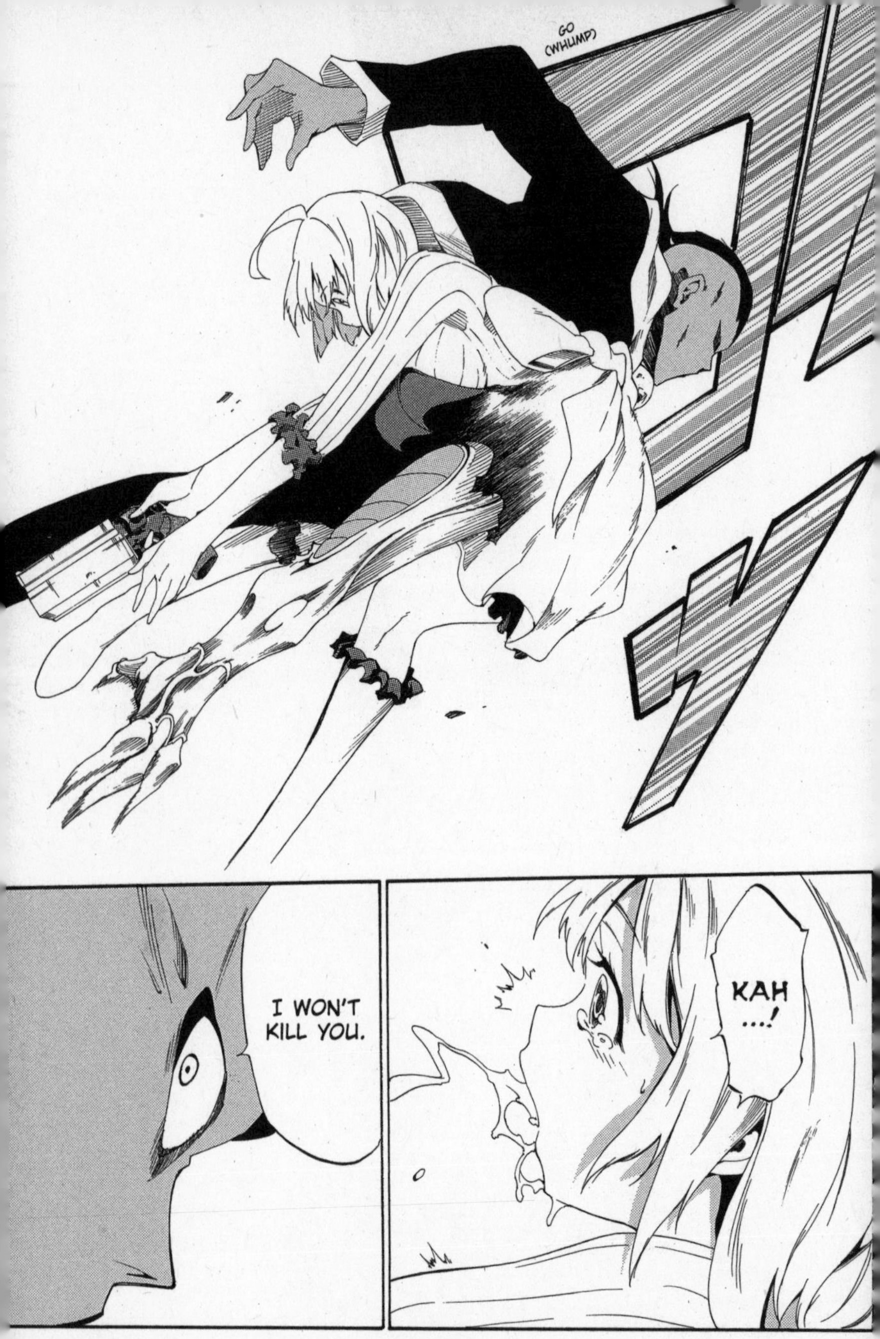
GO
(WHUMP)
KAH ...!
I WON'T KILL YOU.

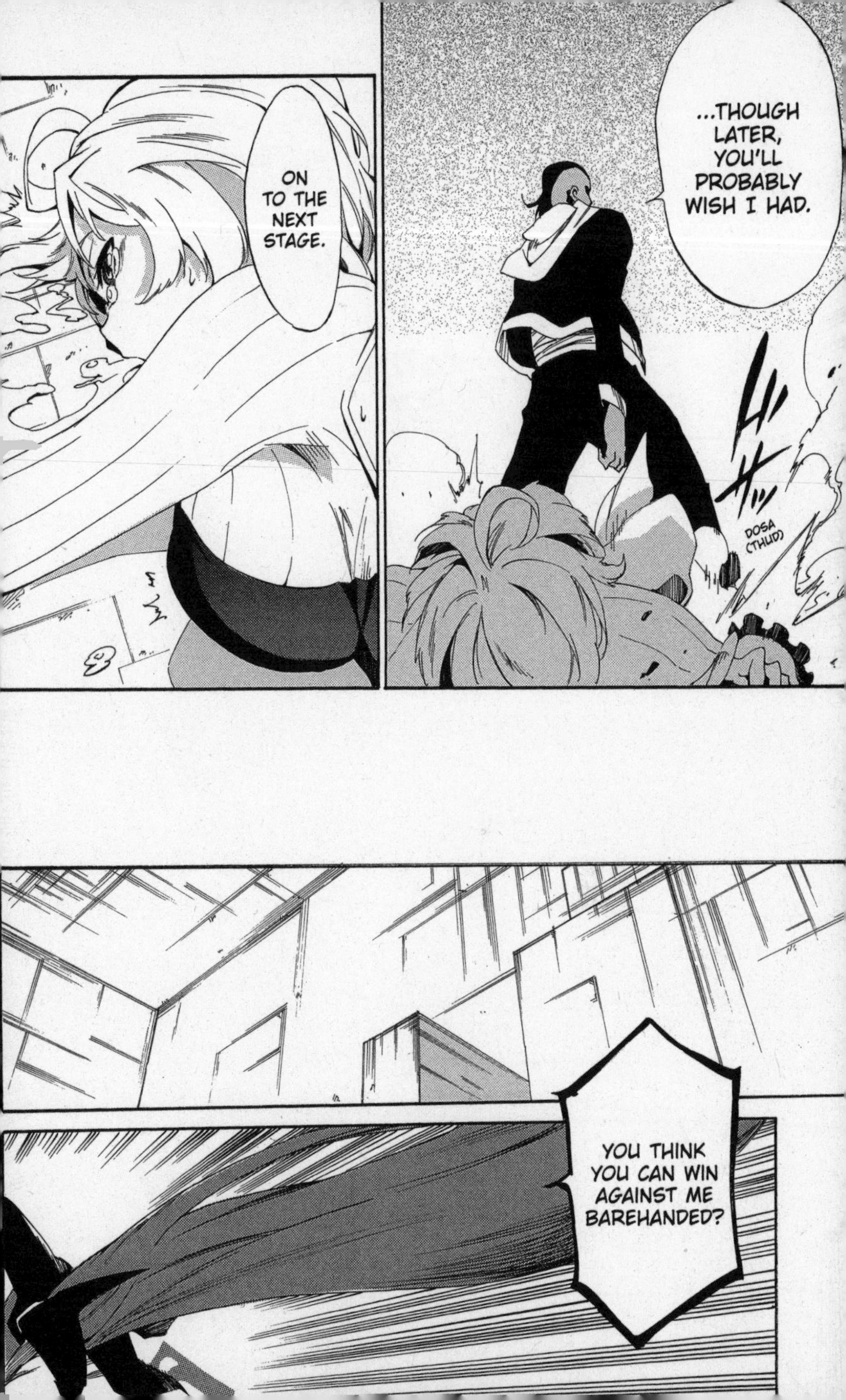
...THOUGH LATER, YOU'LL PROBABLY WISH I HAD.
DOSA (THUD)
ON TO THE NEXT STAGE.
YOU THINK YOU CAN WIN AGAINST ME BAREHANDED?

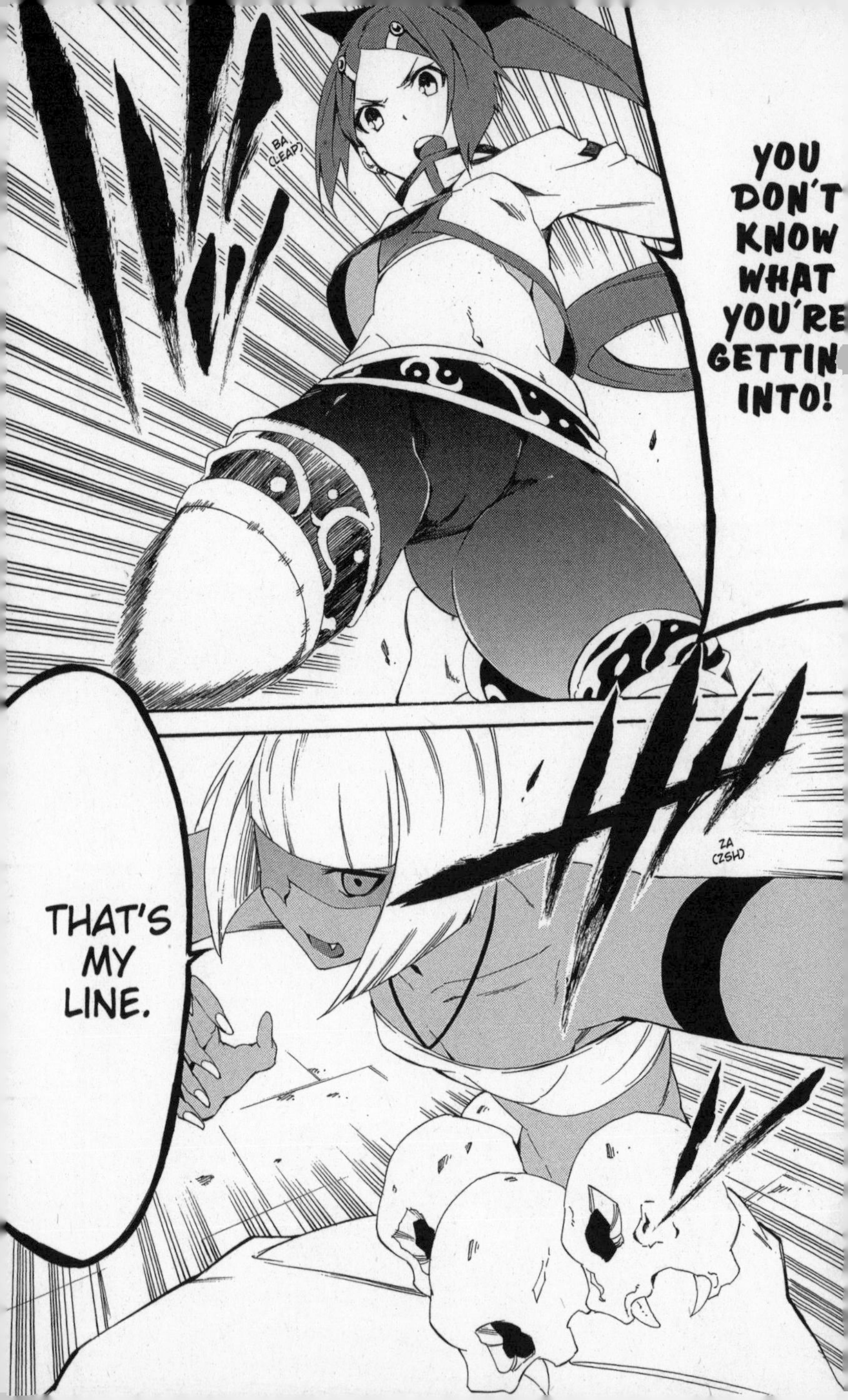
YOU DON'T KNOW WHAT YOU'RE GETTIN INTO!
BA (LEAP)
ZA (ZSH)
THAT'S MY LINE.

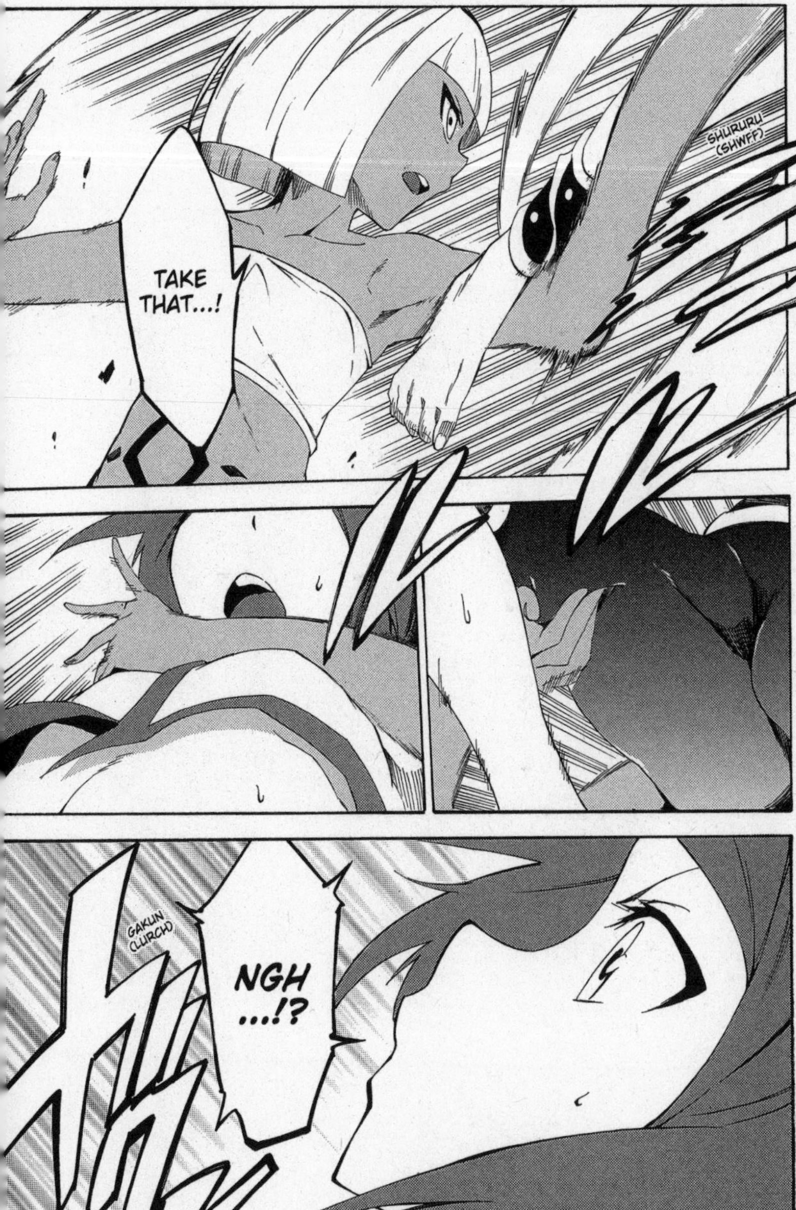
SHURURU (SHWFF)
TAKE THAT...!
GAKUN (LURCH)
NGH ...!?

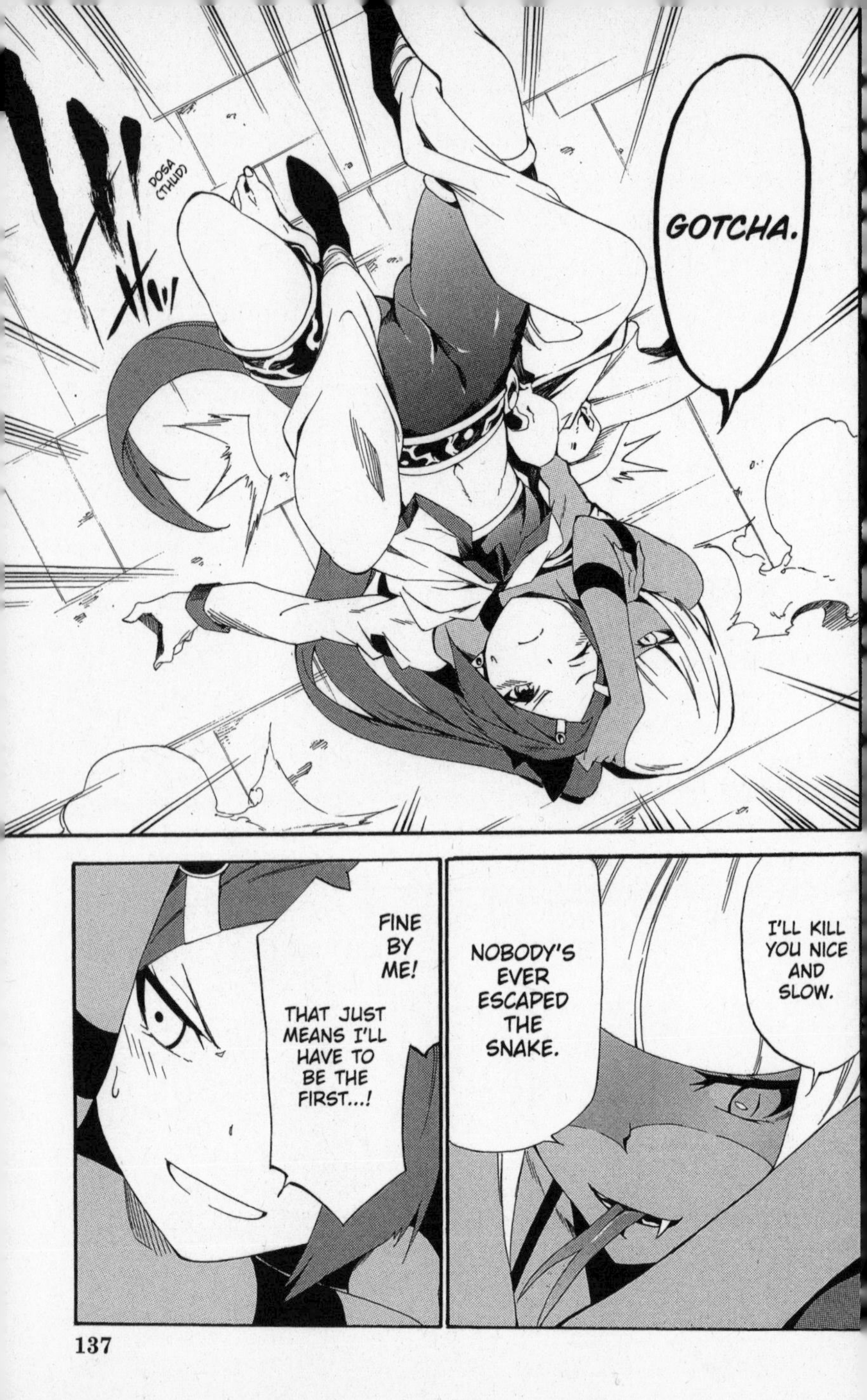
DOSA (THUD)
GOTCHA.
I'LL KILL YOU NICE AND SLOW.
NOBODY'S EVER ESCAPED THE SNAKE.
FINE BY ME!
THAT JUST MEANS I'LL HAVE TO BE THE FIRST...!

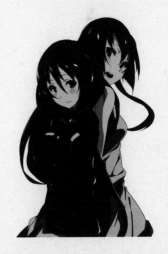

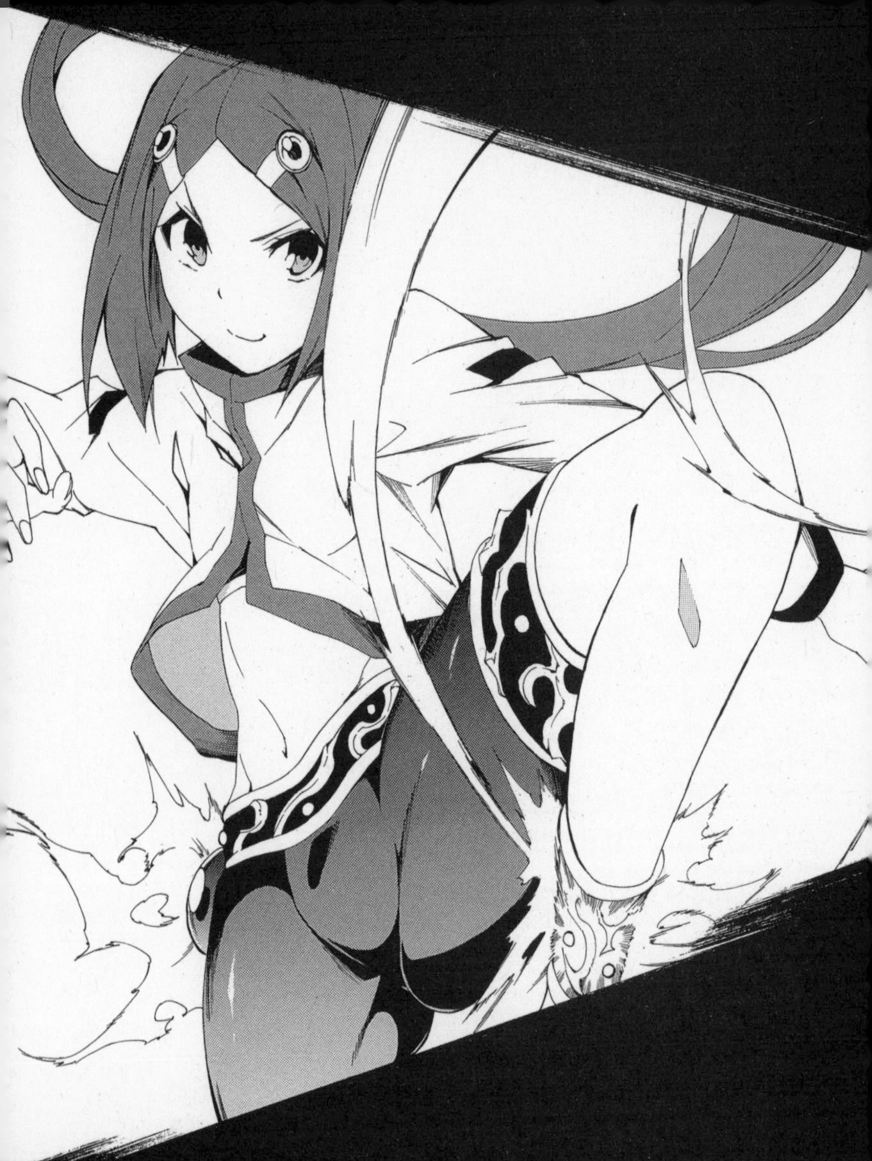

Chapter 19 No. 1

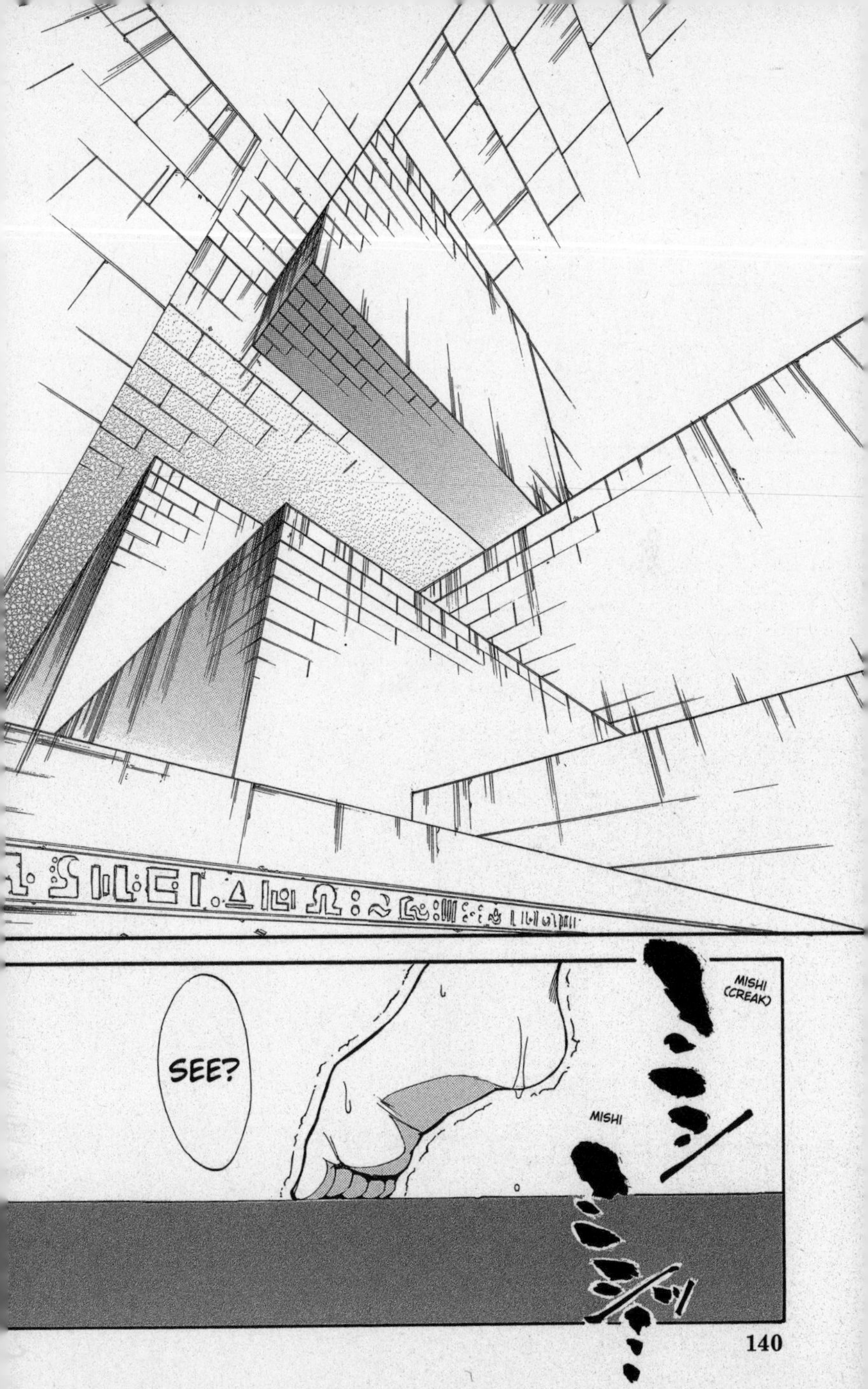
MISHI (CREAK)
MISHI
SEE?

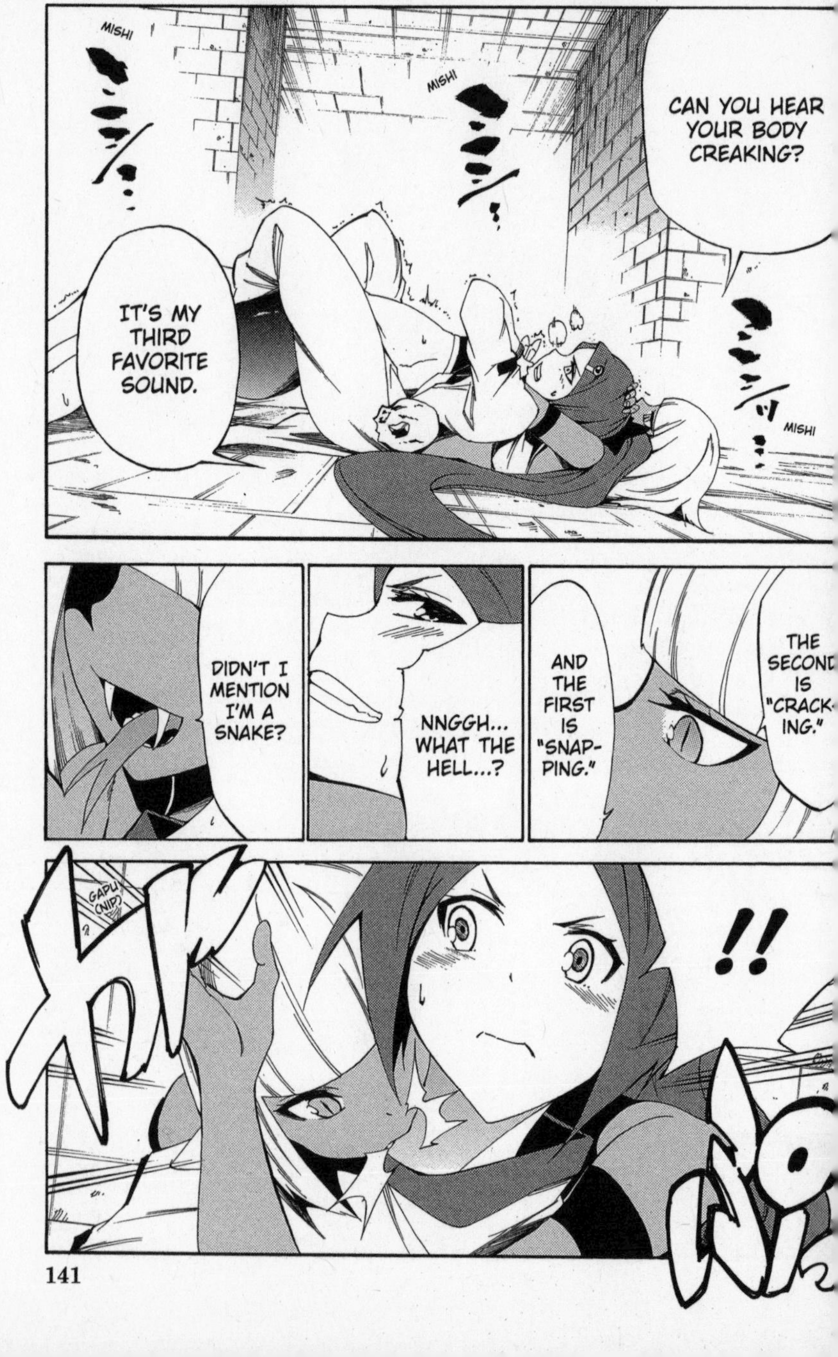
CAN YOU HEAR YOUR BODY CREAKING?
MISHI
MISHI
MISHI
IT'S MY THIRD FAVORITE SOUND.
THE SECOND IS "CRACK-ING."
AND THE FIRST IS "SNAP-PING."
NNGGH... WHAT THE HELL...?
DIDN'T I MENTION I'M A SNAKE?
!!
GAPU (NIP)

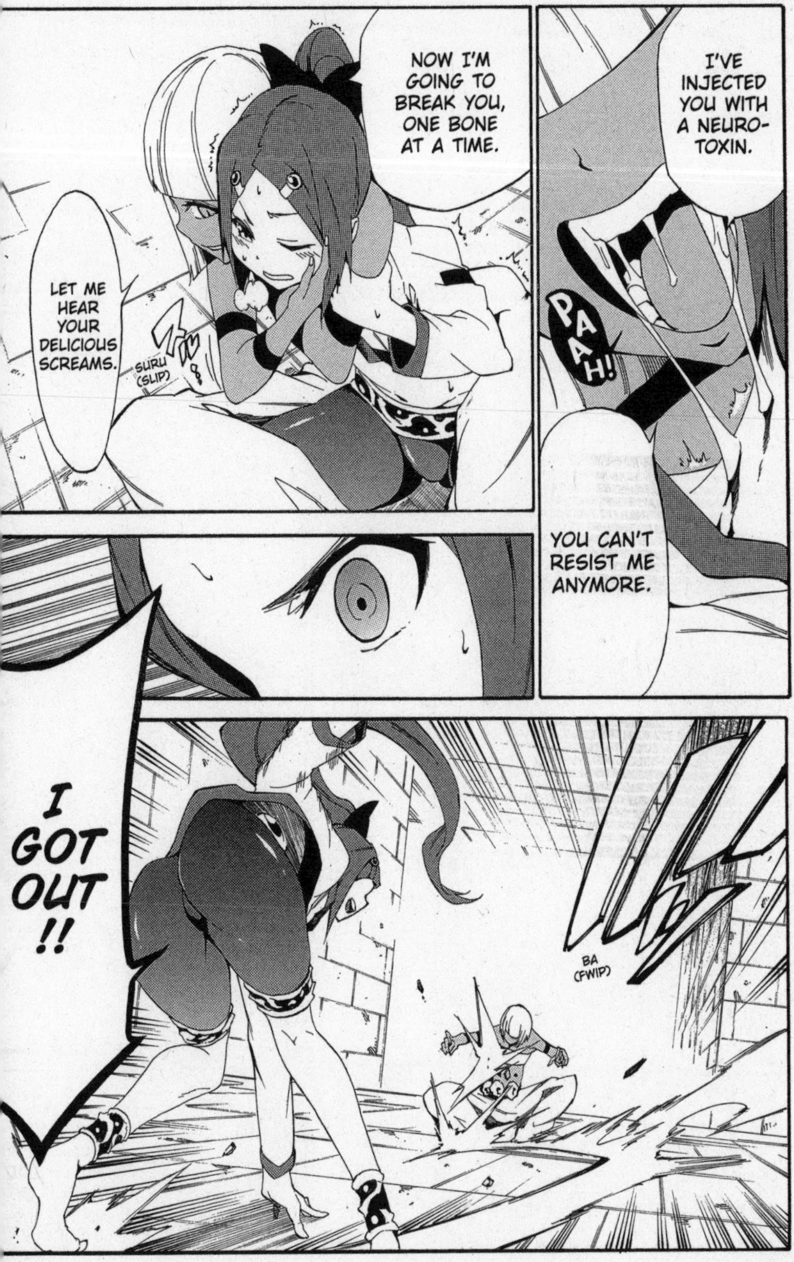

I'VE INJECTED YOU WITH A NEURO-TOXIN.
PAAH!
YOU CAN'T RESIST ME ANYMORE.
NOW I'M GOING TO BREAK YOU, ONE BONE AT A TIME.
LET ME HEAR YOUR DELICIOUS SCREAMS.
SURU (SLIP)
I GOT OUT!!
BA (FWIP)

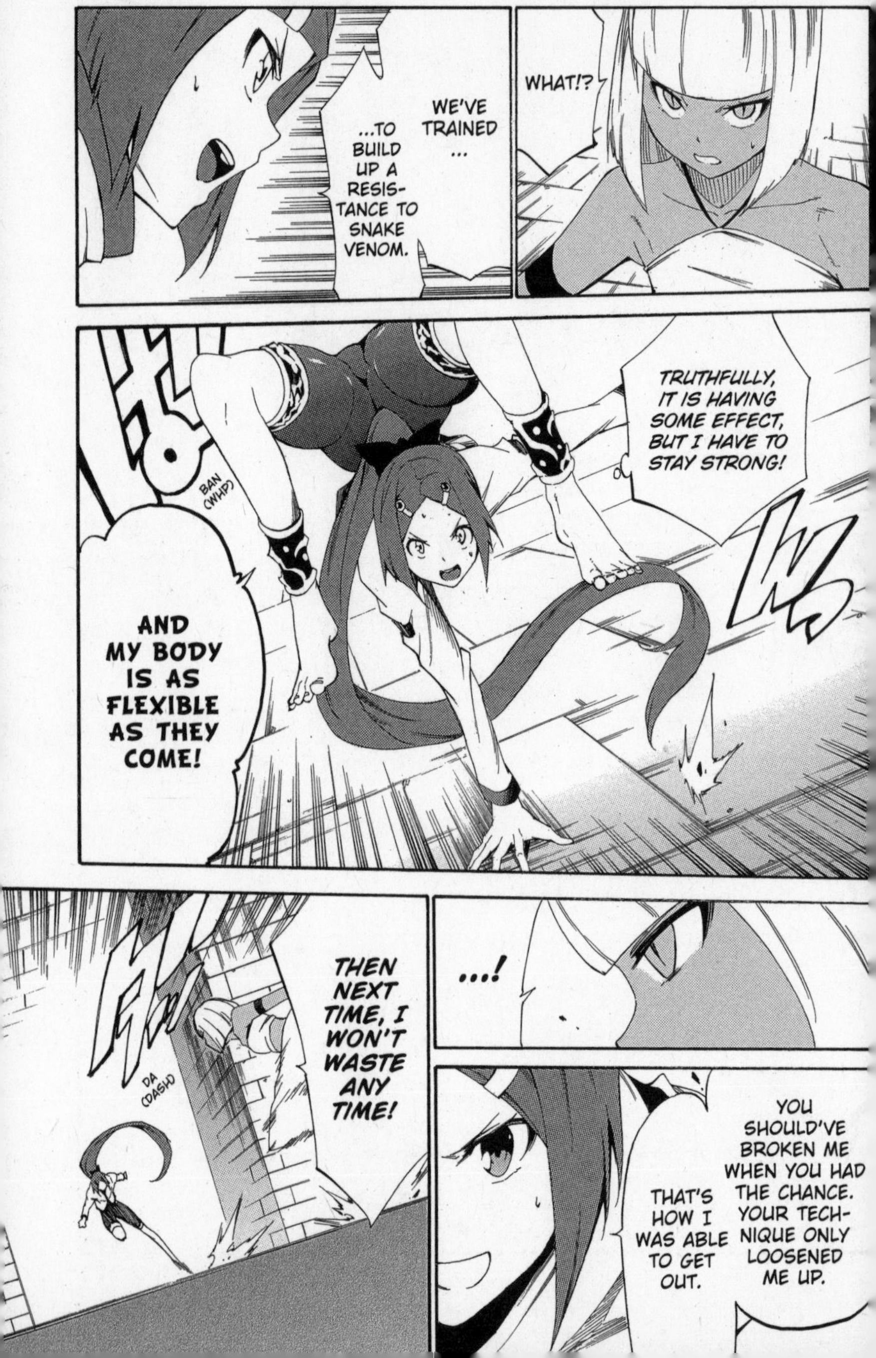
WHAT!?
WE'VE TRAINED ...
...TO BUILD UP A RESIS-TANCE TO SNAKE VENOM.
TRUTHFULLY, IT IS HAVING SOME EFFECT, BUT I HAVE TO STAY STRONG!
BAN (WHP)
AND MY BODY IS AS FLEXIBLE AS THEY COME!
...!
YOU SHOULD'VE BROKEN ME WHEN YOU HAD THE CHANCE. YOUR TECH-NIQUE ONLY LOOSENED ME UP.
THAT'S HOW I WAS ABLE TO GET OUT.
THEN NEXT TIME, I WON'T WASTE ANY TIME!
DA (DASH)

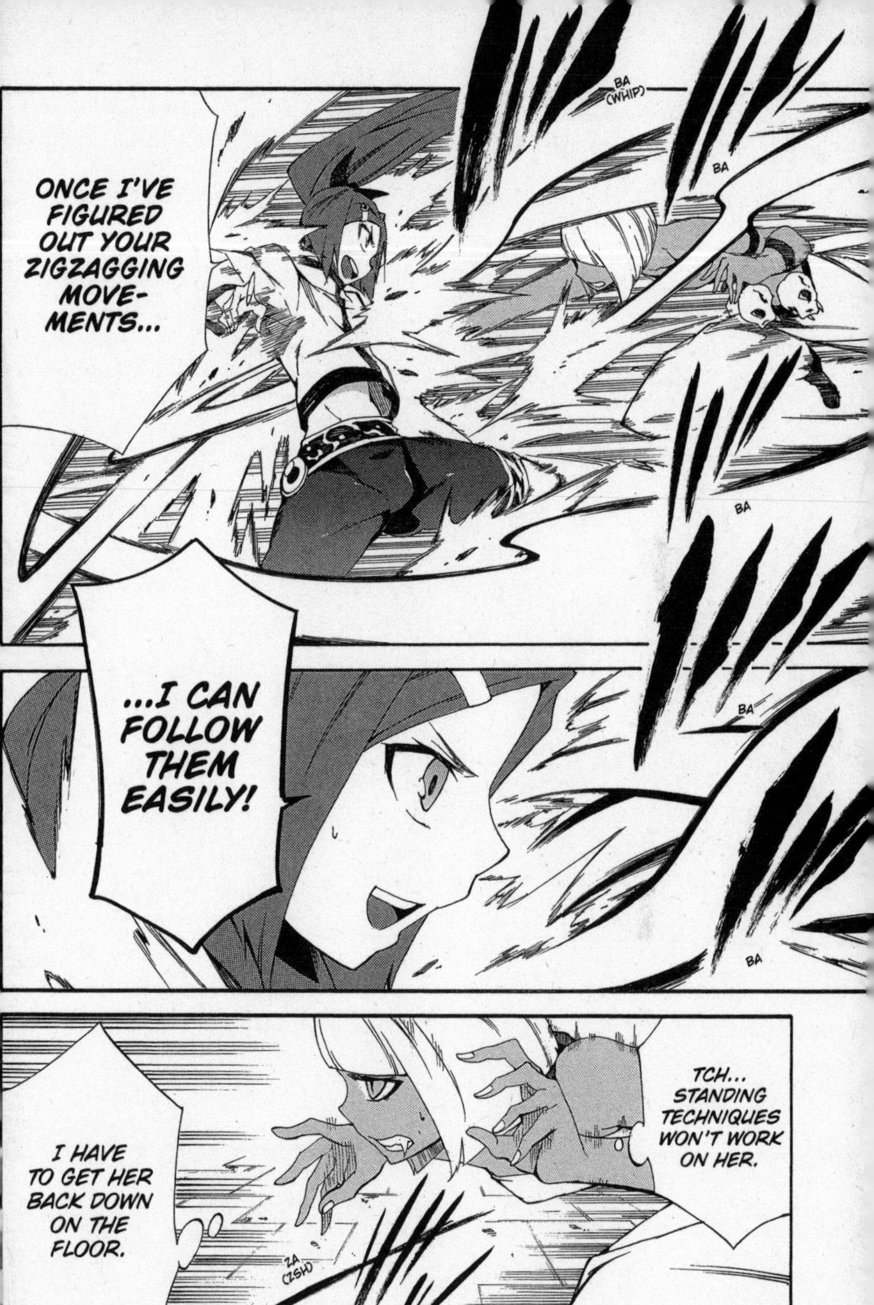
BA (WHIP)
BA
ONCE I'VE FIGURED OUT YOUR ZIGZAGGING MOVEMENTS...
BA
BA
...I CAN FOLLOW THEM EASILY!
BA
TCH... STANDING TECHNIQUES WON'T WORK ON HER.
ZA (ZSH)
I HAVE TO GET HER BACK DOWN ON THE FLOOR.

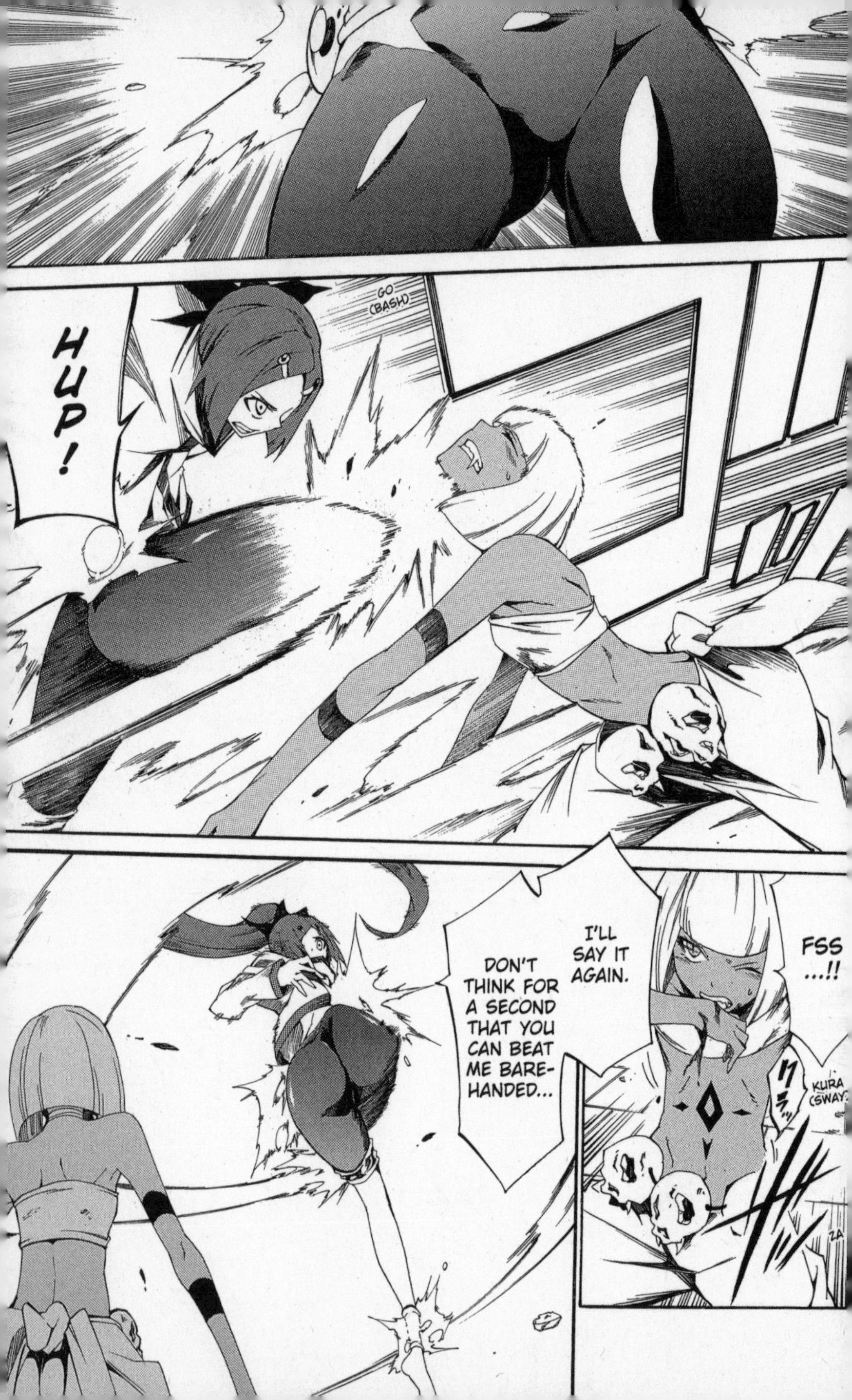
GO (BASH)
HUP!
FSS ...!!
KURA (SWAY)
ZA
I'LL SAY IT AGAIN.
DON'T THINK FOR A SECOND THAT YOU CAN BEAT ME BARE-HANDED...

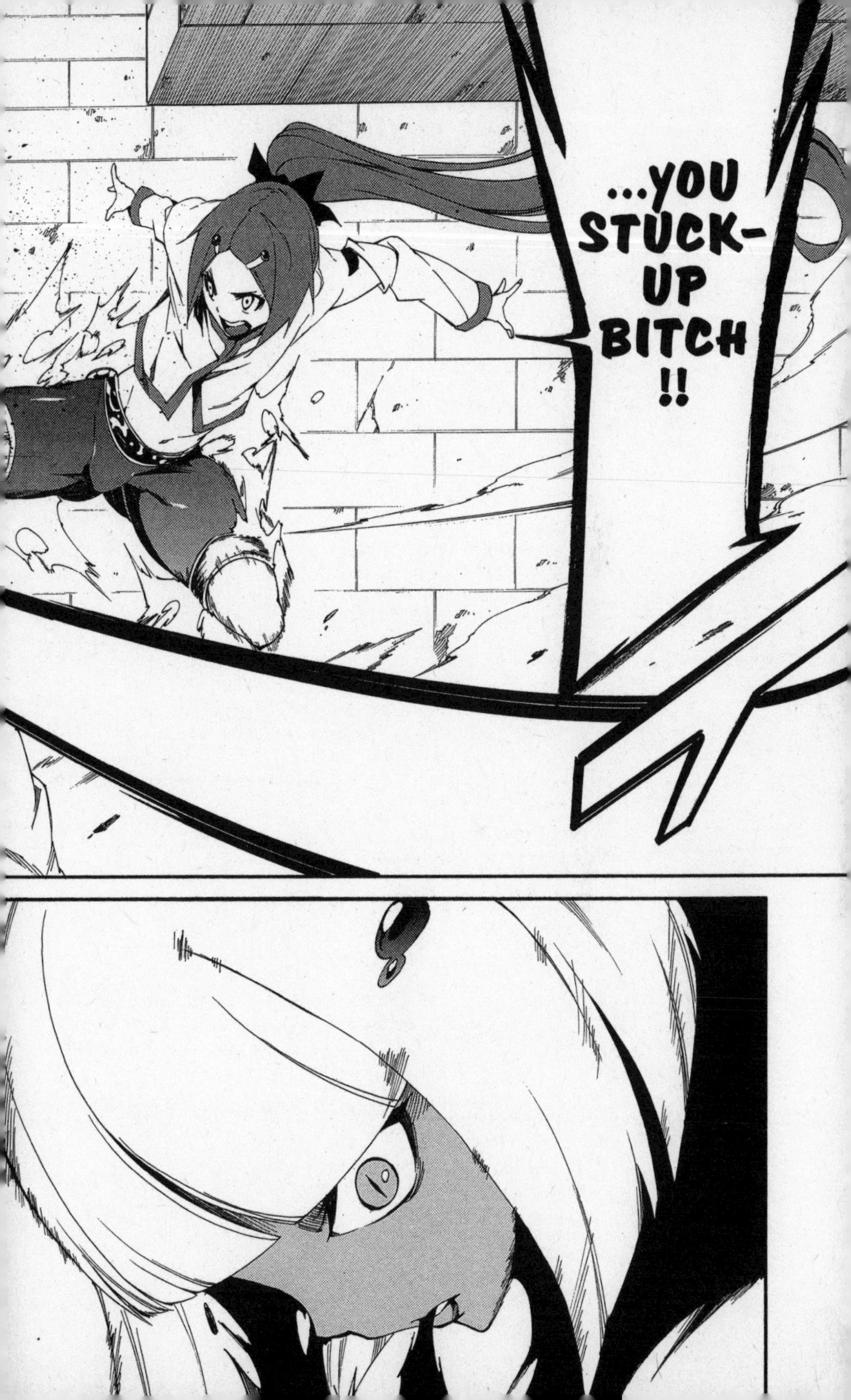
...YOU STUCK-UP BITCH!!

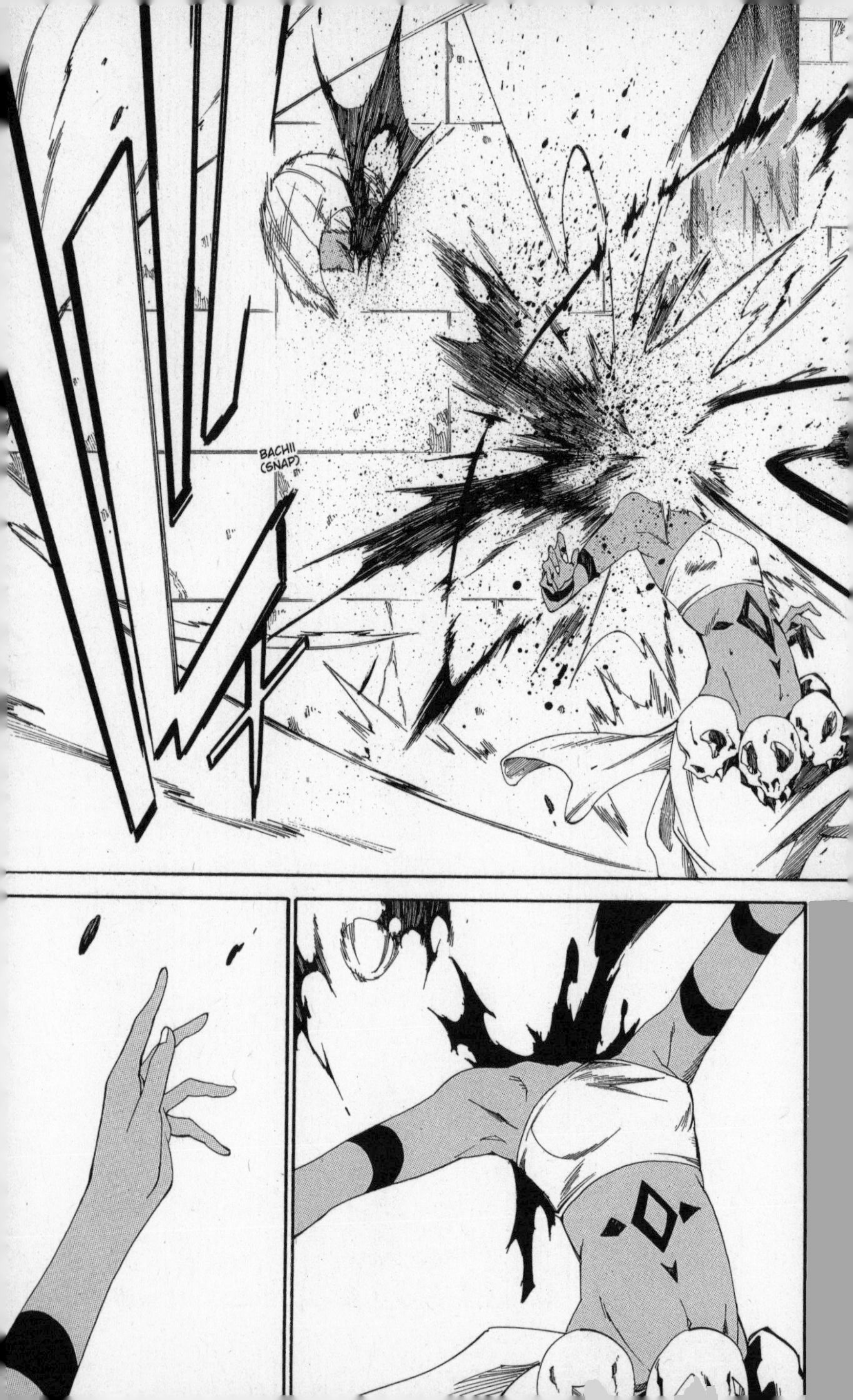
BACHII
(SNAP)

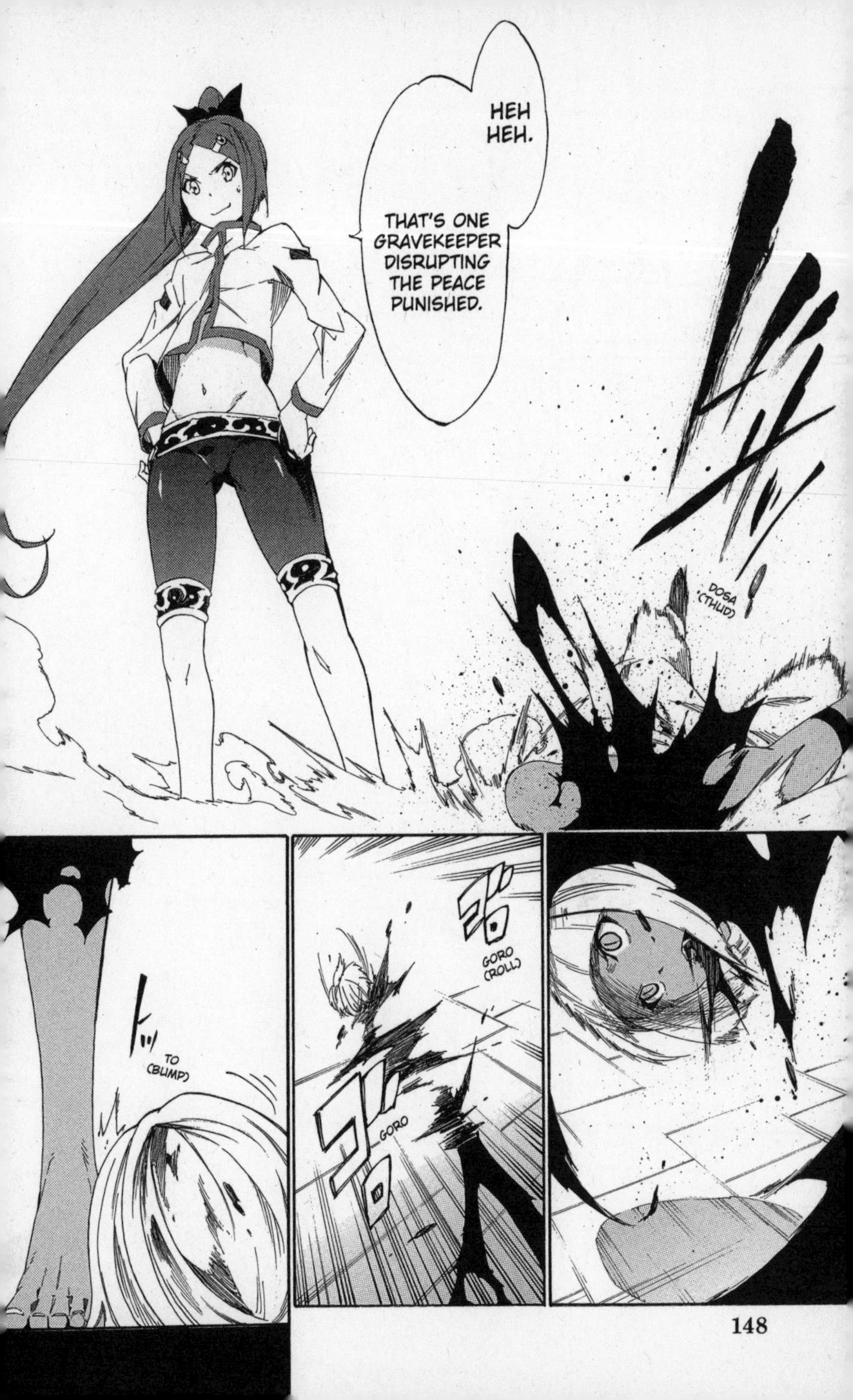
HEH HEH.
THAT'S ONE GRAVEKEEPER DISRUPTING THE PEACE PUNISHED.
DOSA (THUD)
GORO (ROLL)
GORO
TO (BUMP)

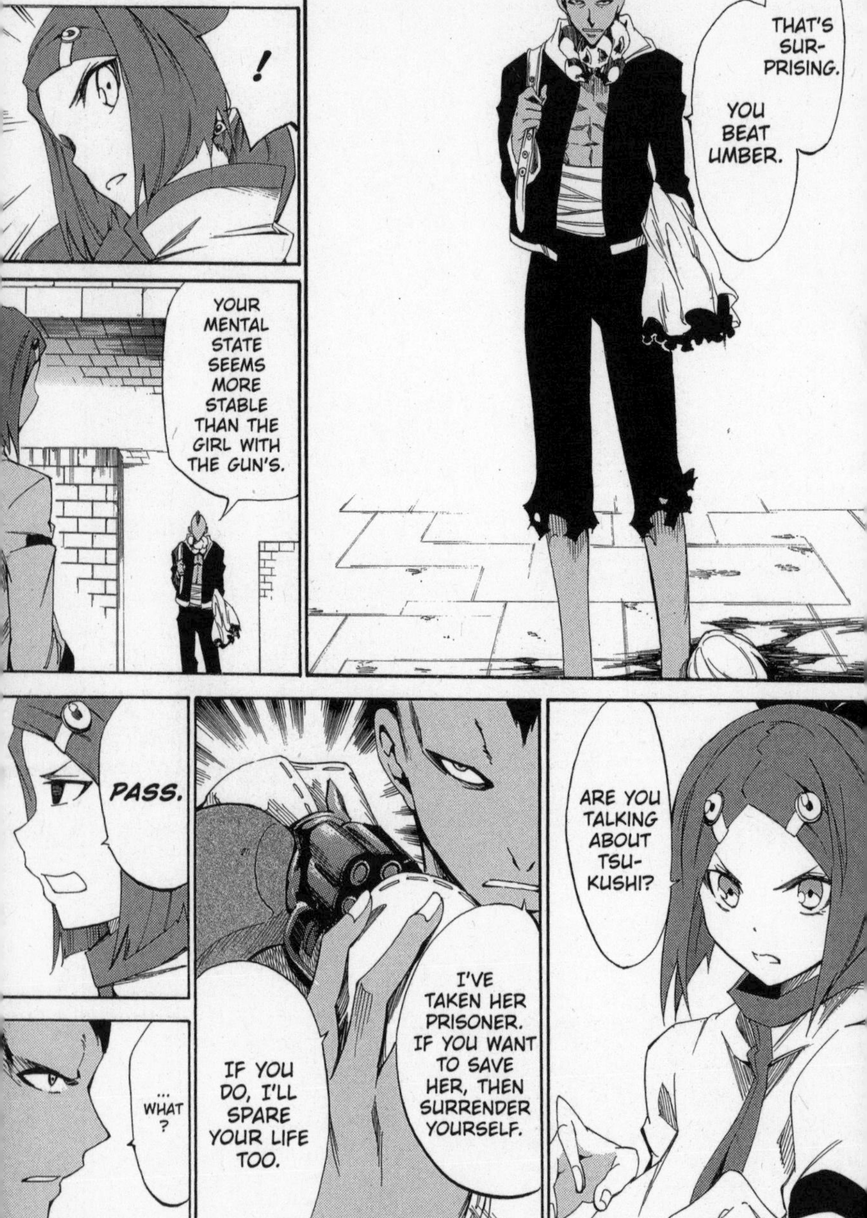
THAT'S SUR-PRISING.
YOU BEAT UMBER.
!
YOUR MENTAL STATE SEEMS MORE STABLE THAN THE GIRL WITH THE GUN'S.
ARE YOU TALKING ABOUT TSU-KUSHI?
I'VE TAKEN HER PRISONER. IF YOU WANT TO SAVE HER, THEN SURRENDER YOURSELF.
IF YOU DO, I'LL SPARE YOUR LIFE TOO.
PASS.
... WHAT?

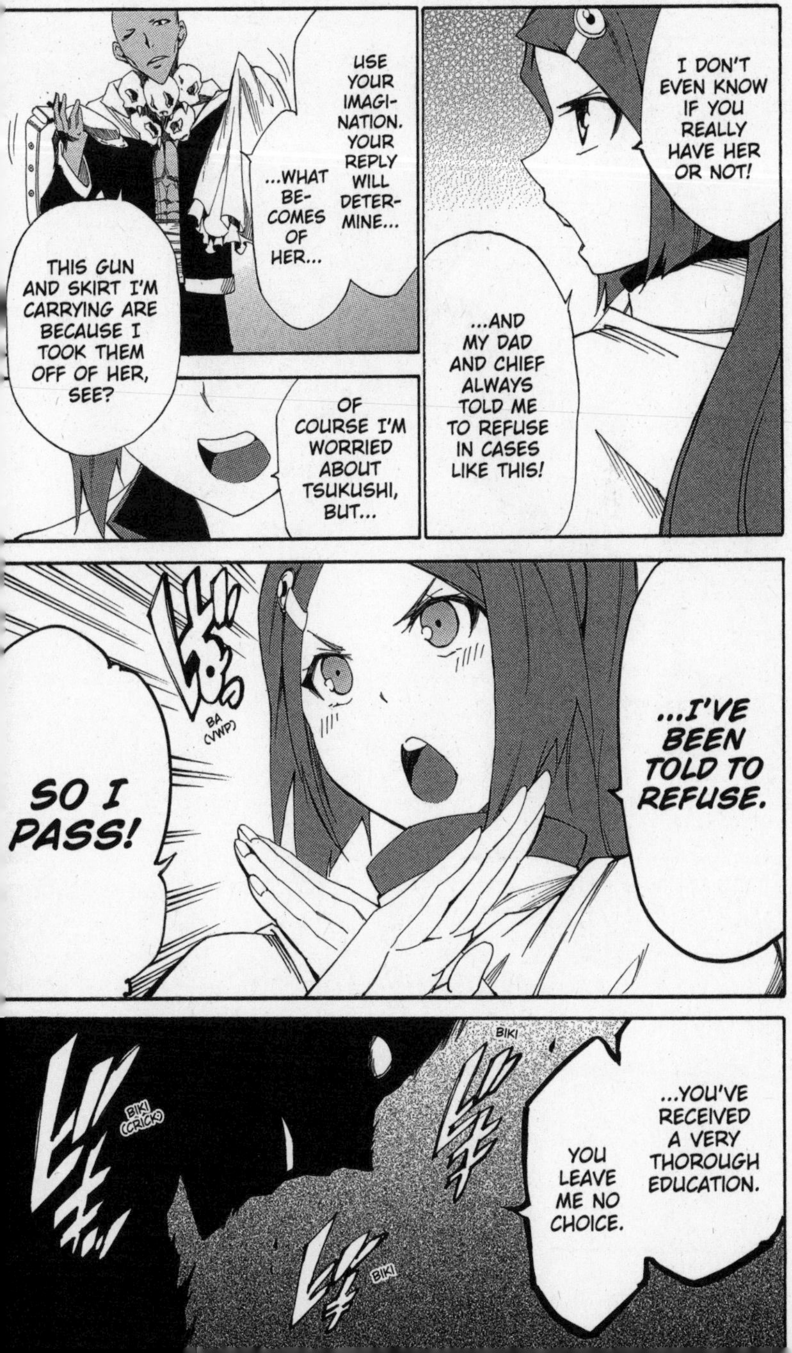
I DON'T EVEN KNOW IF YOU REALLY HAVE HER OR NOT!
...AND MY DAD AND CHIEF ALWAYS TOLD ME TO REFUSE IN CASES LIKE THIS!
USE YOUR IMAGINATION. YOUR REPLY WILL DETERMINE...
...WHAT BECOMES OF HER...
THIS GUN AND SKIRT I'M CARRYING ARE BECAUSE I TOOK THEM OFF OF HER, SEE?
OF COURSE I'M WORRIED ABOUT TSUKUSHI, BUT...
...I'VE BEEN TOLD TO REFUSE.
BA (VWP)
SO I PASS!
...YOU'VE RECEIVED A VERY THOROUGH EDUCATION.
YOU LEAVE ME NO CHOICE.
BIKI
BIKI (CRICK)
BIKI

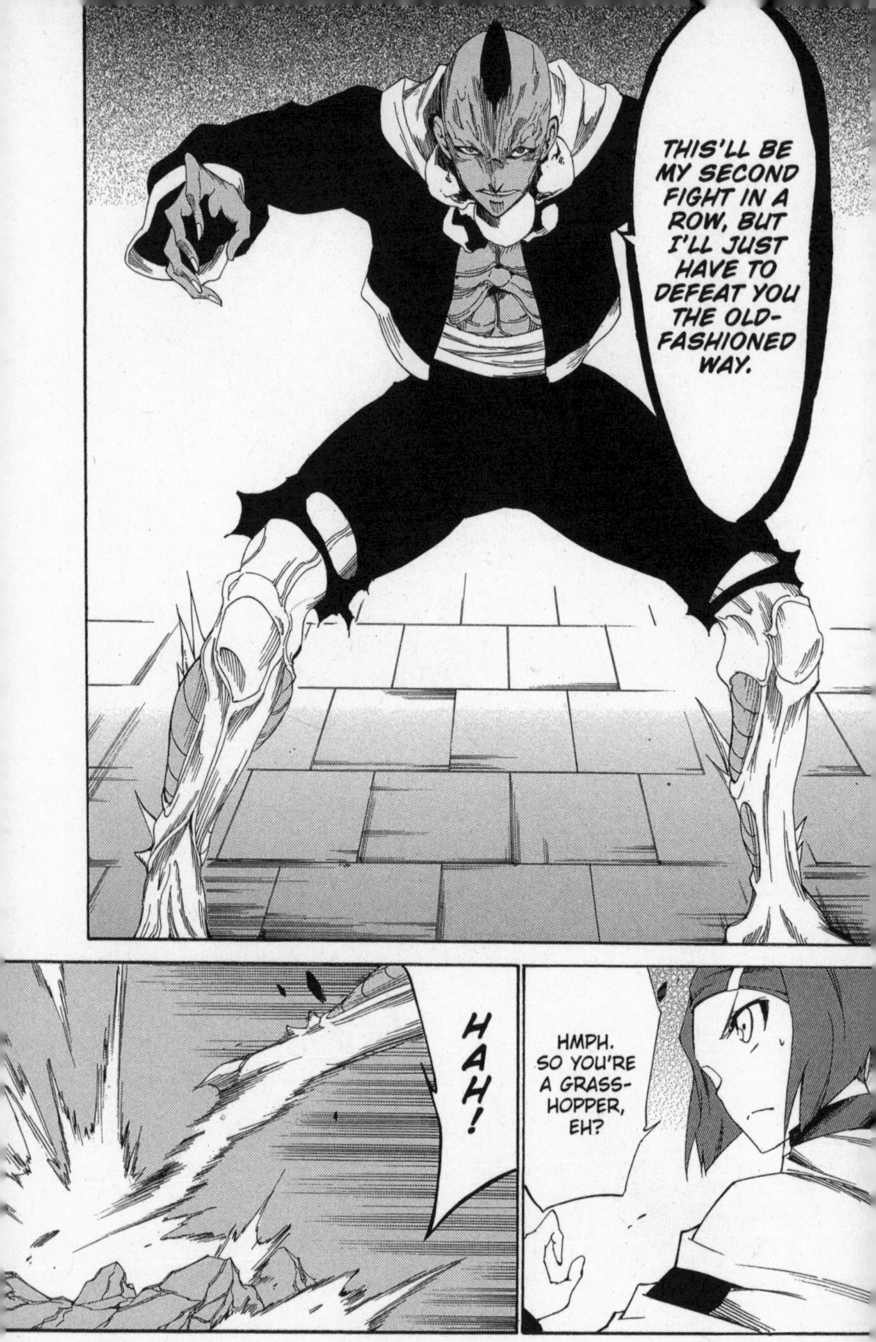
THIS'LL BE MY SECOND FIGHT IN A ROW, BUT I'LL JUST HAVE TO DEFEAT YOU THE OLD-FASHIONED WAY.
HMPH. SO YOU'RE A GRASS-HOPPER, EH?
HAH!

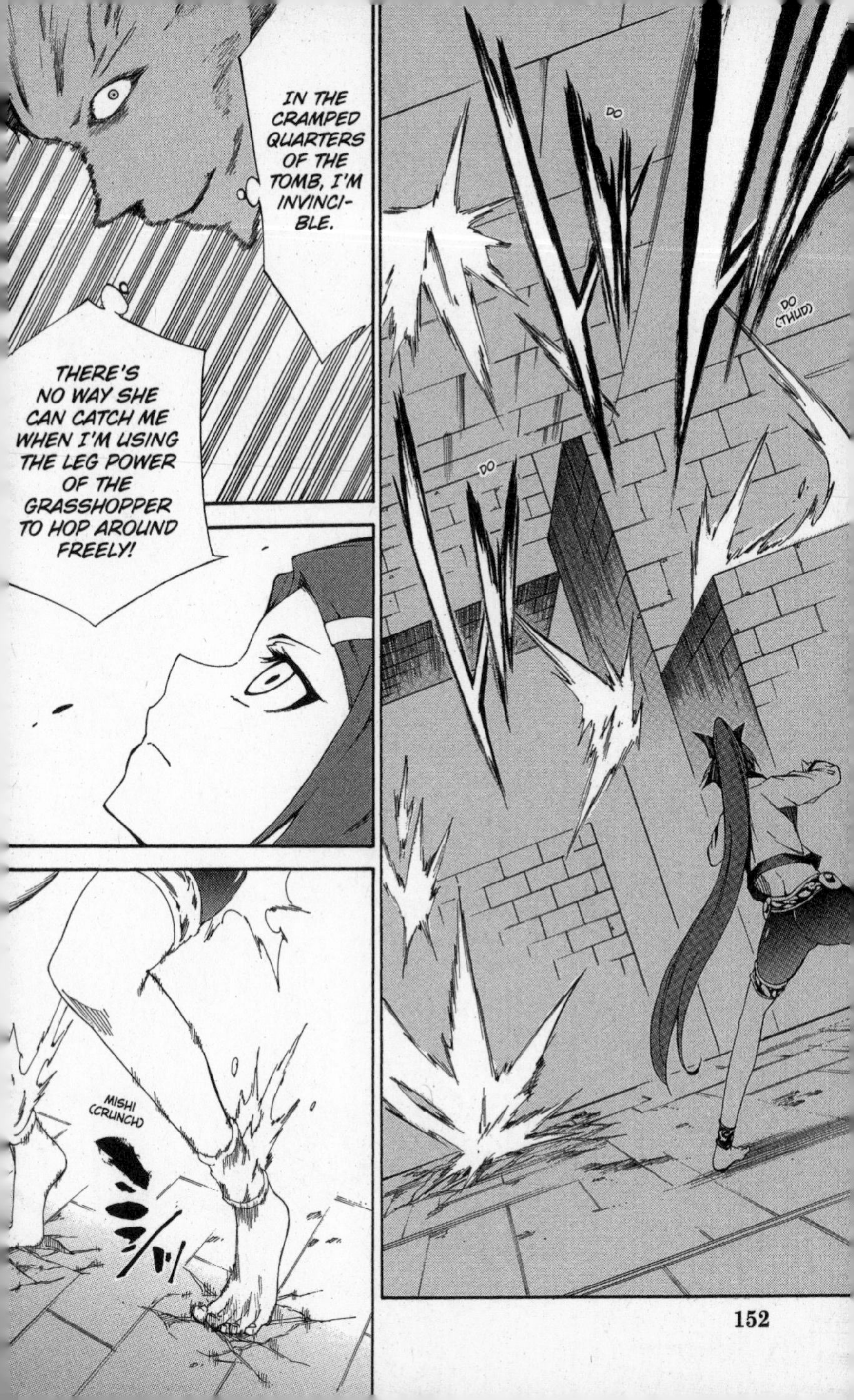
DO
DO (THUD)
DO
IN THE CRAMPED QUARTERS OF THE TOMB, I'M INVINCIBLE.
THERE'S NO WAY SHE CAN CATCH ME WHEN I'M USING THE LEG POWER OF THE GRASSHOPPER TO HOP AROUND FREELY!
MISHI (CRUNCH)

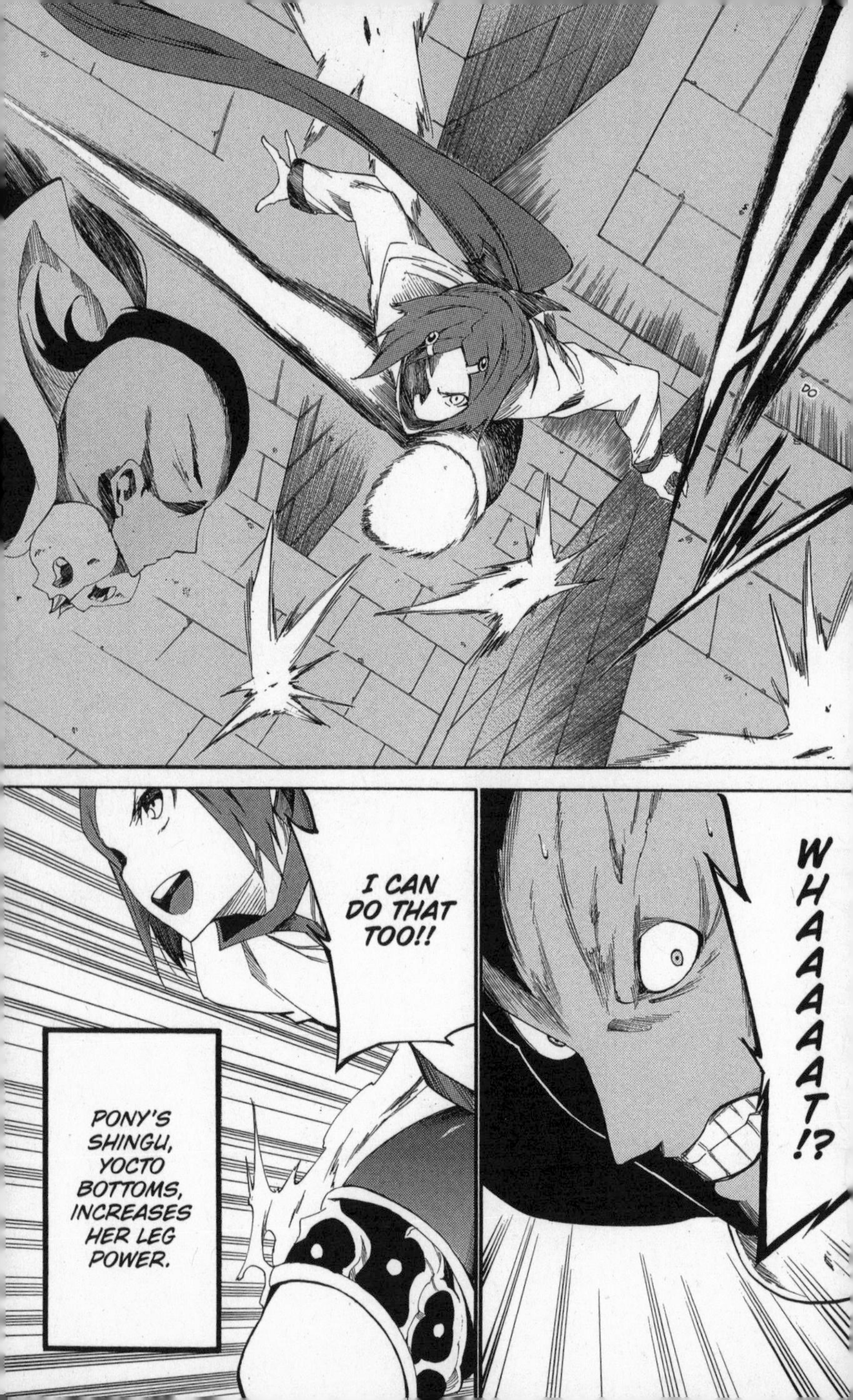
DO
WHAAAAAAT!?
I CAN DO THAT TOO!!
PONY'S SHINGU, YOCTO BOTTOMS, INCREASES HER LEG POWER.

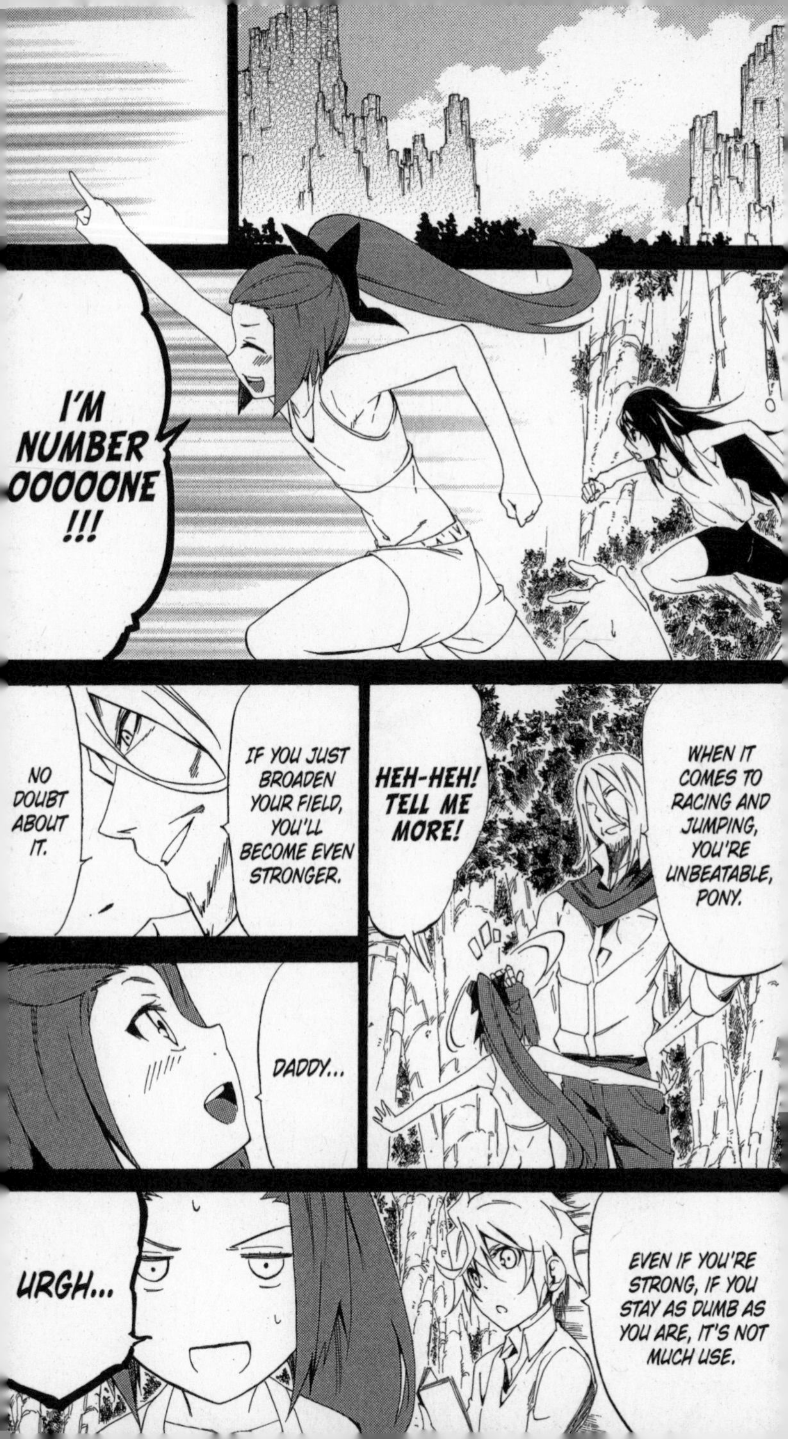

I'M NUMBER OOOOONE!!!
WHEN IT COMES TO RACING AND JUMPING, YOU'RE UNBEATABLE, PONY.
HEH-HEH! TELL ME MORE!
IF YOU JUST BROADEN YOUR FIELD, YOU'LL BECOME EVEN STRONGER.
NO DOUBT ABOUT IT.
DADDY...
EVEN IF YOU'RE STRONG, IF YOU STAY AS DUMB AS YOU ARE, IT'S NOT MUCH USE.
URGH...

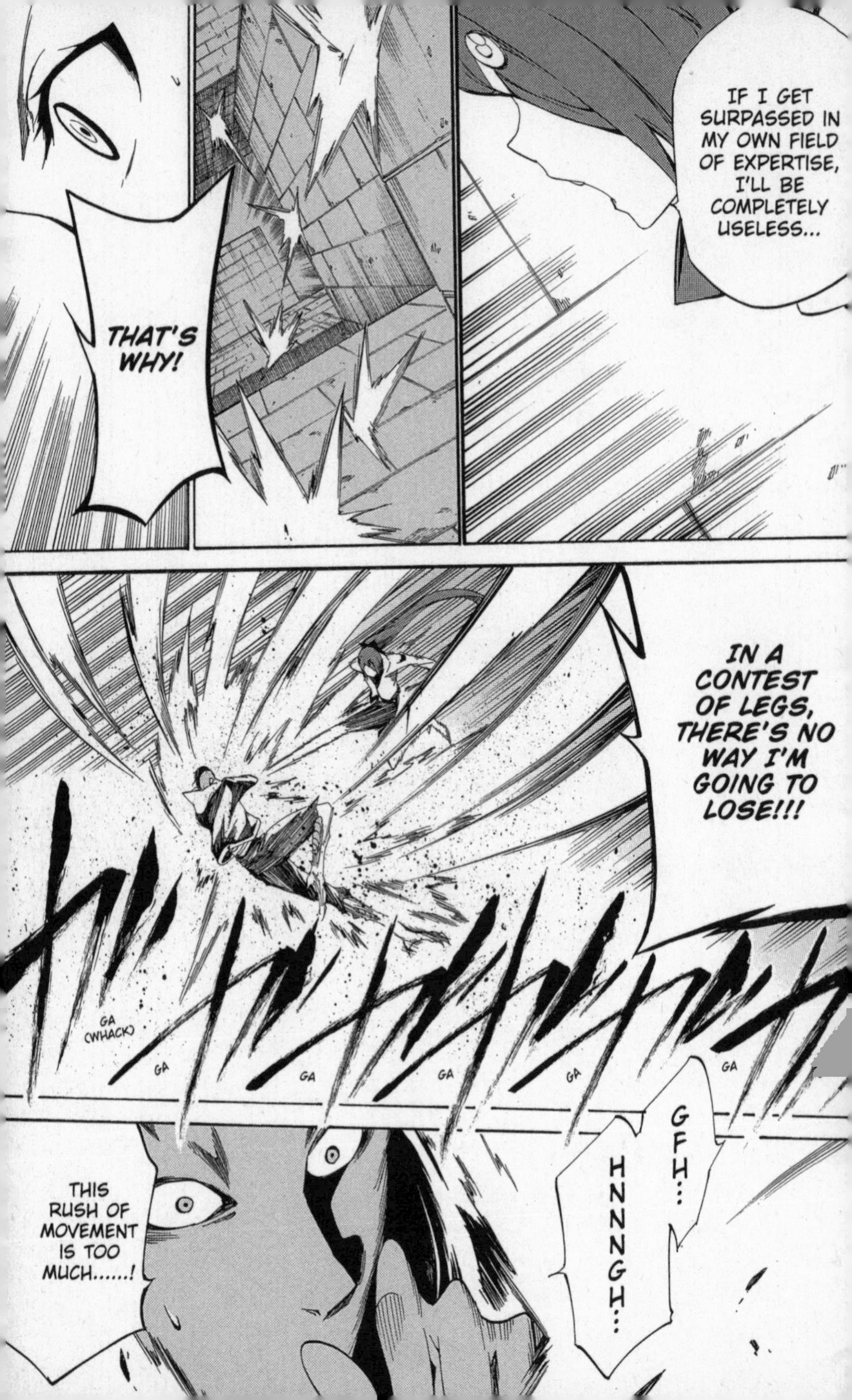
IF I GET SURPASSED IN MY OWN FIELD OF EXPERTISE, I'LL BE COMPLETELY USELESS...
THAT'S WHY!
IN A CONTEST OF LEGS, THERE'S NO WAY I'M GOING TO LOSE!!!
GA
GA
GA
GA
GA
GA (WHACK)
GFH...
HNNNGH...
THIS RUSH OF MOVEMENT IS TOO MUCH......!

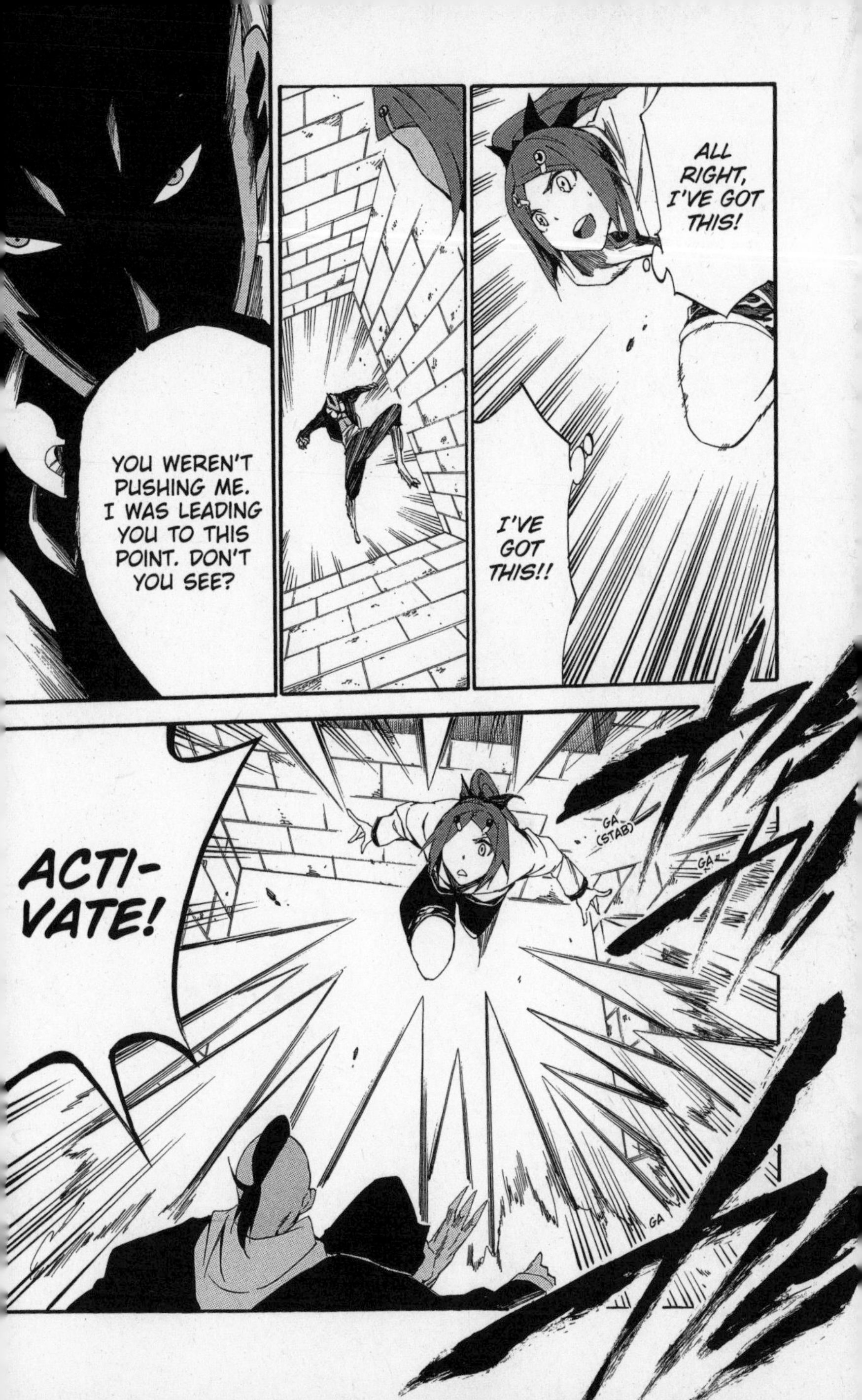
ALL RIGHT, I'VE GOT THIS!
I'VE GOT THIS!!
YOU WEREN'T PUSHING ME. I WAS LEADING YOU TO THIS POINT. DON'T YOU SEE?
GA (STAB)
GA
ACTI-VATE!
GA

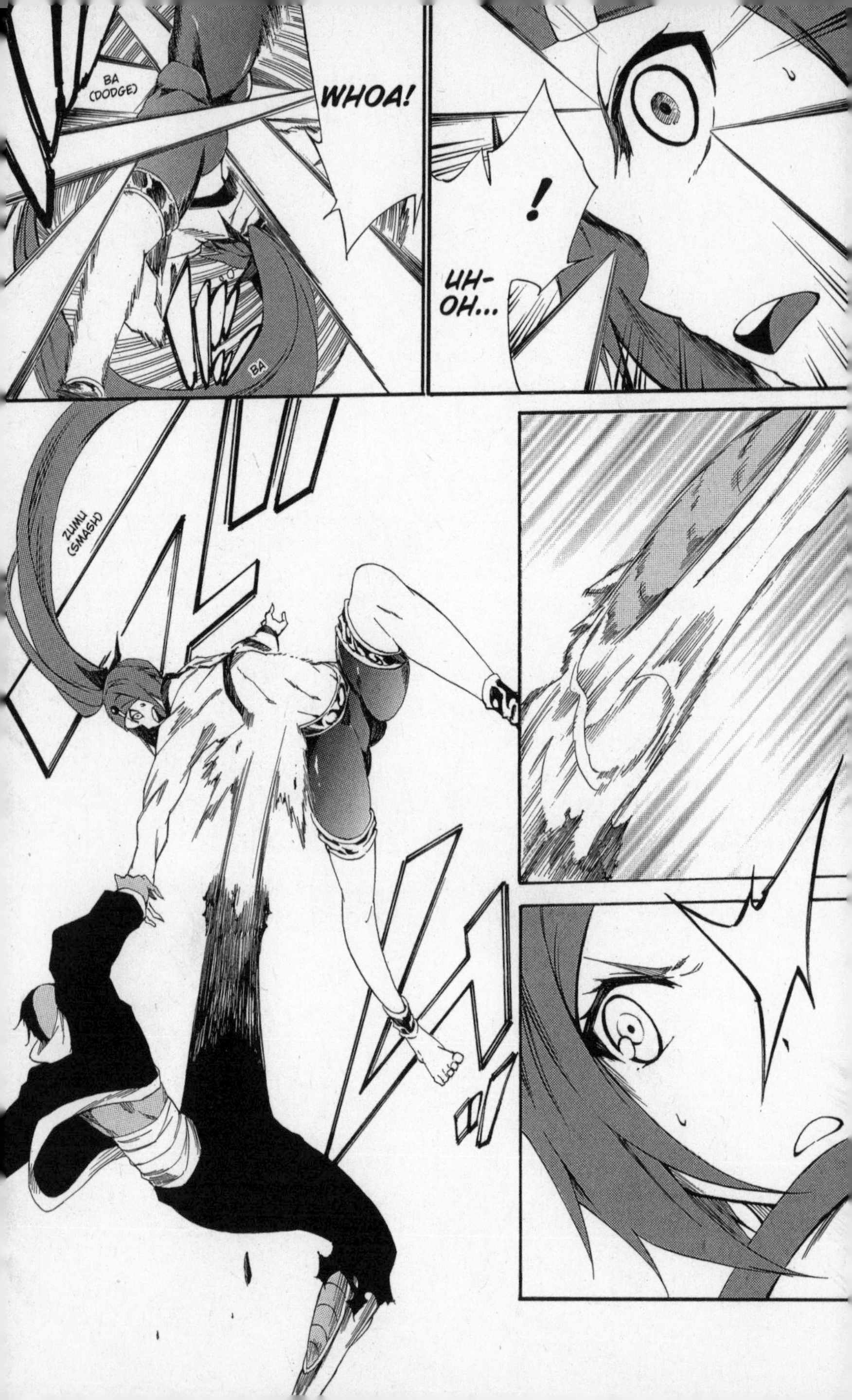
!
UH-OH...
WHOA!
BA (DODGE)
BA
ZUMU (SMASH)

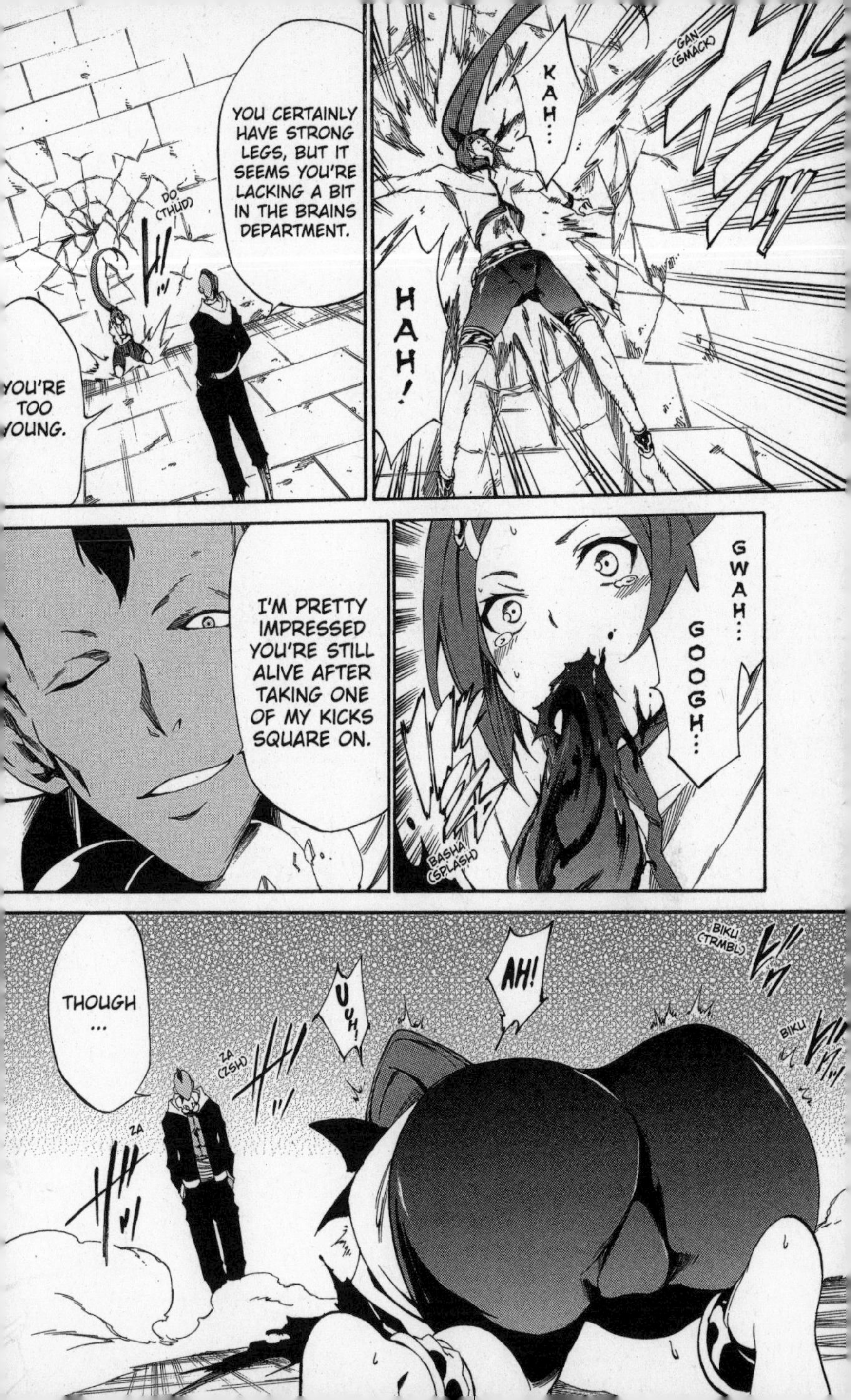
GAN (SMACK)
KAH...
HAH!
YOU CERTAINLY HAVE STRONG LEGS, BUT IT SEEMS YOU'RE LACKING A BIT IN THE BRAINS DEPARTMENT.
DO (THUD)
YOU'RE TOO YOUNG.
GWAH... GOOGH...
BASHA (SPLASH)
I'M PRETTY IMPRESSED YOU'RE STILL ALIVE AFTER TAKING ONE OF MY KICKS SQUARE ON.
BIKU (TRMBL)
BIKU
AH!
UUH!
ZA (ZSH)
ZA
THOUGH...

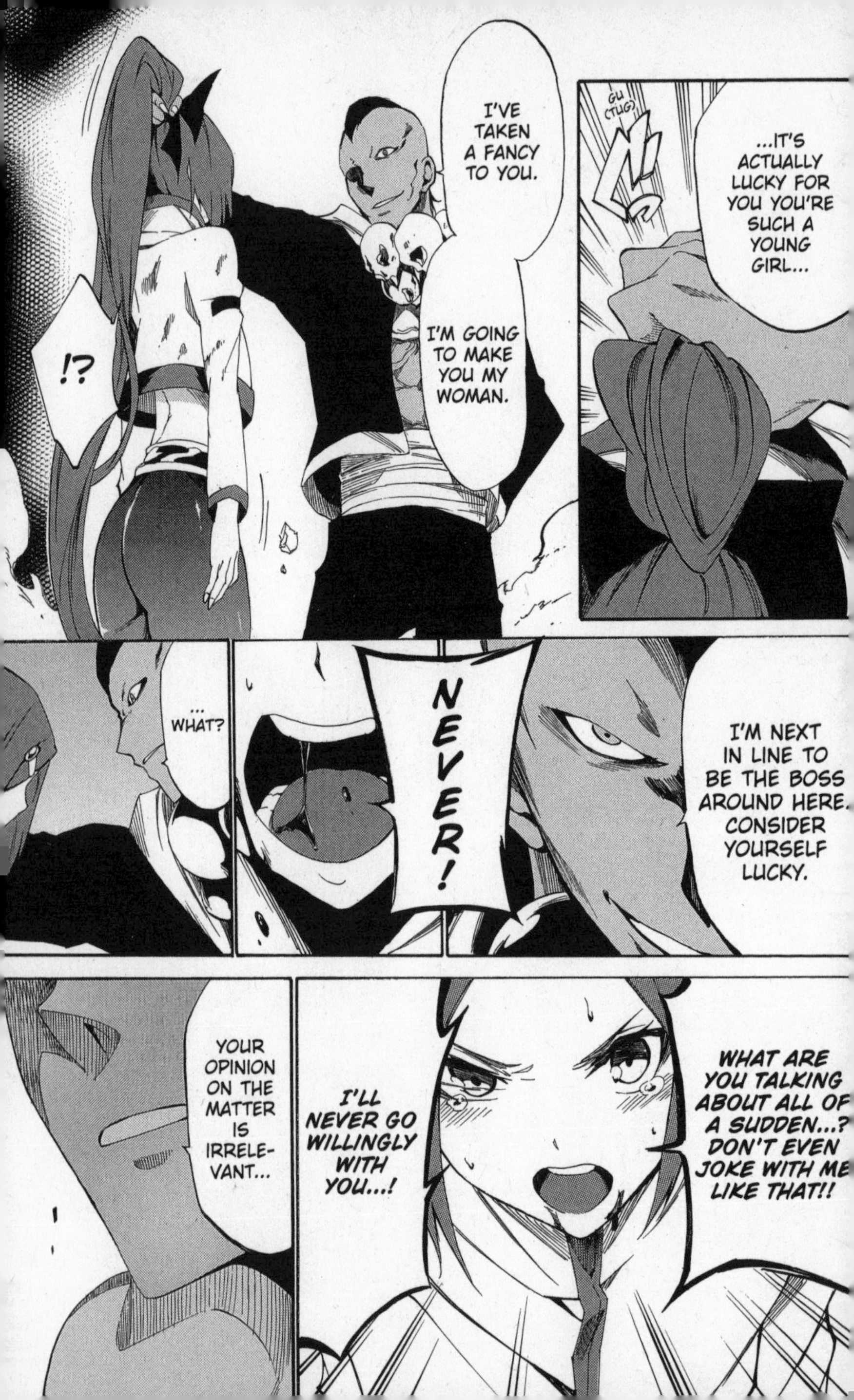
GU (TUG)
...IT'S ACTUALLY LUCKY FOR YOU YOU'RE SUCH A YOUNG GIRL...
I'VE TAKEN A FANCY TO YOU.
I'M GOING TO MAKE YOU MY WOMAN.
!?
I'M NEXT IN LINE TO BE THE BOSS AROUND HERE. CONSIDER YOURSELF LUCKY.
NEVER!
... WHAT?
WHAT ARE YOU TALKING ABOUT ALL OF A SUDDEN...? DON'T EVEN JOKE WITH ME LIKE THAT!!
I'LL NEVER GO WILLINGLY WITH YOU...!
YOUR OPINION ON THE MATTER IS IRRELEVANT...

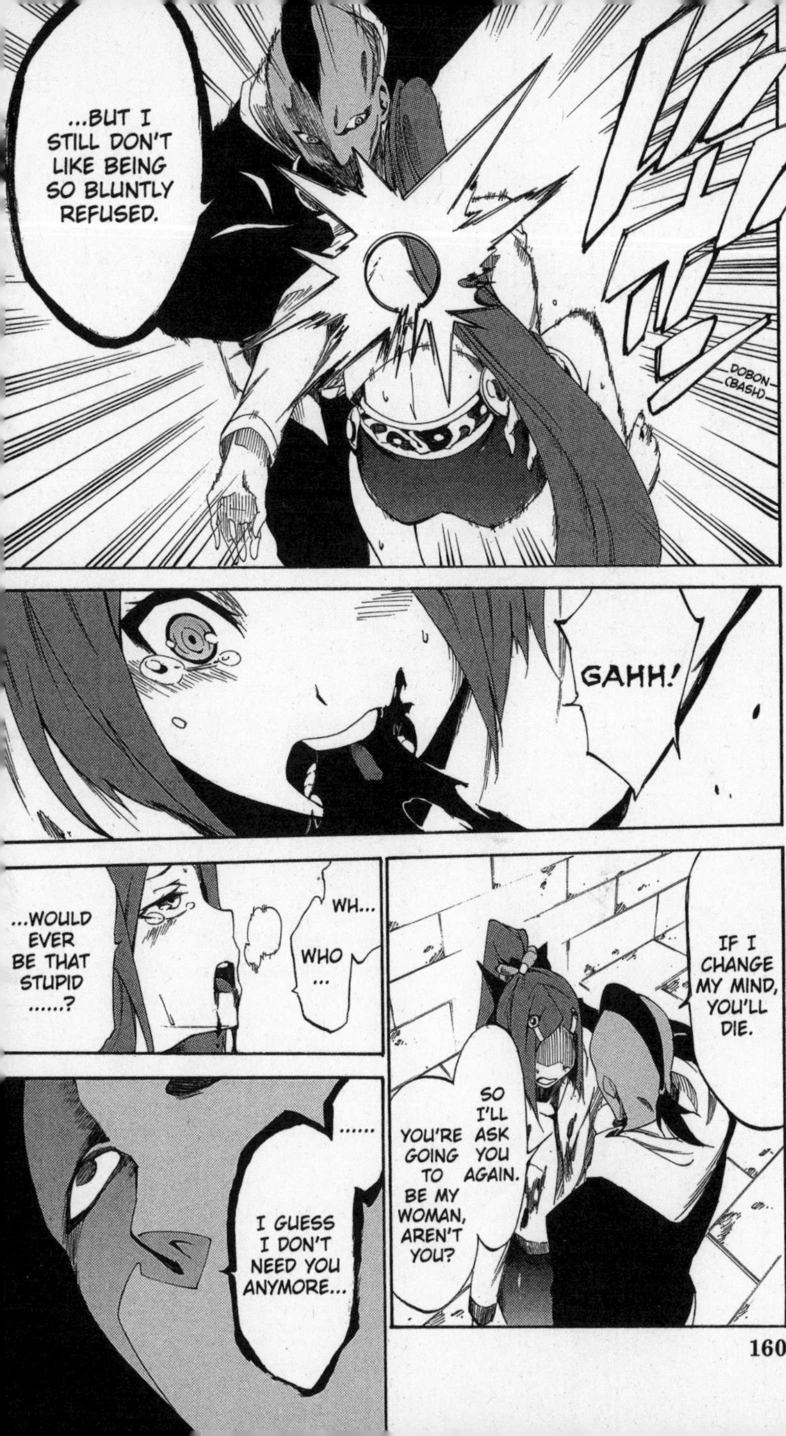
...BUT I STILL DON'T LIKE BEING SO BLUNTLY REFUSED.
DOBON (BASH)
GAHH!
IF I CHANGE MY MIND, YOU'LL DIE.
SO I'LL ASK YOU AGAIN.
YOU'RE GOING TO BE MY WOMAN, AREN'T YOU?
WH... WHO ...
...WOULD EVER BE THAT STUPID ......?
......
I GUESS I DON'T NEED YOU ANYMORE...

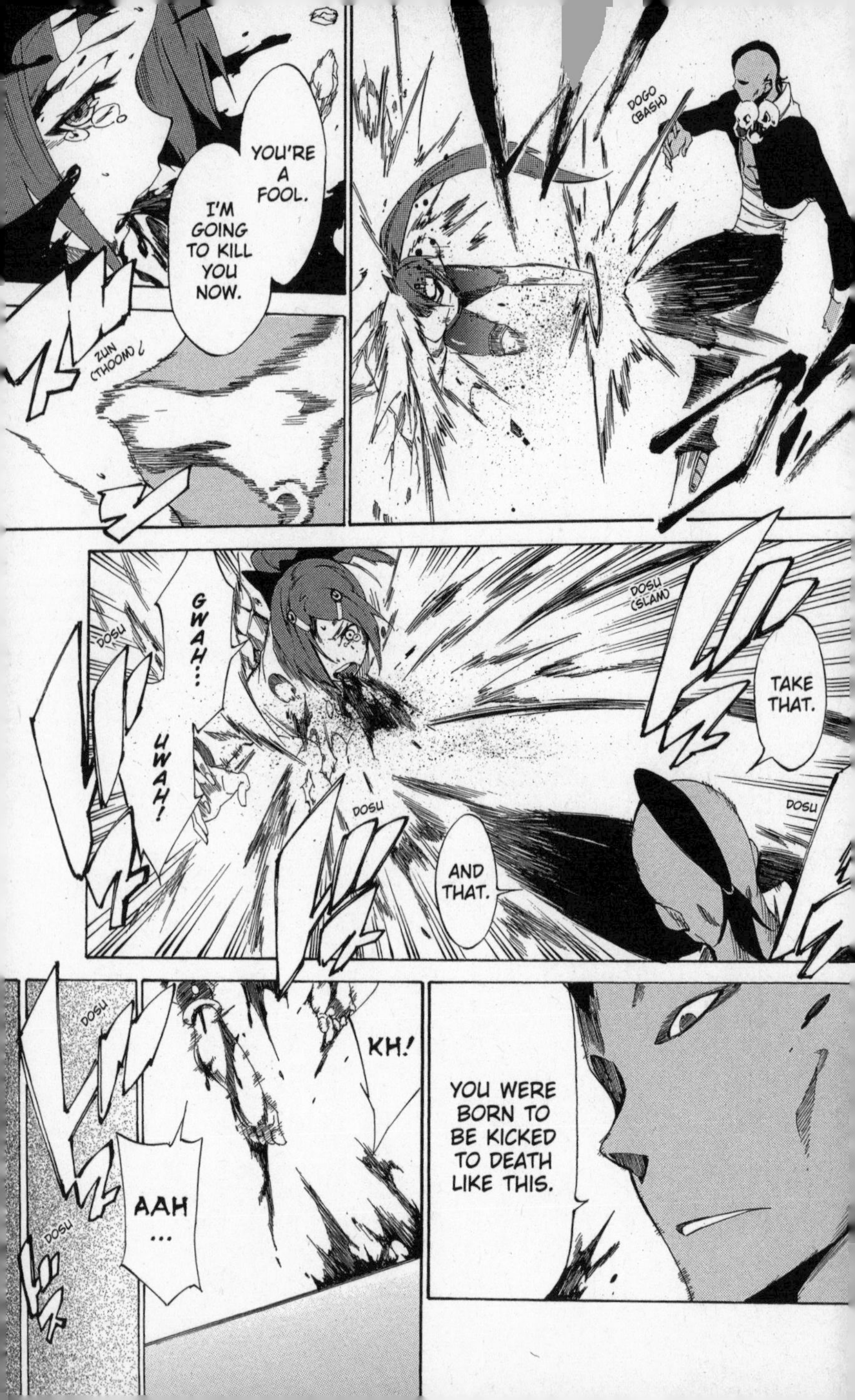
DOGO (BASH)
YOU'RE A FOOL.
I'M GOING TO KILL YOU NOW.
ZUN (THOOM)
DOSU (SLAM)
TAKE THAT.
DOSU
AND THAT.
DOSU
GWAH...
DOSU
UWAH!
YOU WERE BORN TO BE KICKED TO DEATH LIKE THIS.
KH!
DOSU
AAH ...
DOSU

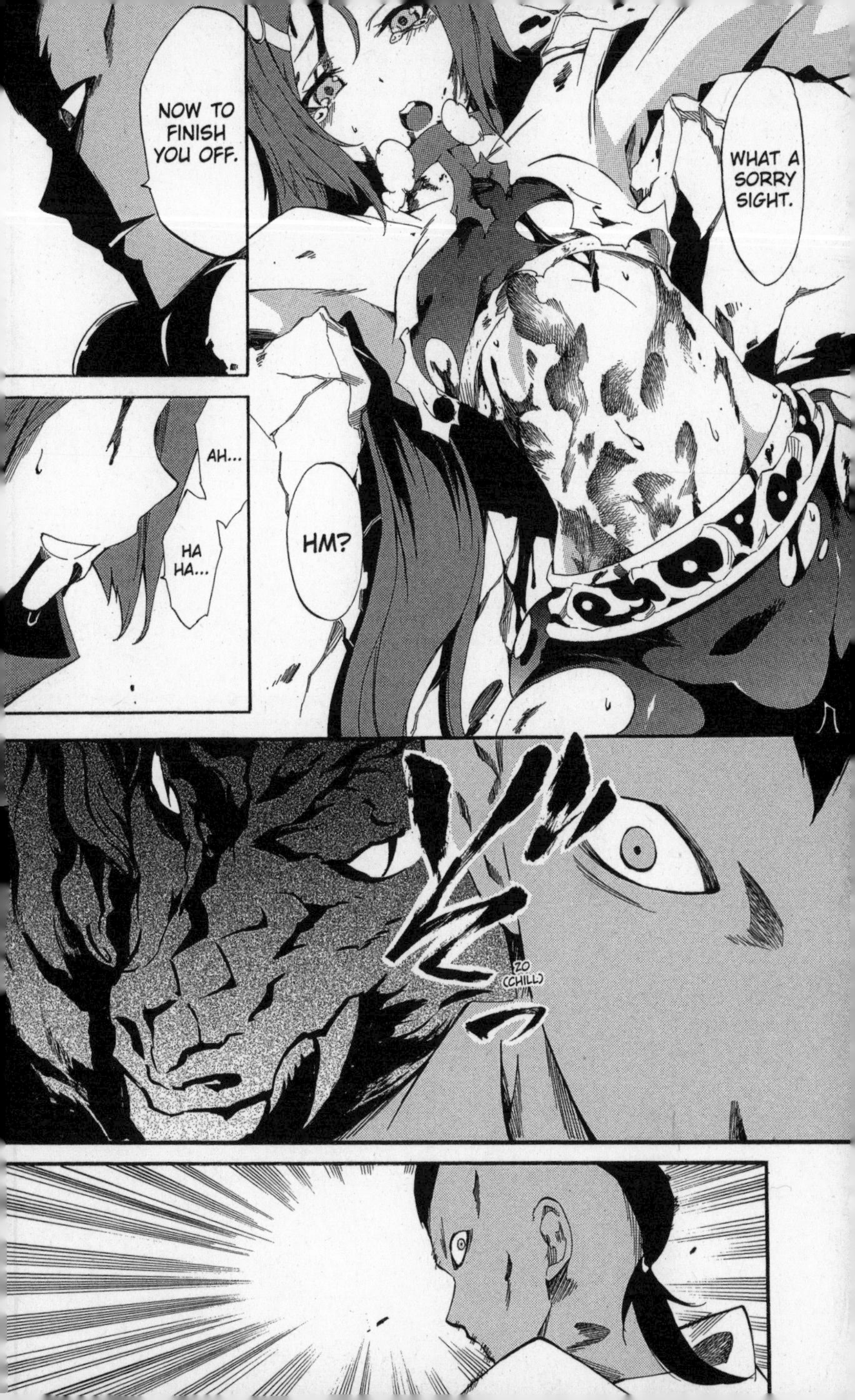
WHAT A SORRY SIGHT.
HM?
NOW TO FINISH YOU OFF.
AH...
HA HA...
ZO (CHILL)

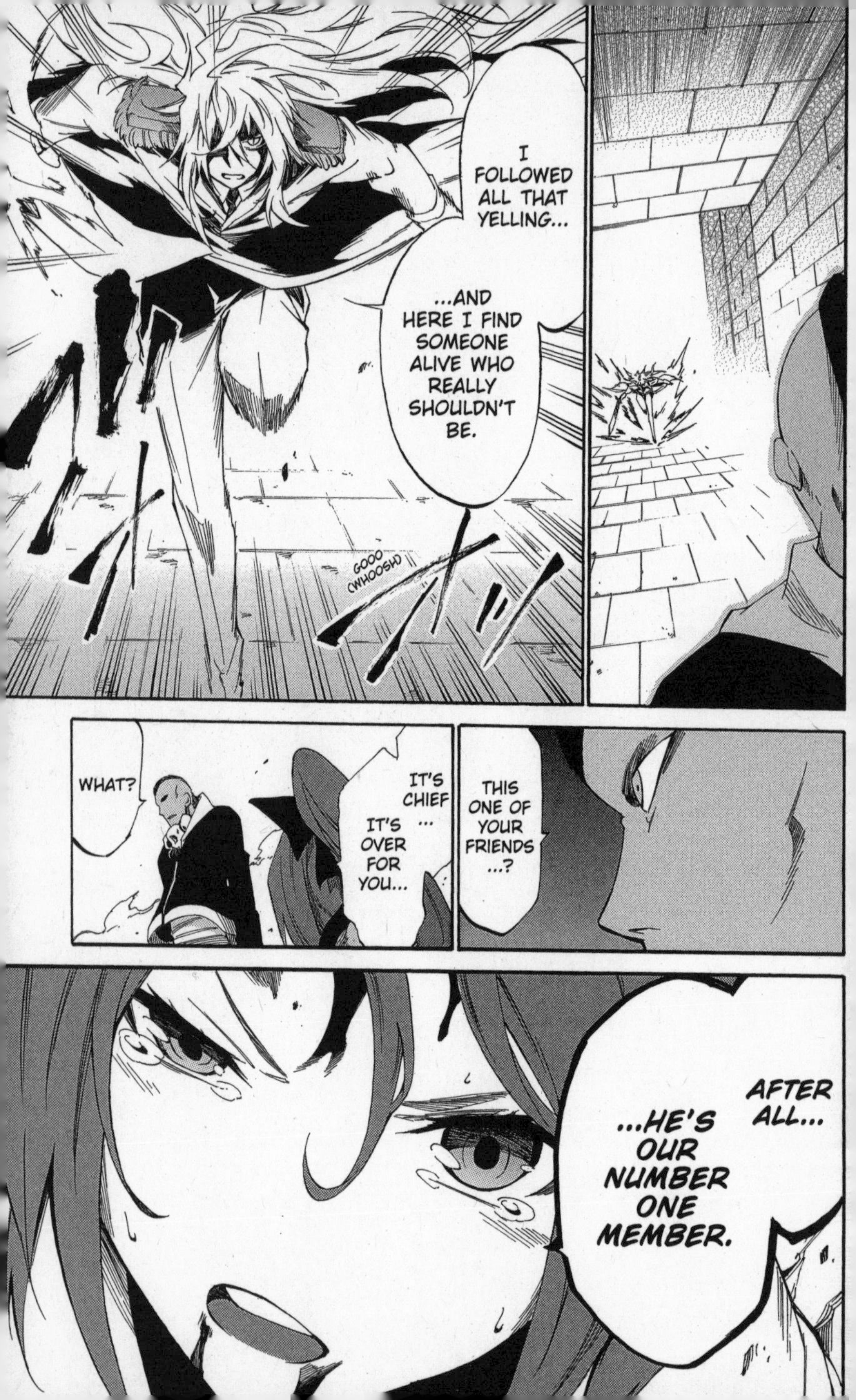
I FOLLOWED ALL THAT YELLING...
...AND HERE I FIND SOMEONE ALIVE WHO REALLY SHOULDN'T BE.
GOOO (WHOOSH)
THIS ONE OF YOUR FRIENDS ...?
IT'S CHIEF ...
IT'S OVER FOR YOU...
WHAT?
AFTER ALL...
...HE'S OUR NUMBER ONE MEMBER.

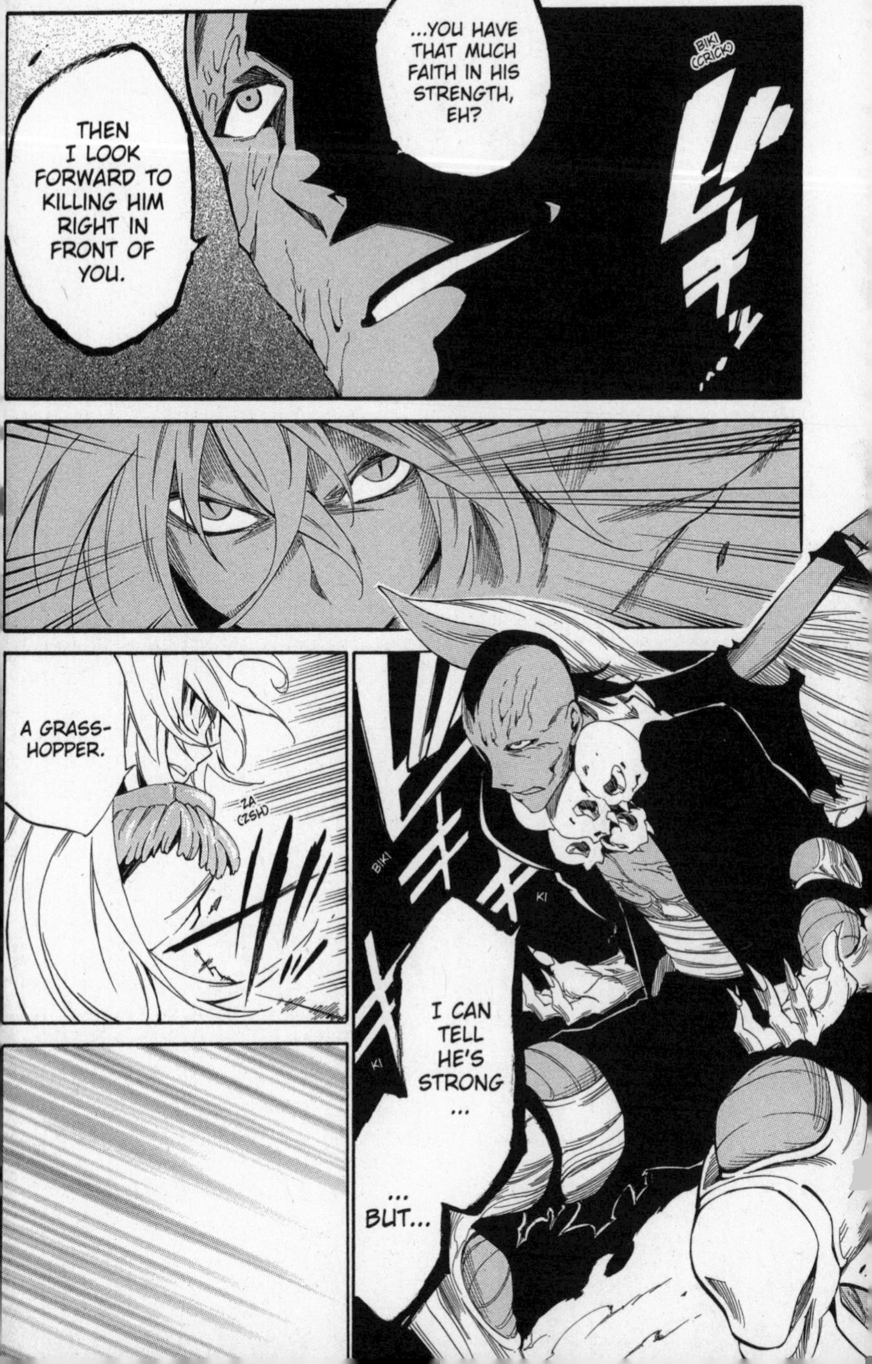
BIKI (CRICK)
...YOU HAVE THAT MUCH FAITH IN HIS STRENGTH, EH?
THEN I LOOK FORWARD TO KILLING HIM RIGHT IN FRONT OF YOU.
BIKI
KI
KI
I CAN TELL HE'S STRONG ...
... BUT...
A GRASS-HOPPER.
ZA (ZSH)

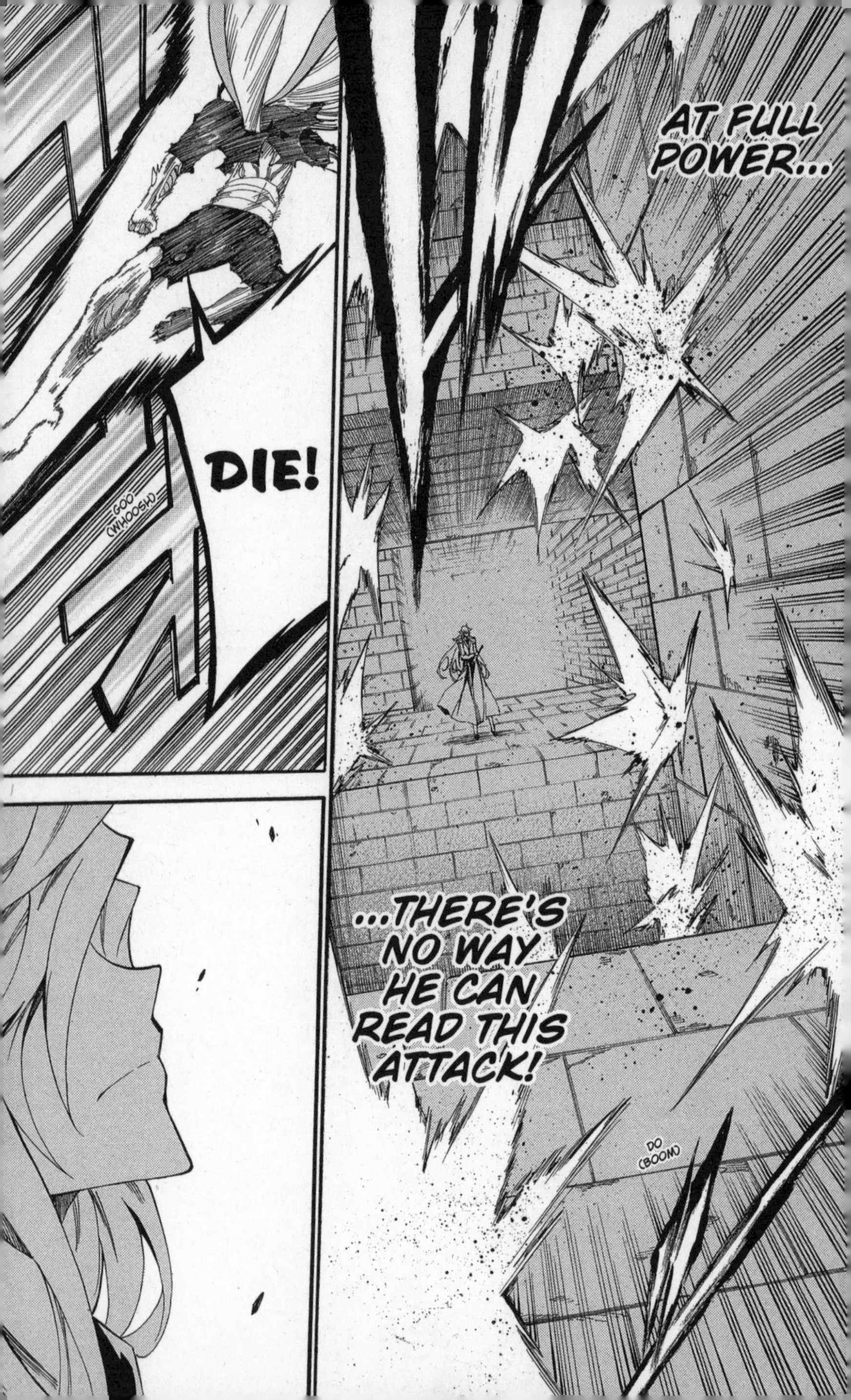
AT FULL POWER...
...THERE'S NO WAY HE CAN READ THIS ATTACK!
DO (BOOM)
DIE!
GOO (WHOOSH)

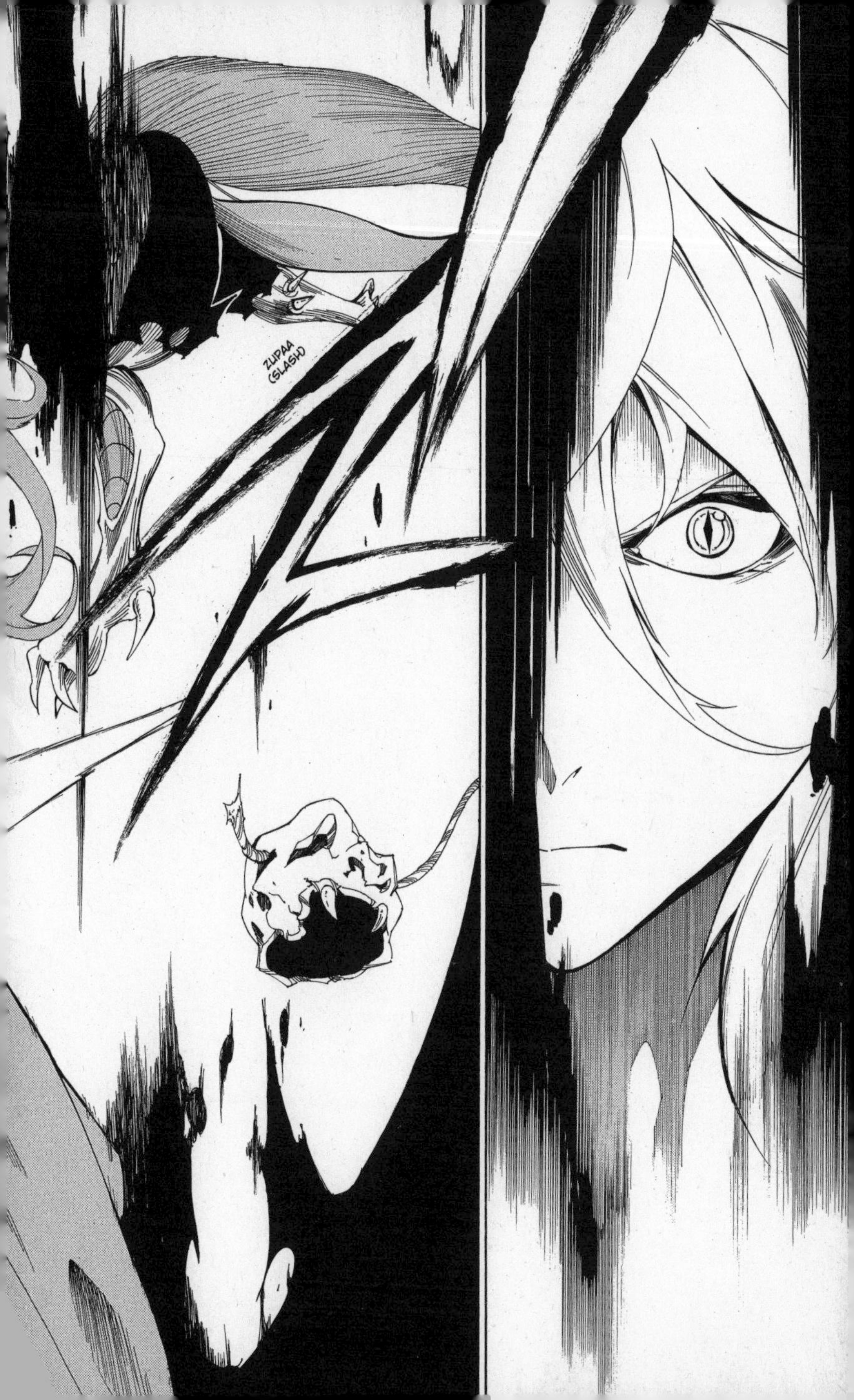
ZUPAA
(SLASH)

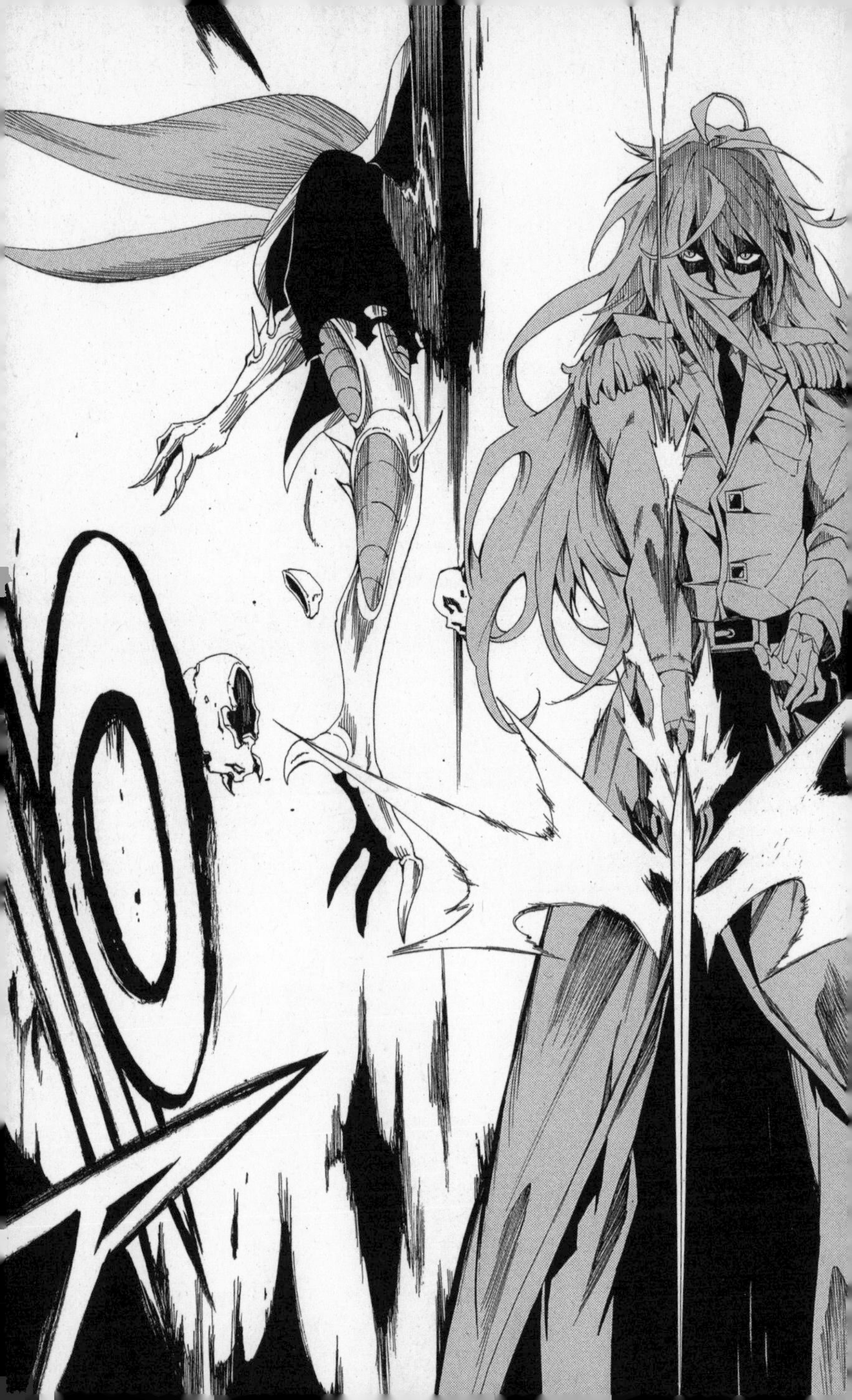

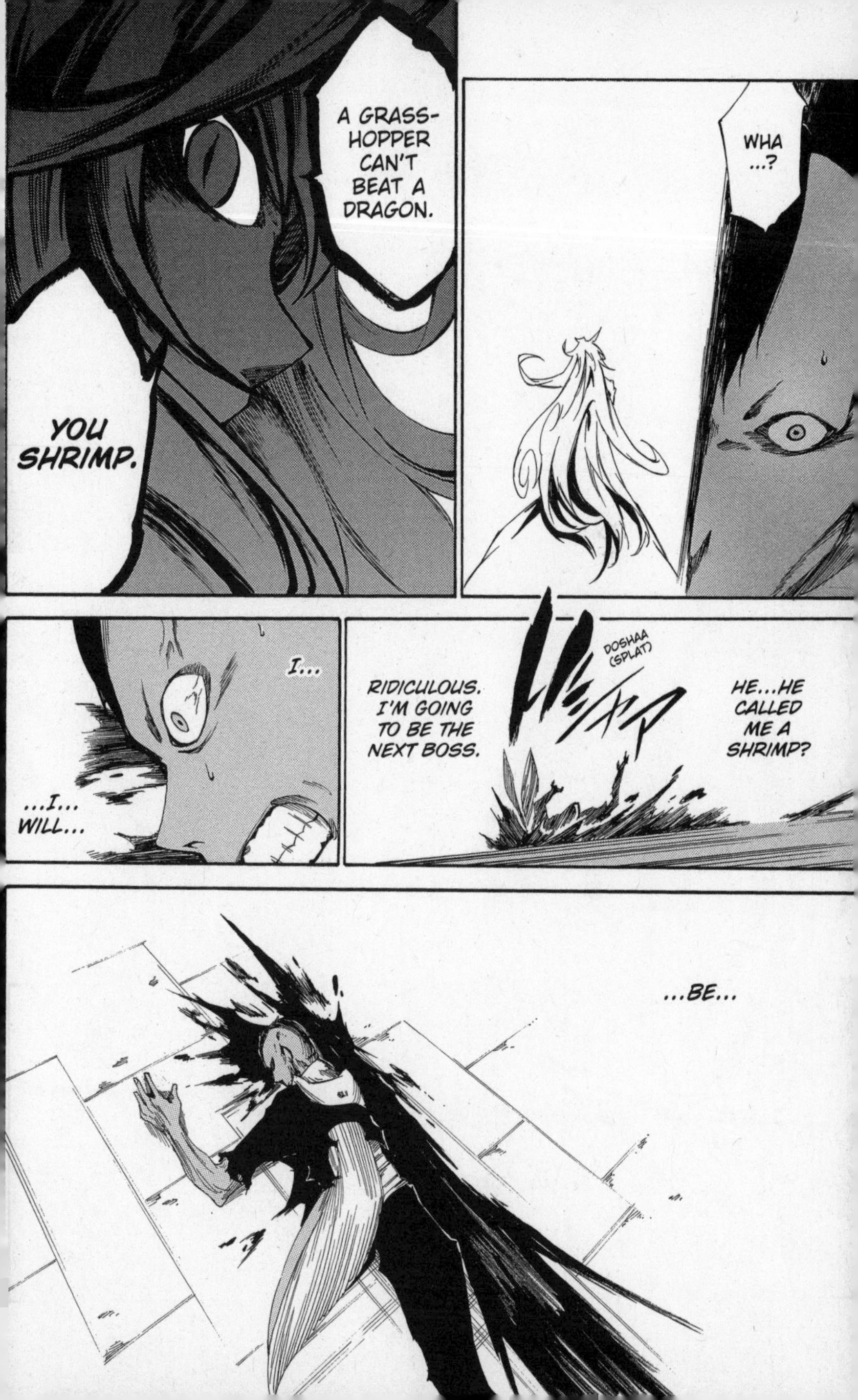
WHA ...?
A GRASS-HOPPER CAN'T BEAT A DRAGON.
YOU SHRIMP.
HE...HE CALLED ME A SHRIMP?
DOSHAA (SPLAT)
RIDICULOUS. I'M GOING TO BE THE NEXT BOSS.
I...
...I... WILL...
...BE...

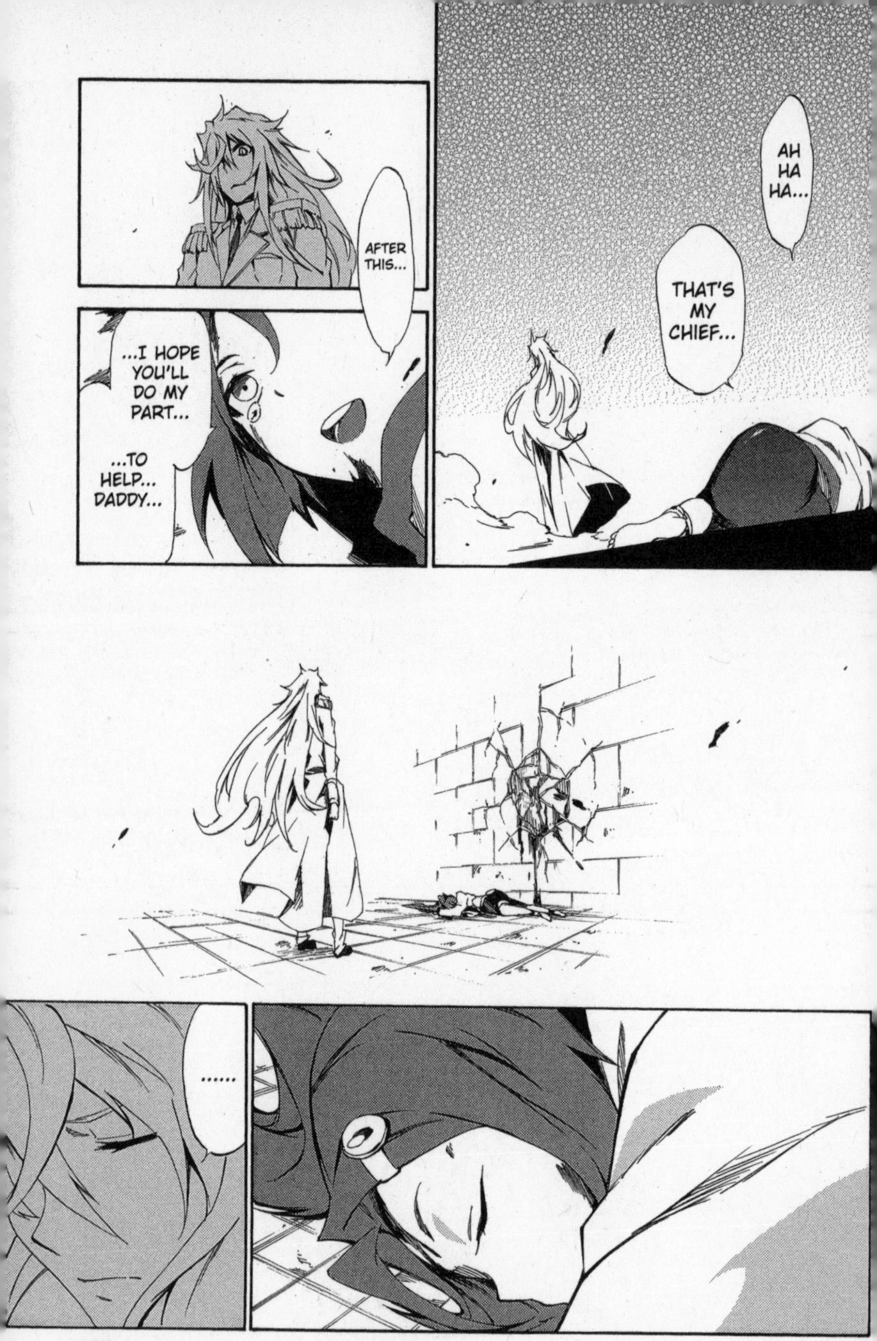
AH HA HA...
THAT'S MY CHIEF...
AFTER THIS...
...I HOPE YOU'LL DO MY PART...
...TO HELP... DADDY...
......

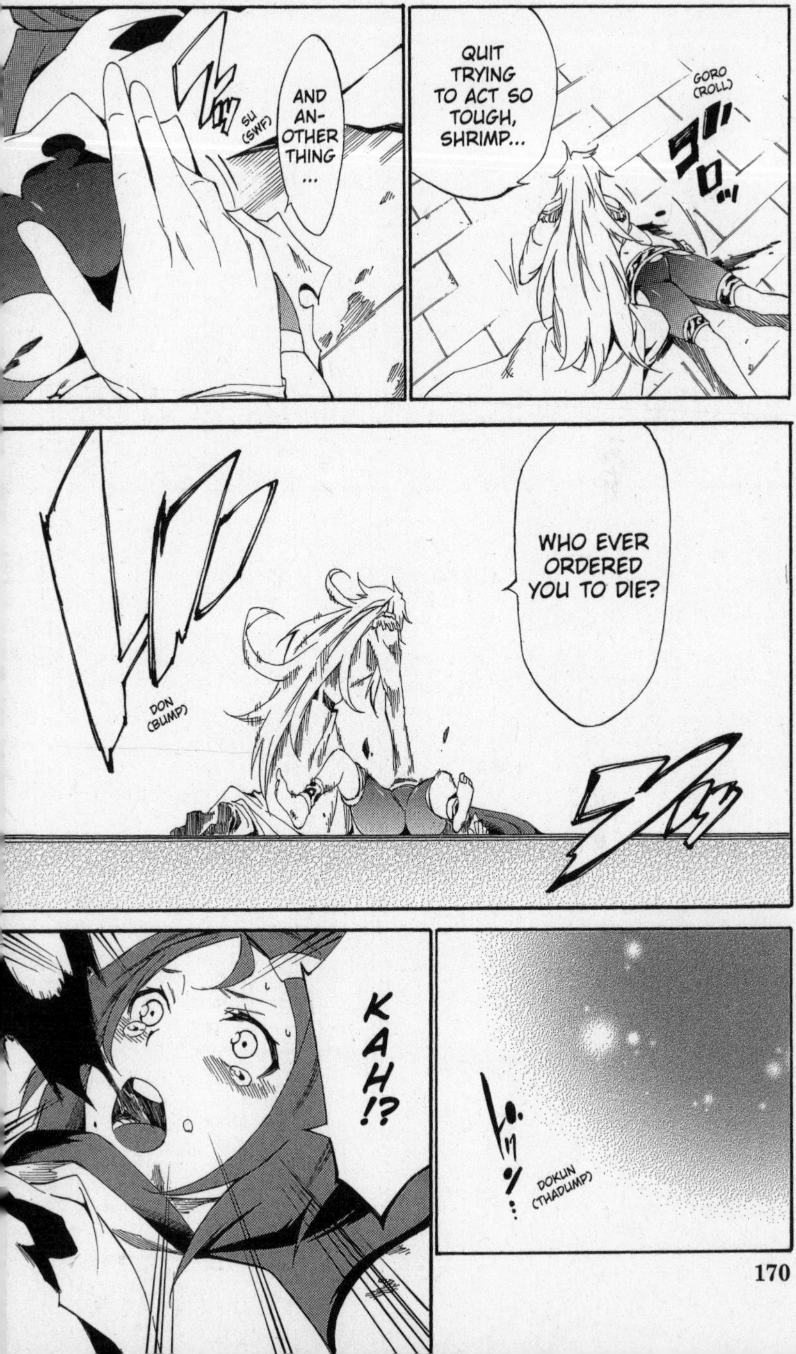
QUIT TRYING TO ACT SO TOUGH, SHRIMP...
GORO (ROLL)
AND AN-OTHER THING ...
SU (SWF)
WHO EVER ORDERED YOU TO DIE?
DON (BUMP)
DOKUN (THADUMP)
KAH!?

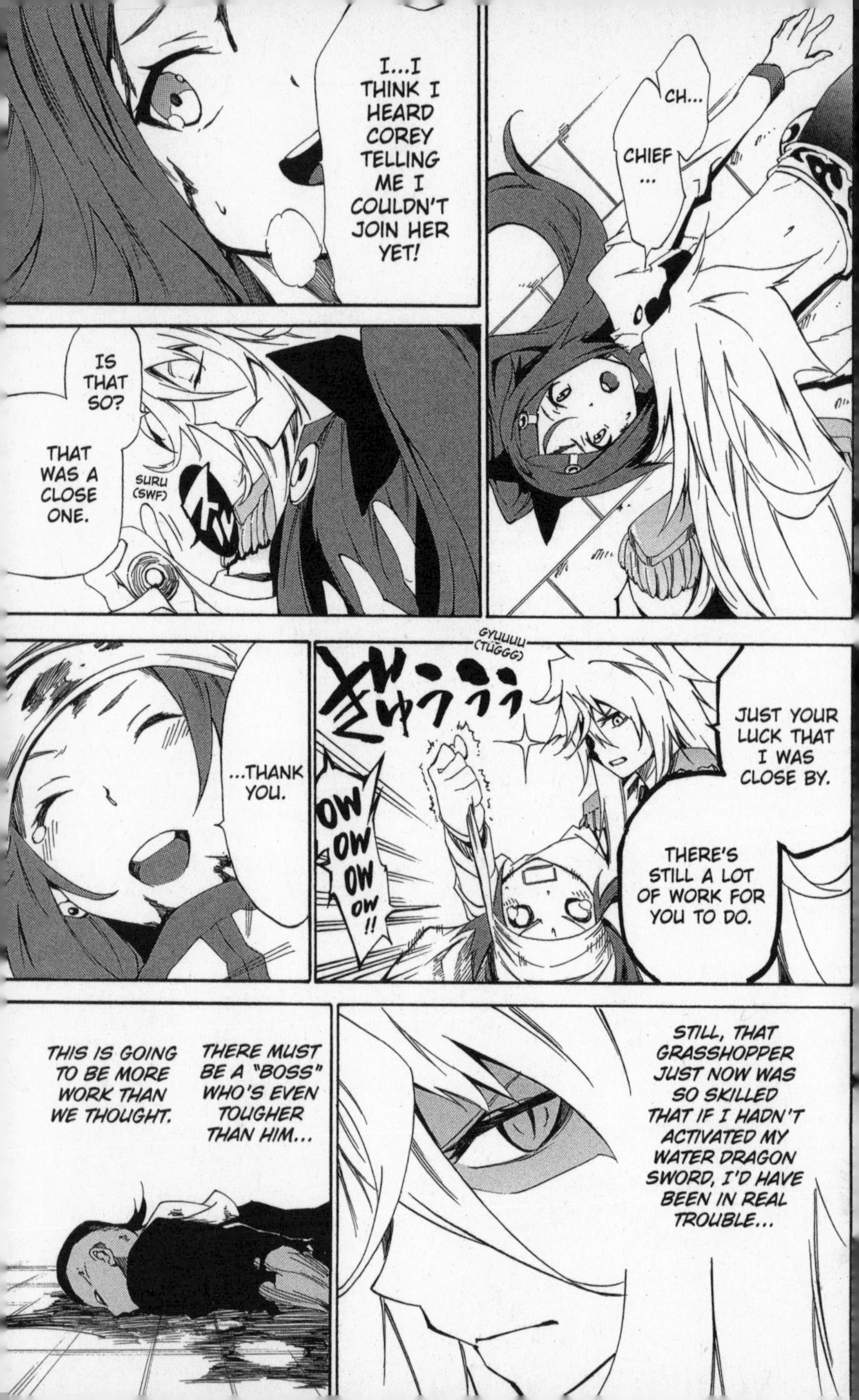

CH...
CHIEF...
I...I THINK I HEARD COREY TELLING ME I COULDN'T JOIN HER YET!
IS THAT SO?
SURU (SWF)
THAT WAS A CLOSE ONE.
GYUUUU (TÜGGG)
JUST YOUR LUCK THAT I WAS CLOSE BY.
THERE'S STILL A LOT OF WORK FOR YOU TO DO.
OW OW OW OW!!
...THANK YOU.
STILL, THAT GRASSHOPPER JUST NOW WAS SO SKILLED THAT IF I HADN'T ACTIVATED MY WATER DRAGON SWORD, I'D HAVE BEEN IN REAL TROUBLE...
THERE MUST BE A "BOSS" WHO'S EVEN TOUGHER THAN HIM...
THIS IS GOING TO BE MORE WORK THAN WE THOUGHT.

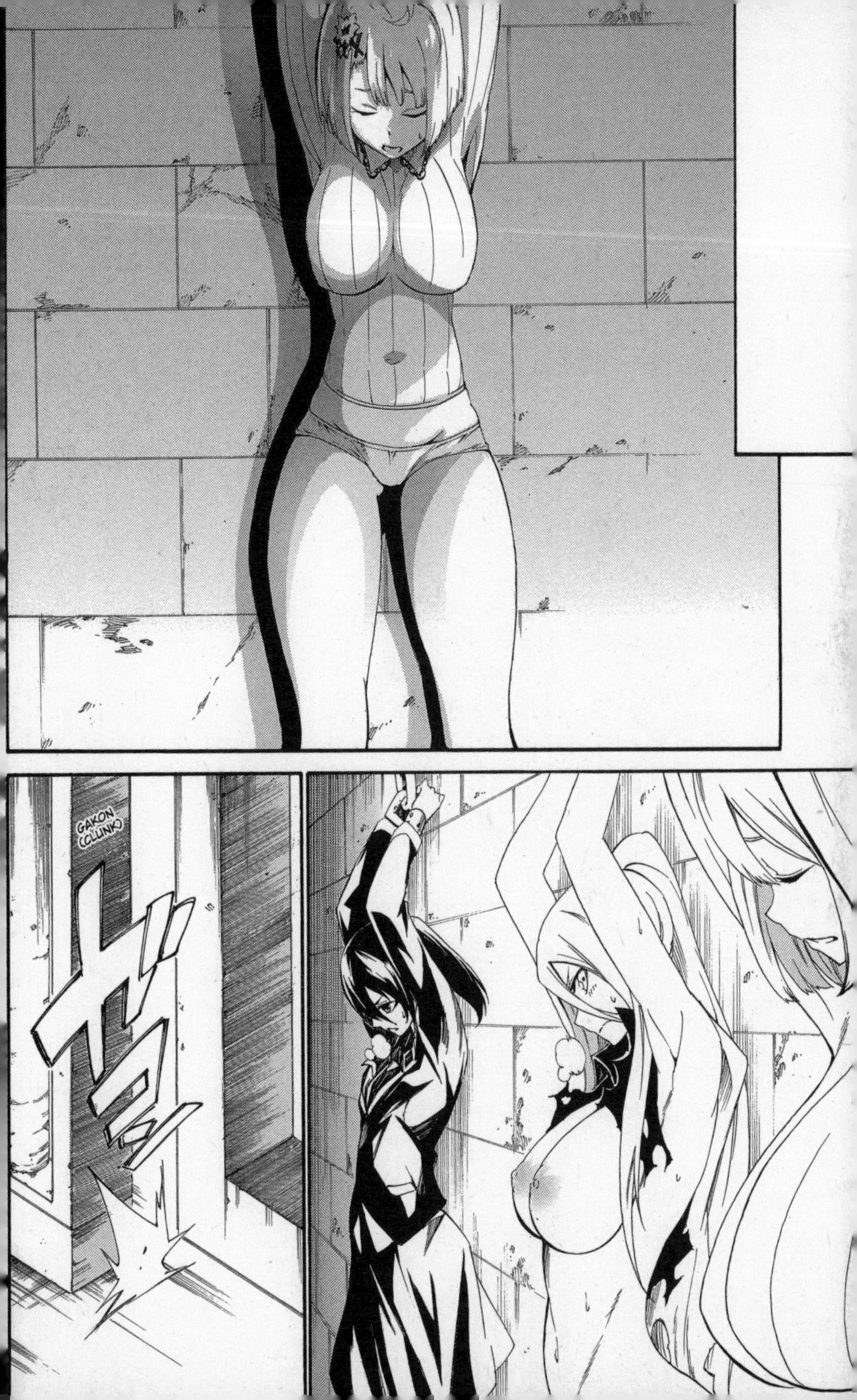
GAKON
(CLUNK)

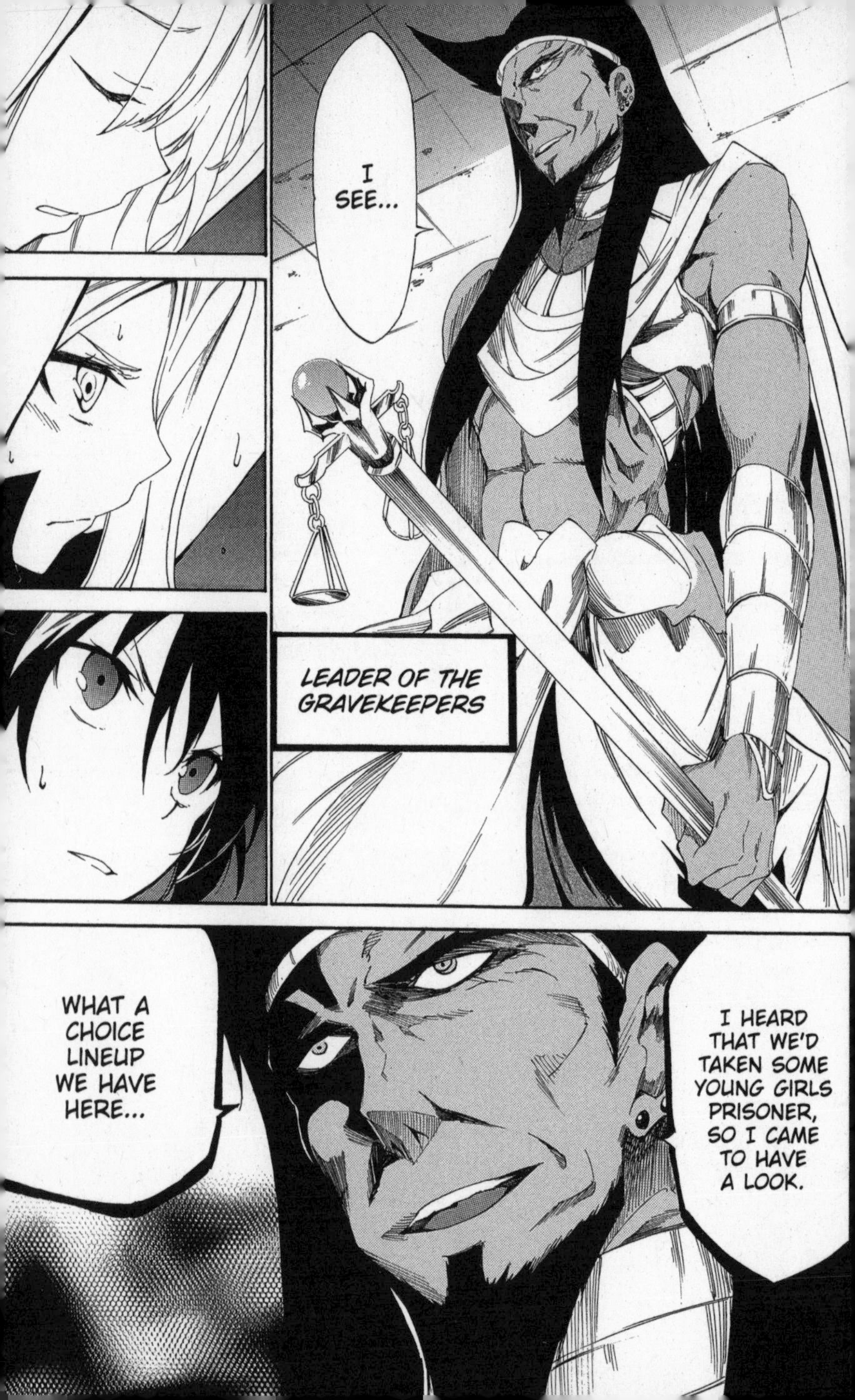
I SEE...
LEADER OF THE GRAVEKEEPERS
I HEARD THAT WE'D TAKEN SOME YOUNG GIRLS PRISONER, SO I CAME TO HAVE A LOOK.
WHAT A CHOICE LINEUP WE HAVE HERE...

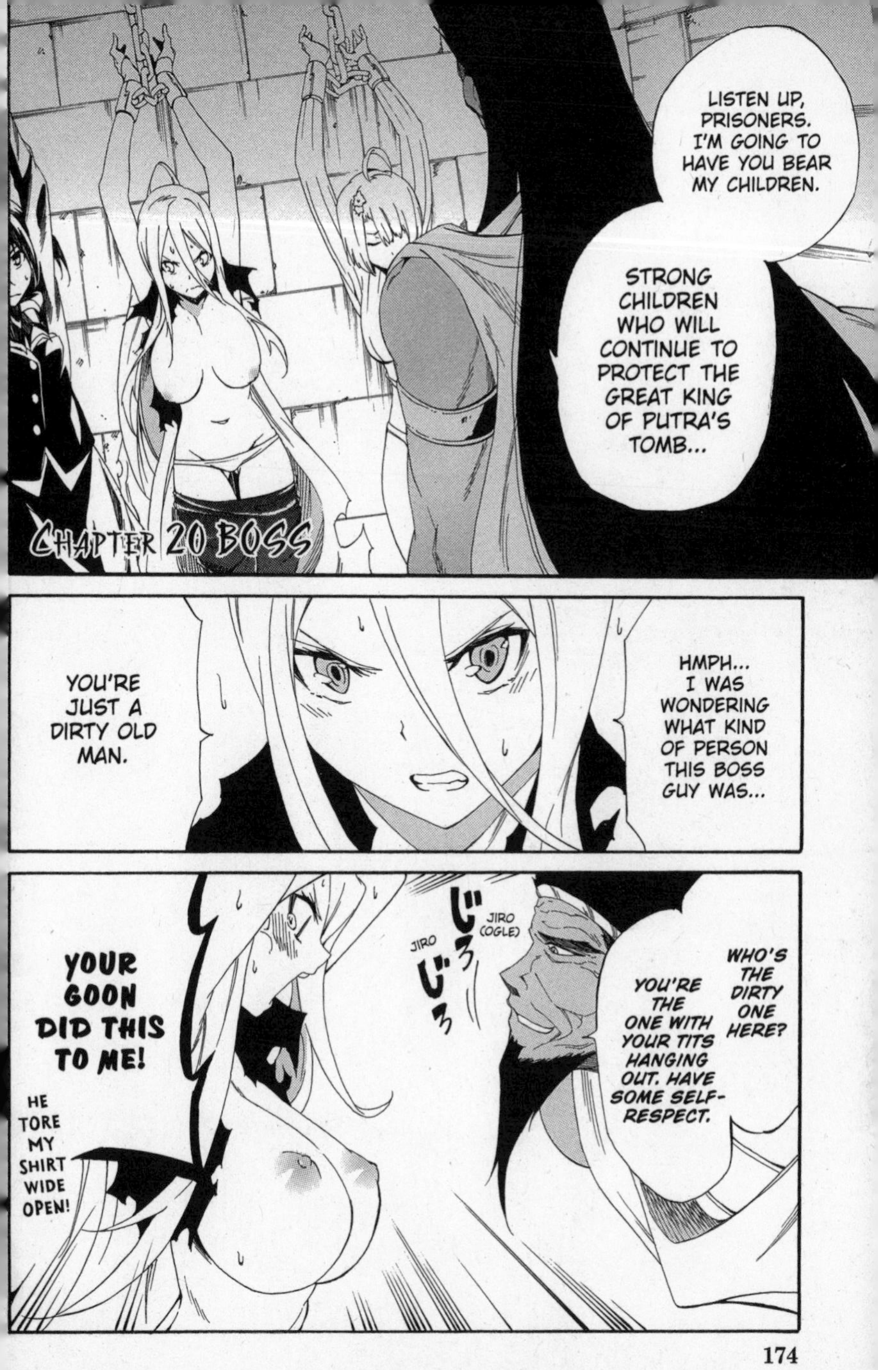
LISTEN UP, PRISONERS. I'M GOING TO HAVE YOU BEAR MY CHILDREN.
STRONG CHILDREN WHO WILL CONTINUE TO PROTECT THE GREAT KING OF PUTRA'S TOMB...
CHAPTER 20 BOSS
HMPH... I WAS WONDERING WHAT KIND OF PERSON THIS BOSS GUY WAS...
YOU'RE JUST A DIRTY OLD MAN.
WHO'S THE DIRTY ONE HERE?
YOU'RE THE ONE WITH YOUR TITS HANGING OUT. HAVE SOME SELF-RESPECT.
じろ
JIRO (OGLE)
じろ
JIRO
YOUR GOON DID THIS TO ME!
HE TORE MY SHIRT WIDE OPEN!

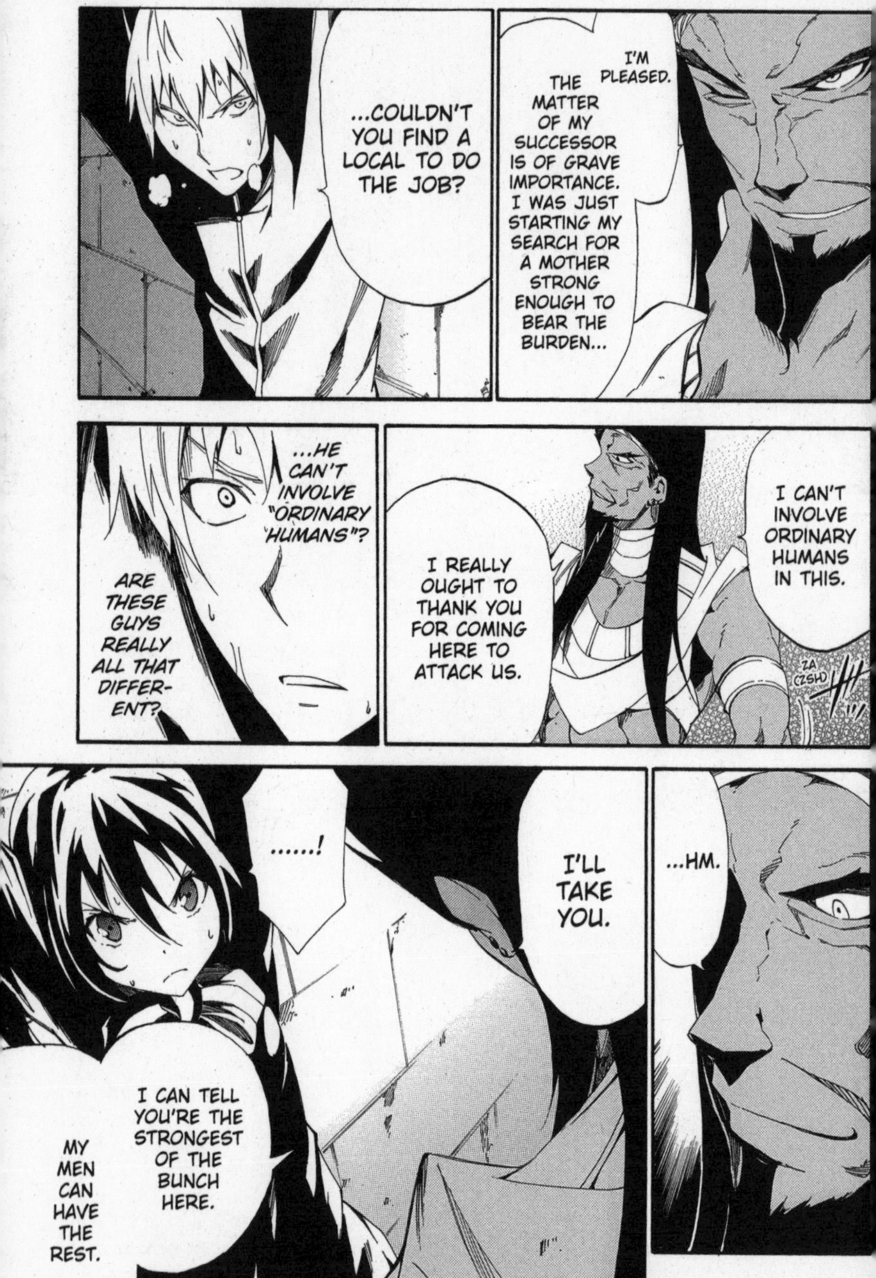
I'M PLEASED.
THE MATTER OF MY SUCCESSOR IS OF GRAVE IMPORTANCE. I WAS JUST STARTING MY SEARCH FOR A MOTHER STRONG ENOUGH TO BEAR THE BURDEN...
...COULDN'T YOU FIND A LOCAL TO DO THE JOB?
I CAN'T INVOLVE ORDINARY HUMANS IN THIS.
ZA CZSH
I REALLY OUGHT TO THANK YOU FOR COMING HERE TO ATTACK US.
...HE CAN'T INVOLVE "ORDINARY HUMANS"?
ARE THESE GUYS REALLY ALL THAT DIFFER-ENT?
...HM.
I'LL TAKE YOU.
......!
I CAN TELL YOU'RE THE STRONGEST OF THE BUNCH HERE.
MY MEN CAN HAVE THE REST.

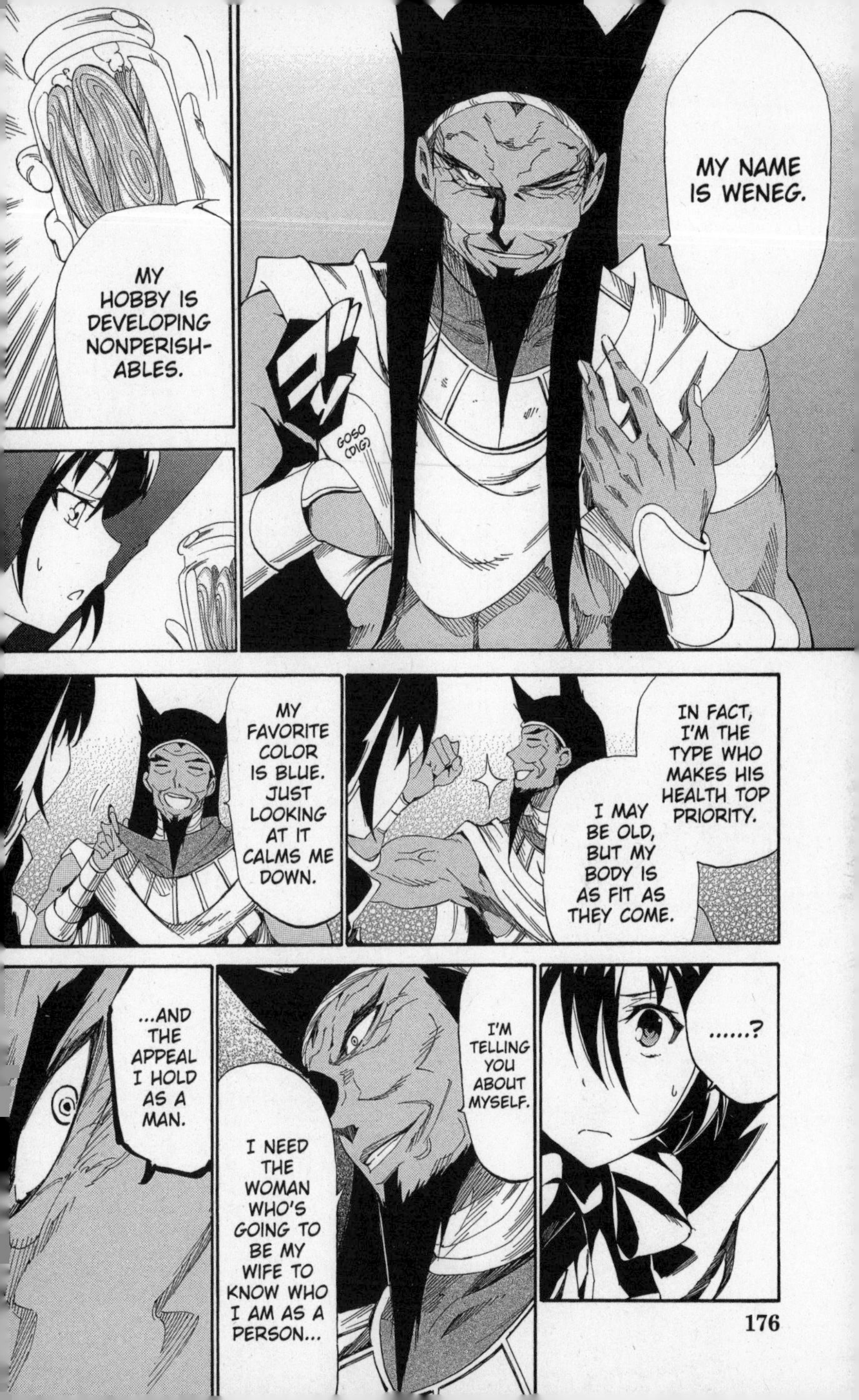
MY NAME IS WENEG.
GOSO (DIG)
MY HOBBY IS DEVELOPING NONPERISH-ABLES.
IN FACT, I'M THE TYPE WHO MAKES HIS HEALTH TOP PRIORITY.
I MAY BE OLD, BUT MY BODY IS AS FIT AS THEY COME.
MY FAVORITE COLOR IS BLUE. JUST LOOKING AT IT CALMS ME DOWN.
......?
I'M TELLING YOU ABOUT MYSELF.
I NEED THE WOMAN WHO'S GOING TO BE MY WIFE TO KNOW WHO I AM AS A PERSON...
...AND THE APPEAL I HOLD AS A MAN.

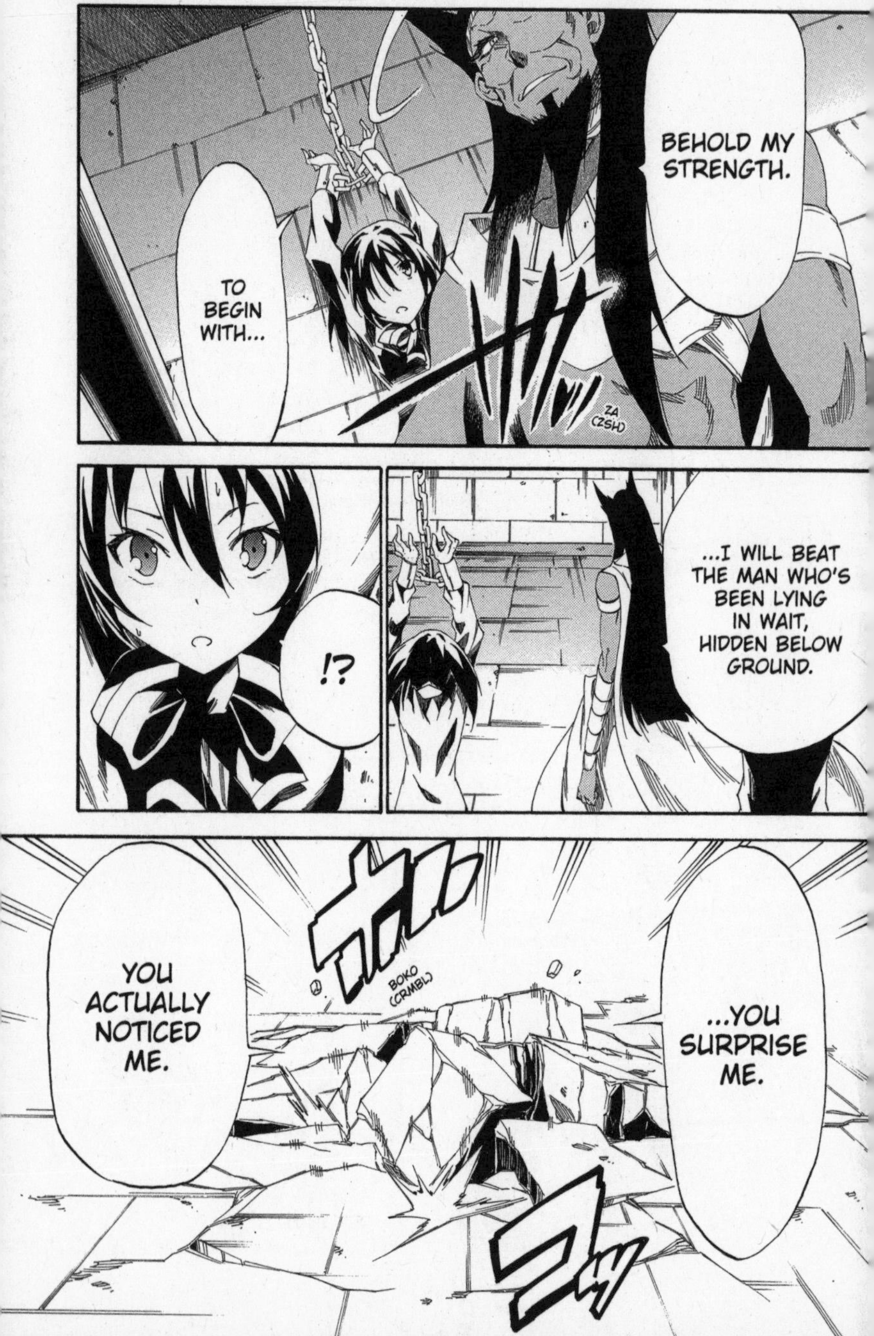
BEHOLD MY STRENGTH.
TO BEGIN WITH...
ZA (ZSH)
...I WILL BEAT THE MAN WHO'S BEEN LYING IN WAIT, HIDDEN BELOW GROUND.
!?
...YOU SURPRISE ME.
BOKO (CRMBL)
YOU ACTUALLY NOTICED ME.

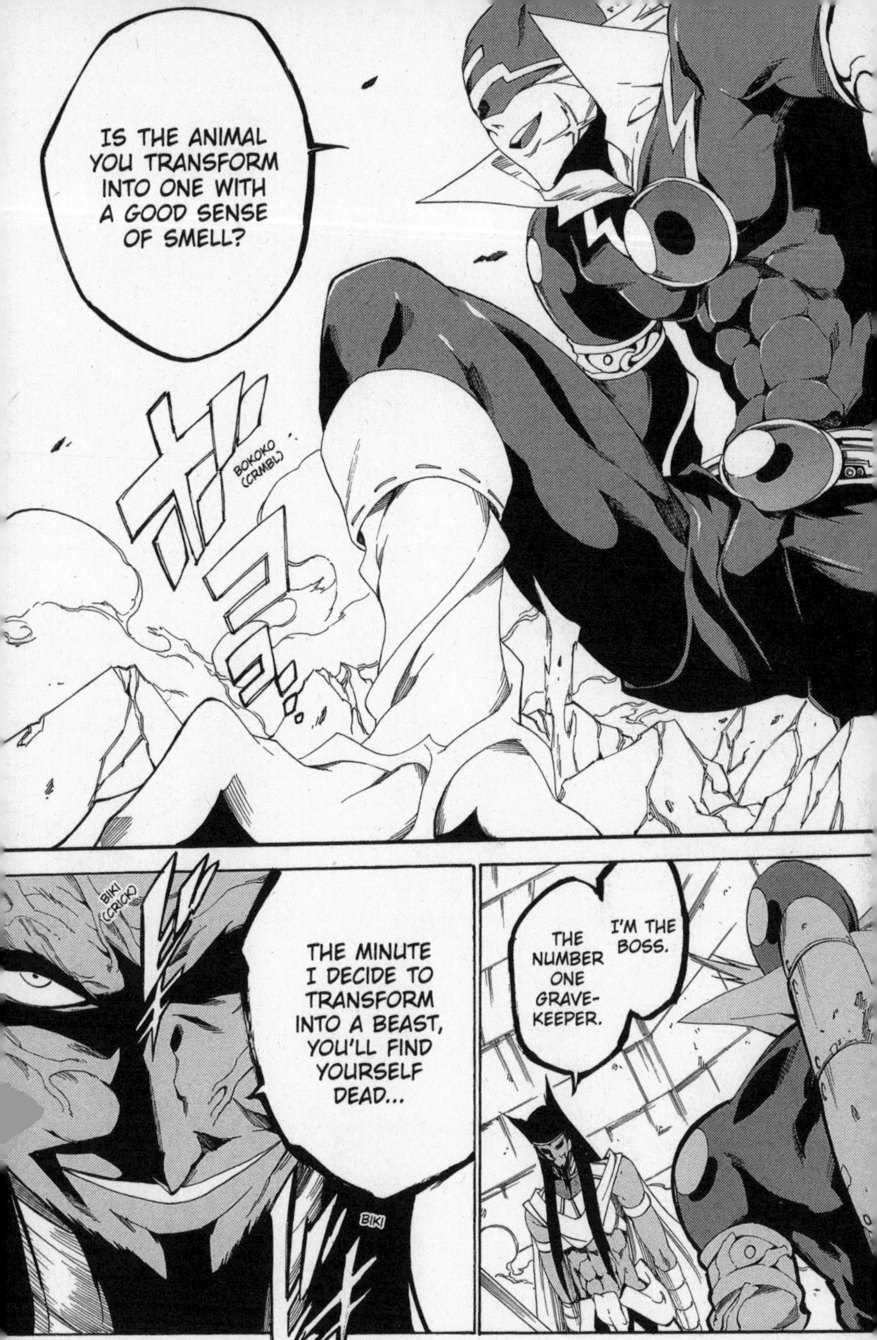
IS THE ANIMAL YOU TRANSFORM INTO ONE WITH A GOOD SENSE OF SMELL?
BOKOKO (CRMBL)
I'M THE BOSS.
THE NUMBER ONE GRAVE-KEEPER.
BIKI (CRICK)
THE MINUTE I DECIDE TO TRANSFORM INTO A BEAST, YOU'LL FIND YOURSELF DEAD...
BIKI

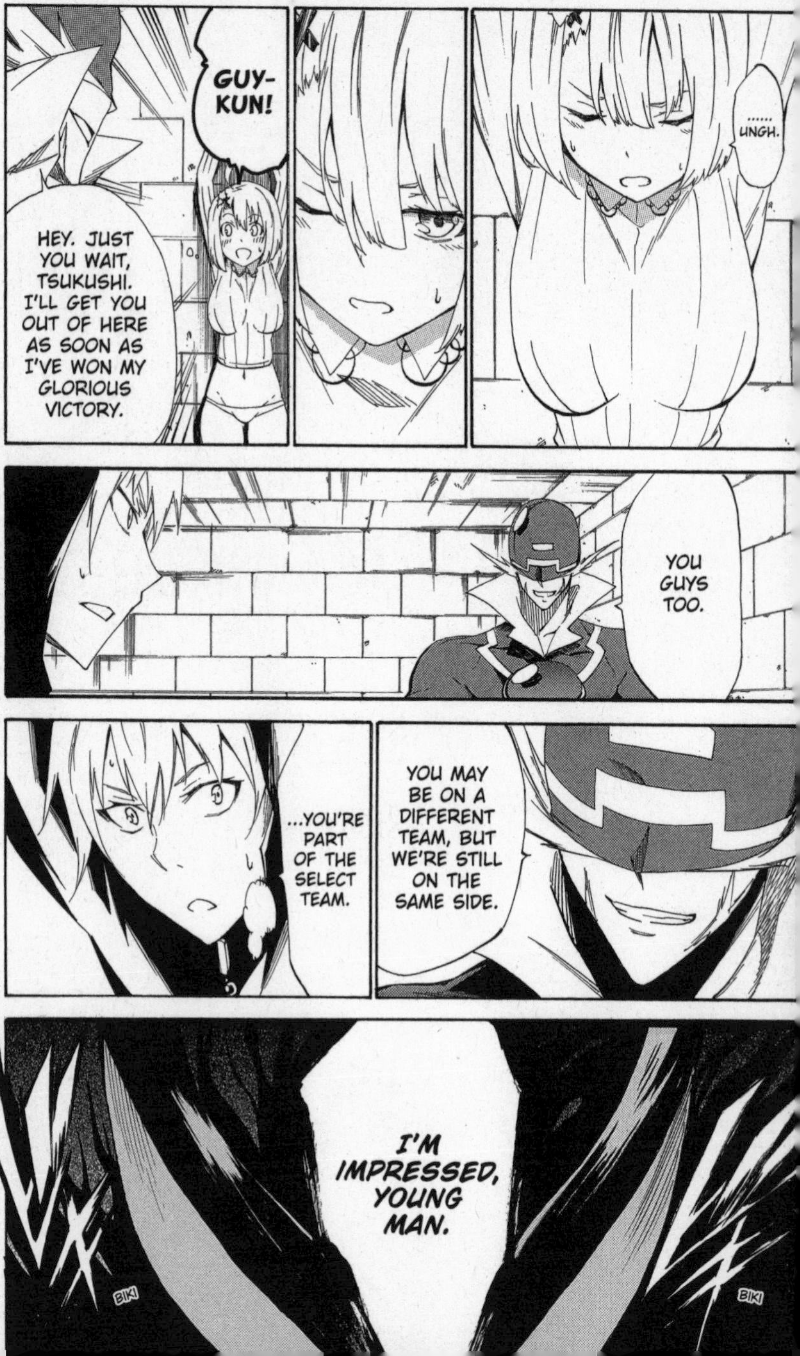
......
UNGH.
GUY-KUN!
HEY. JUST YOU WAIT, TSUKUSHI. I'LL GET YOU OUT OF HERE AS SOON AS I'VE WON MY GLORIOUS VICTORY.
YOU GUYS TOO.
YOU MAY BE ON A DIFFERENT TEAM, BUT WE'RE STILL ON THE SAME SIDE.
...YOU'RE PART OF THE SELECT TEAM.
I'M IMPRESSED, YOUNG MAN.
BIKI
BIKI

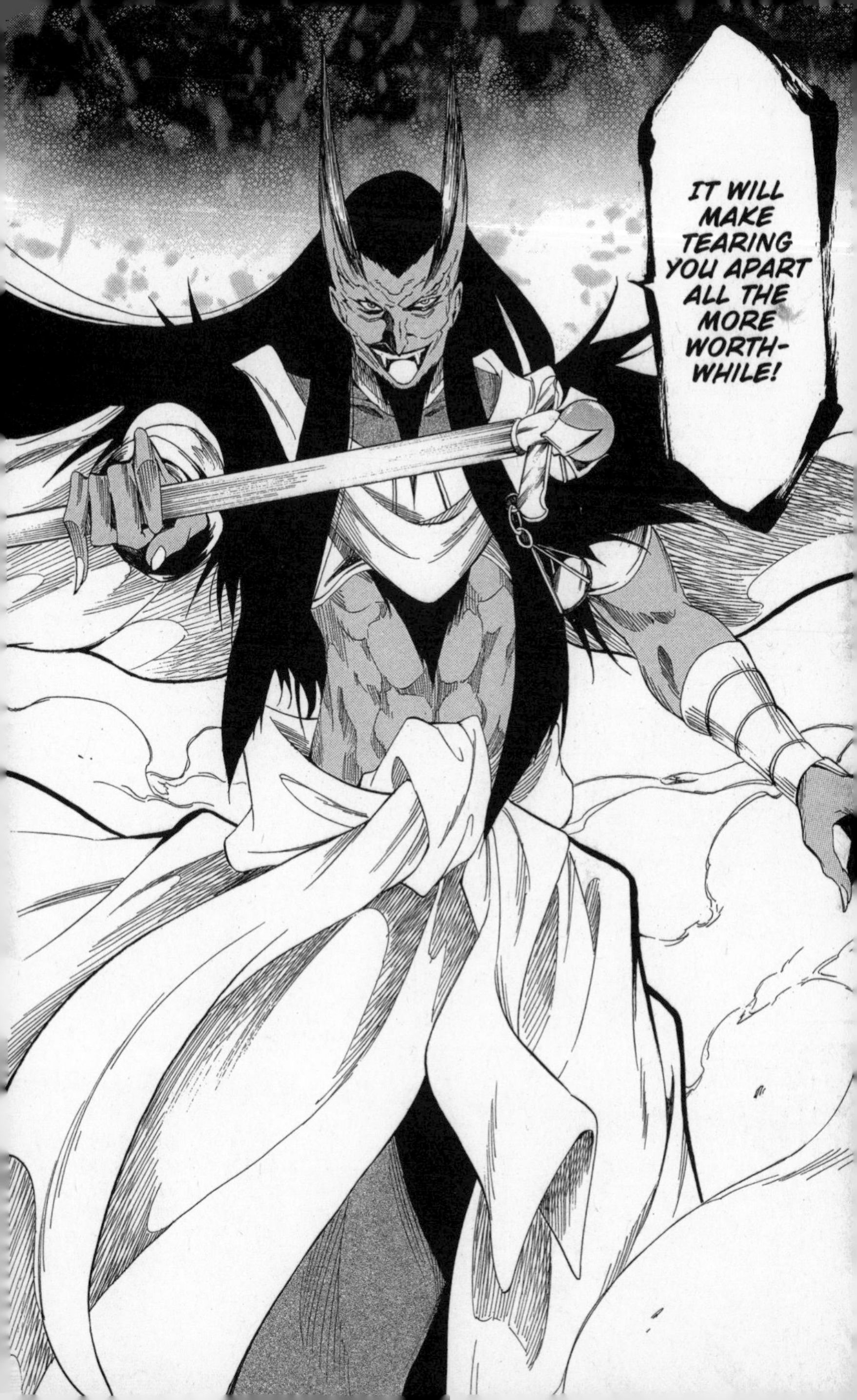
IT WILL MAKE TEARING YOU APART ALL THE MORE WORTH-WHILE!

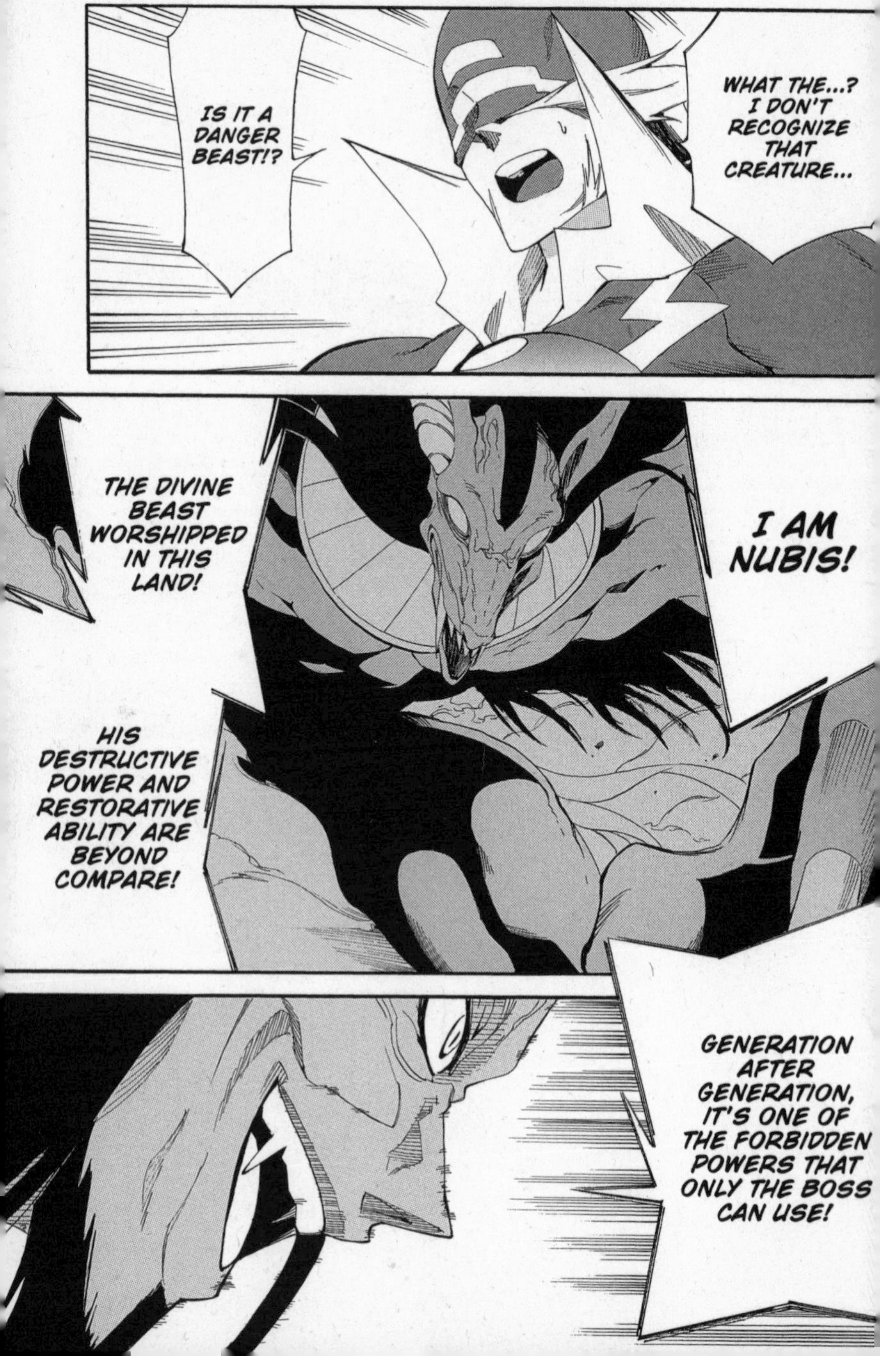
WHAT THE...? I DON'T RECOGNIZE THAT CREATURE...
IS IT A DANGER BEAST!?
I AM NUBIS!
THE DIVINE BEAST WORSHIPPED IN THIS LAND!
HIS DESTRUCTIVE POWER AND RESTORATIVE ABILITY ARE BEYOND COMPARE!
GENERATION AFTER GENERATION, IT'S ONE OF THE FORBIDDEN POWERS THAT ONLY THE BOSS CAN USE!

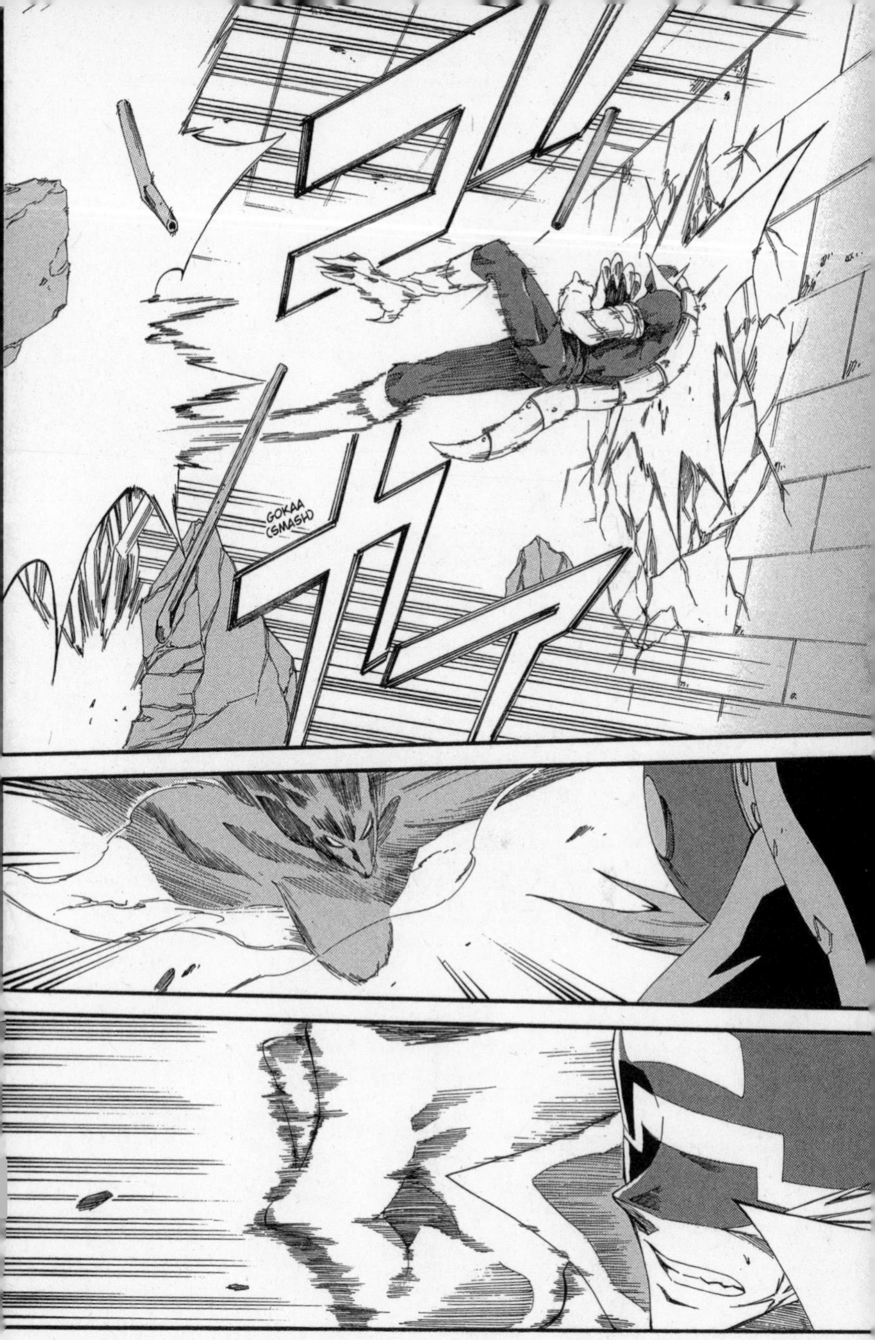
GOKAA
(SMASH)

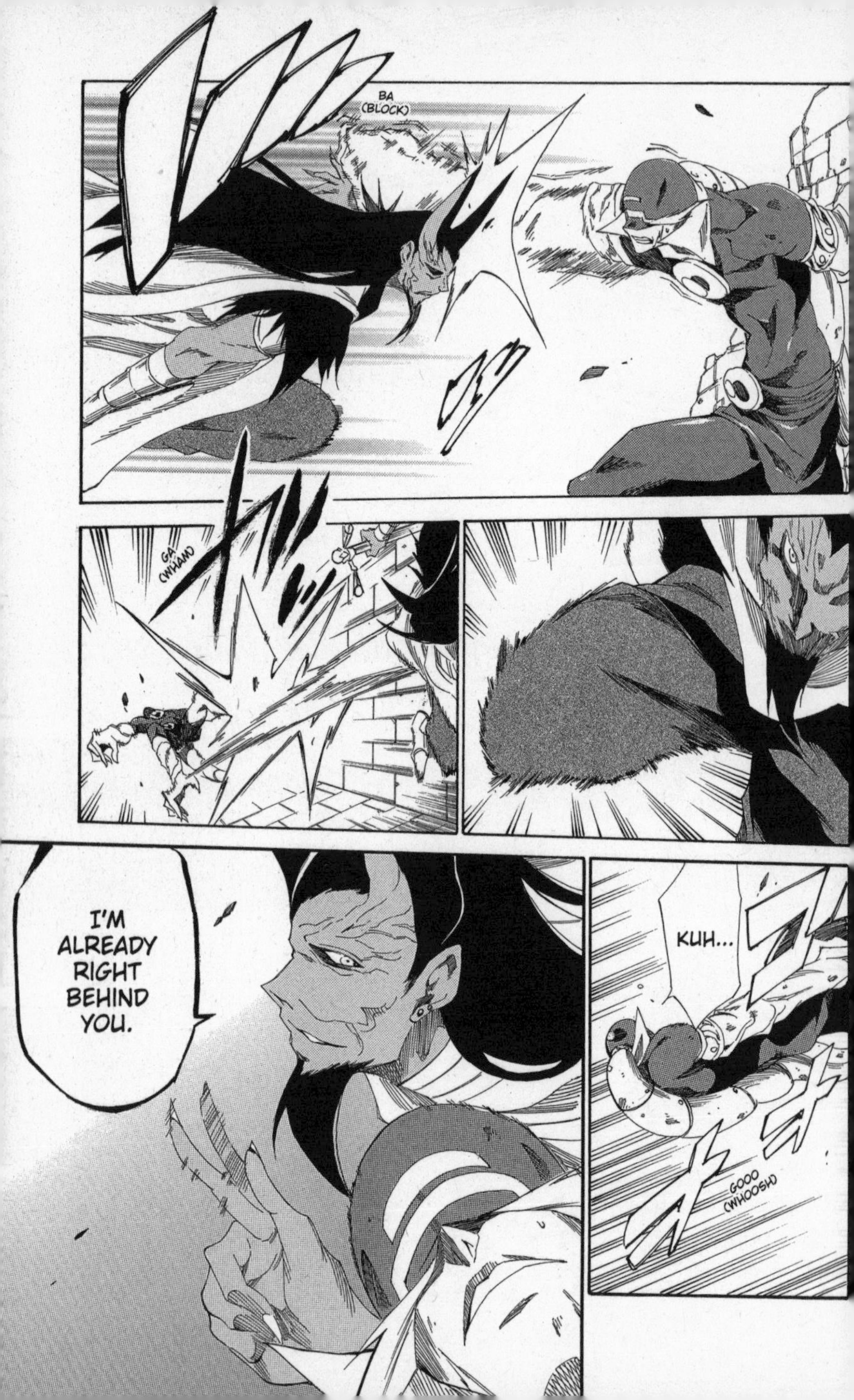
BA (BLOCK)
GA (WHAM)
KUH...
GOOO (WHOOSH)
I'M ALREADY RIGHT BEHIND YOU.

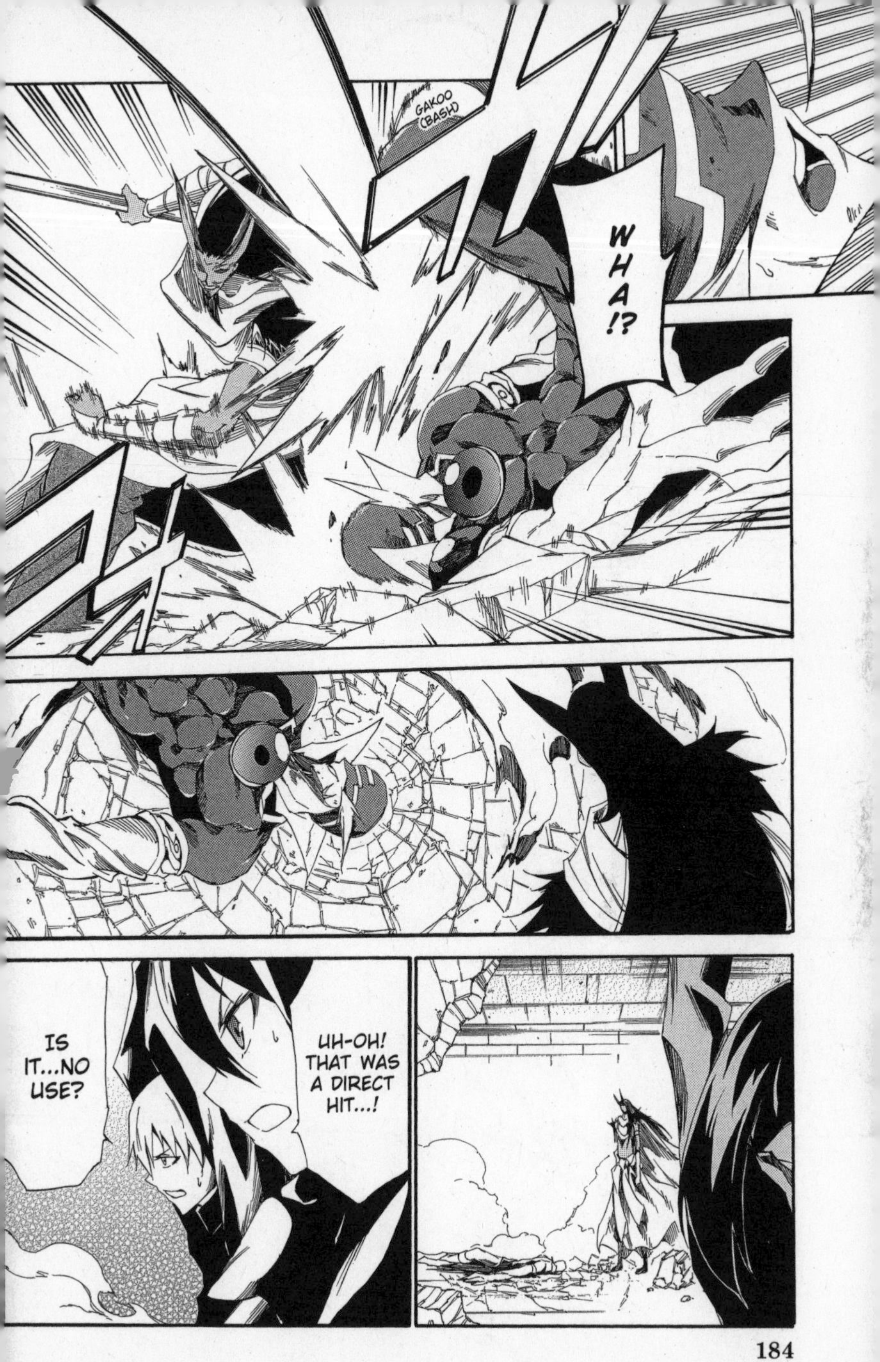
GAKOO (BASH)
WHA!?
UH-OH! THAT WAS A DIRECT HIT...!
IS IT...NO USE?

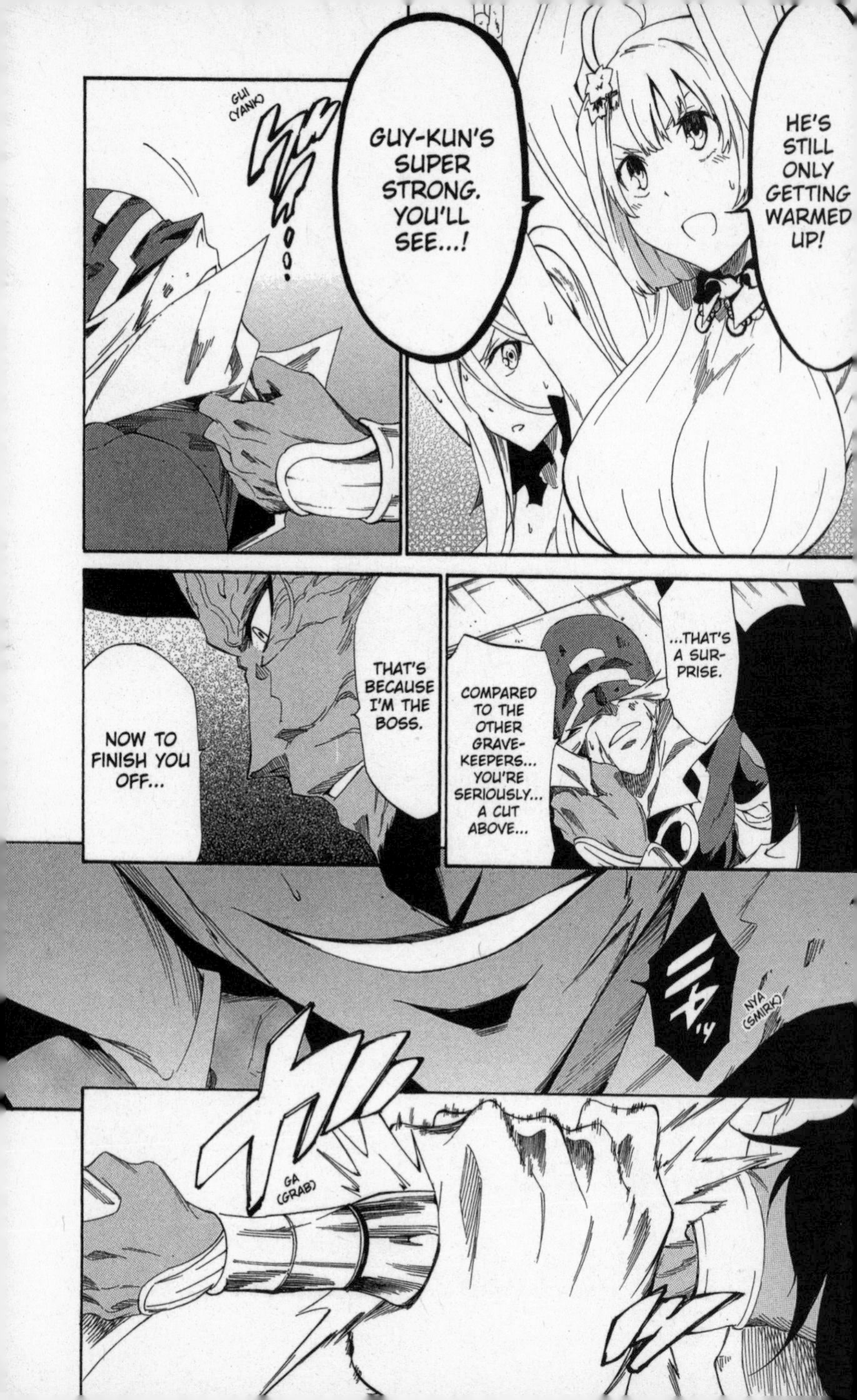
HE'S STILL ONLY GETTING WARMED UP!
GUY-KUN'S SUPER STRONG. YOU'LL SEE...!
GUI (YANK)
...THAT'S A SUR-PRISE.
COMPARED TO THE OTHER GRAVE-KEEPERS... YOU'RE SERIOUSLY... A CUT ABOVE...
THAT'S BECAUSE I'M THE BOSS.
NOW TO FINISH YOU OFF...
NYA (SMIRK)
GA (GRAB)

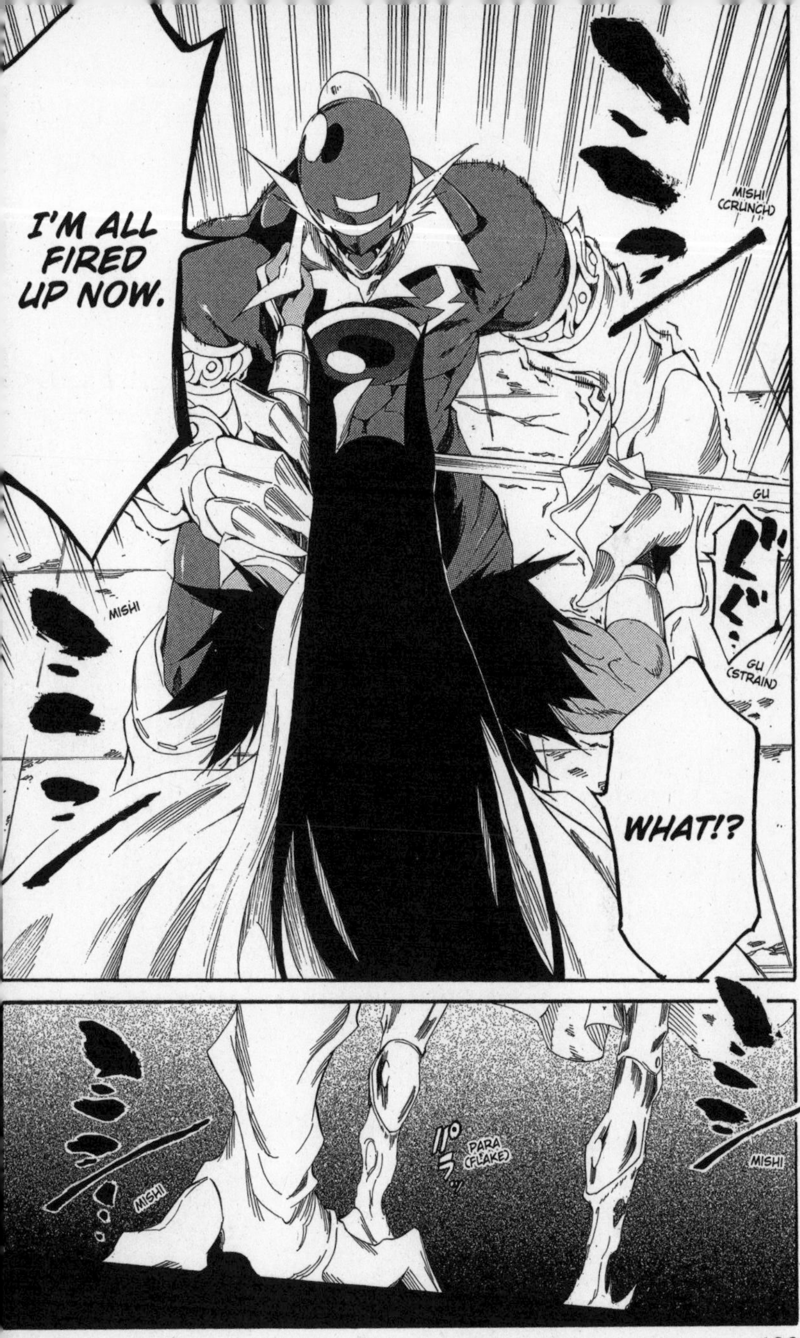
MISHI (CRUNCH)
I'M ALL FIRED UP NOW.
GU
GU (STRAIN)
MISHI
WHAT!?
MISHI
PARA (FLAKE)
MISHI

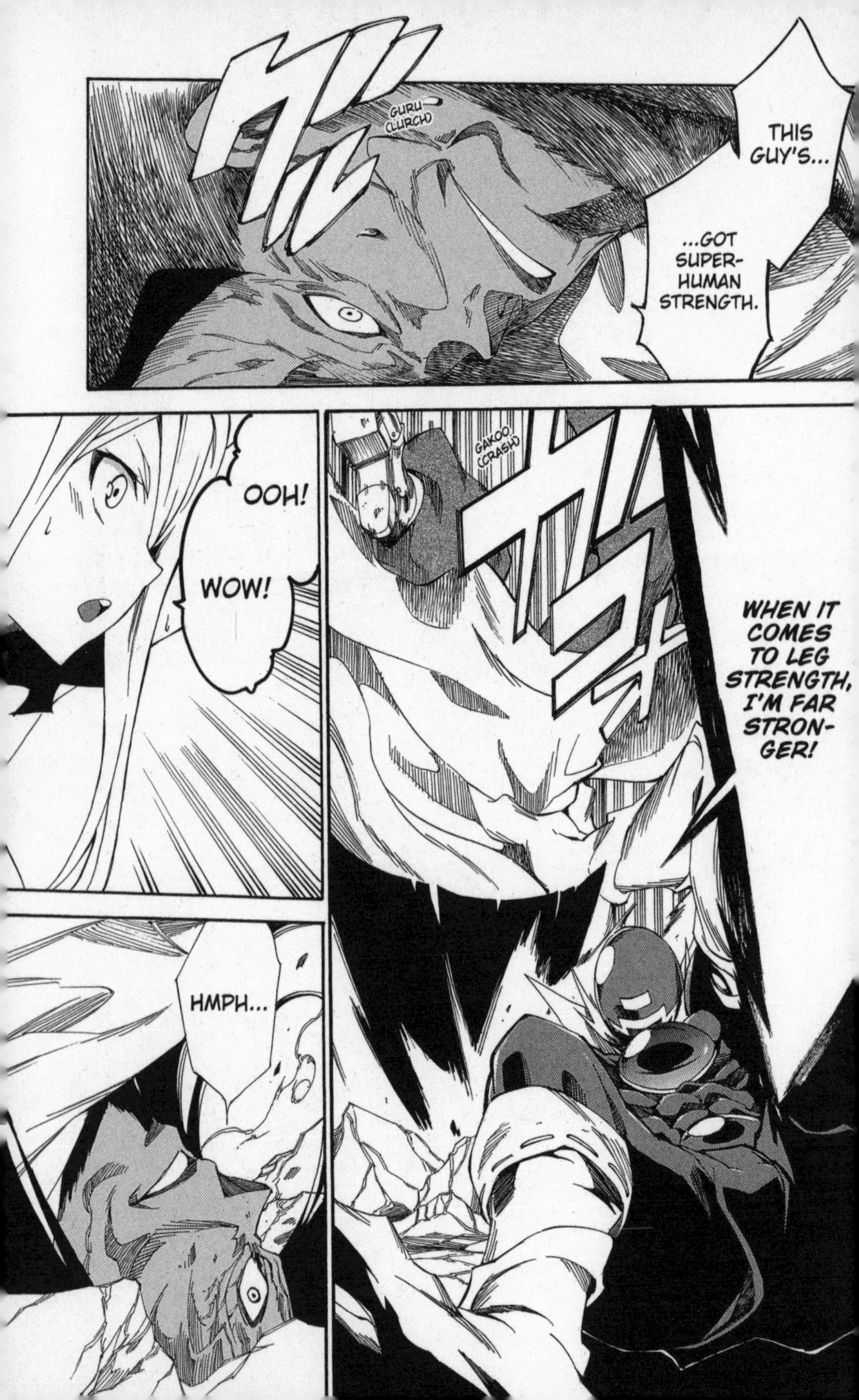
THIS GUY'S...
...GOT SUPER-HUMAN STRENGTH.
GURU (LURCH)
GAKOO (CRASH)
WHEN IT COMES TO LEG STRENGTH, I'M FAR STRON-GER!
OOH!
WOW!
HMPH...

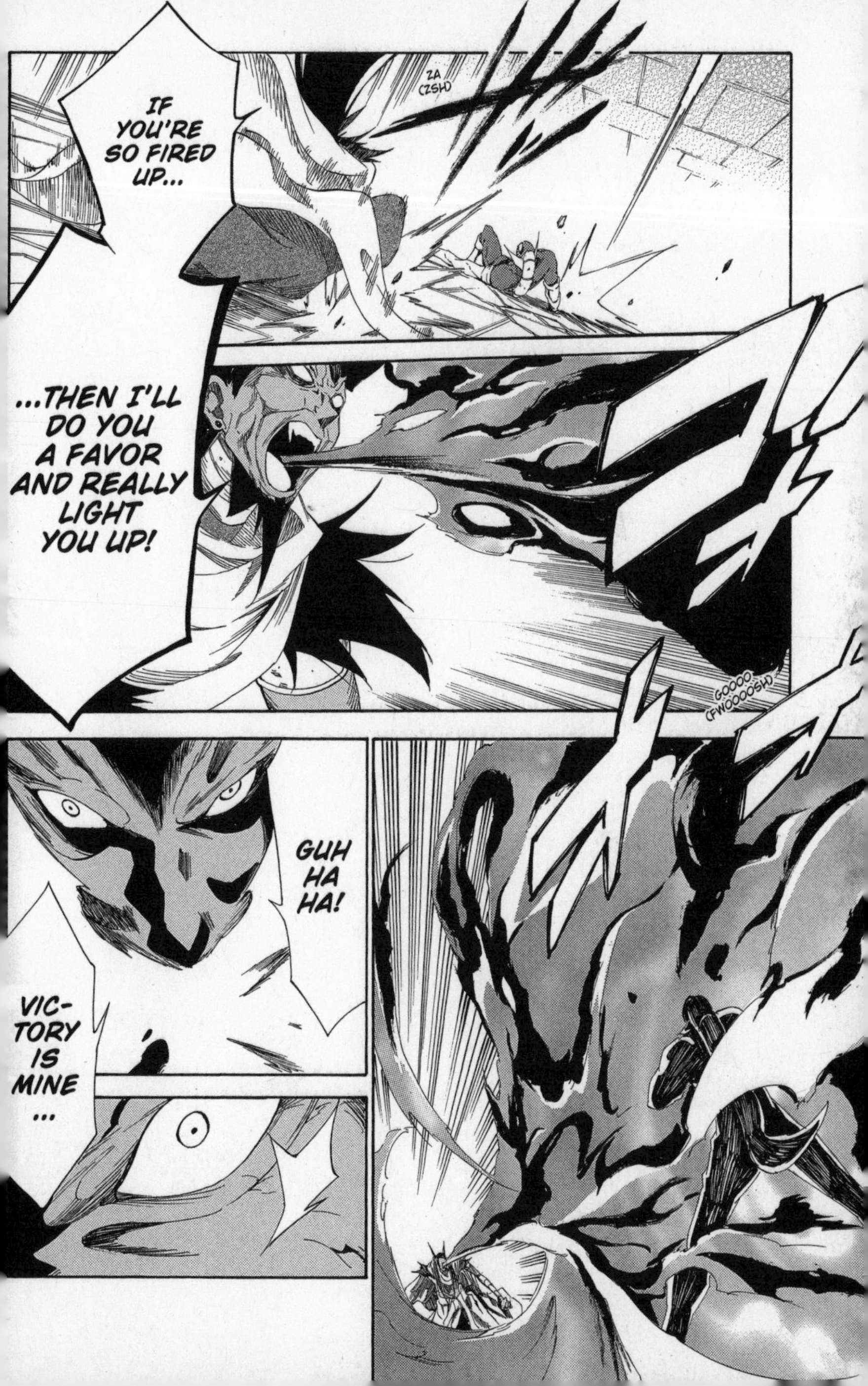
ZA
(ZSH)
IF YOU'RE SO FIRED UP...
...THEN I'LL DO YOU A FAVOR AND REALLY LIGHT YOU UP!
GOOOO
(FWOOOOSH)
GUH HA HA!
VIC-TORY IS MINE ...

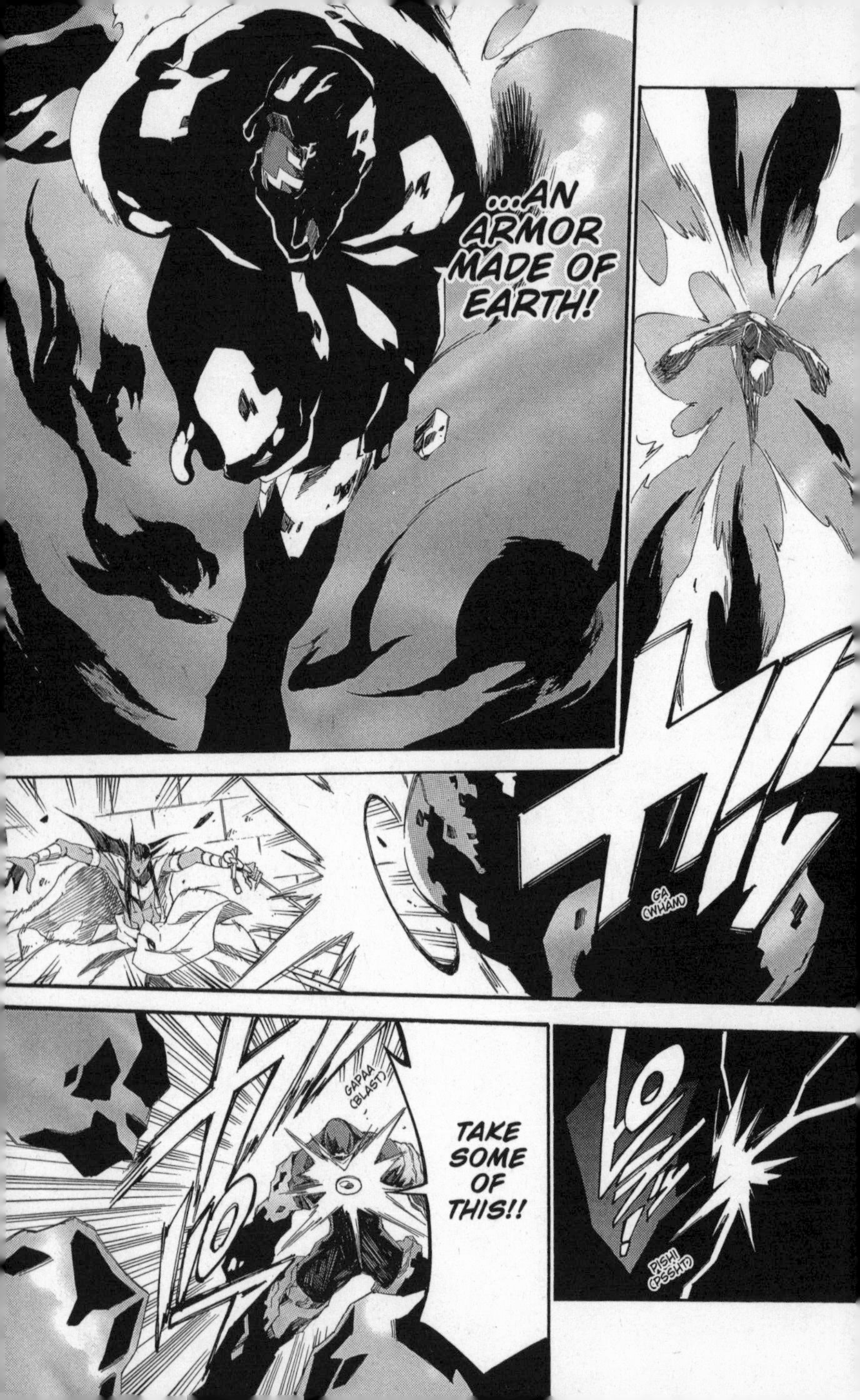
...AN ARMOR MADE OF EARTH!
GA (WHAM)
PISHI (PSSHT)
GAPAA (BLAST)
TAKE SOME OF THIS!!

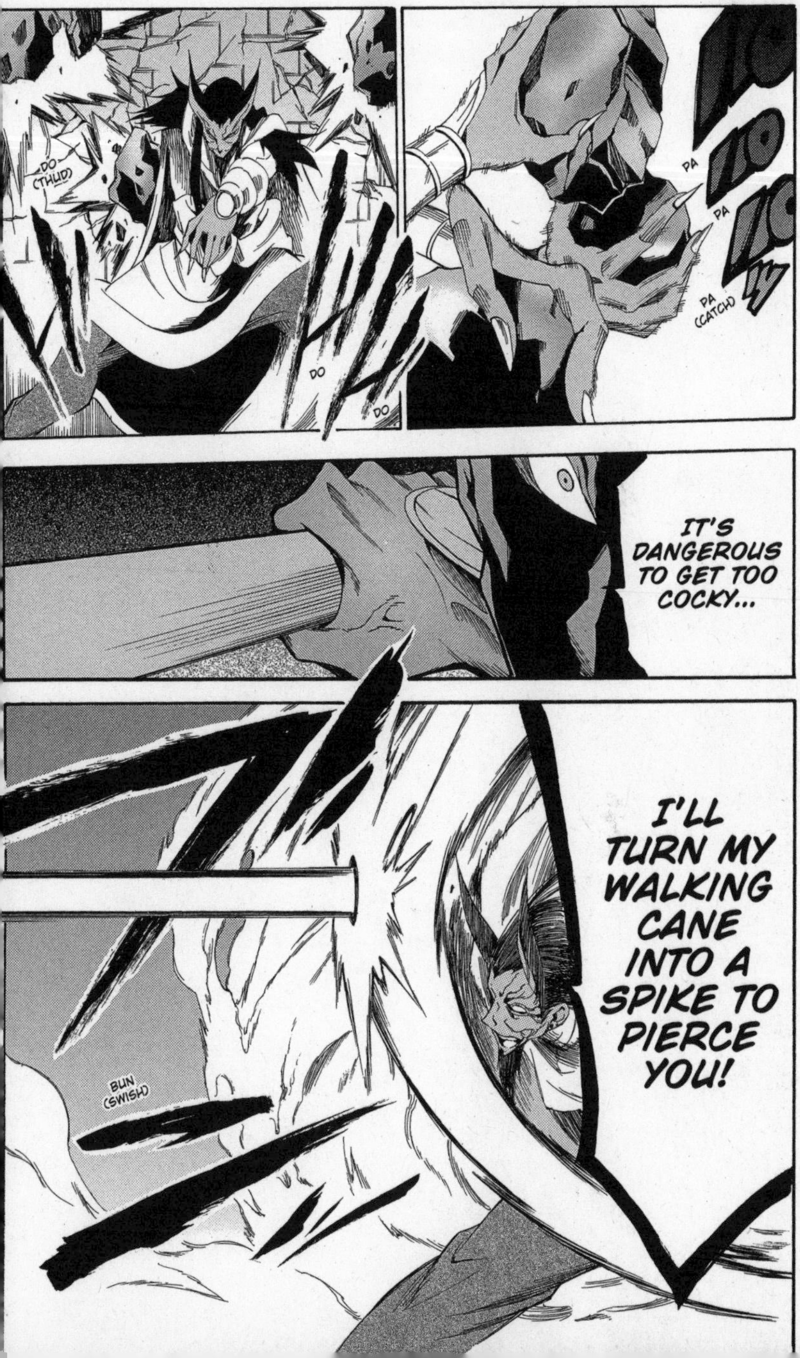
PA
PA
PA (CATCH)
DO (THUD)
DO
DO
IT'S DANGEROUS TO GET TOO COCKY...
I'LL TURN MY WALKING CANE INTO A SPIKE TO PIERCE YOU!
BUN (SWISH)

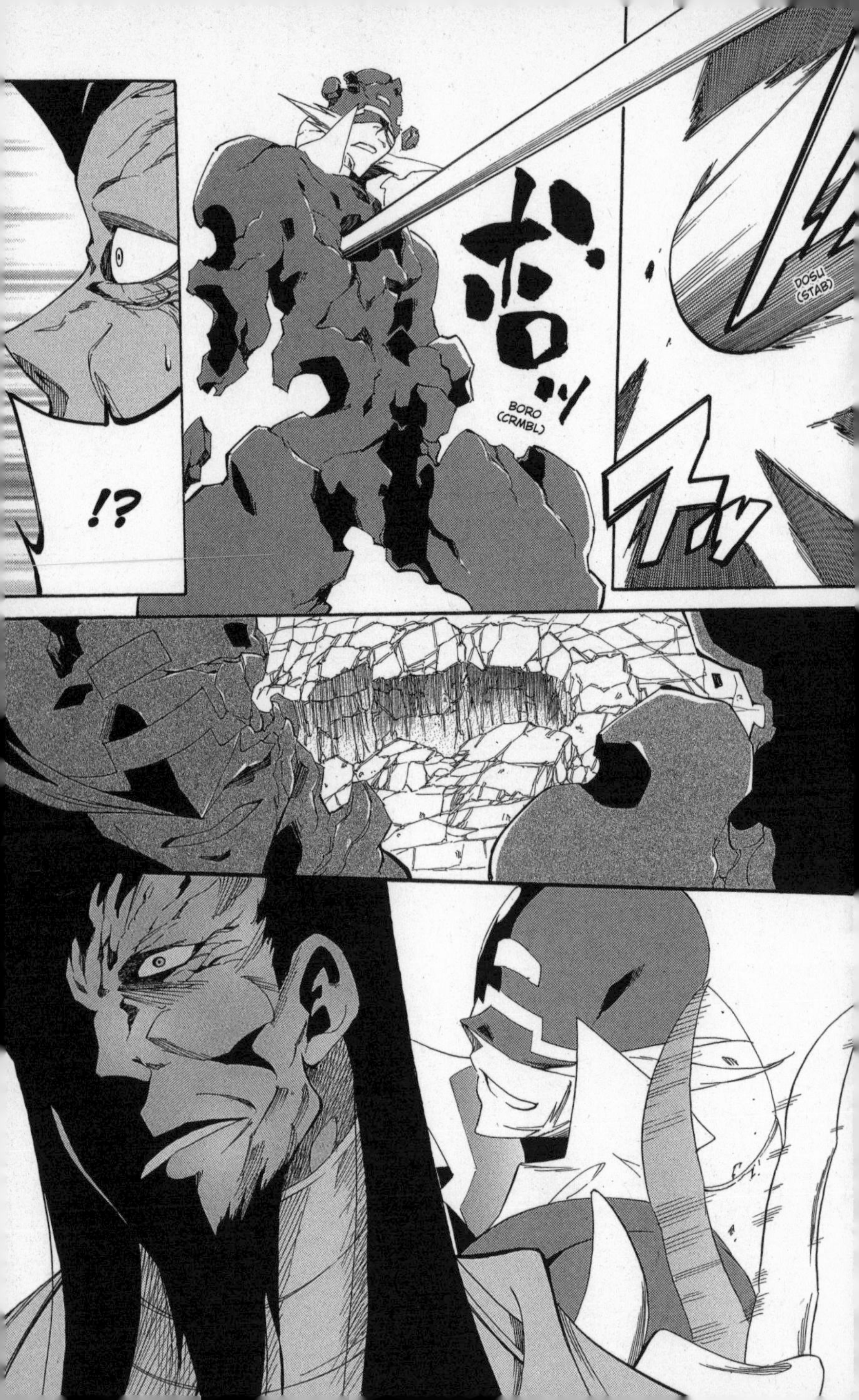
DOSU (STAB)
ボロッ
BORO (CRMBL)
!?

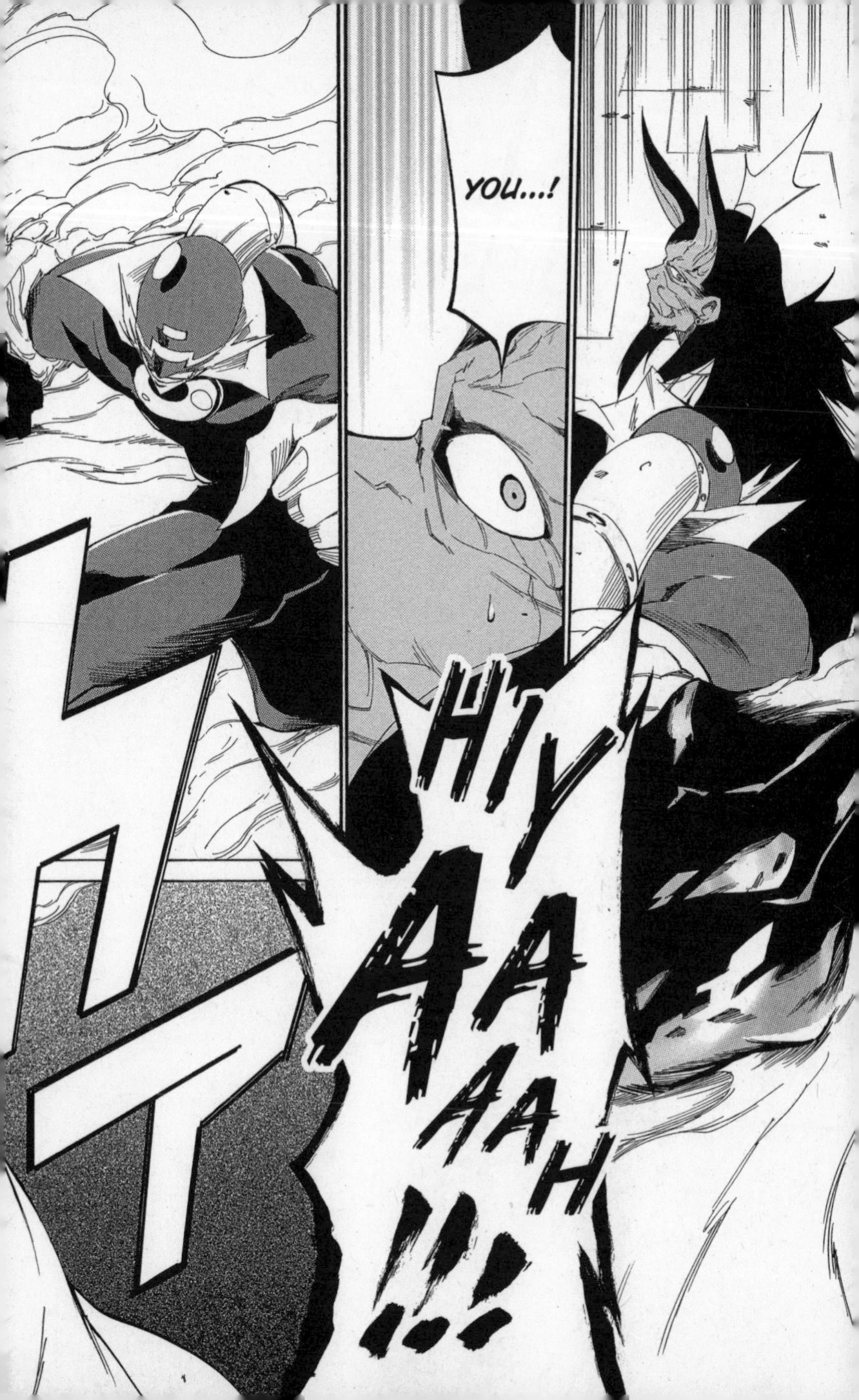
YOU...!
HIYAAAAH!!!

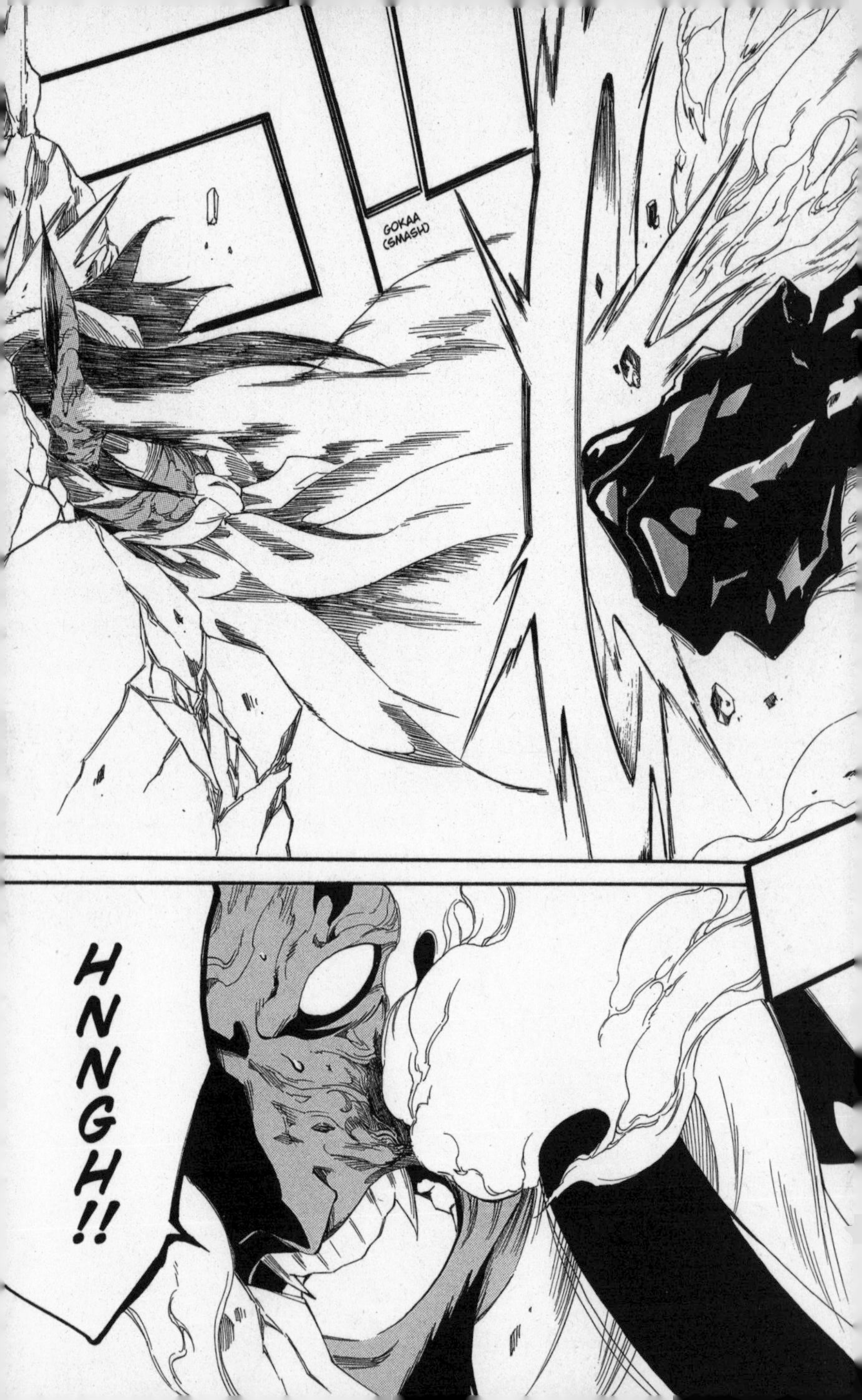
GOKAA
(SMASH)
HNNGH!!

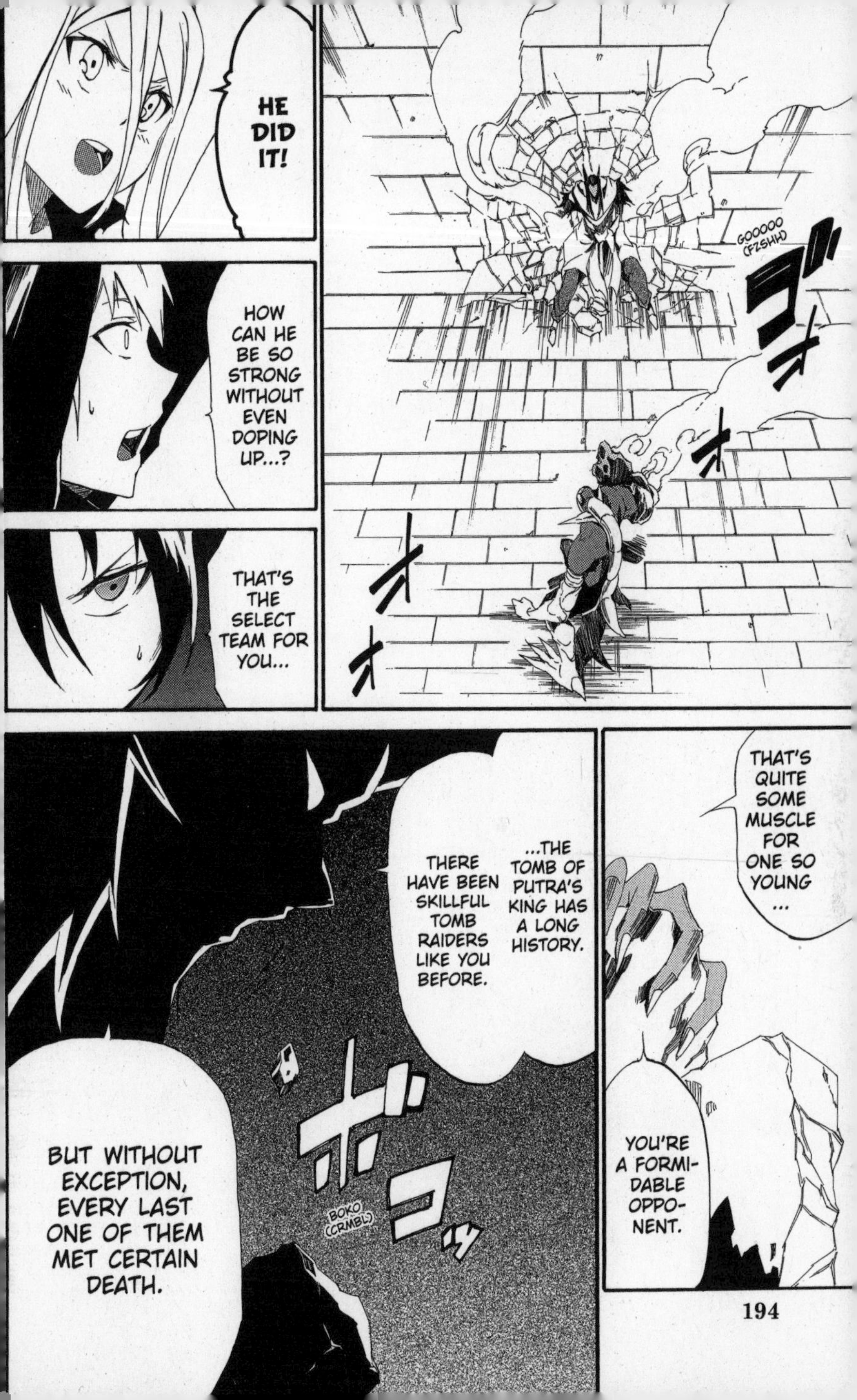

GOOOOO (FZSHH)
HE DID IT!
HOW CAN HE BE SO STRONG WITHOUT EVEN DOPING UP...?
THAT'S THE SELECT TEAM FOR YOU...
THAT'S QUITE SOME MUSCLE FOR ONE SO YOUNG ...
YOU'RE A FORMIDABLE OPPONENT.
...THE TOMB OF PUTRA'S KING HAS A LONG HISTORY.
THERE HAVE BEEN SKILLFUL TOMB RAIDERS LIKE YOU BEFORE.
BOKO (CRMBL)
BUT WITHOUT EXCEPTION, EVERY LAST ONE OF THEM MET CERTAIN DEATH.

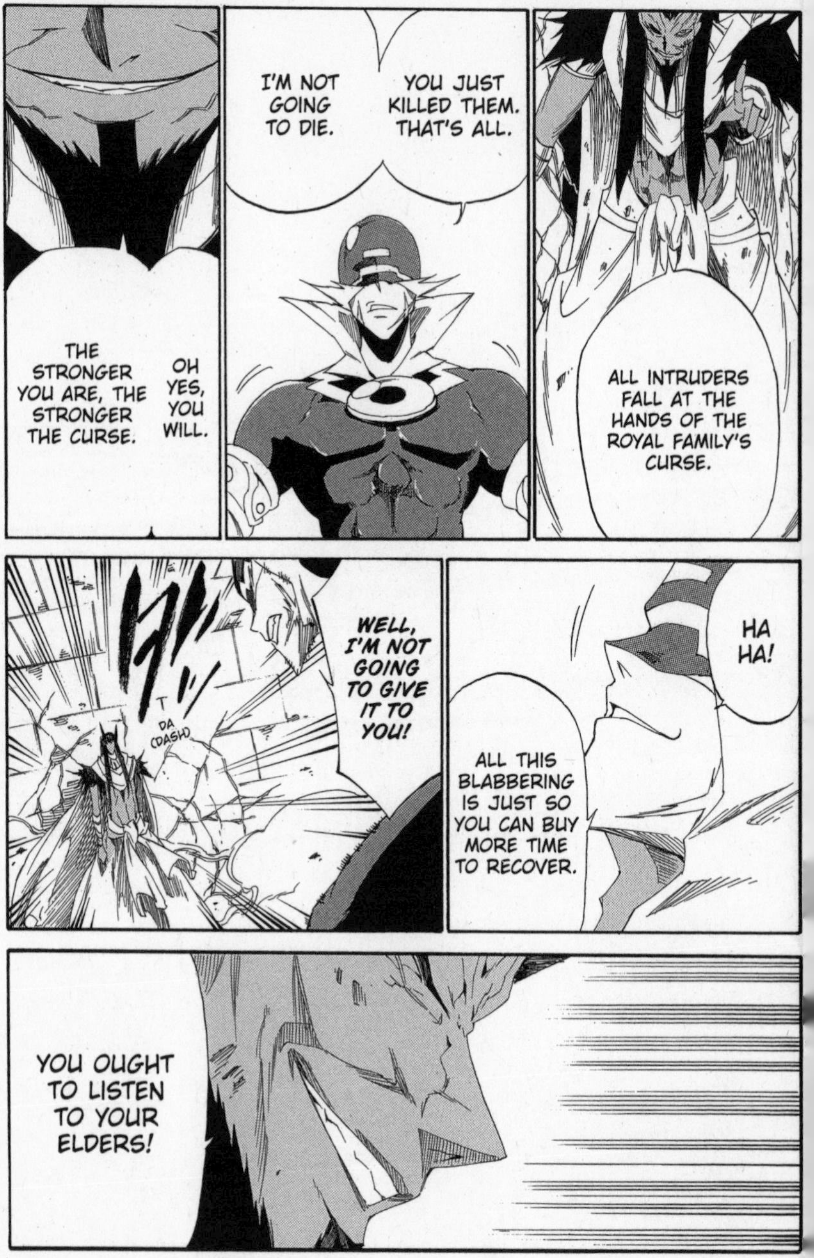
ALL INTRUDERS FALL AT THE HANDS OF THE ROYAL FAMILY'S CURSE.
YOU JUST KILLED THEM. THAT'S ALL.
I'M NOT GOING TO DIE.
OH YES, YOU WILL.
THE STRONGER YOU ARE, THE STRONGER THE CURSE.
HA HA!
ALL THIS BLABBERING IS JUST SO YOU CAN BUY MORE TIME TO RECOVER.
WELL, I'M NOT GOING TO GIVE IT TO YOU!
DA (DASH)
YOU OUGHT TO LISTEN TO YOUR ELDERS!

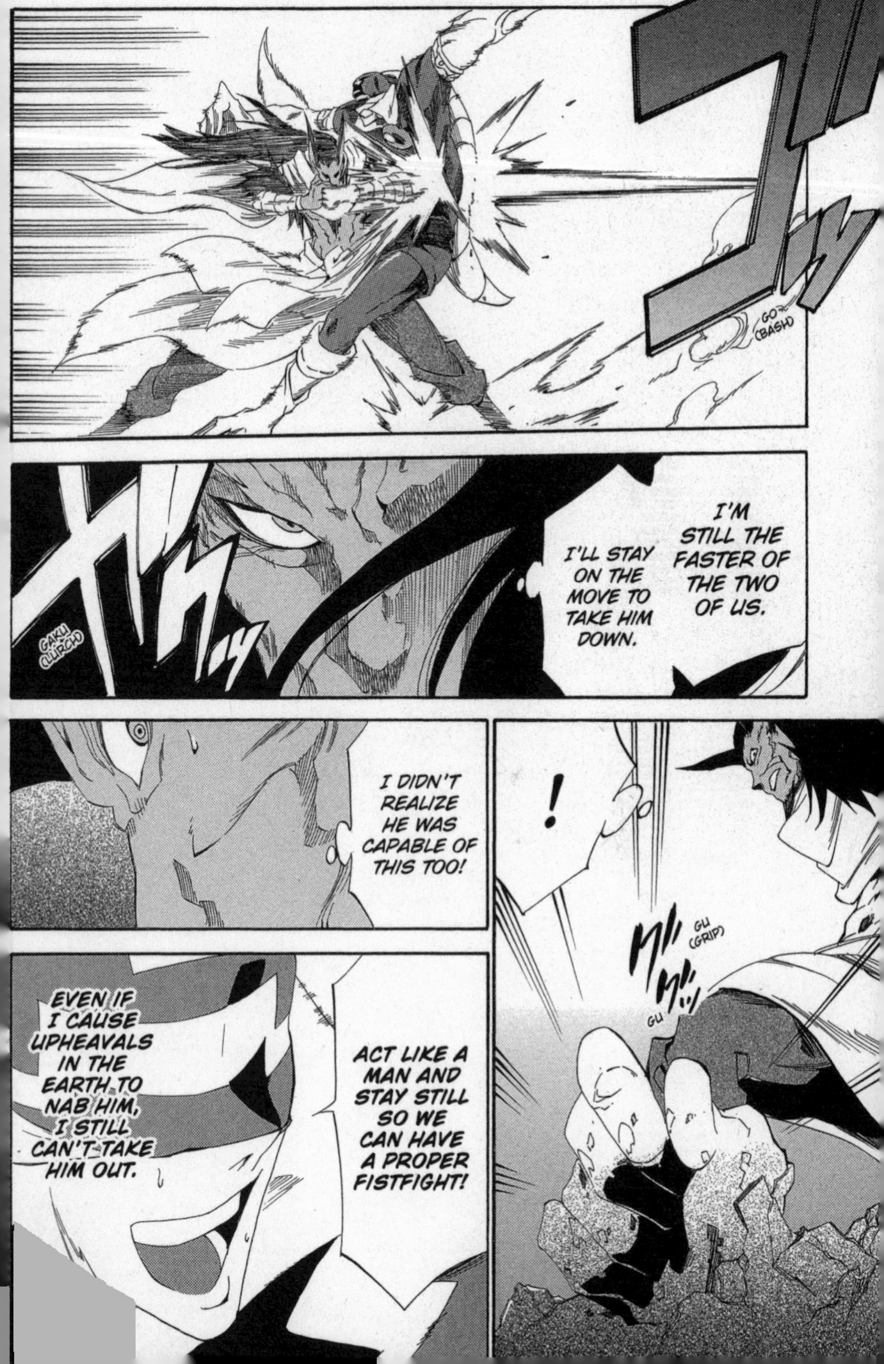
GO (BASH)
I'M STILL THE FASTER OF THE TWO OF US.
I'LL STAY ON THE MOVE TO TAKE HIM DOWN.
GAKU (LURCH)
!
GU (GRIP)
GU
I DIDN'T REALIZE HE WAS CAPABLE OF THIS TOO!
ACT LIKE A MAN AND STAY STILL SO WE CAN HAVE A PROPER FISTFIGHT!
EVEN IF I CAUSE UPHEAVALS IN THE EARTH TO NAB HIM, I STILL CAN'T TAKE HIM OUT.

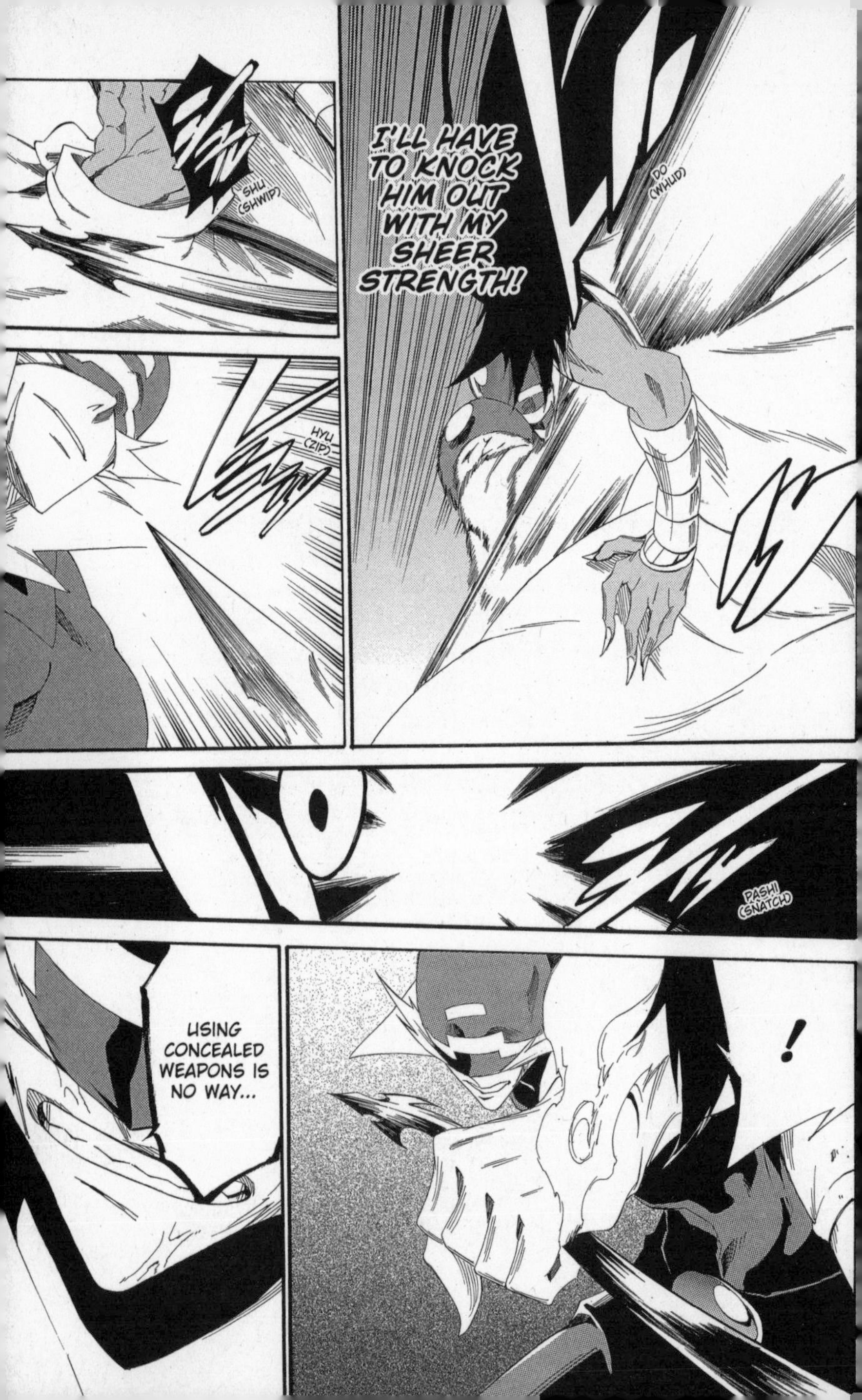
DO (WHUD)
I'LL HAVE TO KNOCK HIM OUT WITH MY SHEER STRENGTH!
SHU (SHWIP)
HYU (ZIP)
PASHI (SNATCH)
!
USING CONCEALED WEAPONS IS NO WAY...

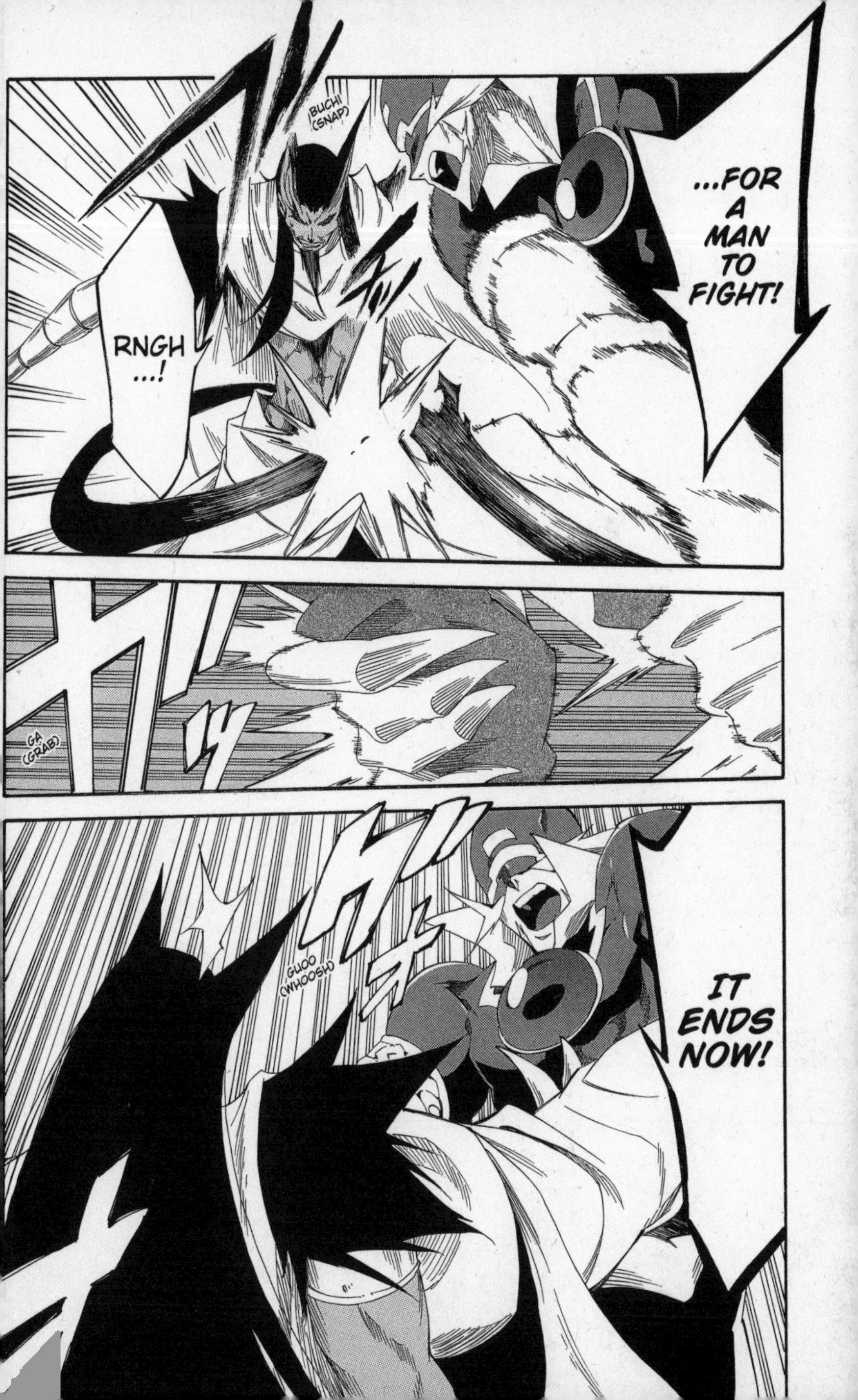
...FOR A MAN TO FIGHT!
BUCHI (SNAP)
RNGH ...!
GA (GRAB)
IT ENDS NOW!
GUOO (WHOOSH)

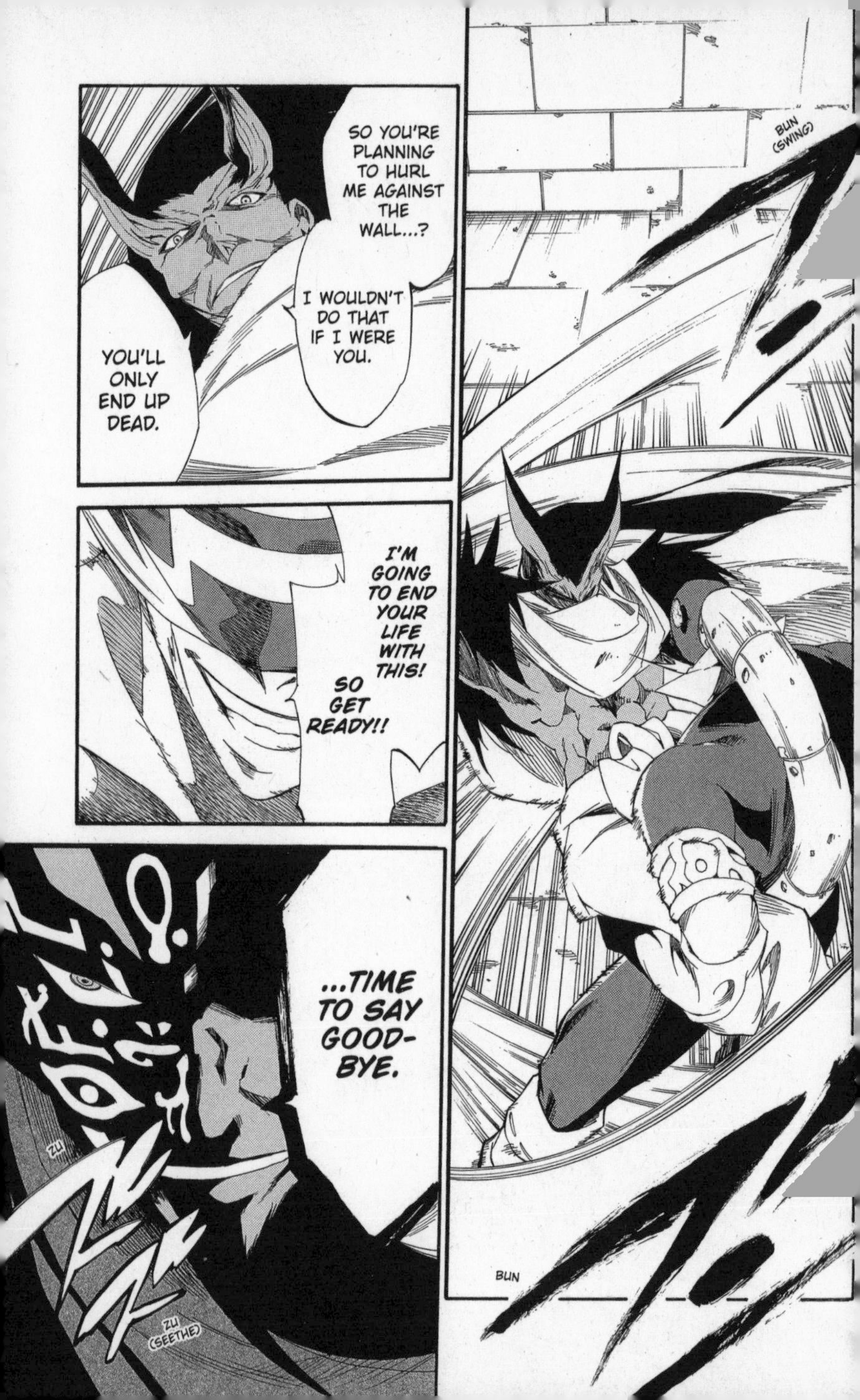
BUN (SWING)
BUN
SO YOU'RE PLANNING TO HURL ME AGAINST THE WALL...?
I WOULDN'T DO THAT IF I WERE YOU.
YOU'LL ONLY END UP DEAD.
I'M GOING TO END YOUR LIFE WITH THIS!
SO GET READY!!
...TIME TO SAY GOOD-BYE.
ZU
ZU (SEETHE)

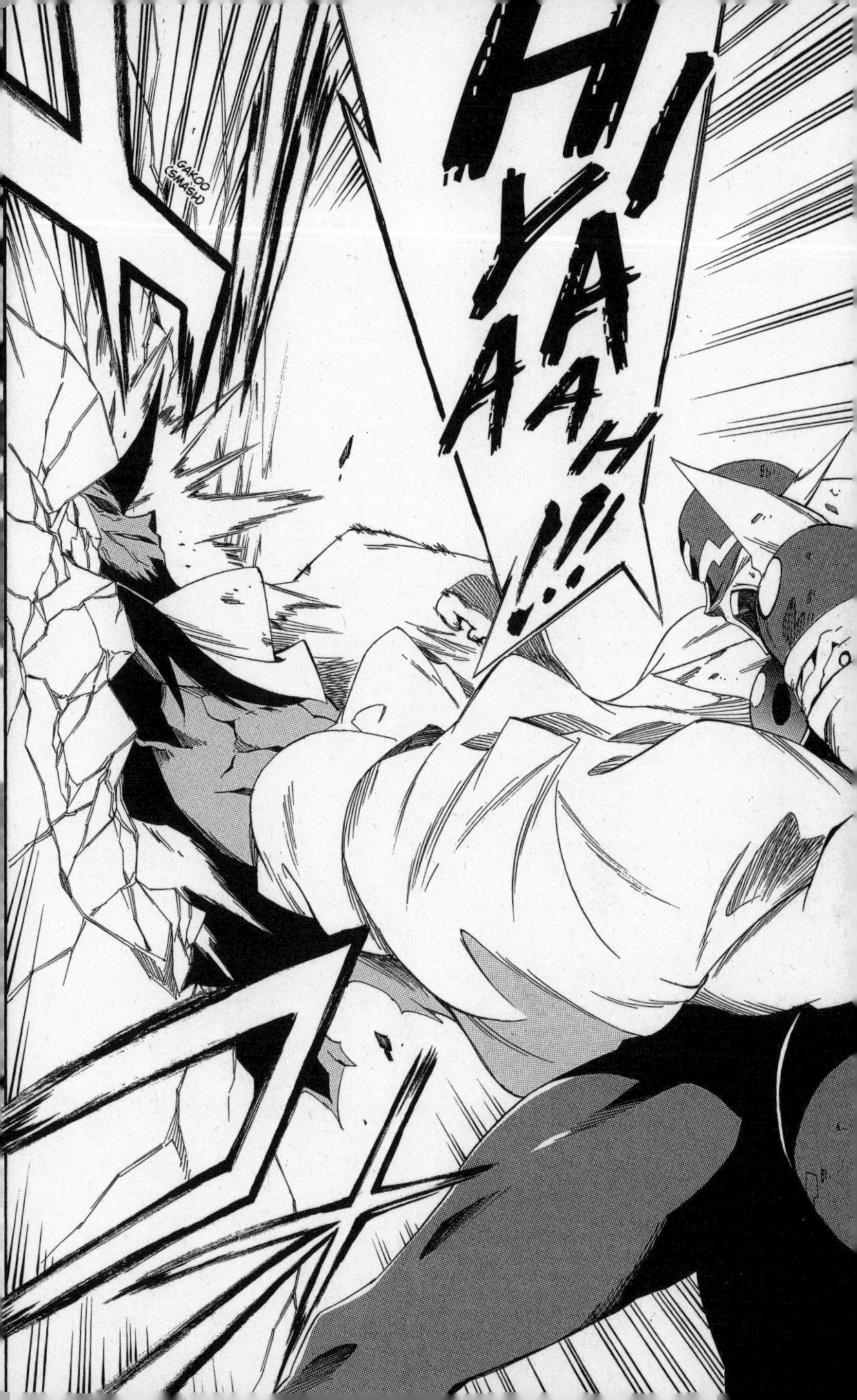
HIYAAAH!!!
GAKOO (SMASH)

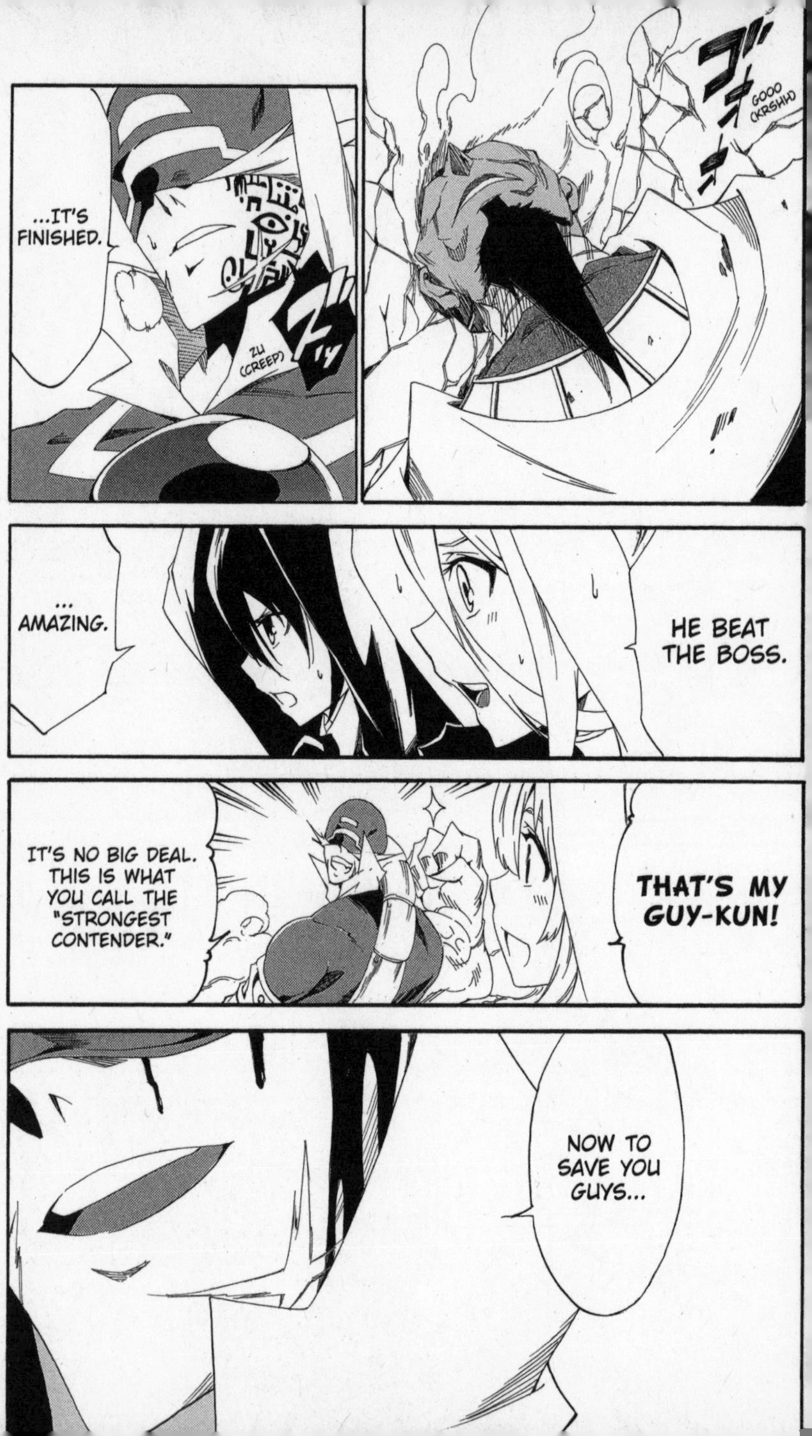

GOOO (KRSHH)
...IT'S FINISHED.
ZU (CREEP)
HE BEAT THE BOSS.
...
AMAZING.
THAT'S MY GUY-KUN!
IT'S NO BIG DEAL. THIS IS WHAT YOU CALL THE "STRONGEST CONTENDER."
NOW TO SAVE YOU GUYS...

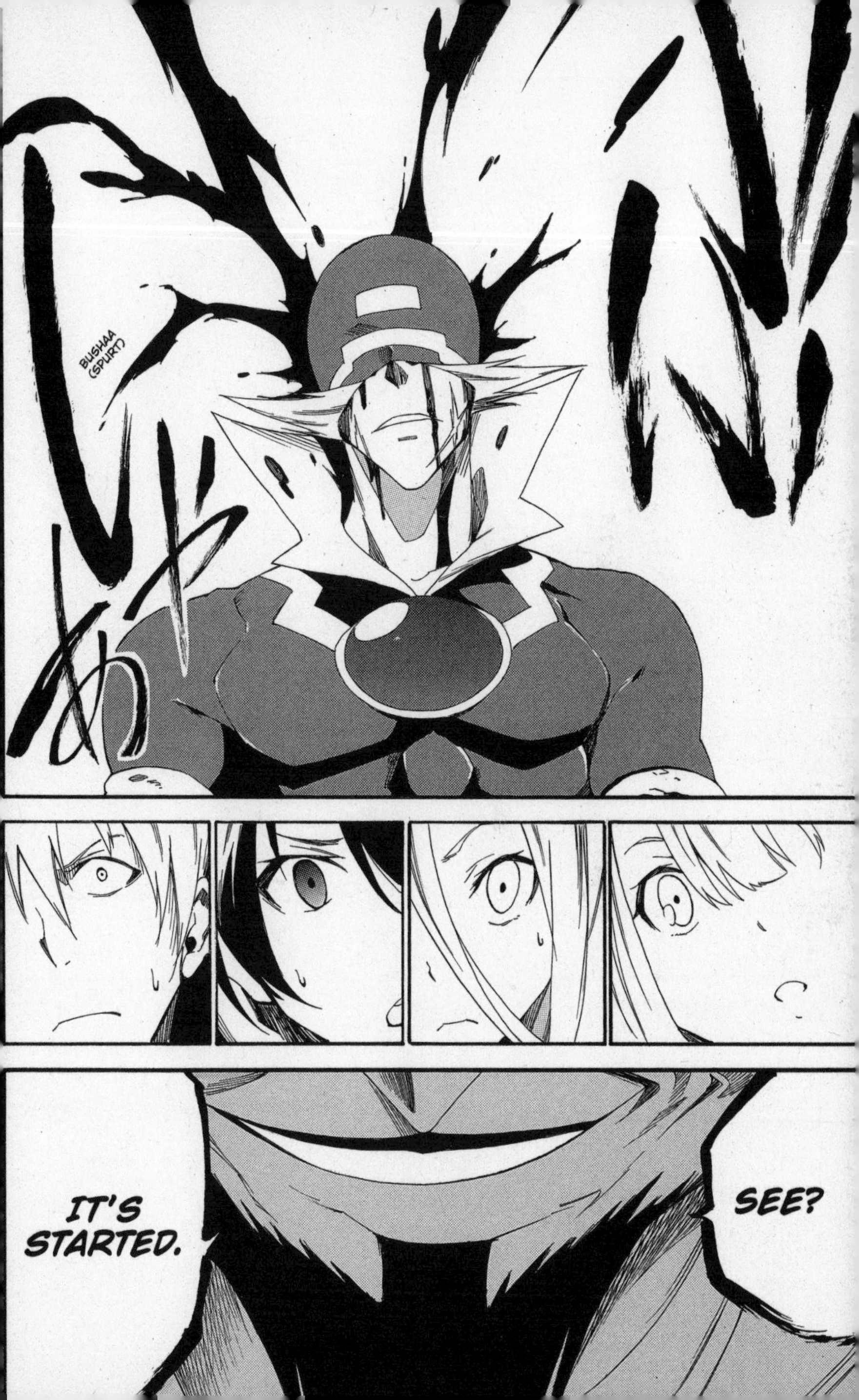
BUSHAA
(SPURT)
SEE?
IT'S
STARTED.

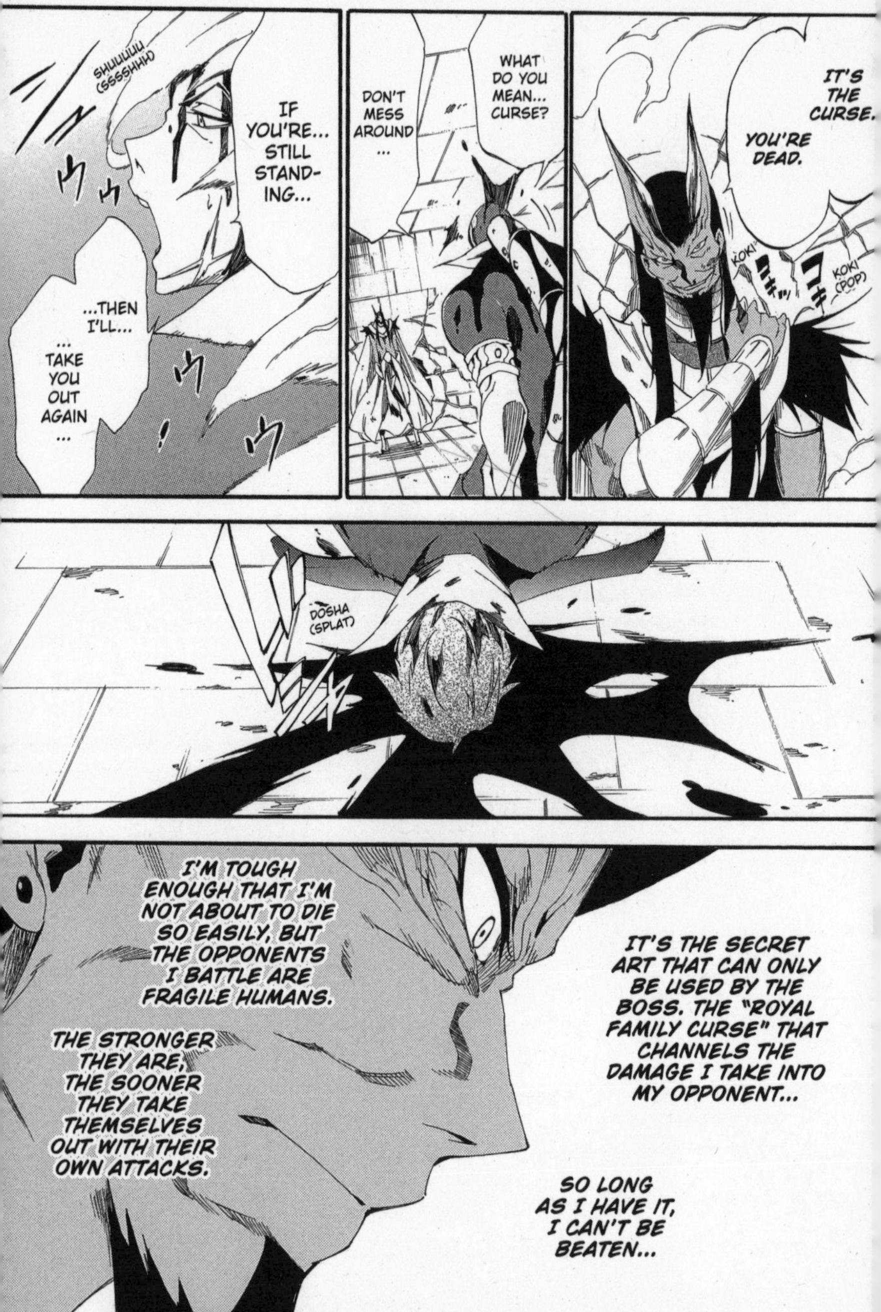
IT'S THE CURSE.
YOU'RE DEAD.
KOKI
KOKI (POP)
WHAT DO YOU MEAN... CURSE?
DON'T MESS AROUND...
SHUUUUU (SSSSHHH)
IF YOU'RE... STILL STANDING...
...THEN I'LL...
...TAKE YOU OUT AGAIN...
DOSHA (SPLAT)
IT'S THE SECRET ART THAT CAN ONLY BE USED BY THE BOSS. THE "ROYAL FAMILY CURSE" THAT CHANNELS THE DAMAGE I TAKE INTO MY OPPONENT...
I'M TOUGH ENOUGH THAT I'M NOT ABOUT TO DIE SO EASILY, BUT THE OPPONENTS I BATTLE ARE FRAGILE HUMANS.
THE STRONGER THEY ARE, THE SOONER THEY TAKE THEMSELVES OUT WITH THEIR OWN ATTACKS.
SO LONG AS I HAVE IT, I CAN'T BE BEATEN...

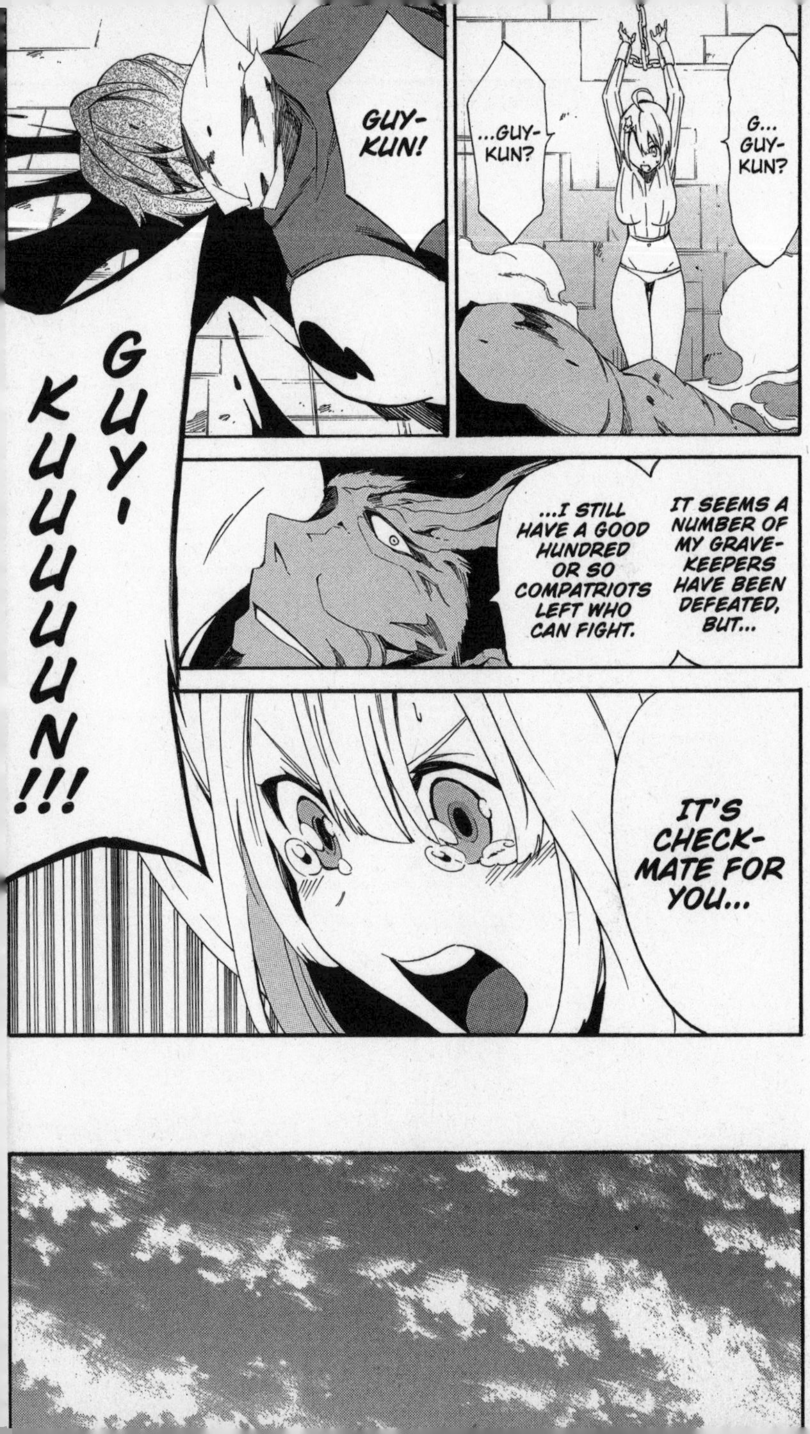
G... GUY-KUN?
...GUY-KUN?
GUY-KUN!
IT SEEMS A NUMBER OF MY GRAVE-KEEPERS HAVE BEEN DEFEATED, BUT...
...I STILL HAVE A GOOD HUNDRED OR SO COMPATRIOTS LEFT WHO CAN FIGHT.
IT'S CHECK-MATE FOR YOU...
GUY-KUUUUUUUN!!!

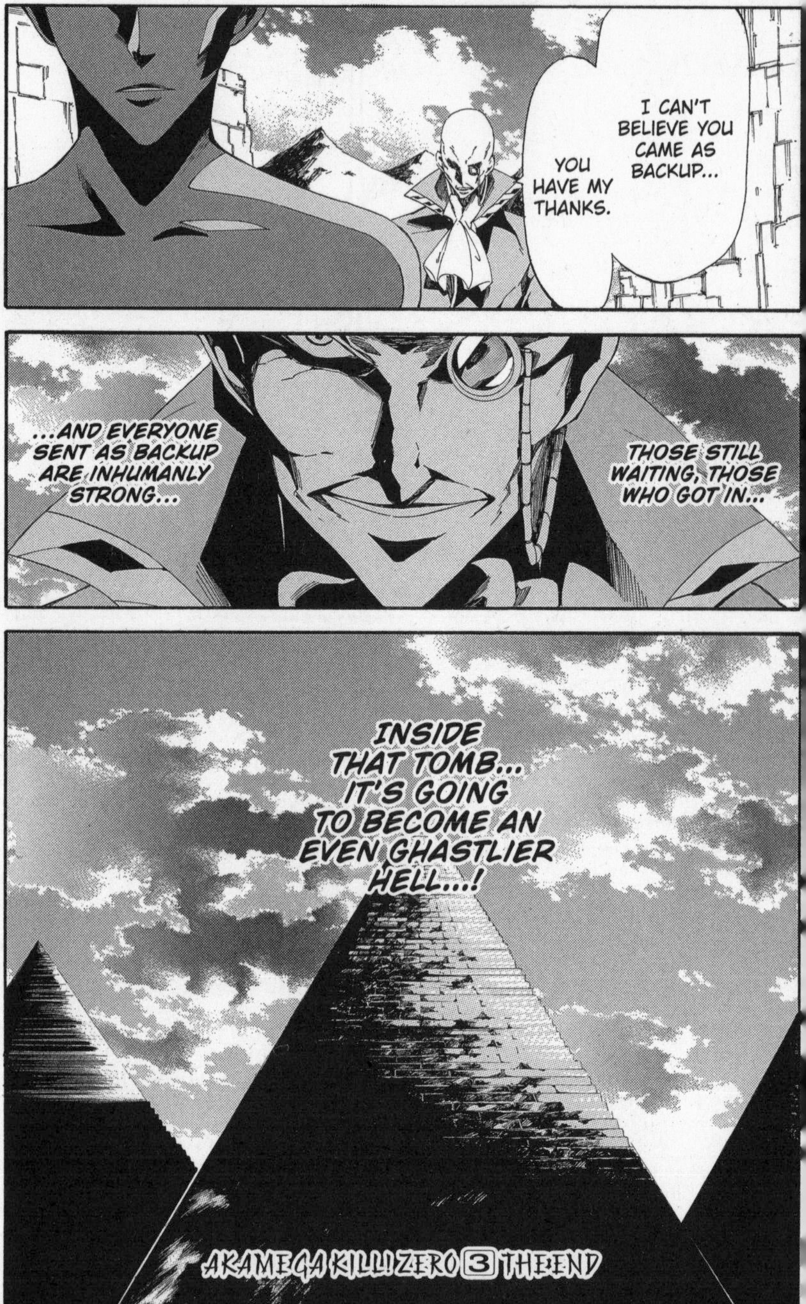
I CAN'T BELIEVE YOU CAME AS BACKUP...
YOU HAVE MY THANKS.
THOSE STILL WAITING, THOSE WHO GOT IN...
...AND EVERYONE SENT AS BACKUP ARE INHUMANLY STRONG...
INSIDE THAT TOMB... IT'S GOING TO BECOME AN EVEN GHASTLIER HELL...!
AKAME GA KILL! ZERO 3 THE END

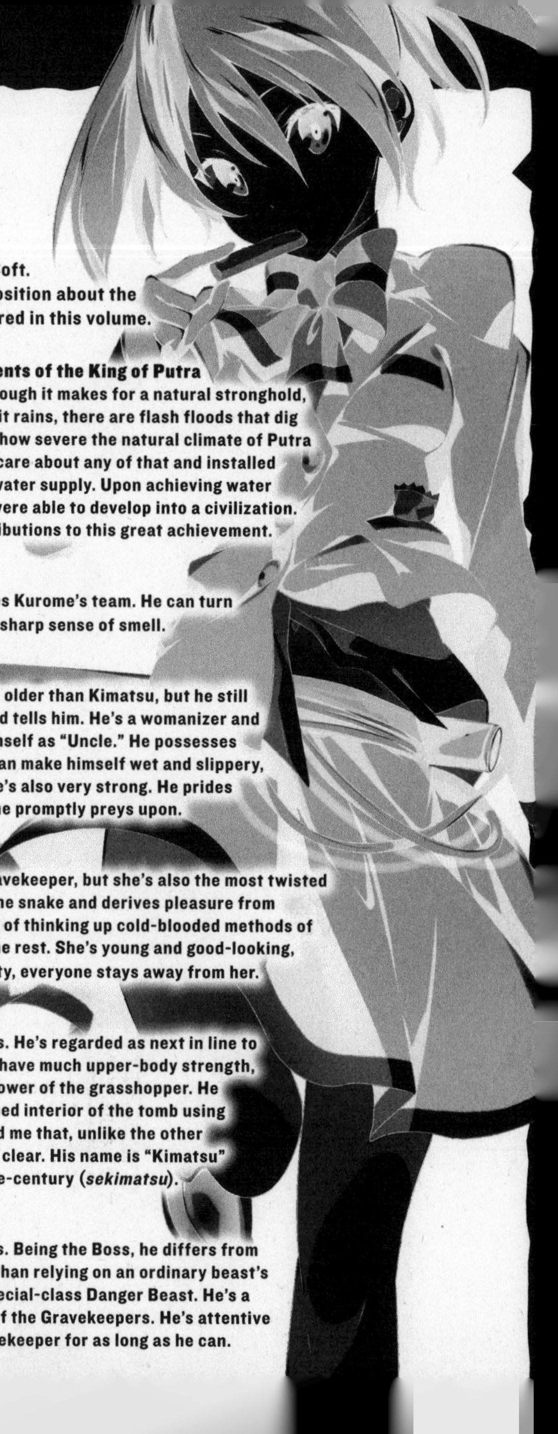

TAKAHIRO's PostScript

Hello, this is Takahiro from Minato Soft.
I'm going to do a supplementary exposition about the characters and locations that appeared in this volume.

◆The Land of Putra and achievements of the King of Putra
Putra's nothing but rocks, so even though it makes for a natural stronghold, it's not suited for agriculture. When it rains, there are flash floods that dig out ravines, which goes to show just how severe the natural climate of Putra is. But long ago, the first king didn't care about any of that and installed dams and water lines to establish a water supply. Upon achieving water security, the people of the canyons were able to develop into a civilization. The king is still revered for his contributions to this great achievement.

◆Storm
He's a young Gravekeeper who battles Kurome's team. He can turn his hair into a flying storm and has a sharp sense of smell.

◆Jamo
This is Kimatsu's best friend. Jamo's older than Kimatsu, but he still listens to whatever his younger friend tells him. He's a womanizer and all-around jokester who refers to himself as "Uncle." He possesses the power of the squid. Because he can make himself wet and slippery, it's hard to land a blow on him, and he's also very strong. He prides himself on his tentacles, which Akame promptly preys upon.

◆Umber
She's a cool and collected female Gravekeeper, but she's also the most twisted inside. She possesses the power of the snake and derives pleasure from squeezing her prey to death. Her way of thinking up cold-blooded methods of murder makes her stand out above the rest. She's young and good-looking, but because of her warped personality, everyone stays away from her.

◆Kimatsu
The youthful ace of the Gravekeepers. He's regarded as next in line to be the Boss. He talks big but doesn't have much upper-body strength, possessing instead the lower-body power of the grasshopper. He attacks by hopping around the cramped interior of the tomb using his prized leg strength. My editor told me that, unlike the other characters, his name's origin isn't as clear. His name is "Kimatsu" because his hairstyle is so end-of-the-century (*sekimatsu*).

◆Boss
The leader of the Putra Gravekeepers. Being the Boss, he differs from the rest of his team because, rather than relying on an ordinary beast's powers, he can use the power of a special-class Danger Beast. He's a traditionalist who lives by the rules of the Gravekeepers. He's attentive to his health so that he can be a Gravekeeper for as long as he can.

AKAME GA KILL! ZERO, VOL. 3!

THANK YOU FOR BUYING THIS VOLUME!

SINCE THIS IS A STORY THAT TAKES PLACE IN A FOREIGN LAND, ALL THE NEW CHARACTERS WHO APPEAR HAVE A DARK COMPLEXION. YEP... IT'S AS OPEN-AND-SHUT A CASE AS THAT! AS FAR AS THE DRAWINGS GO, I'M NOT THE TYPE WHO USES MUCH SCREEN TONE, SO IT WAS A NEW EXPERIENCE FOR ME. THE GRAVEKEEPERS ARC WILL BE CONTINUING IN THE NEXT VOLUME AS WELL, SO AKAME AND THE TEAM OUGHT TO BE GETTING A BIT MORE TANNED, WHICH MEANS EVERYONE WILL BE BROWN-SKINNED FROM VOLUME 4 ON. (J/K)

TAKAHIRO-SAN, WHO WRITES THE STORY; TASHIRO-SENSEI; OUR EDITOR, KOIZUMI-SAN; NAKAMURA-SAN, WHO HELPED WITH THE PICTURES; AND TO ALL THE READERS OUT THERE: THANK YOU VERY MUCH! AND BEST REGARDS HERE ON OUT!

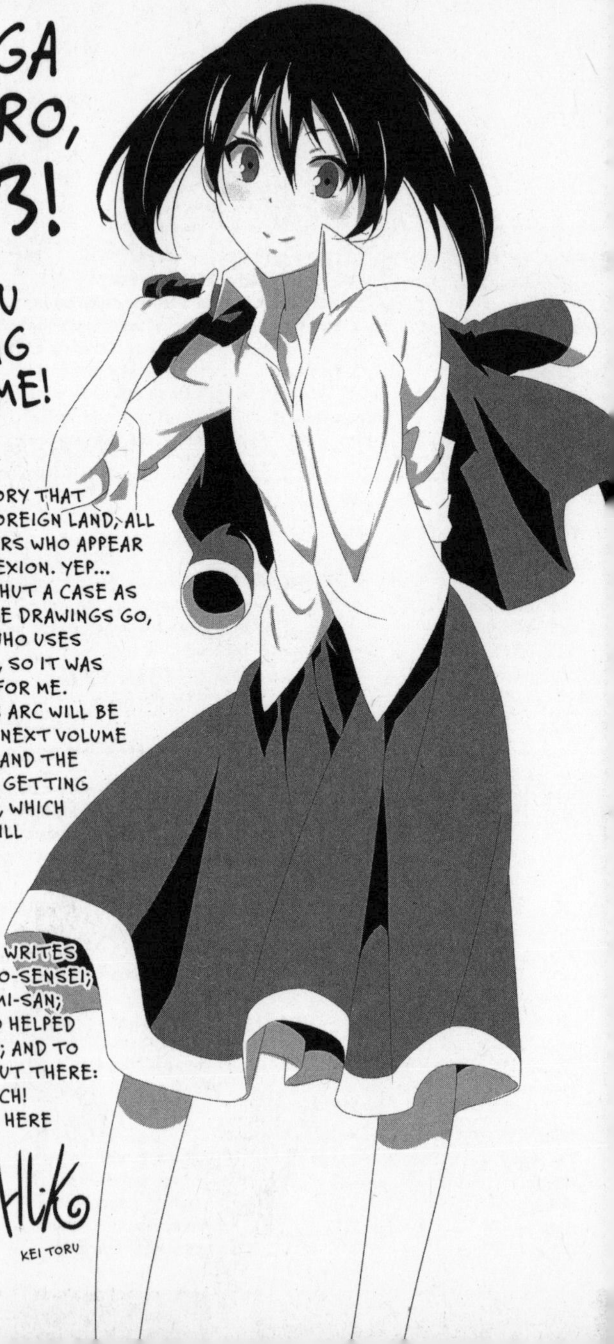

KEI TORU

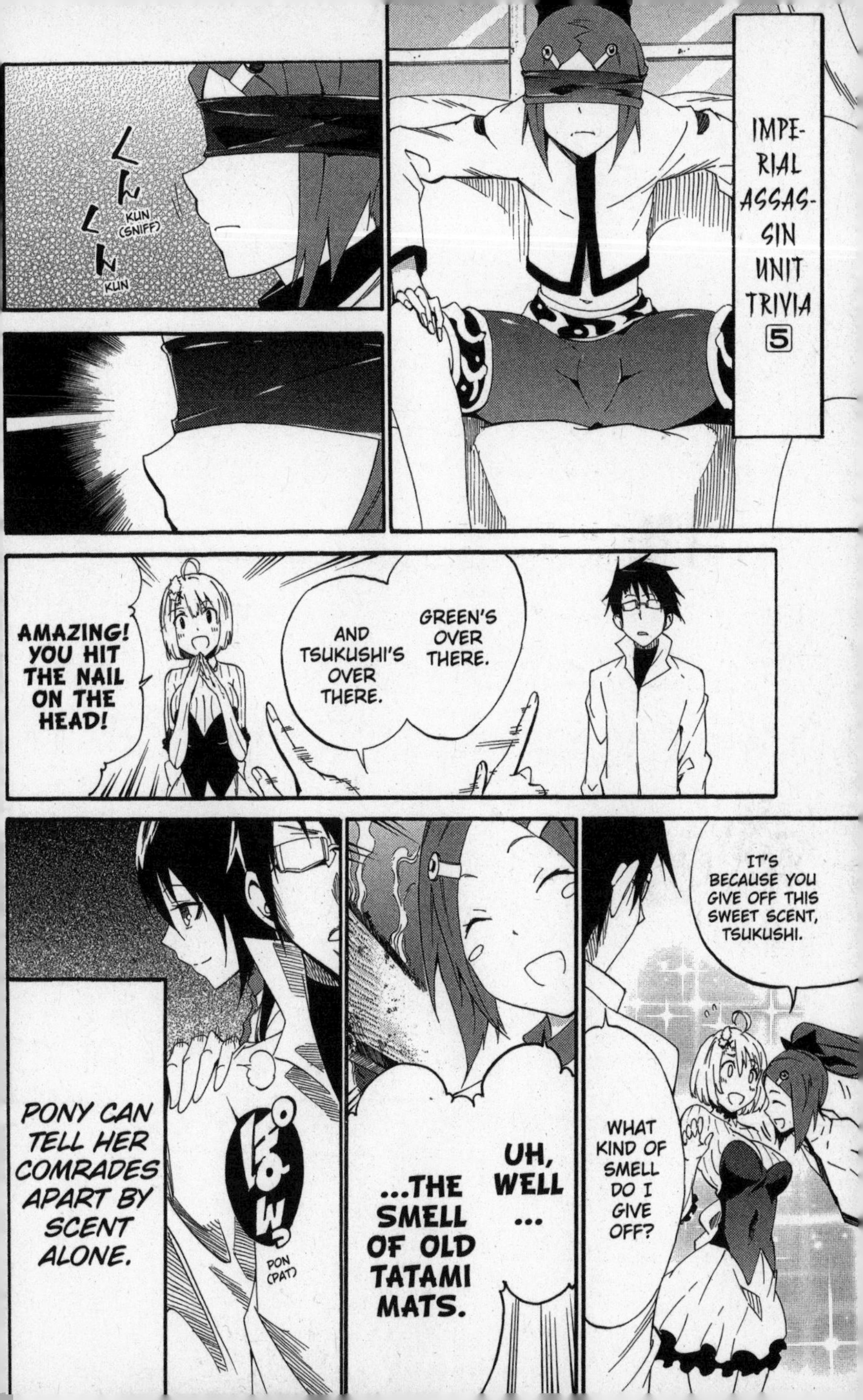
IMPERIAL ASSASSIN UNIT TRIVIA 5
くん
KUN (SNIFF)
くん
KUN
GREEN'S OVER THERE.
AND TSUKUSHI'S OVER THERE.
AMAZING! YOU HIT THE NAIL ON THE HEAD!
IT'S BECAUSE YOU GIVE OFF THIS SWEET SCENT, TSUKUSHI.
WHAT KIND OF SMELL DO I GIVE OFF?
UH, WELL ...
...THE SMELL OF OLD TATAMI MATS.
PON (PAT)
PONY CAN TELL HER COMRADES APART BY SCENT ALONE.

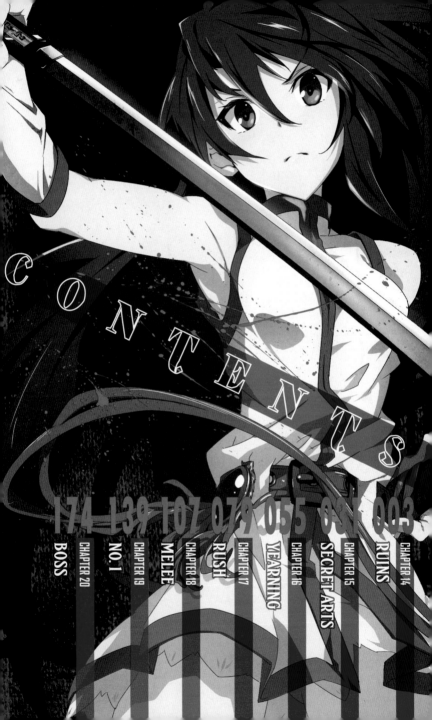

CONTENTS

174 139 107 079 055 031 003

BOSS
CHAPTER 20

NO.1
CHAPTER 19

MELEE
CHAPTER 18

RUSH
CHAPTER 17

YEARNING
CHAPTER 16

SECRET ARTS
CHAPTER 15

RUINS
CHAPTER 14

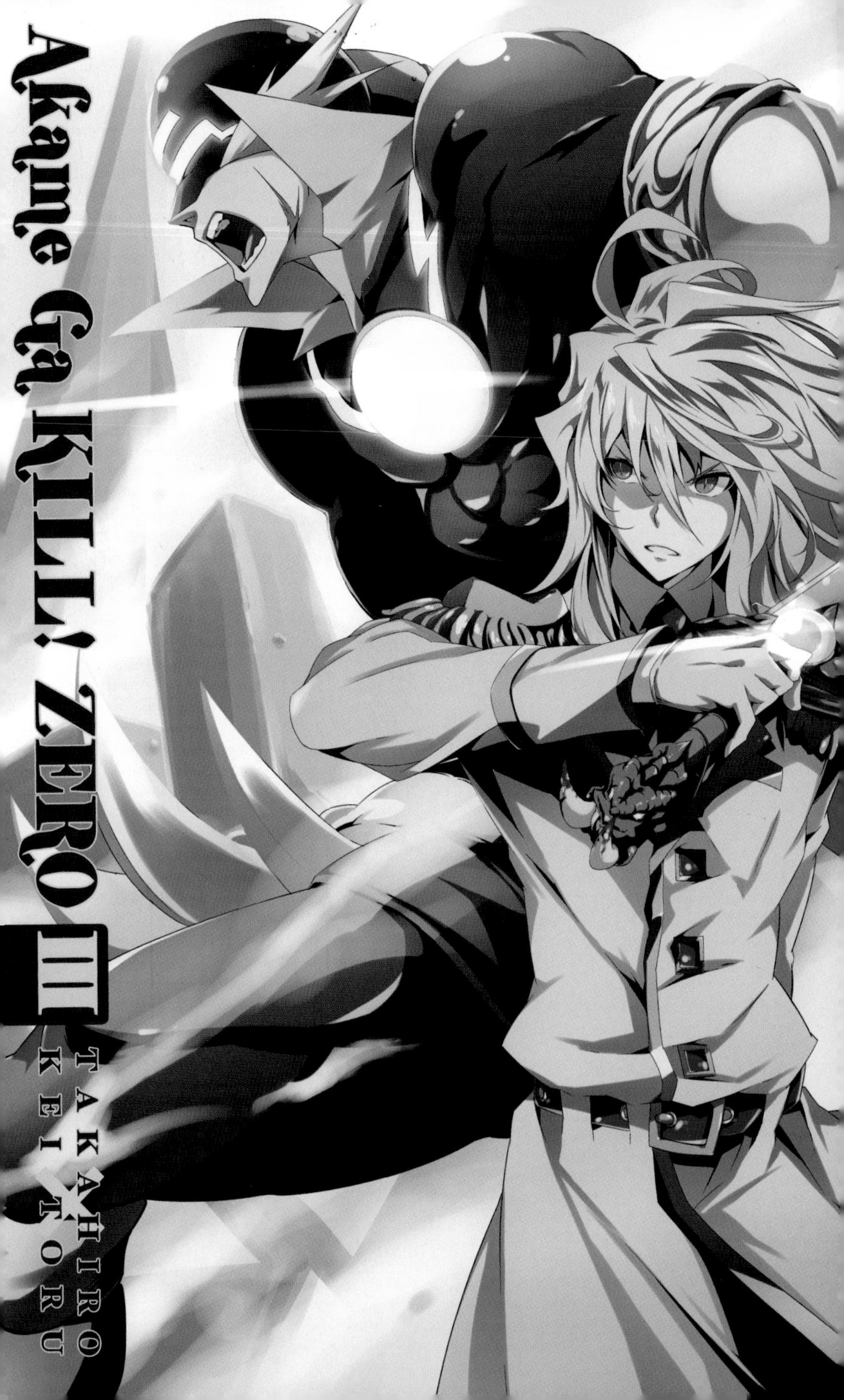
Akame ga KILL! ZERO III
TAKAHIRO × KEI TORU

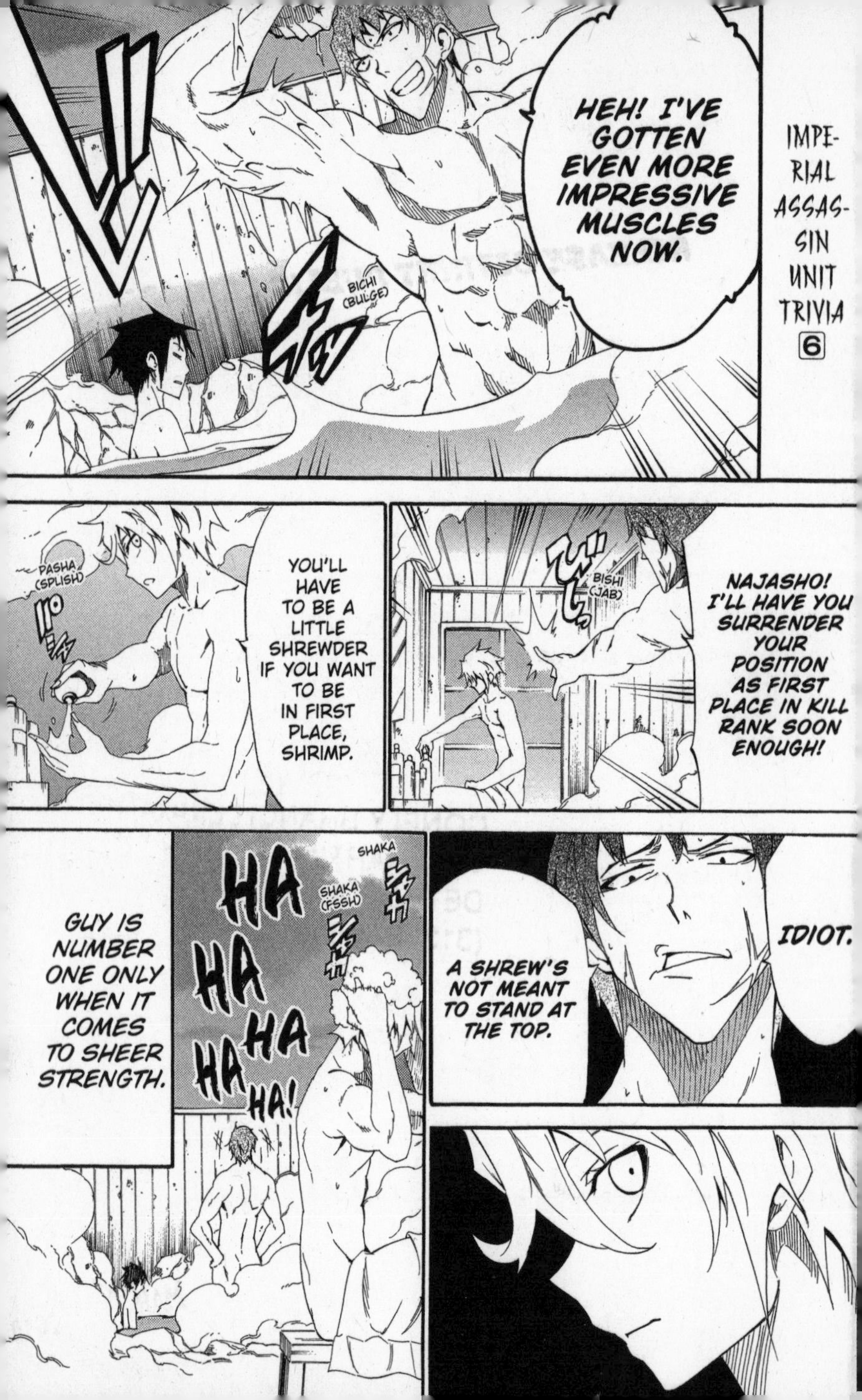
IMPERIAL ASSASSIN UNIT TRIVIA 6
HEH! I'VE GOTTEN EVEN MORE IMPRESSIVE MUSCLES NOW.
BICHI (BULGE)
BISHI (JAB)
NAJASHO! I'LL HAVE YOU SURRENDER YOUR POSITION AS FIRST PLACE IN KILL RANK SOON ENOUGH!
YOU'LL HAVE TO BE A LITTLE SHREWDER IF YOU WANT TO BE IN FIRST PLACE, SHRIMP.
PASHA (SPLISH)
IDIOT.
A SHREW'S NOT MEANT TO STAND AT THE TOP.
SHAKA SHAKA (FSSH)
HA HA HA HA HA HA HA!
GUY IS NUMBER ONE ONLY WHEN IT COMES TO SHEER STRENGTH.

AKAME GA KILL! ZERO 3

**TAKAHIRO
KEI TORU**

Translation: Christine Dashiell • Lettering: Erin Hickman

This book is a work of fiction. Names, characters, places, and incidents are the product of the author's imagination or are used fictitiously. Any resemblance to actual events, locales, or persons, living or dead, is coincidental.

AKAME GA KILL! ZERO Vol. 3
© 2015 Takahiro, Kei Toru / SQUARE ENIX CO., LTD. First published in Japan in 2015 by SQUARE ENIX CO., LTD. English translation rights arranged with SQUARE ENIX CO., LTD. and Yen Press, LLC through Tuttle-Mori Agency, Inc., Tokyo.

English translation © 2016 by SQUARE ENIX CO., LTD.

Yen Press
1290 Avenue of the Americas
New York, NY 10104

Visit us at yenpress.com
facebook.com/yenpress
twitter.com/yenpress
yenpress.tumblr.com

First Yen Press Edition: September 2016

Yen Press is an imprint of Yen Press, LLC.
The Yen Press name and logo are trademarks of Yen Press, LLC.

The publisher is not responsible for websites (or their content) that are not owned by the publisher.

Library of Congress Control Number: 2015956843

ISBNs: 978-0-316-39786-5 (paperback)
978-0-316-54373-6 (ebook)
978-0-316-54376-7 (app)

10 9 8 7 6 5 4 3 2 1

BVG

Printed in the United States of America